# Innovative
# forms of
# Organizing

# Innovative
# forms of
# Organizing

## international perspectives

Edited by

Andrew M Pettigrew

Richard Whittington

Leif Melin

Carlos Sánchez-Runde

Frans van den Bosch

Winfried Ruigrok

and

Tsuyoshi Numagami

SAGE Publications
London • Thousand Oaks • New Delhi

Chapters One and Seven © Andrew
  M. Pettigrew and Silvia Massini
Chapter Two © Richard Whittington and Leif
  Melin
Chapter Three © Leona Achtenhagen, Leif
  Melin, Tomas Müllern and Thomas Ericson
Chapter Four © Leona Achtenhagen, Leif
  Melin and Tomas Müllern
Chapter Five © Marjolijn S. Dijksterhuis,
  Frans A.J. Van den Bosch and Henk
  W. Volberda
Chapters Six and Eight © Andrew M.
  Pettigrew and Richard Whittington

Chapter Nine © Evelyn M. Fenton and
  Andrew M. Pettigrew
Chapter Ten © Carlos J. Sánchez-Runde and
  Andrew M. Pettigrew
Chapter Eleven © Carlos J. Sánchez-Runde,
  Silvia Massini and Javier Quintanilla
Chapter Twelve © Arie Y. Lewin, Silvia
  Massini, Winifried Ruigrok and Tsuyoshi
  Numagami
Chapter Thirteen © Leona Achtenhagen and
  Leif Melin
Chapters Fourteen and Fifteen © Andrew
  M. Pettigrew

First published 2003

SAGE Publications Ltd
6 Bonhill Street
London EC2A 4PU

SAGE Publications Inc
2455 Teller Road
Thousand Oaks, California 91320

SAGE Publications India Pvt Ltd
B-42, Panchsheel Enclave
Post Box 4109
New Delhi 110 017

**British Library Cataloguing in Publication data**

A catalogue record for this book is available
from the British Library

ISBN 0 7619 6435 5
ISBN 0 7619 6436 3 (pbk)

**Library of Congress Control Number 0000000**

Typeset by C&M Digitals (P) Ltd., Chennai, India
Printed and bound in Great Britain by the Athenaeum Press, Gateshead

# Contents

# Notes on Contributors

**Leona Achtenhagen**
is a Research Fellow at Jönköping International Business School in Sweden and affiliated to the University of Bamberg, Germany. Previously, she was a Visiting Fellow at Warwick Business School, UK. She received her doctorate from the University of St Gallen, Switzerland. Her thesis focused on co-ordination in innovating organizations. Her current research projects are on organizational growth and entrepreneurship. She teaches courses in International and Strategic Management as well as Organization Theory.

**Frans A.J. van den Bosch**
is Professor of Management at the Department of Strategic Management and Business Environment, Rotterdam School of Management, Erasmus University, Rotterdam. He holds a master's degree (*cum laude*) in Economics from the Erasmus University, Rotterdam and a PhD in Law from Leyden University. His current research interests include managerial and knowledge-based theories of the firm; strategic renewal; intra- and inter-organizational governance structures; corporate governance and corporate responsiveness, and integrative strategy frameworks. He has published several books and papers in journals such as *Journal of Management Studies, Long Range Planning, Organization Science, Organization Studies* and *Business and Society*. He is co-director of the Erasmus Strategic Renewal Center (ESRC) and of the Erasmus Research Institute of Management (ERIM) research program, 'Managing Strategic Renewal of Multiunit Firms and Networks in Turbulent International Environments'.

**Marjolijn Dijksterhuis**
is a Research Associate at the Department of Strategic Management and Business Environment, Rotterdam School of Management, Erasmus University, Rotterdam. She is currently completing her doctoral research which deals with the role of cognition in organizational adaptation processes. How managerial and organizational cognition and action are related is key in this research.

**Thomas Ericson**
took his PhD in Business Administration at Linköping University in 1998. He then continued his research as a research fellow at Jönköping International Business School. His research has focused on sensemaking in organizations. He has contributed to the understanding of strategic change through studies of the meanings that prevail among organizational members, as well as the processes whereby these meanings change and coincide. At present he is working with organizational development at The Swedish Agency for Public Mangement in Stockholm.

**Evelyn Fenton**
is a lecturer in the Department of Management at the University of Reading School of Business. She gained a PhD in strategic agenda building and change in the water industry from Warwick Business School where she was a Senior Research Fellow at the Centre for Creativity, Strategy and Change. Her current research interests are in professional services, the management of organizational networks, and strategies for leveraging their social and intellectual capital.

**Arie Lewin**
is Professor of Business Administration and Sociology and IBM Research Fellow at the Fuqua School of Business, Duke University. He is the Editor in Chief of *Journal of International Business Studies* (2002–), Director of the Center for International Business Education and Research (CIBER) and lead Principal Investigator for the International Project on New Organizational Forms. Professor Lewin has been Program Director for Decision, Risk and Management Science at the National Science Foundation (1986–88); Departmental Editor of *Management Science* for the department of Organization Analysis, Performance and Design (1974–87); founding Editor-in-Chief emeritus of *Organization Science* (1989–98); Visiting Research Professor, Erasmus University (1999–), Visiting Professor International Management, Cranfield School of Management 2000–02), DKB Visiting Professor, Keio University Graduate School of Business (Spring 1993, 1994); Visiting Research Professor, Institute for Business Research, Hitotsubashi University (1994–95) and Chair of Duke University Academic Council (1982–86). Professor Lewin's primary research interests involve the co-evolution of new organizational forms and management of strategy and organization change in times of increasing disorder. He leads a cross-national research collaboration (Germany, Japan, Korea, Spain, Sweden, Switzerland, Denmark, the Netherlands, UK, and the USA) research consortium – New Organization Forms for the Information Age (NOFIA), involving longitudinal comparative studies of strategic re-orientations and organization restructurings and international competitiveness.

**Silvia Massini**
is lecturer in Economics and Technology Management at the Manchester School of Management at UMIST. Previously she has been a researcher at CNR (Rome) and CCSC (Warwick Business School), and visiting fellow at SPRU (Brighton) and CRIC (Manchester). Her research spans the areas of the economics of innovation and technological change, the management of technology and organizational aspects of technological change. She has published in *Small Business Economics, European Management Journal, Research Policy* and the *Journal of Evolutionary Economics*, and has contributed to a number of book chapters.

**Leif Melin**
is Professor of Strategy and Organization at Jönköping International Business School, Jönköping University. Earlier he was Professor of Strategic Management at Linköping University where he led the Strategic Change Research Group. His current research interests concern strategizing in renewal processes, organizing aspects of growth, and governance and cultural issues in family businesses. He has published widely in edited books and international journals. He serves on the editorial boards of many journals, such as *Organization Studies* and *Strategic Organization*.

**Tomas Müllern**
is Associate Professor at Jönköping International Business School. His research interests cover innovative forms of organizing, leadership and rhetoric, and organizational renewal and learning. All three areas, in different ways, highlight a need for understanding new and innovative organizational practices.

**Tsuyoshi Numagami**
is Professor at the Department of Commerce, Hitotsubashi University, Tokyo, Japan. His recent publications include 'Infeasibility of Establishing Invariant Laws in Management Studies', (*Organization Science*, 9, (1), (1998)) and 'Flexibility Trap: A Case Analysis of U.S. and Japanese Technological Choice in the Digital Watch Industry,' (*Research Policy*, 25 (1996)).

**Andrew Pettigrew**
is Associate Dean, Research and Professor of Strategy and Organization at Warwick Business School, Warwick University. Between 1985 and 1995 he founded and directed the Centre for Corporate Strategy and Change. He has held previous academic positions at Yale University, London Business School and Harvard Business School, where in the academic year 2001 he was a Visiting Professor. He is a Fellow of both the Academy of Management and the British Academy of Management. He was the first Chairman of the British Academy of Management (1987–90) and then President (1990–93). In 1998 he was elected a Founding Academician of the Academy of the Social

Sciences. In 2002 he was elected Distinguished Scholar of the Academy of Management, the first European scholar to be so honoured. His latest book is *The Handbook of Strategy and Management* (2002). London, Sage (co-editor, with Howard Thomas and Richard Whittington).

### Javier Quintanilla

has a PhD from the University of Warwick and is Assistant Professor at IESE Business School, University of Navarra, Madrid. His current research interests are international human resource management and the management of professional service firms. He has published widely in scholarly journals. He is also the author of *Dirección de recursos humanos en empresas multinacionales; Las subsidiaries al descubierto*, published by Prentice Hall-Financial Times, and several chapters in monographs.

### Carlos Sánchez-Runde

is Associate Professor and Associate Director for Faculty at IESE Business School in Barcelona. He received his PhD in Management from the University of Oregon. He has also taught in the USA, Chile, Argentina, Peru, Uruguay and China. He has published a book and several papers on strategic human resource management and cross-cultural organizational behaviour.

### Winfried Ruigrok

is a Professor of International Management at the University of St Gallen (Switzerland). He previously worked at the Erasmus University, Rotterdam, the University of Amsterdam (both in the Netherlands), the European Commission (Belgium) and Warwick Business School (UK). His current research focuses on internationalization and international restructuring, the role of foreigners in top management teams and boards, and corporate governance.

### Henk W. Volberda

is Professor of Strategic Management and Business Policy and Chairman of the Department of Strategic Management and Business Environment, Rotterdam School of Management, Erasmus University, Rotterdam. In 1992, he earned his PhD *cum laude* in Business Administration from the University of Groningen. For his research on strategic flexibility, he received several awards, one of which was the Igor Ansoff Award, 1993. His research interests include strategic flexibility, new organizational forms, and strategic management of innovation. He has published in journals such as *Journal of Management Studies, Long Range Planning, Organization Science, Organization Studies* and *Omega*. His published books are *'Building the Flexible Firm: How to remain competitive'* (Oxford University Press, 1998) and *On Rethinking Strategy* (Sage, 2001). He is co-director of the research program 'Managing Strategic Renewal of Multiunit Firms and Networks in Turbulent International Environments'. He is currently studying the process of strategic renewal within large European corporations.

**Richard Whittington**

is Millman Fellow of New College and Professor of Strategic Management at the Saïd Business School, University of Oxford. With Andrew Pettigrew and Martin Conyon, he was one of the original co-applicants of the INNFORM programme. He is currently working on how senior managers learn to strategize and the practice of organizing. His single and co-produced books include *Corporate Strategies in Recession and Recovery, What Is Strategy – and Does It Matter? Rethinking Marketing, The European Corporation*, and *The Handbook of Strategy and Management*. He is on the editorial boards of the *Academy of Management Review*, the *British Journal of Management*, the *European Management Journal, Long Range Planning, Organization Studies*, and *Strategic Organization*.

# Preface

This book is the second and summative volume from the study of Innovative Forms of Organizing (INNFORM) programme of research. The first book from the programme was published in 2000 by Sage Publications. That book was titled *The Innovating Organization* and was edited by Andrew M. Pettigrew and Evelyn M. Fenton. Like the first book, this one is very much a collective and collaborative effort, as signalled by the seven co-editors listed on the title page.

The aims of the INNFORM research were to map the contours of contemporary organizational innovation, to examine the performance benefits and other consequences of innovative forms of organizing, and to explore the managerial and organizational processes of moving from more traditional forms of organizing. The programme was initiated from Warwick Business School in a successful research submission to the Economic and Social Research Council's (ESRC) Innovation Programme. Coopers & Lybrand Europe (now part of the merged entity, PricewaterhouseCoopers) also contributed to the research funding, as did the consortium of organizations who supported the Centre for Corporate Strategy and Change at Warwick Business School. The research was carried out in co-operation with colleagues from Erasmus University (the Netherlands), ESSEC (France), Hitotsubashi University (Japan), IESE (Spain), Jönköping University (Sweden), Oxford University (UK) and St Gallen University (Switzerland). Duke University joined the team in 1997 to carry out the US survey component of the programme. The lead researchers from each of the institutions are: Frans van den Bosch, Hamid Bouchikhi, Tsuyoshi Numagami, Carlos Sánchez-Runde, Leif Melin, Richard Whittington, Winfried Ruigrok and Arie Lewin.

The initial funding for the research was made possible by generous grants from the ESRC and Coopers & Lybrand. These initial awards were supplemented by additional awards by both organizations to extend the scope of the work and to support dissemination activities. We are most grateful for this financial support. We would also like to recognize the wholehearted support given our work by Dr Fiona Steele, the co-ordinator of the ESRC Innovation Programme.

Paul Batchelor, then the partner in charge of Coopers & Lybrand Europe, helped us prepare the initial submission to the ESRC and offered co-funding and considerable direct assistance in other ways. Vic Luck (Managing Partner for PWC in Europe, the Middle East and Africa) supported the fourth year of funding and joined the UK team in a high-profile dissemination event. We would also like to acknowledge the support of Andy Embury of PWC. Crucial to the success of the research has been PWC's willingness to act not just as co-funders, but also co-producers and co-disseminators of knowledge. Chris David and David Shaw, both Directors of PWC, have been great week-by-week collaborators and, in different ways, have greatly enriched the INNFORM team. We thank you.

The collaborating teams from Europe and Japan have also had to commit considerable financial and people resources to the research. This commitment made the international collaborative side of the INNFORM programme work.

Case study research can be very demanding for researcher and host company alike and we never take research access for granted. We would like to thank all the representatives of the 18 European companies who helped us to gain access to people and documentary information. The companies concerned were: ABB, AGBAR, BP, Coopers & Lybrand Europe, Davis Langdon Everest, Fremap, Hilti AG, Internationale Nederlanden Groep, Östgöta Enskilda Bank, Ove Arup & Partners, Rabobank, Saab Training Systems, Siemens AG, Spencer Stuart, Trumpf and Unilever. BP and Unilever allowed us to carry out two cases in each of their wide network of businesses.

Not all the colleagues who worked on the INNFORM programme are represented as editors or authors of this volume. From the original Warwick team we would like to thank Martin Conyon (now of the Wharton School) and Simon Peck (now of Case Western University) for their help with the survey design and econometric analysis. It was Martin and Simon who first introduced us to the economics of complementarities, one of the important theoretical themes in this book. William Pettigrew (then an Oxford history undergraduate) helped with the archival collection and analysis that informed the BP case in Chapter 8 of this volume. Dr Andres Hatum (now of IAE, Argentina) and Sotirios Paroutis at various times supported the Warwick team with literature reviews. Their contribution was always willingly given and always of great practical value.

The St Gallen team benefited from the empirical and theoretical contributions of Professor Johannes Rüegg-Stürm and Mathias Wagner. Professor Tsuyoshi Numagami would like to acknowledge the support of NISTEP in Tokyo. He also wishes to express his thanks to Professor Akira Goto of Tokyo University, Associate Professor Akiya Nagata of the Japanese Institute of Science and Technology, and Associate Professor Yaichi Aoshima of Hitotsubashi University. Professors Sánchez-Runde and Javier Quintanilla gratefully acknowledge support from the Division of Research of IESE, University of Navarra.

Understandably perhaps, most of the intellectual, administrative and secretarial pressures of producing this volume have fallen upon Warwick Business School. Even with collaborative and shared tasks, the buck has to stop somewhere. I would like to express my thanks to Caroline Conneely, Janet Biddle and Sheila Frost who, at various times and in various ways, helped with the production of the manuscript. My greatest appreciation is to Gill Drakeley who has word processed large sections of the book and has also helped to refashion and reformat successive drafts from contributors as they have arrived at my office at Warwick Business School.

Thank you all, and forgive us if we have inadvertently missed out someone who has supported what is certainly the most complex and challenging piece of research I have had the privilege to engage in over 35 years of trying to do management research.

Andrew M. Pettigrew
Warwick Business School

Chapter 1

# Innovative Forms of Organizing:

## Trends in Europe, Japan and the USA in the 1990s

*Andrew M. Pettigrew and Silvia Massini*

## INTRODUCTION

Here at the beginning of the twenty-first century the trumpets of change are heralding the appearance of innovative forms of organization. Some management writers have suggested a widespread sense of revolution in the form, character and process of contemporary organizations. In their attempts to capture and portray these changes in form there has been a notable tendency to invent new phrases. These phrases often imply the appearance of new types of organizations, but the emphasis is not just on new organizational forms or structures, but also new processes and systems. Thus we are variously persuaded of the rise of the network and cellular form, (Miles et al., 1997), the federal organization (Handy, 1992), the postmodern flexible firm (Volberda, 1998) and the individualized corporation (Ghoshal and Bartlett, 1998). In the accounts of Hammer and Champy (1993, pp. 14–15), Miles et al. (1997) and Ghoshal and Bartlett (1998, pp. 6–8), the contemporary shift in organizational paradigm is equivalent to the emergence of the multidivisional structures (M-Form) of Du-Pont and General Motors in the 1920s. The M-Form is being overtaken by the N-Form (Hedlund, 1994). These are important claims which thus far have not been subject to substantial and broadly based empirical inquiry.

But why are organizations in transition? As ever, big questions are rarely answered by single causes. There appears to be a convergence of economic, technological, informational, industrial and political factors driving the emergence of innovative forms of organizing (Hitt et al., 1998; Fenton and Pettigrew, 2000a). Heightened international competition in a globalizing economy is pushing firms to think and act globally and locally. (Hamel and Prahalad 1996). There are efficiency drives to reduce costs, pressures to concentrate manufacturing resources regionally and to simplify complex matrix structures by de-emphasizing country organizations. Internationalizing firms are strengthening internal networks between functions, divisions, countries and regions in order to speed the transfer of skill and knowledge and are investing in alliances and other partnerships to compete through co-operation. Technological change is shortening product life cycles in many industries and pressurizing firms to build organizations with greater flexibility. Advances in information and communication technologies are enabling network formation and utilization and permitting a quantity and quality of hierarchical control and lateral knowledge sharing previously considered impossible. Deregulation has also been an enormous driver both of increased economic competition and of cultural and people change in organizations. New skills, knowledge, attitudes and standards are now required in industries and firms previously sheltered from competition (Pettigrew and Whipp, 1991).

These multifactor explanations for the emergence of new forms of organizing are clearly suggestive of broader and deeper explanations for change than just the efficiency motives of managers and entrepreneurs. Max Weber (1927) had, of course, long since contended that particular forms of organization appear at specific moments in time embedded within existing social, economic and technological conditions. Thus the industrial age gave rise to the bureaucratic organization with its emphasis on hierarchy, stability and control. The present era of change is portrayed by Heydebrand (1989) as the result of the transition from industrial to post-industrial capitalism. Drawing on Bell's (1973) analysis, Heydebrand notes that this shift from commodity production to service delivery and intellectual technologies is the defining characteristic for the emergence of post-industrial forms. Heydebrand's (1989) particular form of political–economic explanation prophesizes the 'reappearance of clanlike, neopatrimonial, flexible, informal, decentralized yet culturally integrated network relations in postmodern organizations.' (1989: 327). But the rise of such practices is never linear, universal and complete. The traces of the previous era in terms of formal rationality, fixed hierarchies and division of labour and norms of formal interaction and deference may persist to different degrees into the new era. Old forms may persist and coexist with new variants thus demanding from the analyst of change observational lenses which include historical sensitivity within particular societies and organizations and comparative awareness between societies and organizations.

The above kind of international comparative and longitudinal research is still rare in the social and management sciences. This book is the summative representation of a programme of research designed and executed to deliver such comparative and time series data on Innovative Forms of Organizing (INNFORM). The INNFORM programme was a collective endeavour of an international research network led from Warwick Business School in the UK, but involving six other European universities and one university each from the USA and Japan. The programme of research had a progress aim, a performance aim and a process aim:

- The progress aim was to map the extent of innovation in forms of organizing in a large sample of firms in Europe, Japan and the USA in 1992–93 and 1996–97.
- The performance aim was to test the performance consequences of these new forms of organizing.
- The process aim was to examine the managerial and organizational processes of moving from more traditional forms of organizing.

These ambitious aims involved making substantial commitments of people and other resources and taking some big intellectual and managerial risks. Most of the risks paid off but some didn't, and we devote Chapter 15 of this volume to discussing the lessons learnt from this multidisciplinary, multi-methods and multiresearch-site study.

Beyond the above three aims the INNFORM programme was guided by an evolving set of core questions and a particular form of organizational analysis which we hoped would deliver theoretical insights and empirical findings on the *what*, *why* and *how* of the emergence of innovative forms of organizing. Later in this chapter, when we have assessed some of the most important literature on innovative forms, we will outline some of the specific questions and frameworks which shaped and derived from our work. Here it is enough to say that we were curious about four classes of questions:

- the origins of innovative forms;
- trends in their emergence in firms in different national, industrial and regional contexts;
- the very micro processes of their development in organizations adopting innovative forms;
- the consequences for the organizations and managers who experimented with changes in their organizational forms and practices.

Behind these four classes of questions lay some deeper prerequisites which shaped our form of organizational analysis. We started with the organization as the unit of analysis, for that is obviously where any experimentation with innovative forms was taking place. We used the literature as it was in

1995–96 when our programme started (plus some early pilot case studies) to identify demonstrable indicators of the emergence of new forms. After a flirtation with some of the early ideal types being touted in the literature, we set aside any search for network forms of organizing, or 'n' or cellular form. We concentrated our search for patterns in the emergence of the indicators rather than assuming a priori that those indicators coalesced into new types of organizations. We sought to map trends in these organizational innovations in firms with different degrees of knowledge intensity and internationalization. Our international comparative analysis in Europe, Japan and the USA allowed us to explore whether there was any convergence in the patterns of innovating between regions and nation states, or whether divergent forms of capitalism (Whitley, 1999) were shaping alternative innovation pathways in different parts of the world.

Time was also a crucial enabler of our analysis. An essential principle of our method was to catch reality in flight (Pettigrew, 1997a, 1998a). Trends in the emergence of innovative forms can only be assessed in the light of a temporal analysis. So our survey instrument tried to map the emergence of innovative forms at two time points 1992–93 and 1996–97. And our case studies, to different degrees, had a retrospective and a real time component. In some of our cases these temporal observations allowed a process analysis where we could examine the origins, development, decay and further evolution of innovative forms. We also dealt directly with important questions of consequence. This occurred most obviously in our assessment of the performance implications of experimentation with new forms. We also addressed consequence questions in examining cycles of on-going organizing and strategizing in some of our firms and the implications of heightened organizational complexity triggered by innovative forms.

This second and summative book from the INNFORM programme of research is different in scale and intellectual character from *The Innovating Organization* which was edited by Pettigrew and Fenton and published in 2000. The earlier book had three purposes:

- to offer a comprehensive and critical assessment of the literature on innovative forms of organizing;
- to present 8 of our 18 European case studies as illustrations of innovative organizational transformations;
- to offer a cross-case analysis of those eight case studies.

In tackling these three purposes, *The Innovating Organization* only addressed the process aim of our research and hinted (through our European surveys data set) of the progress aim. In this summative volume we directly tackle all three aims of the INNFORM programme. We offer analyses of trends in innovative forms of organizing in Europe, Japan and the USA and draw on comparative case analysis from the majority of our 18 European case studies.

Crucially we illuminate these empirical analyses by raising and developing three core analytical and theoretical themes in our work. Thus Part 1 of this volume focuses on the theme of organizing/strategizing and illustrates and develops this theme with a set of case studies from Swedish, German, Swiss and Dutch firms. Part 2, meanwhile, picks up the crucial consequences and performance theme in examining complementarities, change and performance. After the introductory Chapter 6, which establishes the theme, there are again three chapters which, in different ways, develop the complementarities and performance link. Chapter 7 does this through the econometric analysis of our survey findings and Chapters 8 and 9 by offering complementary analyses of the *what*, *why* and *how* of building systems of innovation. This complementarities theme is illustrated by six of the eight UK case studies from the INNFORM database. Part 3 of this volume picks up the issue of Managing Dualities. A key finding from our survey and case study work was that as firms are building more innovative and flexible forms so they are making simultaneous and apparently contradictory changes. This tendency for modernizing firms to be building hierarchies and networks and attempting to both centralize and decentralize (among other dualities) illustrates well the consequence and process dimensions of our inquiry. Again in Part 3, after the introductory Chapter 10, we draw on both our survey and case study findings to develop the crucial practical theme of managing dualities.

Part 4, the concluding part of this volume, comprises two chapters. Chapter 14 draws together many of the theoretical and empirical threads from the INNFORM programme and offers a range of concluding thoughts about the content of our work. Given the scale, complexity and challenges of the INNFORM programme, in Chapter 15 we decided to offer an account and analysis of the social production of knowledge in conducting this programme of research. Here we provide some analysis and concluding observations on the how of our work, including the special challenges of international collaborative inquiry enriched also by a partnership with PricewaterhouseCoopers.

## INNOVATIVE FORMS OF ORGANIZING

At the beginning of their comprehensive review of the research and writing on new or innovative forms of organizing Fenton and Pettigrew (2000a) offered the following conclusions: the body of literature on new forms is proliferating in scale and intellectual diversity and has yet to be united under an overarching theory or perspective and therefore may only be weakly classified as a research focus. They catalogue the field's theoretical diversity and note that the range of contributions cover perspectives such as inter-organizational theory (Powell, 1990; Perrone, 1997); network theory (Granovetter, 1982, 1992; Uzzi, 1997; Polodny and Page, 1998); knowledge-based views (Hedlund, 1994; Nonaka, 1994; Grant, 1996); complementarities (Milgrom and Roberts, 1995; Ichniowski et al., 1997) and relational perspectives (Ghoshal and Bartlett, 1990; Roth and Nigh, 1992; Ghoshal and Nohria, 1993; Easton and Araujo, 1994). However, in among this diversity of levels of analysis, conceptual language and theoretical perspectives is the agreement that the form, process and role of organizations had fundamentally changed at the end of the twentieth century, and continue to do so.

But if the direction of change is so evident why is there such diversity of language and emphasis to capture the content and process and often assumed speed of change? There are many candidate explanations for this conundrum. It appears that the loose focus of interest in innovative forms has built into it a double ambiguity. Different scholars choose to define organizational form differently and where they offer a definition of what is new or innovative in forms, there may also be multiple definitions on offer. This double ambiguity has led us on the INNFORM programme to attempt precision in defining organizational form (below we focus on changing structures, processes and boundaries) and also what is new or innovative. Thus we propose four instances of innovation as guidelines in choosing our 18 case studies. In the first instance, innovation may refer to a genuine widespread organizational innovation, such as the development of the multi-divisional form in the 1930s, or the possibility of its equivalent in the 1990s. Secondly, innovation may be some novel combination of organizational processes and/or structures not previously associated. Thirdly innovation could refer to some novel combination of previously associated structures and/or processes. Finally, innovation could be some organizational initiative which is new for the industry sector in that particular economy but more generally may not be new. The important criterion was that the changes which the organization adopted were perceived as new by their members. Thus the INNFORM view of organizational form and of newness of form attempts to capture both the features and indicators of form and recognizes that such indicators are sensitive to the perceptions and opinions of those creating and responding to the forms (McKendrick and Carroll, 2001; Ruef, 2000; Polos, Hannan and Carroll, 2002).

In our original successful proposal to the UK Economic and Social Research Council (ESRC) for funding for this research (Pettigrew, Whittington and Conyon, 1995), we scanned the literature on innovative forms at that time and identified the following linked characteristics or features:

- radical decentralization of profit responsibility to operating units, and reliance on internal contracting mechanisms;
- flattened organizational hierarchies;
- restricted head office roles, with top management focused on knowledge creation and dissemination;

- a shift from 'command and control' management styles to 'facilitate and empower';
- highly elaborate formal and informal internal communication systems, lateral as well as hierarchical;
- extensive use of ad hoc interdivisional and interfunctional conferences, task forces and teams rather than rigid organizational compartmentalization;
- the deliberate construction and use of internal labour markets for the dissemination of knowledge.

This list of indicators seemed plausible at the time, but it was based upon a shaky and somewhat untheorized empirical base. Part of the problem was that in the mid-1990s in the field of organization structure and design, practice had far accelerated ahead of empirical analysis. This is, of course, a familiar enough issue in the various fields of management research where there is a long tradition of practitioners taking action and research agendas than following the practice. In this kind of situation it is somewhat easy for the researchers to be beguiled by the trumpets of novelty being loudly blown by the consultants influencing the early adoption of new managerial innovations. As many have commented, management theory and practice is a fashion industry and at the early stages of proclaiming novelty a new mobilizing language has to be found to capture the attention of practitioners and scholars alike. So the 1990s literature on innovative forms has been replete with attention-directing language such as the rise of the boundaryless organization, the centreless organization, the federal and network organization. Amplified by a limited set of case study examples, such imagery often drives home a strong and resonant aspect of any novel set of organizational practices, but such writing gives us only a limited picture of the wider landscape of change.

Nevertheless, as DiMaggio (2001) and others have argued, this imagery of the innovating firm began to coalesce around some core themes. There seemed to be three obvious emphases in this practice-based literature: first, the emphasis on greater permeability of organizational boundary and the development of networks, co-operative relations and alliances within and between organizations; secondly, the trend to flatten the hierarchies of more traditional organizations and to build more co-operative forms of managerial style; and thirdly the associated drive to develop more creative, responsive and learning orientated organizations which could cope with the tougher competitive conditions at the end of the twentieth century.

Drawing on a range of literature way beyond the practice based writing on innovative forms, Fenton and Pettigrew (2000a) also identify three highly interrelated themes permeating these literatures. The three themes are labelled by Fenton and Pettigrew (2000a) as:

- the globalizing firm and its changing boundaries;
- the knowledge firm in the knowledge economy;
- networks and the socially embedded firm.

The first of these themes picks up the pressures on globalizing firms to shift their goals from economizing to adding value. Thus the economies of scale derived from vertically integrated firms are giving way to a focus on core competencies while other activities are being outsourced. The work of Ghoshal and Bartlett, 1990, 1995 in particular has led to a reconceptualization of the global firm as an entity for capturing and utilizing strategic internal competencies. In these kinds of global firms there is a heightened emphasis on organizing requiring complementary changes in processes and structures.

The knowledge firm in the knowledge economy has been successfully refined to become more inclusive, not just of the preoccupations of so-called knowledge intensive firms in newer industries, but also of the knowledge and learning related needs of more mature firms in older industries. Deep within this theme is the recognition that competitive performance is no longer just about positioning based upon tangible assets, but is also an innovation contest resting on combinations of tangible and intangible resources. The emphasis on learning and knowledge creation and use is now explicitly built into organizational analysis and development as firms seek both to collect and connect knowledge within and without their traditional organizational boundaries.

The theme of networks and the socially embedded firm places inter-organizational relations and network formation and use at the heart of the organizational agenda. Here the focus of organizing is on the character and patterns of relationships and exchange which occur in a variety of intra-firm and inter-firm networks, alliances, and other co-operative engagements. The belief is that such network and relational practices will provide a context for learning and offer rapid transfer of knowledge and ideas into action, hence increasing the responsiveness and creativity of the firm. As firms add value via relationships and require even greater internal and external interdependence to create, share and transfer knowledge, so the basis for organizational activity and configuration is centred on relationships and the wider social context in which the firm is embedded.

There is a clear overlap between the three themes identified by Fenton and Pettigrew (2000a) and DiMaggio (2001). Both sets of authors also recognize the interconnections between three elements. Whittington et al. (1999) also argue that features of new forms of organizing maybe mutually reinforcing: 'Flatter structures demand more interactive processes; interaction is concentrated within more tightly drawn organizational boundaries; narrower focus reduces the need for tall hierarchies of control' (Whittington et al., 1999: 588). All this is suggestive that new forms of organizing may have to proceed in a systemic and related way and not in a piecemeal fashion. We will return to this issue of holistic and complementary change in Part 2 of this volume.

As we write in 2002 the two widest and deepest assessments of the literature on innovative forms of organizing are to be found in Fenton and Pettigrew (2000a) and DiMaggio (2001). These authors come to a remarkably similar set of conclusions about the state of knowledge of the emergence of new organizational forms. Both catalogue the diverse, fragmented and limited nature of empirical inquiry and theoretical development; both note the absence of a unifying theory to interpret the empirical findings which do exist; and both recognize the, at times, prescriptive and apocalyptic writing in the practitioner orientated literature and the consequent difficulty for the reader to disentangle what has been found from what the author would like to see.

These authors also comment strongly on the partial nature of empirical enquiry on innovative forms. Fenton and Pettigrew (2000a) refer to the predominance of exceptional cases in and out of extraordinary sectors or geographical locations, while DiMaggio (2001) refers to the study of eccentric companies in idiosyncratic competitive environments.

There is the additional challenge in studying an emergent process that truth is the daughter of time (Pettigrew, 1990). Few of the empirical studies prior to the INNFORM programme had either spatial width or temporal depth. Observations and prophesies were being made about a complex and possibly discontinuous process of change from limited cases, often in a single society and predominantly from atemporal data sets. At the beginning of his analysis of the twenty-first century firm DiMaggio (2001: 5) notes the absence of mapping studies of innovative forms, 'the literature is far richer in striking examples of purported trends than in careful empirical studies documenting the scope and incidence of change'. He follows this (2001: 6) by bemoaning the lack 'of careful analyses that take into mutual account business firms (other than the largest multinationals) in different regions of the globe'. And then at the end of his treatise (2001: 215) he brings together the spatial and temporal deficiencies of new forms of organizing research by proclaiming, 'a major priority for the research community should be to establish systems that collect trend data on the structure, governance and behaviour of organizations comparable to that now collected routinely for human beings'. Five years earlier it was these sorts of challenges which motivated the INNFORM network to design and execute a study of innovative organizational forms which put spatial and temporal context at the very heart of the research.

## THE INNFORM PROGRAMME

As we have indicated, the INNFORM programme of research had a progress, a performance and a process aim. The goal was to map the extent of development of innovative forms in the 1990s, test for the performance consequences of any such changes and study the process of emergence of the new forms. These aims required a multimethod research strategy and the collection of time series data. Survey methods and multivariate statistical analyses were used to achieve the progress and performance aims of the research, and case studies of 18 European firms were utilized to achieve the process aims. The core funding for the research team in the UK was provided by the ESRC and PricewaterhouseCoopers, supplemented by funds from the consortium of organizations who supported the Centre for Corporate Strategy and Change at Warwick Business School. Further additional funding was supplied by the other university teams who were part of the INNFORM network. PricewaterhouseCoopers were not just co-funders of the research, they were also co-producers and co-disseminators. Two directors of PricewaterhouseCoopers, Chris David and David Shaw made notable contributions to the development and impact of the research.

Crucially, the research also required the active and sustained co-operation of colleagues from Duke University (the USA), Erasmus University (the Netherlands), ESSEC (France), Hitotsubashi University (Japan), IESE (Spain), Jönköping University (Sweden) and St Gallen University (Switzerland). The lead researchers from each of these institutions are respectively Arie Lewin, Frans van den Bosch, Hamid Bouchikhi, Tsuyoshi Numagami, Carlos Sanchez-Runde, Leif Melin and Winfried Ruigrok. Richard Whittington, the co-principal investigator of the research, was at Warwick Business School when the research was initiated, but worked at Oxford University throughout the conduct of the research. The Warwick team at various times has involved Martin Conyon, Evelyn Fenton, Silvia Massini and Simon Peck.

We often portray the INNFORM programme as a network studying networks. How this network was built, maintained and motivated was a crucial input to the progress and impact of this research effort and some of the intellectual and managerial challenges of making this network work are discussed in the concluding chapter of this volume. It goes without saying that this programme could not have achieved its aims without the active and sustained commitment of all members of the international network.

## SURVEYING INNOVATIVE FORMS OF ORGANIZING IN EUROPE, JAPAN AND THE USA

The INNFORM survey design began from an examination of the literature on new organizational forms and three mini-case studies of innovative organizations. We also benefited from the strengths and limitations of survey instruments developed to identify patterns of restructuring in US firms (for example, Markides, 1996) in the late 1980s and early 1990s. Many of these instruments appeared ill-adapted to the new competitive landscape and, in any case, were not developed specifically to test for new forms of organizing. Accordingly, our own survey instrument was eclectic and adaptive in design. In the intellectual debates (initially in the Warwick team) and then more widely in our international network, we decided it was premature to follow the managerial literature at that time, which was attempting to portray the evolution of new forms of organizing as the emergence of various ideal types such as network or federal or horizontal forms of organization. Instead we searched the literature for patterning in terms of likely indicators of emergent change and then sought some validation of the relative importance of such empirical indicators in the three UK pilot case studies and the experiences of our international collaborators. This early intellectual debate was a crucial stepping stone in the project's development and a key part of the early team building for the research.

The review of literature we did on new forms of organizing to prepare the INNFORM survey instrument revealed a wide list of indicators of organizational change. (See Whittington et al. (1999) for a more in-depth presentation of this literature.) We decided to cluster these indicators of contemporary change under the headings of *changing structures*, *changing processes*, and *changing boundaries*. Here we define the three main dimensions, draw out some of the significant interdependencies between them and also indicate the limited extent of systematic and large-sample surveys of innovative forms of organizing. Figure 1.1 summaries nine areas of change measured in the INNFORM survey.

## CHANGING STRUCTURES

The new competitive environment has put traditional hierarchical structures under a dual pressure. First, the heavy hierarchical layers of middle managers have become too expensive; second, these layers have impeded the information flows and quickness of response necessary for flexibility and innovation. As a result, firms have apparently been resorting to widespread delayering in order to remove these expensive barriers to action (Freeman and Cameron, 1993; Zeffane, 1992).

The removal of layers has been accompanied by increased decentralization, both operational and strategic. Increased operational decentralization – for example in areas such as product design and marketing – has been necessary both to improve response times and to harness the on-the-ground knowledge of operating managers. Strategic decentralization – for example, increased responsibility for investment decisions – increases the profit-orientation and accountability of business managers, incentivizing them in an increasingly competitive environment (Pettigrew, 1999b). ABB's business managers are even reported to be able to retain profits in their local balance sheets from year

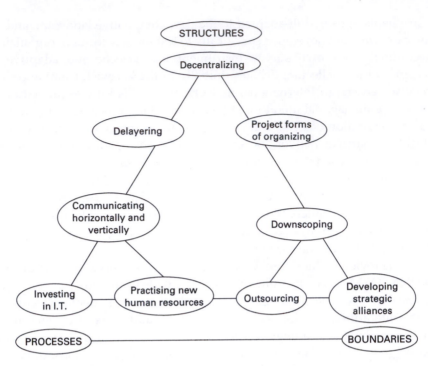

FIGURE 1.1   *New forms of organizing: the multiple indicators*

to year (Bartlett and Ghoshal, 1993). Decentralization into smaller units promotes cross-functional and cross-boundary teams. In place of rigid traditional structures, organizations are increasingly shifting towards more flexible, project-based forms of organization. Structures are therefore taking on a more horizontal character, projects being the vehicle for bridging the 'divisions' of traditional divisional organization (Ghoshal and Bartlett, 1995).

## CHANGING PROCESSES

The flexibility and knowledge required in the new knowledge economy requires intensive interaction, vertical and horizontal. Learning organizations are communication-intensive, requiring new investments in information technology (IT). These unite different parts of the organization in intense exchanges of information. A key dimension of these flows is horizontal, promoting 'co-adaptive' exploitation of cross-business synergies. These flows of information are moving outwards as well, to embrace suppliers and customers through electronic data interchange (EDI) and similar initiatives (Jarvenpaa and Ives, 1994). The new communication-intensive organization allows still further process innovation, in terms of participation, polycentricity and flexibility (Fulk and DeSanctis, 1995).

For these processes to work, the hard infrastructure of IT needs to be underpinned by 'softer' investments in human resources. As Ghoshal and Bartlet (1998) have insisted, the new strategies and structures require new ways of managing and new kinds of managers. Whittington and Mayer (1997) suggest that the human resources (HR) function has become central to making the new forms of organization work. These new human resource management (HRM) practices have two broad dimensions for the emerging model of organization: those concerned with supporting horizontal networking and those concerned with maintaining organizational integration.

The new HR fosters horizontal processes in a variety of ways. Growing use of corporate-wide conferences, seminars and similar events is reported, as companies seek occasions on which to bring together key personnel for exchange. Companies are increasingly seeing their key resource as their people and the knowledge they carry, so that corporate-wide management of careers across organizational boundaries is becoming important (Quintanilla and Sánchez-Runde, 2000). These horizontal processes need integration, too, within a corporate sense of purpose (Van Wijk and Van den Bosch, 2000). High profile leadership and corporate mission building are necessary to provide the sense of shared corporate identity on which exchange can be built. Investment in managerial development plays a key part in cementing a common purpose within a 'boundaryless organization', as at GE. Here the deliberate cultivation of cross-unit teams and cross-unit communications are key functions (Nohria and Ghoshal, 1997; Pettigrew, 1999b; Fenton and Pettigrew, 2000).

## CHANGING BOUNDARIES

Large scale drives high hierarchies; wide scope stretches horizontal relationships (Jacques, 1990). Delayering and more interactive processes are likely to be accompanied, therefore, by decreased scale and increased focus on narrower spans of activities. This correlate of changing structures and processes is reinforced by increased competitive pressures forcing companies to focus on 'core competencies', redrawing their boundaries around what constitutes or supports their true competitive advantage (Prahalad and Hamel, 1990).

This pressure is reflected in the widely observed shifting of business towards smaller, decentralized units (Zenger and Hesterley, 1997). Hierarchy and scale can hamper the strategic flexibility required for competing in increasingly hyper-competitive environments. The shift in scale is often reinforced by strategic downscoping and the abandonment of conglomerate strategies, leaving firms focused on areas of advantage (Hoskisson and Hitt, 1994). Even within particular product-market domains, firms appear increasingly to be outsourcing value-chain activities of low value or strategic significance, with a wide range of non-core activities from training and research and development (R&D) subcontracted. Where superior skills or resources exist outside the firm, firms are making increased use of strategic alliances to supplement and sometimes enhance their own competencies. In sum, whether by alliances, outsourcing or downscoping, firms appear to be drawing in their boundaries around narrower spheres of activity.

The above review of trends in organizational change reveals a patch-work quilt of conjecture and pockets of evidence to suggest that some dimensions of change may be occurring faster than others. The distinctive contribution of our survey was, first, to measure all the indicators of change together, secondly to measure them over two time points (1992–93 and 1996–97) and thirdly to examine the extent to which the dimensions cohere: were some firms innovating predominantly in the areas of structures, or processes, or boundaries? And what is the extent of these changes?

Unusually for a survey instrument of this kind, respondents were asked to compare their organization in 1992 with 1996. (In the US study the two time points were 1993 and 1997.) This is, of course, a limited timescale within a process of organizational change which probably started some time before and is continuing now. However, problems of reliable respondent recall precluded a longer period of retrospection, and the periods 1992–96 and 1993–97 certainly included considerable pressure for change in Europe, Japan and the USA.

An initial questionnaire was tested with a large group of executive MBA students; a further refined version was piloted on a small sub-sample of large UK firms. After certain adjustments, the questionnaire was mailed during 1997 to the chief executives of large and medium-sized (that is, with more than 500 employees) independent, domestically owned firms through-out Western Europe. For the UK, these were the largest 1500 independent businesses by employment; for the remainder of Western Europe, there were 2000 large and medium-sized firms sampled in proportion to home-country GDP. Although relying on single respondents, our targeting of chief execu-tives was designed to elicit as comprehensive a view as possible and is in line with widespread practice given the difficulties of obtaining multires-pondent returns from large-scale surveys. Except for the Dutch and Scandinavian samples, the Continental European questionnaires were trans-lated by native speakers into German, Italian, Spanish or French, as most appropriate, and checked for accuracy by local team members. We re-mailed to initial non-respondents and subsequently used telephone follow-ups. The overall response rate was 13.1 per cent, comparable to other recent European surveys of organizational change (Ezzamel et al., 1996).

Corresponding to their original sampling proportions, the largest group of respondents were UK (40.7 per cent) and German (15.9 per cent); no other country accounted for more than 10 per cent of responses. Tests for the UK sample indicated no response biases for size, industry or profitability.

The Japanese survey instrument was translated into Japanese by col-leagues from Hitotsubashi University. Only very minor changes were made in the survey instrument to reflect the Japanese context. In order to improve the response rate, the survey was sent out with an appropriate covering letter by the Japanese Institute of Science and Technology Policy (NISTEP). The questionnaire was mailed in 1997 to the chief executives of 1000 large and medium-sized companies with more than 500 employees/independent domestically owned firms in Japan. The response rate for the Japanese survey was a commendable 25.7 per cent.

With the UK, Western European and Japanese surveys completed in 1997 the decision was made early in 1999 to carry out a US survey. Agreement was reached with colleagues at Duke University in the USA to administer the INNFORM standardized survey instrument and PricewaterhouseCoopers provided additional financial support. In the summer of 1999, the US survey was mailed to a sample of the 1500 largest independent domestically owned firms in the USA. This time (to reflect the timing of the survey) CEOs were asked to report on the same indicators of organizational change, but at the five-year time points 1993 and 1997. Seventy-nine useable survey instruments were returned – a response rate of 5.3 per cent. Tests for this US sample indicated no response biases for size, sector or profitability indicating that the sample who responded to the survey instrument were representative of the 1500 firms surveyed.

There are no large-scale published surveys mapping the extent of development of new forms of organizing in Europe, Japan and the USA and no studies comparing the three regions. There are, of course, a number of good studies (particularly done by Lincoln and his colleagues, for example, Lincoln and Kalleberg, 1990) comparing US and Japanese organizations in the 1980s and then in the 1990s. These studies variously indicate that, compared to the US, Japanese manufacturing organizations have taller hierarchies, less functional specialization, less formal delegation of authority but more de facto participation in decisions by lower levels of management. The picture presented in these studies of Japanese firms is of a highly integrated and interdependent set of factors embedded in Japanese institutions, the interlinkages between large and medium-sized firms in the Keiretsu arrangements, and the form and processes within Japanese firms which accumulatively help to build a highly adaptive and flexible form of organizing in Japan. Thus in large Japanese firms, life-term employment and promotion through seniority are said to provide a platform for the building of generalist skills which are enabled by frequent job rotation and regular training. Innovation in product development is said to be encouraged by elaborate processes of organizational and individual learning. Strong hierarchies are combined with equally strong processes of horizontal co-ordination which encourage both knowledge creating and sharing (Aoki, 1990; Nonaka and Takeuchi, 1995). The above features of Japanese organizations led us to expect that at least some of the innovative forms of organizing in Europe and the USA were already present in some of the Japanese firms. But were the economic and business pressures in Europe in the 1990s pushing European firms towards greater change in their structures, processes and boundaries? And what impact, if any, were equivalent pressures in Japan and the USA in the 1990s having on the content and pace of organizational change there?

## COMPLEMENTARITIES AND PERFORMANCE

In addition to surveying trends in the emergence of new forms of organizing, we also sought to examine any associations between organizational change and performance. Here we have built upon recent theorizing about the potential virtues of complementary change (Milgrom and Roberts, 1990, 1995). Our approach in using complementarities thinking is analytically broader than previous research which thus far has tended to focus on functional areas such as HRM (for example, Ichniowski et al., 1997).

The notion of complementarities develops a line of thought in organizational theory that leads through contingency theory to configuration theory. Complementarities thinking follows contingency theory in seeing performance as dependent on 'fit' between key organizational variables, such as size and structure (Donaldson, 1996). However, it goes beyond the reductionist, disaggregated one-to-one comparisons of contingency theory to address the multilateral kinds of fit required for organizational effectiveness (Drazin and Van de Ven, 1985; Meyer et al., 1993). Here the notion of complementarities comes close to configuration theory, with its emphasis on the holistic, aggregated and systemic nature of organizational phenomena (Miller, 1987, 1996). This configurational approach has pushed performance analysis beyond simple interactions between disaggregated variables to a more aggregated comparison of the performance of whole types (Miles and Snow, 1978; Hambrick, 1983; Drazin and Van de Ven, 1985).

The complementarities notion starts from this configurational appreciation of the holistic nature of organizations, but adds two twists. The first twist is to stress the dangers of transitions. Milgrom and Roberts (1995: 181) describe the basic notion of complementarity as 'doing *more* of one thing *increases* the returns to doing *more* of another' (italics in original). The performance benefits of any change are dependent, therefore, upon the nature of other potentially complementary changes. In analysing the 'modern manufacturing' model, for example, Milgrom and Roberts (1990) suggest that the introduction of computer-aided design (CAD) technology pays best when associated with complementary inventory production, marketing and management policies. Here Milgrom and Roberts are not making the simple pairwise assumptions about performance relationships found in much contingency theory; rather they are insisting on the potential for complex, multiple interactions between changes, so that performance relationships are likely to be at least three-way and practices may reinforce the effects of other practices in either a positive or negative direction according to what else is going on at the same time. This interdependence is very characteristic of configurational theory, but complementarities stresses the implications for change: 'changing only a few of the system elements at a time to their optimal values may not come at all close to achieving all the benefits that are available through a fully co-ordinated move, and may even have negative payoffs' (Milgrom and Roberts, 1995: 191). The focus shifts from comparison between whole types to the gap in between, where the transition from one type to another is incomplete. The complementarities notion warns strongly of a possible J-curve relationship between change and performance, with partial implementation potentially worse than the starting point.

Complex interdependence also suggests the second twist on traditional configurational analysis, a reintroduction of the disaggregated approach to performance testing. Typically, configurational research has compared the relative performance of configurations as a whole (Ketchen et al., 1997). Configurations are treated as something of a black box, with no analysis of the contribution of individual elements to the performance of the whole or testing of systemic effects over and above the sum of individual contributions. However, the claim from complementarities that performance benefits depend upon combining the full set of complements suggests a simultaneously aggregated and disaggregated approach that compares the contribution of individual practices with the performance payoffs of them all together. Practices that are associated with positive performance when combined with their complements may be found to have negative effects when taken individually. Moreover, as Ichniowski et al. (1997) argue, complementarity among practices implies that the magnitude of the performance effect of the full system is larger than the sum of the marginal effects from adopting each practice individually. When analysed together, the individual effects on performance should be exhausted by the full-system effects.

The complementarities notion therefore extends the configurational approach in two ways. First, complementarity theory makes performance predictions that go beyond simple binary-type comparisons of one configuration with another and emphasize the problems of being caught with partial initiatives in between. Second, complementarity theory insists on a simultaneously aggregated and disaggregated analysis, both to define the conditionality of individual effects on other effects and to ensure that full-system effects outweigh individual component effects.

Overall, complementarity theory proposes both that high-performing firms are likely to be combining a number of practices at the same time and that the payoffs, to a full system of practices, are greater than the sum of its parts, some of which taken on their own might even have negative effects. The survey-based and case study findings on complementarities and performance are presented in full in Part 2 of this volume.

## THE CASE STUDY QUESTIONS AND ANALYSIS

The research strategy of the INNFORM programme has been to use complementary methods to pose complementary questions with the aim of identifying complementary findings. The third aim of our research required posing a different set of process questions from those used in the survey and implementing the comparative longitudinal case study methodology (Pettigrew, 1990, 1997a).

The survey findings could tell us a great deal about the what of innovation by exposing trends in the pattern of change within and between our nine indicators at our two time points of 1992–93 and 1996–97, but the survey results are silent on the how and why of innovation. The main purpose of our case study work was to pose and answer a series of process questions about the origins, initiation, sequencing, development, decay, consequence and impact of innovative forms of organizing. Figure 1.2 lists the 18 European case studies.

Given the scale of the BP and Unilever organizations, we decided to use these large systems as sources of two cases each. One case explored the overall process of corporate organization change and the other case took a slice across the organization to examine network formation and use.

The 18 case studies above were designed with three main objectives:

1   To analyse the processes and practices of the emergence, development and management of innovating forms
2   To examine how and why the subset of our firms who attempted complementary change managed that process over the time period from the late 1980s to 2002
3   To offer a wider platform for empirical analysis and theoretical development than that which was possible given the feasible length and necessary restrictive set of indicators of change in our survey instrument.

We have already discussed the four criteria of 'newness' we used to choose our cases in order that they would consistently and adequately illustrate movement towards, or conceivably away from, innovative forms. In addition to debating and agreeing the criteria for choice of case studies, the INNFORM network also discussed and agreed a set of analytical questions for each case. The questions included: an analysis of the drivers for innovation; the content, scope, sequencing and depth of change; the process sequencing of the innovation; barriers and facilitators of change; instances of differential pace of change and consequences and unresolved management

BP Organization Development 1985–2002 – UK
BP Knowledge Management Network – UK
Unilever Organization Development 1987–2002 – UK/Netherlands
Unilever Global Hair Products Network – UK/Netherlands
Ove Arup and Partners – UK
Coopers & Lybrand Europe – UK
Spencer Stuart – UK
Davis, Langdon & Everest – UK
ABB – Swiss/Swedish
Hilti – Swiss/Lichtenstein
Siemens – German
Trumpf – German
Internationale Nederlanden Groep (ING) – Netherlands
Rabobank – Netherlands
Fremap – Spanish
AGBAR – Spanish
Saab Training Systems – Swedish
Östogöta Eskilde Bank – Swedish

FIGURE 1.2  *The 18 case studies of the INNFORM programme*

issues in implementing the new forms of organizing. Each case also had theoretical objectives to provoke and inspire debate in the field of organization design (Fenton and Pettigrew, 2000a).

Sets of cases were also chosen with the objective of illustrating and developing theoretical and empirical ideas, in particular thematic areas. Previous research and writing on professional service organizations (PSOs) by, for example, Hinings et al. (1991), Greenwood and Lachman (1996); and Lowendahl (1997) has focused attention on organizational change. The global and networked character for PSOs also suggested that they were settings where experimentation would be taking place with innovative forms of organizing. The Warwick team thereby chose four global PSOs with aspirations to become global networks as a focal point for their investigations. (See, for example, Fenton and Pettigrew in Chapter 9 of this volume.)

The second objective in using our case study work has been to build on our statistical findings regarding the association between complementary change initiatives and firm performance. From our survey results we knew little of the *what*, *why* and *how* of the creation and re-creation of complementary change in firms over time, and of how managerial choices and changes may deliver performance improvement. Four of our 18 case studies offered the potential to pose and answer analytical questions about the relationship between complementary change and performance. Two of these, BP and Unilever, are used to explore complementarities in action in Chapter 8 of this volume.

The greater contextual depth and temporal quality of case study research provides opportunities to pose and answer *how* and *why* questions. The inductive and interpretative quality of case study work also provides scope for theory building and novel empirical pattern recognition. Probably the two best examples of this in the INNFORM programme are developed in Parts 1 and 3 of this volume, where we explore theoretical ideas and some illustrative case examples on organizing/strategizing and also develop the empirical and managerial theme of dualities in the modern corporation.

## PATTERNS IN THE EMERGENCE OF INNOVATIVE FORMS OF ORGANIZING IN EUROPE, JAPAN AND THE USA 1992–97

Building on a range of theoretical traditions in organizational analysis, we expected to find both slow and unequal diffusion of new forms of organizing across our three regions (Fligstein and Freeland, 1995; Calori et al., 1997; Whitley, 1999; Whittington et al., 1999; Whittington and Mayer, 2000). Large firms only slowly adopted the M-form, the previous substantial organizational innovation (Dyas and Thanheiser, 1976; Whittington and Mayer, 2000) and population ecologists have long argued for the liabilities of newness consequent upon change and its corollary that novelty was most likely to come from either new entrants in a population of firms, or firms associated with radical technical innovations (Baum, 1996).

There is also some evidence and theoretical interpretation that the particular historical legacies and institutional structures of different national environments may influence the diffusion of organizational practices. In their review of the literatures on corporate forms and governance arrangements in 1995, Fligstein and Freeland contend that the world is not converging on a single form of organization. This conclusion is echoed to some degree in DiMaggio (2001), but he is more open in assessing the dual pressures for convergence and divergence in organizational practices between nations. DiMaggio's review recognizes pressures from globalization processes and the international system, which encourage convergence. He also argues that the idea systems of management today have such an international quality that they may be encouraging convergence in the beliefs of managers and then in their actions. This convergence is a movement towards 'project-based work and team organization; flatter, more horizontal organizations that rely on long-term interdependent relations with external parties; and extensive efforts to leverage capabilities across a wide range of activities' (DiMaggio, 2001: 68). But these convergent pressures at the international system level are in turn faced by issues of receptivity and resistance at the nation state and organizational levels of analysis, which in turn create different forms and speed of adaptation at local levels. Later in this volume Lewin et al. argue for the potency of natural institutional configurations in explaining variation in the diffusion of novel organizational practices between nations. This line of argument had previously been developed by Whitley (1999), who noted that divergent forms of capitalism were enabled by significant differences in societal institutions and agencies such as the state, capital and labour markets, and dominant beliefs about trust, loyalty and authority.

A second force for the unequal diffusion of new organizational practices may be different business environments and sectoral conditions. Thus Hedlund (1994) and Nonaka and Takeuchi (1995) have linked new initiatives in organizations to the knowledge intensity of sectors and firms. Equally, exposure to the dynamics of international competition (Zahra and O'Neill, 1998) and the complexity of multinational operations (Bartlett and Ghoshal, 1989) are identified as drivers of innovative organizational forms. International businesses can therefore be expected to be more innovative organizationally than more local ones.

In analysing our survey findings we thereby were curious about any convergence or divergence in the patterns of change in structures, processes and boundaries across the three regions. Were we seeing parallel change, convergent change or divergent change across the three regions? Was there any evidence of differential pace of change across the regions? And for the commentators who had projected revolutionary change in the development of new forms of organizing, were these forms supplanting or supplementing existing organizational arrangements? Finally, did the knowledge intensity and degree of internationalization of the firm appear to be strong drivers for the adoption of the new organizational practices we were measuring?

In order to make our research findings as accessible as possible we have used a series of five figures (Figures 1.3 through 1.7) to present descriptive trends of change statistics. Underpinning these figures are statistical tables which include tests for statistical significance. There is no space in this introductory chapter to include all these tables but we have included Table 1.1, Organizational indicators in Europe and Japan and the USA, as an example. In Table 1.1 the statistically significant differences between regions are shaded in grey. The reader may also wish to be reminded that, because the time point of surveying varied across the three regions, the European and Japanese results are for 1992 and 1996 and the US results are for 1993 and 1997.

The answers to questions in the INNFORM survey were mostly structured in a five-point Likert scale for both 1992–93 and 1996–97. For example, the question on the adoption of a project-based structure asked chief executives to indicate the extent to which the corporate structure was organized according to that form.

The possible answers for both 1992–93 and 1996–97 were: 1 = none; 2 = little; 3 = moderate; 4 = much; 5 = great. In general, the percentages in the following figures represent the proportion of organizations answering 4 or 5 in the five-point Likert scale. The missing data under HR (human resource innovations) in Figure 1.4 and outsourcing in Figure 1.5 are because of the way those questions were posed in the survey instrument. The INNFORM survey instrument is included as an Appendix at www.sagepub.co.uk/resources/pettigrew.htm

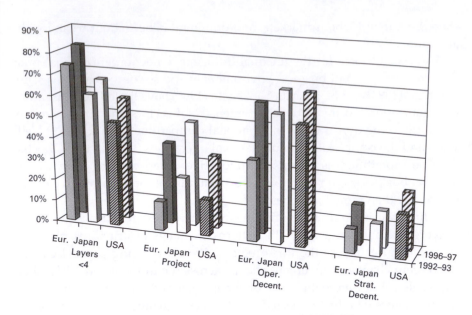

FIGURE 1.3   *Organizational structures, 1992–93 and 1996–97*

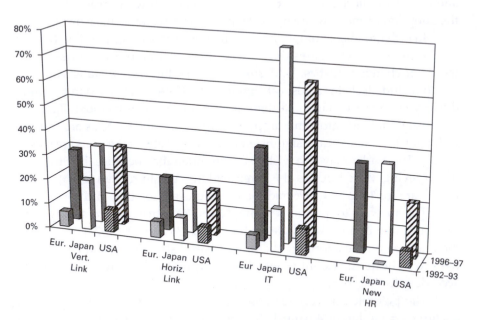

FIGURE 1.4   *Organizational processes, 1992–93 and 1996–97*

Figures 1.3, 1.4, 1.5 and 1.6 and Table 1.1 show the adoption of organizational innovations in structure, processes and boundaries across the three regions for 1992–93 and 1996–97. The nine indicators of new forms of

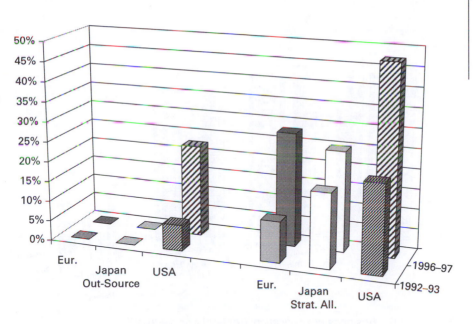

FIGURE 1.5  *Organizational boundaries, 1992–93 and 1996–97*

organizing correspond to the categories pictured in Figure 1.1. The overwhelming finding is a common direction of change, but from different starting points and involving some variation in pace across the three regions. Figure 1.3 shows that between 1992–93 and 1996–97 there is evident structural change with movement towards flatter, more fluid and decentralized structures with strong development of project structures and operational decentralization in Europe. Figure 1.4 indicates that underlying these structural changes were considerable process changes, most notably in the development of both vertical and horizontal linkages and investment in IT. The picture on boundary changes is more complex and will be discussed below.

Table 1.1 shows the descriptive statistics across the regions at the two time points and, in the grey shading, the main statistically significant differences. At 1992–93 and again at 1996–97, the most significant differences are between Europe and Japan and Japan and the USA. Japan had the most developed operational decentralization, project form development, and vertical and horizontal linkages at 1992. US firms claimed the most strategic alliance formulation in 1993 and this pattern was perpetuated in 1997. Over the two time points, European firms relatively speaking increased their adoption of project forms, operational decentralization, and both vertical and horizontal links, but in 1996 there were still statistically significant differences between Europe and Japan in number of hierarchical layers, project formation and operational decentralization. The most notably statistically significant differences between Europe and the USA at the two time points

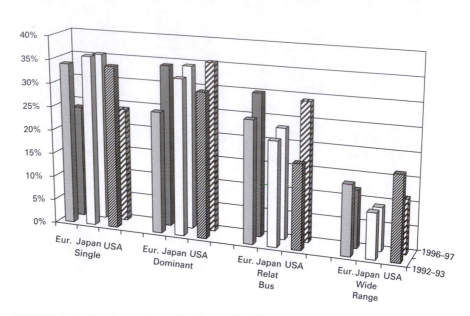

FIGURE 1.6   *Business diversification 1992–93 and 1996–97*

were greater hierarchical levels, more IT investment and greater alliance formation in the US firms.

Figure 1.6 Business diversification, 1992–93 and 1996–97 shows the responses to our survey question on the extent of diversification across the three regions. This figure (and Table 1.1) show that there was downscoping (de-diversification) among the firms with the widest product portfolios, but also a reduction in the number of firms with single product businesses – overall indicating some movement towards related diversification across the sample as a whole.

Figures 1.3 through 1.6 revealed the form of organizational arrangements in the three regions at 1992–93 and 1996–97. We have also examined elsewhere (Whittington et al., 1999; Pettigrew et al., 2000) the extent of change between the two time points within Europe and between Europe and Japan. Here we add the picture of change with the US trends. Relative to Japanese and US firms, European firms indicated a greater increase in emphasis or importance to changes in project formation, and operational and strategic decentralization over the period 1992–93 to 1996–97. Very high levels of process changes were indicated in all three regions with the biggest increases in IT being in Japan and the USA and the biggest increases in vertical and horizontal linkages and the HR innovations occuring in Europe and the USA. There was a tremendous increase in emphasis given to outsourcing across all three regions in the period 1992–93 to 1996–97 and a greater attachment to alliance formation in Europe and the USA compared with Japan. US

TABLE 1.1 Organizational indicators in Europe and Japan, 1992 and 1996, and USA, 1993 and 1997

| | Europe 1992 | Japan 1992 | US 1993 | Chi-2 (prob.) | Chi-2 (prob.) EUR-JP | Chi-2 (prob.) EUR-US | Chi-2 (prob.) JP-US | Europe 1996 | Japan 1996 | US 1997 | Chi-2 (prob.) | Chi-2 (prob.) EUR-JP | Chi-2 (prob.) EUR-US | Chi-2 (prob.) JP-US |
|---|---|---|---|---|---|---|---|---|---|---|---|---|---|---|
| Layers: median | 3 | 4 | 5 | | | | | 3 | 4 | 4 | | | | |
| Less than 4 | 74.3 | 61.1 | 48.7 | 25.084 (0.000) | 11.762 (0.001) | 20.103 (0.000) | 3.561 (0.169) | 81.8 | 65.9 | 57.7 | 31.595 (0.000) | 19.962 (0.000) | 22.210 (0.000) | 1.672 (0.434) |
| Projects | 13.5 | 25.8 | 16.7 | 14.853 (0.002) | 14.735 (0.000) | 0.481 (0.488) | 2.340 (0.126) | 38.0 | 48.8 | 33.8 | 8.475 (0.014) | 6.929 (0.008) | 0.405 (0.525) | 4.541 (0.033) |
| Op Dec | 37.3 | 59.1 | 55.3 | 30.306 (0.000) | 27.473 (0.000) | 8.580 (0.003) | 0.340 (0.560) | 60.9 | 67.4 | 67.1 | 3.172 (0.205) | 2.687 (0.101) | 1.061 (0.303) | 0.003 (0.960) |
| Str Dec | 11.0 | 14.6 | 20.0 | 5.200 (0.074) | 1.740 (0.187) | 4.746 (0.029) | 1.208 (0.272) | 18.4 | 16.8 | 26.3 | 3.421 (0.181) | 0.259 (0.611) | 2.549 (0.110) | 3.277 (0.070) |
| Vert links | 6.2 | 20.1 | 9.0 | 31.191 (0.000) | 30.170 (0.000) | 0.824 (1.000) | 5.104 (0.024) | 29.0 | 31.5 | 32.1 | 0.614 (0.736) | 0.468 (0.494) | 0.293 (0.588) | 0.009 (0.927) |
| Horiz links | 6.4 | 9.1 | 6.4 | 1.696 (0.428) | 1.568 (0.211) | 0.000 (0.991) | 0.541 (0.462) | 21.6 | 17.7 | 17.9 | 1.679 (0.432) | 1.461 (0.227) | 0.519 (0.471) | 0.002 (0.963) |
| IT | 5.6 | 16.9 | 10.3 | 23.204 (0.000) | 23.293 (0.000) | 2.483 (0.115) | 2.010 (0.156) | 37.2 | 76.6 | 64.1 | 104.422 (0.000) | 99.929 (0.000) | 19.758 (0.000) | 4.783 (0.029) |
| New HR | – | – | 6.3 | – | – | – | – | 34.9 | 35.4 | 21.5 | 5.845 (0.045) | 0.022 (0.882) | 5.398 (0.020) | 5.345 (0.069) |
| Outsourcing | – | – | 6.4 | | | | | – | – | 25.6 | – | | | |
| Str all (>10% Totass) | 10.2 | 18.5 | 22.0 | 7.889 (0.019) | 4.853 (0.028) | 6.057 (0.014) | 0.314 (0.575) | 28.3 | 25.0 | 47.5 | 10.363 (0.006) | 0.454 (0.500) | 8.166 (0.017) | 9.108 (0.003) |
| Diversification: Single | 34.3 | 35.9 | 34.2 | 0.234 (0.890) | 0.226 (0.634) | 0.001 (0.980) | 0.076 (0.783) | 23.7 | 35.4 | 24.1 | 10.668 (0.005) | 10.118 (0.001) | 0.005 (0.941) | 3.449 (0.063) |
| Dominant | 25.4 | 32.7 | 30.4 | 4.067 (0.131) | 3.874 (0.049) | 0.853 (0.356) | 0.147 (0.701) | 34.1 | 34.4 | 35.4 | 0.053 (0.974) | 0.004 (0.948) | 0.053 (0.818) | 0.030 (0.862) |
| Rel. bus. | 25.6 | 21.8 | 17.7 | 2.890 (0.236) | 3.410 (0.065) | 2.268 (0.132) | 0.594 (0.441) | 29.9 | 23.2 | 29.1 | 3.380 (0.185) | 3.316 (0.069) | 0.021 (0.884) | 1.098 (0.295) |
| Wide range | 14.7 | 9.5 | 17.7 | 4.678 (0.096) | 1.154 (0.283) | 0.478 (0.489) | 3.760 (0.053) | 12.1 | 9.1 | 11.4 | 1.314 (0.518) | 1.310 (0.252) | 0.029 (0.866) | 0.352 (0.553) |

Observations: Europe = 439; Japan = 257; USA = 79
Source: INNFORM programme

firms increased their downscoping activities the most over the period 1993 to 1997, with only 11 per cent of European firms doing so and a minimal number of Japanese firms attempting de-diversification.

We now extend our analysis and explore the pace of change between organizations in the three regions and examine whether changes in organizational practices are adopted in an incremental or more radical way. The literature on technological innovation characterizes radical innovations as fundamental and clear departures from existing practice. Incremental innovations are defined as minor improvements or simple adjustments in current technology (Dewar and Dutton, 1986). We compared the percentage profiles of the changes in the adoption of organizational innovations during the period 1992–93 to 1996–97. As we have seen, most organizations were moving towards an increasing adoption of the innovations measured in our survey. We defined the changes between 1992 and 1996 as follows: a negative value in the difference between the value reported in 1996 and the value in 1992 in the five-point Likert scale corresponds to a reduction of the emphasis of certain organizational innovations. We denote this negative value as *Against the trend*. A positive difference of 1 in our scaled questions is an *Incremental* change; and a difference greater than one is a *Radical* change. *No change* indicates the percentage of companies which did not change the emphasis of the organizational indicators during the four years.

In Table 1.2 we compare the profiles of European, Japanese and US firms over the period 1992–93 to 1996–97 and test for statistically significant differences between the percentage profiles of each organizational innovation.

Table 1.2 indicates that all the innovation profiles (structures, processes and boundaries) show statistically significant differences between Europe and Japan and all the profiles with the exception of adoption of project forms show statistically significant differences between Japan and the USA. Only in two of the structural indicators (de-layering and project) and one process indicator (new HR practices) are there statistically significant differences between Europe and the USA.

The relatively low percentages in the *Against the trend* category for all three regions confirms that there is parallel change occurring between 1992–93 and 1996–97. European and US firms show much higher percentages of radical change compared with their Japanese comparators over this period. The only notable exception to this is in IT innovations, where 38.8 per cent of Japanese firms claim radical changes between the two time periods, although this is much less than the equivalent European (49.7 per cent) and US (57.7 per cent) percentages.

There is now a well-established literature in organization theory (Child, 1984) indicating that many large firms simultaneously adopt more than one logic of organizing in grouping their activities. Thus firms can be seen to be grouping their assets by product and service, geographical region, function and in terms of project form. The INNFORM survey instrument

TABLE 1.2  *Incremental and radical changes in European, Japanese and US organizations, 1992–96*

| | Structures | | | | Processes | | | | | Boundaries | | | |
|---|---|---|---|---|---|---|---|---|---|---|---|---|---|
| | De-layer | Proj-form | Oper. Dec. | Strat. Dec. | Vert. Links | Horiz. Links | Info. Tech. | New HR | Out-source | Strat. Alli. | Down-scope | R&D intens | Internat. |
| **Europe** | | | | | | | | | | | | | |
| Against trend | 14.3 | 6.1 | 9.6 | 6.9 | 2.9 | 4.3 | 2.1 | 3.4 | 5.5 | 1.7 | 19.2 | 2.5 | 3.2 |
| No change | 54.0 | 46.2 | 46.5 | 55.5 | 18.3 | 22.9 | 8.8 | 4.1 | 31.4 | 68.1 | 69.4 | 70.0 | 63.5 |
| Incremental | 18.6 | 23.3 | 21.4 | 25.8 | 57.4 | 53.9 | 39.4 | 48.9 | 53.0 | 23.8 | 2.3 | 24.2 | 29.4 |
| Radical | 13.1 | 24.3 | 22.4 | 11.7 | 21.4 | 18.9 | 49.7 | 43.6 | 10.1 | 6.4 | 9.1 | 3.3 | 3.9 |
| Radic + incr | 31.7 | 47.6 | 43.8 | 37.5 | 78.8 | 72.8 | 89.1 | 92.5 | 63.1 | 30.2 | 11.4 | 27.5 | 33.3 |
| **Japan** | | | | | | | | | | | | | |
| Against trend | 8.0 | 3.2 | 2.8 | 4.7 | 2.0 | 1.2 | 0.0 | 8.7 | 3.6 | 0.7 | 2.4 | 4.9 | 2.4 |
| No change | 77.5 | 63.6 | 81.5 | 80.6 | 40.6 | 40.6 | 8.2 | 20.1 | 34.0 | 89.6 | 94.5 | 89.0 | 87.7 |
| Incremental | 12.1 | 23.2 | 13.0 | 11.9 | 53.9 | 56.3 | 52.9 | 64.6 | 57.3 | 9.6 | 3.1 | 6.1 | 9.9 |
| Radical | 2.4 | 10.0 | 2.8 | 2.8 | 3.5 | 2.0 | 38.8 | 6.7 | 5.1 | 0.0 | 0.0 | 0.0 | 0.0 |
| Radic + incr | 14.5 | 32.2 | 15.8 | 14.7 | 57.4 | 58.3 | 91.8 | 71.3 | 62.4 | 9.6 | 3.1 | 6.1 | 9.9 |
| **US** | | | | | | | | | | | | | |
| Against trend | 23.7 | 0.0 | 18.4 | 13.3 | 1.3 | 2.6 | 1.3 | 1.3 | 3.8 | 3.4 | 25.3 | 4.0 | 2.5 |
| No change | 39.5 | 73.8 | 48.7 | 50.7 | 15.4 | 20.5 | 6.4 | 15.2 | 37.2 | 55.9 | 57.0 | 72.0 | 53.2 |
| Incremental | 15.8 | 20.0 | 17.1 | 25.3 | 59.0 | 50.0 | 34.6 | 45.6 | 44.9 | 35.6 | 15.2 | 21.3 | 35.4 |
| Radical | 21.1 | 6.2 | 15.8 | 10.7 | 24.4 | 26.9 | 57.7 | 38.0 | 14.1 | 5.1 | 2.5 | 2.7 | 8.9 |
| Radic + incr | 36.9 | 26.2 | 32.9 | 36.0 | 83.4 | 76.9 | 92.3 | 83.6 | 59.0 | 40.7 | 27.7 | 24.0 | 44.3 |
| Chi-2 (prob) | 42.4 | 28.4 | 89.8 | 46.7 | 64.6 | 46.5^ | 11.9^ | 88.8 | 6.8 | 20.7^^ | 60.6^ | 45.2^ | 48.3^ |
| EU-JP | (0.000) | (0.000) | (0.000) | (0.000) | (0.000) | (0.000) | (0.000) | (0.000) | (0.079) | (0.000) | (0.000) | (0.000) | (0.000) |
| Chi-2 (prob) | 9.4 | 10.5^^ | 6.5 | 3.6 | 0.9^ | 3.0 | 1.9^ | 6.7^ | 2.1^ | 2.4^^ | 6.5 | 0.8 | 5.5^ |
| EU-US | (0.025) | (0.001) | (0.091) | (0.305) | (0.624) | (0.226) | (0.388) | (0.034) | (0.345) | (0.124) | (0.088) | (0.847) | (0.064) |
| Chi-2 (prob) | 55.0 | 1.2^^ | 49.0 | 28.3 | 41.9^ | 53.4^ | 9.1^ | 48.9^ | 8.5^ | 25.6^ | 69.6^ | 66.7^^ | 10.1^ |
| JP-US | (0.000) | (0.277) | (0.000) | (0.000) | (0.000) | (0.000) | (0.011) | (0.000) | (0.014) | (0.000) | (0.000) | (0.000) | (0.001) |

*Source:* INNFORM Programme Survey

^one cell had a frequency <5 and was aggregate to the neighbour; ^^two cells had a frequency <5 and were aggregate to the neighbours included a question which asked our sample to indicate the extent to which their corporate structure was formally organized by product, geography, function and project. Each organization was asked to compare 1992–93 with 1996–97 and indicate the extent of the emphasis on the four structural groupings on a five-point scale: none, little, moderate, much and great. We took the project-based structure to be the closest to the characterization of innovative forms in the literature and were interested in the relative adoption of the four logics of organizing over the time period 1992–93 to 1996–97. If we found over this period an overwhelming change towards the project-based structure, this would represent at least some evidence for the new supplanting the old. If, however, any rise in the project form was occurring alongside the corresponding adoption of the other three logics of organizing then this was some evidence to support a more incremental innovation pathway – organizations would be supplementing the old with the new and not supplanting the old with the new. Figure 1.7 shows some very interesting results about the extent to which innovative forms are supplementing or supplanting existing forms in Europe, Japan and the USA.

The clear picture in Figure 1.7 is of a rise in the emergence of project forms of organizing in all three regions, with Japan having the highest adoption rate in 1996 from the highest base level in 1992. However, the very substantial rise of project forms of organization in Europe, Japan and the USA does not appear to be at the expense of other logics of organization. The clear message from these results is of new forms of organizing supplementing, rather than supplanting, existing forms.

Thus far we have only summarized the general trends in new forms of organizing across the three regions by time period. However, following our earlier discussion, we also expect variation to occur according to company-specific business characteristics such as knowledge intensity and degree of internationalization. We now summarize our results in Table 1.3, linking knowledge intensity (proxied by R&D expenditure as a percentage of total sales) and internationalization (measured by percentage of sales outside the company's domestic market) to the extent of organizational change.

Table 1.3 illustrates the effect of the two business contingencies, knowledge intensity and internationalization, on the adoption of organizational innovations in 1996. Knowledge intensity is proxied by R&D expenditures as a percentage of the firm's turnover. There is an overlap between knowledge intensity and R&D expenditures, but they are not equivalent because R&D is a more specific form of knowledge, a subset of scientific and technological knowledge, whereas knowledge intensity normally refers to a wider set of attributes including information and skills (see for example Tidd et al., 1997; see also the May–June 2002 special issue of Organization Science on Knowledge, Knowing and Organizations, 13 (3)). The knowledge intensity variable used in the regression models is a binary variable which identifies organizations spending more than 3 per cent of their turnover in R&D (they

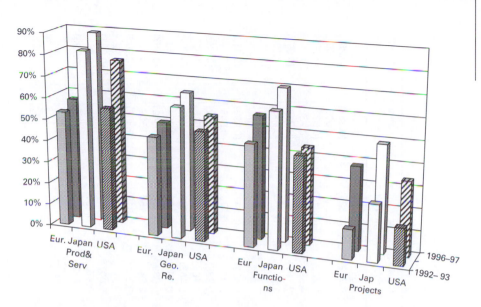

FIGURE 1.7   *Organizational logics, 1992–93 and 1996–97*

are 21 per cent of the European sample, 32 per cent of the Japanese, and 31 per cent of the US). The indicator for high internationalization is also a binary variable which discriminates companies with foreign operating businesses producing products and services in more than ten countries for the Europe and Japan samples, and more than 15 countries for the USA sample. These thresholds correspond to about 30 per cent of the companies in the samples in the three regions. We tested for alternative thresholds, but the results are fairly robust and do not vary substantially when using different cutoffs, except in one case discussed below.

We only find one common result across the three regions: that a high degree of internationalization increases the probability of engaging in strategic alliances. This result is consistent with standard international business and international management literatures according to which multinational enterprises tend to establish international partnerships to explore new markets or to gather knowledge about local markets (see, among others, Contractor and Lorange, 1988 and 2002; Nooteboom, 1999).

Apart from this result, the effects of R&D and internationalization appear to influence the adoption of different organizational innovations in the three regions. In Europe, high R&D intensity increases the probability of organizing by projects, introducing a high degree of strategic decentralization and downscoping, in the US it increases the probability of intensifying horizontal linkages, and in Japan it does not have any effect on the probability of adopting organizational innovations. This last finding may be surprising

TABLE 1.3  *The effect of knowledge intensity and internationalization on the adoption of organizational innovations*

| | Europe | | | Japan | | | USA | | |
|---|---|---|---|---|---|---|---|---|---|
| | Knowledge intensity | Internationalization | Chi-2 (prob) | Knowledge Intensity | Internationalization | Chi-2 (prob) | Knowledge intensity | Internationalization | Chi-2 (prob) |
| De-layering | 0.178 (0.140) | 0.268** (0.136) | 6.73 (0.034) | 0.073 (0.207) | 0.136 (0.212) | 0.68 (0.712) | −0.238 (0.324) | 0.534 (0.333) | 2.68 (0.262) |
| Projects | 0.406*** (0.136) | 0.121 (0.132) | 11.31 (0.004) | 0.280 (0.169) | −0.140 (0.174) | 2.97 (0.226) | 0.239 (0.313) | 0.005 (0.327) | 0.65 (0.722) |
| Operational decentraliz. | −0.053 (0.137) | 0.201 (0.134) | 2.28 (0.320) | 0.184 (0.177) | 0.293 (0.184) | 4.59 (0.101) | 0.329 (0.342) | −0.732** (0.342) | 4.74 (0.094) |
| Strategic decentraliz. | 0.337** (0.151) | 0.548*** (0.146) | 23.06 (0.000) | 0.210 (0.192) | 0.058 (0.200) | 1.49 (0.475) | 0.063 (0.328) | −0.145 (0.347) | 0.18 (0.913) |
| Vertical linkages | 0.211 (0.139) | −0.070 (0.137) | 2.34 (0.311) | 0.010 (0.175) | 0.370** (0.178) | 4.59 (0.101) | 0.478 (0.341) | −1.071*** (0.399) | 8.44 (0.015) |
| Horizontal linkages | 0.227 (0.143) | −0.177 (0.144) | 3.36 (0.186) | −0.115 (0.196) | 0.303 (0.196) | 2.44 (0.295) | 0.778** (0.370) | −0.648 (0.432) | 5.34 (0.069) |
| New HRM practices | 0.178 (0.141) | 0.054 (0.135) | 2.07 (0.356) | 0.226 (0.186) | −0.049 (0.196) | 1.46 (0.482) | 0.806 (0.436) | −0.518 (0.393) | 4.47 (0.107) |
| IT | 0.216(*) (0.136) | 0.226* (0.132) | 6.76 (0.034) | −0.262 (0.185) | 0.477** (0.205) | 6.49 (0.039) | 0.160 (0.323) | 0.324 (0.342) | 1.53 (0.467) |
| Outsourcing | −0.066 (0.139) | 0.367*** (0.138) | 7.16 (0.028) | −0.040 (0.172) | 0.266 (0.180) | 2.21 (0.331) | 0.166 (0.319) | 0.509 (0.339) | 3.17 (0.205) |
| Strategic alliances | 0.073 (0.142) | 0.471*** (0.141) | 12.89 (0.002) | 0.268 (0.171) | 0.414** (0.178) | 9.91 (0.007) | 0.076 (0.349) | 0.977** (0.417) | 6.92 (0.031) |
| Downscoping | 0.354** (0.170) | 0.104 (0.171) | 5.43 (0.066) | — | −0.187 (0.470) | 0.17 (0.682) | 0.136 (0.366) | −0.315 (0.403) | 0.65 (0.723) |

*p < 0.1;** p < 0.05;*** p < 0.01. Europe N = 439; Japan N = 257; USA N = 79

*Source:* INNFORM Programme Survey

because it is commonly accepted that the success of R&D intensive firms also requires greater attention to organizational structures and processes that enhance their absorptive capacity (Cohen and Levinthal, 1990), such as, for example, sharing R&D knowledge, increasing decentralization and introducing information systems. As we discussed elsewhere (Pettigrew et al., 2000), and in the context of the evolution of organizational routines and their comparisons between Western and Japanese organizations (Massini et al., 2002), this might be because Japanese firms tend to adopt the organizational innovations investigated by the INNFORM survey regardless of their main activity and these organizational innovations tend to reflect the institutional context and culture of Japanese organizations.

The degree of internationalization affects a higher number of organizational changes compared to R&D in all three regions, but in contrasting ways. In Europe, highly internationalized firms are more likely to introduce high strategic decentralization, invest in IT, outsource and engage in strategic alliances. In Japan, highly internationalized companies, in addition to strategic alliances and IT, are also more likely to develop stronger vertical linkages. However, in the US, apart from high probability to engage in strategic alliances, we find contrasting and somehow counterintuitive results. Highly internationalized American companies are more likely to have more centralized operational decision making and less strong vertical linkages. These results suggest that although these companies are more likely to have weaker linkages between headquarters and subunits, for example for marketing and advertising or technical personnel, they do not have autonomy to run operations. These results emerge in the USA in the case of 15 or more foreign operations (and also with higher thresholds), but do not appear to be significant when we used the same, lower (ten) number of foreign operations as for the other samples.

Our findings may be summarized as follows:

1 There is evidence of a common direction of change, but from different starting points and with some variation in pace across the three regions.
2 There is evidence of parallel change in structures, processes and boundaries, but little evidence as yet to support the thesis that organizations are converging towards a single type of form.
3 Across the three regions there is greater evidence of boundary and process changes than structural changes in the period 1992–97.
4 Our assessment of incremental and radical change across the three regions allows the following conclusion: European and US organizations show much higher percentages of radical change compared with their Japanese comparators.
5 The findings do not confirm previous conjecture about revolutionary change in forms of organizing. Innovative forms of organizing are emerging across the three regions, but they are supplementing not

supplanting existing forms. The new is emerging alongside and within the old, rather than replacing the old.

6 For our European, Japanese and US samples, strategic alliance formation was positively and significantly related to the extent of internationalization of the firm.

7 By 1997 there were still big statistically significant differences between Japanese, European and US firms in their forms of organizing. In 1996 Japanese firms had more hierarchical levels, more project formation and more operational decentralization than their European comparators. By 1997 US organizations had more hierarchical levels, more IT investment and greater alliance formation than their European comparators.

These empirical findings are among the first attempting to map the extent of diffusion of innovative forms of organizing across three important regions of the globe. They help to clear up some of the conundrums about the emergence of innovative forms, but they, in turn, stimulate further questions. In Chapter 7 of this volume we pose and answer some important questions about complementarities in organizational innovation and performance. In Chapter 12 we return to deepen our exploration of whether forms of organizing are converging or diverging across nation states and regions. Here we should also remind ourselves that our results capture the emergence of innovative forms at two time points only and further research is necessary to make sense of what is still a moving target and an emergent process.

We move on in this volume to broaden and deepen our exposure and interpretation of our findings. In Part 1, which follows, we develop the theme of the inseparability of organizing/strategizing. Part 2 displays and interprets our findings on complementarities, change and performance, in Part 3 we pick up the important empirical and policy theme of managing dualities in the innovating organization. Finally, in Part 4 we offer our two concluding chapters on the content and process of our work.

# I

Organizing/Strategizing

# Chapter 2

# The Challenge of Organizing/Strategizing

*Richard Whittington and Leif Melin*

## INTRODUCTION

This chapter provides a broad theoretical frame to the empirical chapters
that follow in this part of the volume. Its title expresses two core themes in
these chapters. First, as the verbs '*organizing*' and '*strategizing*' emphasize,
the focus will be not so much on organizational strategies and forms in
themselves, but on the continuous processes involved in moving towards
and moving along such strategies and forms. Secondly, as the oblique
mark indicates, *organizing* and *strategizing* will be treated not as two
discrete practices, but as inextricably linked together, a single duality rather
than separable building blocks. This commitment to *organizing/strategizing*
involves a theoretical double-turn that puts the emphasis firmly on holistic
processes.

This theoretical move is, we shall argue, at once driven by recent
changes in the nature of business and underpinned by contemporary
developments in social and economic theory. The business context is radically changing with the increased dynamism and competitiveness of markets (D'Aveni, 1994); business content is shifting from traditional
manufacturing to the management of knowledge (Brown and Duguid,
1998). Theory is grasping these changes in a variety of ways: in
economics, through the notion of complementarities (Milgrom and
Roberts, 1995); in social theory, through structuration theory (Giddens,
1984), the notion of practice (Schatzki et al., 2000), and the postmodern
challenge (Chia, 1997).

The chapter is structured as follows. The next section introduces
what we term the double-turn in contemporary management theory. It
is this double-turn that renders nouns into verbs and elides strategizing

with organizing. The following section considers the business drivers of this double-turn, both the move towards the verb form and the merger of the two elements into a single duality. Subsequent sections examine various developments in social theory and economics, both as they provide theoretical context for our double-turn and as they offer resources for taking it further. We conclude by linking these broader themes to the more focused empirical materials that follow, highlighting issues of knowledge, learning and leadership.

## THE DOUBLE-TURN IN MANAGEMENT THEORY

The strategic management discipline still bears the mark of its founding father, Alfred Chandler. It was Chandler (1962: 11–13) who laid down the fundamental distinctions between strategy and operations, decisions and implementation; it was he who then defined the iconic sequence of structure *following* strategy. Chandler's (1962) approach is understandable. As a pioneer in the development of the strategic management discipline, he was approaching the complexities of big business with very little conceptual apparatus: he needed to cut out some sharp distinctions. As a historian using the past to explain the present (Whittington and Mayer, 2000), his attention is always casting ahead towards the end-states, diversification and divisionalization. The processes of change are described, but only as frustrating frictions on the inevitable path towards the ultimate 'chapter' of American enterprise.

Forty years on, we are ready to supersede the Chandlerian instinct towards distinctions and states. The nouns *strategy* and *organization* are supplanted by verb forms emphasizing processes of becoming and sustaining. And even the verb forms, *organizing* and *strategizing* are no longer left to stand apart, but are merged together in a single duality.

The strategy discipline itself has long fretted over the sharp distinction drawn between strategy and organization. Hall and Siais (1980) began the process by challenging the order of the sequence. As they declared, 'strategy follows structure'. Businesses reflect their pasts, so that old structures influence future strategies. Mintzberg (1990: 183) went further by rejecting the sequential notion altogether: '... structure follows strategy as the left foot follows the right ... Strategy formation is an integrated system, not an arbitrary sequence.'

It is a small step from abolishing the sequence to dissolving the distinction. Although Ghoshal and Moran's (1996) concept of 'organizational advantage' originates in a more general assertion of the value of organizations by comparison to markets, it also leads to a conception of advantage lying not only in the traditional strategic variables (price, differentiation and so on), but also in forms of organization. As Nahapiet and Ghoshal (1998) elaborate, particularly in knowledge-based firms, the ways in which social and intellectual capital are organized can together constitute an organizational advantage capable of beating both market mechanisms and other forms of organization. The point is no longer that organization doesn't necessarily follow strategy; rather, it is that organization *is* the strategy (Whittington, 2002). Or, as Sir John Browne of British Petroleum puts it: 'Our strategy is our organization' (Day, 2001: 4). Strategy and organization form an integrated duality.

The turn towards a more active, processual perspective expressed through the verb form was denoted early by Weick (1969) in his first edition of *The Social Psychology of Organising*. Weick's (1969: 1) opening injunction to readers is to '… assume that there are processes which create, maintain, and dissolve social collectivities, that these processes constitute the work of organizing, and that the ways in which these processes are continuously executed *are* the organization' (emphasis in the original). Among the many important insights that follow from this perspective is that organizations are neither concrete nor static. Rather they need to be continuously 're-accomplished', and as that re-accomplishment is necessarily imperfect, so they must continuously mutate (Weick, 1969: 39; Chakravarthy and White, 2002). In other words, there are no organizational end-states. In his second edition, Weick (1979: 44) is still more emphatic, urging us to stamp out nouns, stamp in verbs. As he elaborates, '… verbs keep things moving' (Weick, 1969: 188). *Organizing* is now an accepted, if not always agreed, term in management studies (Sims et al., 1993; Bate et al., 2000).

*Strategizing* has much less currency. One early important usage is in fact pejorative. Williamson (1991) dismisses 'strategizing' – by which he means the search for winning positions and ploys – as an extravagant and foolish distraction from the real business of 'economizing'. But if strategizing is understood in the more neutral terms of the active processes of strategists engaged in strategy-making (Johnson et al., 2003), then we are close to something more valuable. In a fast-moving world, it is better to invest in fertile strategy-making than in finite strategies. Strategies need to be made and re-made continuously.

Unfortunately we still know little about what makes for effective strategy-making processes. As Hamel (1998: 11) observes: 'Strategists may have a lot to say about the context and content of strategy, but, in recent years, they have had precious little to say about the conduct of strategy – that is, the task of strategy-making … What we need is a deep theory of strategy creation.' Researchers are now beginning to converge on this gap (Whittington, 1996; Eden and Ackerman, 1998; McNulty and Pettigrew, 1999; Roos and Victor, 1999; Floyd and Lane, 2000; Johnson et al., 2003). One early learning from this new research is that the contemporary re-organizing of business into more flexible and decentralized forms is catapulting previously detached middle managers into a more active participation in the strategizing process (Floyd and Lane, 2000). Here organizing is very directly linked to strategizing.

Thus the double-turn in management theory is already moving thinking towards the *organizing/strategizing* duality. Weick has expanded our notions of organization beyond the early static view to include on-going processes of organizing. Strategy is increasingly seen as an activity, a task, in which advantage may be drawn not simply from the superiority of what is adopted, but also from the creative potential of the process. The relationship between the two poles is increasingly recognized as well. On the one hand, organization is seen as a source of strategic advantage in itself; on the other, more decentralized modes of organizing are pressing more managers into the processes of strategizing. All this is no accident. The next section identifies business drivers for this double-turn in contemporary management thinking. The following section goes on to introduce four recent currents in broader social and economic theory that offer valuable theoretical resources for taking this double-turn still further.

## BUSINESS DRIVERS FOR 'ORGANIZING/STRATEGIZING'

Chandler's (1962) subjects were traditional large-scale enterprises, mostly industrial, in the first half of this century. Stable end-states and clear distinctions may have seemed feasible aspirations in the conditions of post-war growth and US leadership when he was writing; less so now. This section outlines three drivers from the changing business context underpinning the more interlinked, verbal formulation we are proposing here.

The first is a substantial increase in the pace of change. D'Aveni (1994) characterizes an increasing number of markets as 'hyper-competitive': instead of long, stable periods in which firms can achieve sustainable competitive advantage, competition allows only short periods of advantage, punctuated by frequent interruptions. In these conditions, stable end-states are illusory and verbs supplant nouns. In terms of organization, the key is not to arrive at a final 'chapter', à la Chandler (1962), but to achieve a permanently flexible form, capable of responding fast and appropriately to a wide variety of changes (Volberda, 1996). Galunic and Eisenhardt (1996) show that even divisionalized corporations do not show the fixed domains envisaged in the traditional theory of the M-form; rather, divisional 'charters' are fluid, with businesses and resources continually being recombined. In other words, organizations require constant re-organizing (Eisenhardt and Brown, 1999; Whittington, 2002). In the area of strategy, Teece et al. (1997) respond to the increasing pace of change by extending the resource-based view of the firm from a static focus on existing stocks of resources, towards the appreciation of innovation and renewal implied by 'dynamic capabilities' (cf. Eisenhardt and Martin, 2000). Under conditions of fast-paced change, particular resources and strategies are soon redundant. Fleeting opportunities for competitive advantage can only be snatched through the continual application of the skill of 'strategizing' (Hamel, 1998).

The second driver for 'Organizing/Strategizing' is the problem of imitation in increasingly competitive markets (Grant, 1991; Rivkin, 2000). Here the interlinkage becomes important, both as superior implementation is less easily copied than clever formulation and as organizing becomes a means of embedding critical resources within the firm to inhibit their transfer. Market positions and innovative products are highly visible and, in themselves, vulnerable to imitation (Williamson, 1991). What is less easy to imitate is the ability to do these things well and to do so repeatedly. This ability relies upon a superiority in both organizing and strategizing that is likely to be deeply entrenched within the firm's structures, cultures and processes. The transfer of critical resources to competitors is likewise dependent upon the degree of embeddedness within the firm. Thus the capacity to appropriate the value of key human resources to the advantage of the firm depends upon curbing their internal bargaining power by reducing their potential mobility and value to other employers. As Liebeskind (1996) shows, the structuring of jobs to ensure the dispersal of key skills among many groups of people and the design of systems by which to capture and routinize otherwise tacit and private information are central to embedding such human resources to the advantage of the firm. In this sense, it is the organizing of resources that makes them strategic.

Human resources have become, of course, sharply more important in the contemporary 'knowledge age' (Miles et al., 1997). The third driver, therefore, is the challenge of managing knowledge, particularly potent in forcing strategizing and organizing closer together. Brown and Duguid (1998), in their article *Organizing Knowledge*, insist: 'All firms are in essence knowledge organizations. Their ability to outperform in the marketplace rests on the continuous generation and synthesizing of knowledge.' In particular, they reprise Ghoshal and Moran's (1996) concept of 'organizational advantage' to emphasize the superiority of firms over markets in organizing knowledge. Again, organizing capability, not just strategic positioning, is central to competitive advantage. It is the active verbal form, moreover, that best applies to the 'emergent' character of knowledge within firms (Tsoukas, 1996). Knowledge cannot be controlled centrally; it is continually changing. The exploitation of knowledge within the firm requires a continuous chase after shifting properties, a process better captured by the dynamics of organizing than the finality of organization.

In short, the organizing/strategizing duality needs to be taken seriously for at least three reasons. First, the environment is now changing too fast to rest upon the fixities of nouns: success no longer depends on having the right strategies or structures, but on having the capability to continuously reinvent them. Secondly, in increasingly competitive and transparent markets, the most secure competitive advantages lie deep inside the firm and their value relies upon how they are organized in order to ensure exclusive and effective appropriation. Finally, the 'knowledge age' underpins and extends both these first two drivers, raising the organizing of knowledge to a central position in competitive advantage and giving to this key resource a fluidity and elusiveness that requires the continuous effort of the verb form. But it is not simply changes in the business environment that prompt this turn towards the duality. As we shall see in the next section, social and economic theory is in tune with these developments and provides powerful intellectual resources for pursuing them.

## THEORETICAL RESOURCES FOR ORGANIZING/STRATEGIZING

If 'organizing/strategizing' deserves to be taken seriously for practical reasons, we shall require deep and robust theoretical resources with which to address it for research. This section will introduce four potentially valuable perspectives. From economics, the concept of complementarities emphasizes the indissolubility of strategizing and organizing. From social theory, the recent postmodern turn both challenges the reductionist instinct towards distinctions and argues for the superseding of nouns by verbs. Structuration theory insists on a related duality between structure and action, leaving organization structures as the continuously re-created and ever precarious product of human activities. The practice perspective is similar in its linkage of action to context, but its notions of practice and habitus emphasize the continuous routine of most such action.

We are not going outside the management disciplines per se, because our disciplines have nothing to say about these questions – the work of Weick, Ghoshal and Hamel clearly suggests they have. Rather, by looking outside to some of the base disciplines we can see that the concern for the problematic suggested by 'organizing/strategizing' is shared and supported widely throughout the social sciences. We shall also find that these base disciplines offer a rich and varied resource in terms of perspectives and methods for research on this theme.

### The economics of complementarities

Since the early 1990s, Stanford economists Paul Milgrom and John Roberts have been addressing the challenge of new forms of business strategy and organization through the concept of 'complementarities'. This concept builds on the proposition that doing more of one thing may increase the returns to doing more of another (Milgrom and Roberts, 1995: 181). When two activities reinforce each other in this way, they are complementary. In highlighting the potential for complementarities, their concept accords with notions of synergy, fit and coherence that are long-recognized within management theory (Pettigrew and Whipp, 1991). But Milgrom and Roberts add precision in modelling, a wider scope and some surprising implications to these earlier notions. We shall explore the implications of complementarities, particularly for change and performance, more extensively in the third part of the volume. Here, though, we shall concentrate on how the complementarities concept both promotes a holistic view of strategy and organization and illuminates the new, more flexible forms of manufacturing that have emerged in the last two decades.

The complementarities concept specifically addresses the new, smaller, more flexible forms of organization that traditional economic notions of scale and scope seem poorly able to explain. Milgrom et al. (1991) suggest that we have been undergoing a simultaneous set of technological and managerial transformations equivalent to that which created Chandler's (1990) large-scale corporations a century before. Just as the coincidence of new communications technologies (the telegraph), new transportation technologies (railways) and new managerial technologies (for example, cost accounting and continuous production lines) allowed the emergence of great corporations such as DuPont or General Motors, so today a mutually reinforcing web of innovations in telecommunications, computing and managerial practice (for example, simultaneous design and just-in-time) have stimulated new forms of flexible, fast-paced manufacturing within advanced economies. These innovations are complementary in the sense that advances in one spark advances off in the others, so that positive feedback between them provides ever-growing momentum.

Such complementary effects are not simply economy-wide but can become embodied in sets of synergistic practices within firms too. Milgrom and Roberts (1990) analyse the economics of 'modern manufacturing' in terms of complementarities between new computer and telecommunications technologies and managerial practices across the whole range from production through inventory to marketing. Thus, in their account, the introduction of computer aided design (CAD) makes more profitable a switch from mass to flexible production; this in turn allows savings from smaller inventories; it becomes easier to design for specific or fleeting customer needs; and marketing strategies can shift from economy in mass markets to quality in niche markets. In other words, at the level of both whole economies and particular firms, the economics of complementarities points to the importance of setting up 'virtuous circles' of mutually reinforcing advantage (Whittington et al., 2000).

These virtuous circles have important implications for the relationship between organization and strategy. It is not just that organization structures should fit strategy, though this is important too (Milgrom and Roberts, 1995). The complementarities concept warns that organizational decentralization can easily trap firms in suboptimal strategies. Organizational units are liable to stick at points below their potential because increased performance relies upon other units making complementary changes, for which none individually has the incentive to be first, and potentially sole, mover. Under these conditions, effective strategy requires strong central co-ordination (Milgrom and Roberts, 1995: 190). Strategy and organization are again closely linked.

The third part of this volume will explore further the implications of the complementarities concept, particularly issues of performance and the need to develop a sense of process. For the moment, however, we note how the economics of complementarities not only furnishes us with an account of the spread of innovative forms of organizing, the empirical subject of this book. It also underlines the intimate connection of strategy and organization implied by our theoretical concept of organizing/strategizing. A similar holistic distrust of distinctions is offered through the postmodern tradition, enlivened, however, by a strong sense of process.

## Postmodernism

Postmodernism as intellectual tradition responds to similar late twentieth-century transformations as the economics of complementarities, only framing them more comprehensively as the transition from modernity to postmodernity. According to Lyotard (1984), at the heart of this transition to 'the postmodern condition' were changes in the importance and character of knowledge that the strategic management discipline would only catch up with a decade or so later. In the conditions of postmodernity, knowledge is a commodity indispensable to the worldwide competition for power (Lyotard, 1984: 5). The prominence of knowledge, its diffusion and its commercialization are profoundly destabilizing, however. This instability both jeopardises hard-won distinctions and shifts attention from states to processes. Both bear on the duality of organizing/strategizing.

The great economic advances of modernity depended upon division and specialization: the division of labour, the specialized functions and responsibilities of bureaucracy (Harvey, 1993). Likewise, the achievements of modernism as a form of intellectual enquiry was its continued refinement of nicer and nicer distinctions (Lash, 1990). Both the subject (divisionalization) and the method (distinction) of Chandler's (1962) work exemplify these principles. Postmodernity as a set of economic conditions and postmodernism as intellectual tradition challenge these head-on. For Harvey (1993), the characteristic of postmodern industry is the move from the rigid specialization of mass production to a flexible specialization in which polyvalent skills re-unite highly divided labour. Likewise, the postmodernist impulse in the sphere of knowledge is one of 'de-differentiation' (Lash, 1990), according to which boundaries such as those between high and low art, image and reality, become increasingly blurred. In short, postmodernism repudiates fragmentation, affirms holism. The distinction between strategy and structure, and the ordering into sequence, are no longer sustainable. Strategy and organization merge.

More than this, postmodernism gives these concepts an essentially processual character. Modernistic thinking, according to Chia (1995; 1997), lends itself easily to the Fallacy of Misplaced Concreteness, the multiplication of conceptual distinctions that, once made, soon take on the status of 'things'. Chia (1995) cites nouns such as 'organizations', 'competition' and 'environment'. Postmodernism suspects distinctions and insists on instability; verb forms are preferred. For Law (1994: 1–2), the verb forms – ordering rather than order, organizing rather than organization – emphasize the incompleteness and precariousness of organizational achievements. Chia (1995: 593) summarizes: '… a postmodern style of thinking is one which eschews thinking in terms of accomplishments, of nouns, end-states, insulated, discrete social entities and events. Instead it is a style which privileges action, movement, process and emergence.' Where modernism reifies, postmodernism destabilizes.

We do not need to take on all its intellectual baggage to recognize in postmodernism some valuable correctives to traditional organizational theory. If we take a position that is simply 'after modernism' (Whittington and Mayer, 2000; Whittington et al., 2002; Pettigrew, 2001), we can repudiate the over-drawn distinctions and misplaced concreteness of modernism without burdening ourselves with the exaggerated relativism and irresponsible detachment of postmodernism's fringe. Our adoption of the verb form, and our elision of 'organizing' and 'strategizing', draw on the postmodern critique. But the concept of 'organizing/strategizing' commits us to being no more than 'after modern'.

One further insight of the postmodernist critique is its re-evaluation of practical, local knowledge as opposed to the hard generalizations of positivism. In the contingent, unstable conditions of postmodernity, Lyotard (1984) advocates the contextual wisdom embodied in the 'little stories' of folk history rather than the grand narratives of modernistic science. In this context, it is not the formal truth conditions of traditional *savoir* that matter, but practical *savoir faire*, the knowing of how to get on in particular situations. Something of the same scepticism of modernistic science, and an equivalent emphasis on the practical, is to be found in the third set of theoretical resources we introduce here, those of the practice perspective.

## The practice perspective

Schatzki et al. (2000) describe a 'practice turn' in contemporary social theory that is displacing traditional concerns for structure and systems as the fundamental elements of inquiry and explanation. This practice turn embraces a good many things, but central is a focus on the active engagement of people as practitioners in shared sets of activities, or practices. As such, the notion of practice has already been taken up widely within management theory, including the fields of technology (Orlikowski, 2000), learning at work (Wenger, 1998), accounting (Hopwood and Miller, 1994), organization structure (Whittington, 2002), and strategy (Whittington, 1996; Hendry, 2000). It can help us here too. The focus on activity resonates clearly with our verbal formula of organizing/strategizing. But the practice notion also helps by balancing the verbal sense of creation with a respect for the ordinary accomplishments of the routine, while at the same time introducing a concern for how practitioners learn.

In an important review of the increasing role of the practice notion in the social sciences, Ortner (1984: 149) gave as definition of practice simply 'anything people do'. Strongly implied is the need to re-embrace the micro activities of ordinary people – what De Certeau (1984) has called the 'murmurings of everyday life'. Thus De Certeau and his students attend to such ordinary activities as 'doing cooking' and 'doing shopping' (De Certeau et al., 1998). Understanding these activities carries with it an appreciation of the individual tricks and stratagems required in the daily business of 'making do' within constrained and shifting circumstances. For Bourdieu (1980: 177), this 'practical sense' entails the capacity for instantaneous reflex actions that respond to the demands of each unique situation without conscious calculation or appeal to precedent. It is these tacit skills and capacities that sort out the effective practitioner from the ineffective.

How well these skills and capacities are learnt, and by what processes, becomes critical to success. But practical skills are elusive to traditional science and hardly to be learnt formally. For Bourdieu (1990), these skills come from the past experience that constitutes the practitioner's 'habitus' – the accumulated schemes of perception, thought and action derived from their pathway through life. This habitus is embodied history, internalized in the actor as second nature and so producing practices in the present both spontaneously and barely consciously. There is a holism here too, as habitus acquires through experience an integrated, if fuzzy, coherence. Acquisition of the tricks and stratagems necessary to effective practice, therefore, is not something that relies a great deal on formal learning, more on accumulated practical experience. 'Agents can adequately master the modus operandi that enables them to generate correctly formulated ritual practices only by making it work practically, in a real situation, in relation to practical functions' (Bourdieu, 1990: 91). Learning is critical to effectiveness, but there are few short-cuts and no final moments. Learning demands laborious engagement in particular contexts, an endless and effortful process.

The practice perspective's emphasis on the tacit and the experiential tends to entail methodologies of deep ethnography, aimed at surfacing what is inaccessible to superficial observers from outside and unconscious to busy practitioners within (Bourdieu, 1990). As the following account of structuration theory implies, we expect enough of both observers and practitioners to allow for broader methodologies. However, we can take from the practice perspective a reinforcement of the active sense denoted by 'organizing/ strategizing', but affirm with it a readiness to include not just the dramas of organization and strategy construction, but the routines of organizational and strategic maintenance. Organizing/strategizing should be seen as a chronic and effortful accomplishment. We take also from the practice perspective an appreciation of how organizing/strategizing relies upon practitioner skills, typically irreducible to scientific formulae and therefore hard to access and transmit. A strong implication of the practice perspective is that organizing/strategizing involves learning processes that are challenging and contextual.

## Structuration theory

The structuration theory developed by Anthony Giddens (1984) takes a similar duality to that of organizing/strategizing, that of structure and action. For Giddens (1984: 20–5), structure is inextricably linked to action as both its medium and its outcome. Actors draw upon structural properties, established rules and resources, in order to act, and as they do so they reproduce and amend these same properties. 'Structuration' refers to the consequent structuring of rules and resources over time, their regularities and their evolution. The neologism is necessary to capture Giddens' (1984) twofold concern: on the one hand, to avoid a lop-sided emphasis on either structure or action; on the other, to convey the active, constructive processes involved in reproducing and amending the patterns of everyday life. The potential of structuration theory has long been recognized in the management disciplines (Ranson et al., 1980; Pettigrew, 1985; Whittington, 1992). But particularly relevant to the organizing/strategizing notion are an empowering sense of structure, a reciprocal view of leadership and a methodological guide.

Duality is a theme throughout this book, and the structurationist duality of action and structure has special resonance here. Structure enables as well as constrains. By implication, organizational structures too are not so much passive drags on strategic action, necessary evils to be regretted and minimized; they are central resources upon which action must draw, demanding equal attention alongside strategy and initiative (Adler and Borys, 1996). Action is not simply fettered by structure, it positively relies on it. This duality has important implications for our view of business leaders, essential to action yet dependent on structure. The model of leaders as heroic individuals downplays – to their own disadvantage – the structural rules and resources on which they must draw for their empowerment (Whittington, 1993). Here, structuration theory points to a delicate reciprocity between those who will lead and those who follow. Even as they play creatively on them, still leaders must subscribe to the structural limits and expectations embodied in their organizations. For leaders, action and structure are tied together.

The structurationist emphasis on the continuous processes of creating and maintaining structures is strongly sympathetic to processual perspectives on organizing (Pettigrew, 1997a). It has therefore been a natural step for processual studies of change to draw explicitly on structuration theory (Pettigrew, 1985: 37; Barley and Tolbert, 1997; Huff and Huff, 2000). Here structuration theory has informed a readiness to extend analysis of organizational change both over long periods of time, to capture long-run structural cumulation, and beyond the firm, to include the broader environment that forms the context and basis for action. While processual studies share the practice perspective's concern for close observation, they differ in taking seriously Giddens' (1984) confidence in the reflexivity of human actors: the processualists expect much more from actors' accounts of their own actions. An ability to trust in actors' own accounts relaxes the requirement for deep ethnography implied by heavy emphasis on unconscious and tacit understanding. The interview-based case study is thereby allowed to access more than typically conceded by the practice approach, and the relative economy of this method makes possible multiple case studies, with all the power yielded by the comparative method (Pettigrew and Whipp, 1991).

The contribution of structuration theory, therefore, is both theoretical and methodological. Theoretically, it sensitizes us to both the enabling aspect of structure and the delicate reciprocity of leadership, each consistent with our notion of organizing/strategizing. Methodologically, it licences comparative case studies, less absorbed than the practice perspective, but respectful of actors' own accounts and concerned for history, process and context. Again, therefore, there are useful resources beyond the strict confines of management theory with which to advance the agenda of organizing/ strategizing.

## SUMMARY AND DISCUSSION

This chapter has introduced the double-turn involved in moving from a concern with organization and strategy towards the duality of *organizing/ strategizing*. This move brings both a strong sense of process, captured in the verb form, and an orientation towards holism, reflected in the oblique. Organizing refers to the processes that both constitute and define the on-going activities of an enterprise, underlining the effortful achievement involved as much in maintaining as in creating these activities. Strategizing likewise refers to continuous processes, this time those of making and re-making the strategies of the enterprise. Running these two into the single duality of organizing/strategizing emphasizes their intimate connection.

Strategizing activity is shaped by organizing; organizing is a crucial variable within the strategizing task.

The chapter argues for the growing relevance of this duality. Rapid environmental change requires not fixity, but continued processes of organizational and strategic creation and re-creation. The dangers of imitation and resource transfer in today's competitive markets argue for the importance to strategy of the relatively opaque organizing processes of implementation and the embedding of critical resources within organizational cultures, structures and routines. The contemporary success of knowledge-based strategies relies upon the continuous organizing of systems for capturing and exploiting critical human resources. In all these ways, for many businesses, resting upon the traditional static distinctions of the strategic management discipline will no longer do.

From the social sciences more generally, we have proposed four theoretical perspectives that both support the notion of 'organizing/strategizing' and provide perspectives for exploring its reality. All four are oriented towards a holistic view in one sense or another: the complementarities approach through its insistence on completeness; postmodernism in its rejection of distinctions; the practice perspective through the assumption of underlying coherence in habitus; structuration theory in its conception of duality. There are differences, of course. Process is central to structuration theory, practice theory and postmodernism, less prominent in the economics of complementarity. Knowledge and learning are strong themes of both the practice and postmodern perspectives, but not intrinsic to structuration and complementarity theories. Complementarity theory cares about the economic performance of the firm; for the others, the performance issue is more salient at the level of the individual actor or practitioner. The strong strategic direction urged by complementarity theory is qualified by structuration theory's reminder of the mutual dependency of leaders and followers.

Just as there are different nuances among the theoretical resources we have introduced here, so there are differences among the chapters that follow. Yet in their own ways they do participate in the sensibilities and themes we have established so far. All are concerned with processes – of leadership, of learning and of knowledge integration. There is clear recognition in all three of the intimate linkage of organizing and strategizing. The chapters on learning and leadership each make full use of the comparative case method, the first considering leading European technology firms, the second a wider comparison of banking and engineering. Concerning leadership, the cases reveal an importance of reciprocity between leaders and followers strongly resonant of structuration theory. As for learning within technology firms, the emphasis on learning-by-doing recalls the practical, experiential wisdom valued by both practice and postmodern approaches, while its continuous, routine nature is in sympathy with theories of structuration and practice alike. Finally, in Chapter 5, our Dutch colleagues demonstrate the mutuality of organizing and strategizing in the transformation of the Dutch financial services firm of ING.

It is our contention that the sensibility implied by the processual duality of organizing/strategizing is of increasingly urgent relevance to business in the contemporary world. Management theory is already beginning to grasp its implications, as exemplified by the double-turn emerging from the work of Weick, Ghoshal and others. Yet economic and social theory more widely has much to give as well, and developing this new sensibility will require all the theoretical resources that we can get. The complexity and dynamism described in the following chapters all make the case for a more sophisticated approach to innovative forms of organizing. This approach will have a caution about distinction and reification, and a sympathy towards process and holism, together encapsulated in the notion 'strategizing/organizing'.

Chapter 3

# Leadership:

## The Role of Interactive Strategizing

*Leona Achtenhagen, Leif Melin,*
*Tomas Müllern and Thomas Ericson*

## INTRODUCTION

What we argue for in this volume is to enhance our understanding of strategic and organizational change by going beyond the 'structure follows strategy' and 'strategy follows structure' perspectives. Instead, organizations can be understood as continuous and intertwined processes of organizing and strategizing, as dynamic entities rather than as static organizational structures and strategic positions. Taking such a dynamic perspective on innovating organizations stresses the importance of actors in the organizing/strategizing processes: who are the key actors and what characterizes their roles?

It is often claimed that the roles of leaders and employees would change with the emergence of innovative forms of organizing. Yet, our knowledge about those new roles, especially in organizing and strategizing processes, remains very scarce. The research question we attempt to address in this chapter is therefore: *what is the role of leadership in the organizing/strategizing processes of innovative forms of organizing?* This chapter aims to investigate this question by focusing on the processes of sensegiving and sensemaking. We will argue that, within innovative forms of organizing, the role of leadership is changing. We are witnessing a move away from leadership with a top management focus and unidirectional, top-down sensegiving towards more *reciprocal sensemaking activities*, which actively involve many organizational actors in the organizing and strategizing processes. The ability to communicate between different, more or less temporary organizational units, across organizational layers, as well as with external stakeholders seems to be of growing importance and presents organizational leaders with new challenges.

Here, *strategizing* can be understood as the continuous formation and transformation of strategic patterns and *organizing* as the on-going activities that contribute to the continuous reproduction of an organization. These concepts are innovative in their underlying assumptions of individual and social activities taking place in organizations, but they may still emphasize the top-down direction of these processes. The leadership perspective and the focus on sensegiving and sensemaking activities would traditionally have implied an interest in how strategizing and organizing are influenced by conscious attempts of top leaders to 'steer' organizations towards a certain 'framed' direction. However, to understand strategizing and organizing processes within innovative forms of organizing, we need to develop further the concepts of sensegiving and sensemaking. Thus, we will elaborate on the notion of *reciprocal sensemaking*, which stresses the potential involvement of a wider arena of actors in strategizing and organizing processes.

The concept of reciprocal sensemaking is connected to many aspects of innovative forms of organizing noticed earlier in the INNFORM programme (Pettigrew and Fenton, 2000a), including flattened hierarchies, increased reliance on project forms of organizing, advanced communication systems, decentralization and organizational learning. This new organizational landscape calls for more participatory and communicative forms of leadership (Müllern and Stein, 2000). Using the notion of reciprocal sensemaking indicates that mutual processes of sharing ideas might be important in complex and dynamic organizational configurations, as opposed to the focus on imposing ideas in a top-down way. Inherent in the organizing/strategizing concept elaborated on in this chapter is a focus on the communicative aspect. *How are ideas invented, developed, shared and destroyed in on-going processes of sensemaking?* The metaphor of a 'communicating organization' (cf. Ruigrok et al., 2000a) seems particularly apt to capture essential elements of reciprocal sensemaking.

In this chapter we firstly introduce the perspective on leadership as a process of framing/sensegiving, as well as sensemaking. We argue that it is crucial to understand why and how members within innovative forms of organizing come to share meanings in strategizing and organizing processes. Referring to innovative forms of organizing, we will then develop the argument of reciprocal sensemaking. Further, we will illustrate and give empirical evidence of this line of thought by analysing two case studies. The case analyses focus on how organizing is intertwined with strategizing, and how the leadership roles and groups of actors influencing these processes may change with the emergence of innovative organizing modes. One case is a Scandinavian bank, Östgöta Enskilda Bank (the independent Swedish division of Danske Bank). The bank organizes its activities in a unique way in order to combine small and big, as well as global and local, and employs corresponding strategizing processes, which involve many different actors in the company. The second case illustrates the construction tool manufacturer Hilti AG, which has its headquarters in Liechtenstein but conducts its business on a worldwide scale. These cases of communicating organizations are analysed regarding the reciprocal sensemaking processes taking place.

## LEADERSHIP – BEYOND UNIDIRECTIONAL PROCESSES OF INFLUENCE

Leadership can be understood as a social process in which actors (try to) influence others. In fact, a common denominator in most definitions of leadership is the concept of influence (for example, Yukl, 1998; Daft, 1999; Hughes, Ginnett and Curphy, 1999): the leader is assumed to exert some form of influence over others, often denominated the followers. Recently, there has been a noticeable shift away from focusing mainly on the influencing attempts exerted by the leaders towards a focus on how the followers perceive these processes and the change initiatives they trigger. The top-down influencing attempts have earlier been described in terms of *framing* and *sensegiving* (for example, Gioia and Chittipeddi, 1991; Fairhurst and Sarr, 1996), and the perception and action by a wider group of actors in relation to change initiatives have been described in terms of *sensemaking* (for example, Weick, 1995); these concepts will be further discussed in the following.

With the aim of conceptually separating the top-down influencing process from the sensemaking process involving a wider group of actors, the concept of *framing* and *sensegiving* has been introduced by different authors. Framing has been defined as 'the skill that is required to manage meaning' (Fairhust and Sarr, 1996: 3), relating to the concept of management of meaning (Smircich and Morgan, 1982). Leaders, on different hierarchical levels, can be more or less influential in framing the perceptions of others. In accordance with existing literature, framing and sensegiving can be considered as synonyms. The framing/sensegiving process, thus, is the process through which managers attempt to influence the sensemaking and meaning construction of others towards a preferred redefinition of organizational reality (Gioia and Chittipeddi, 1991). For instance, a vision may function as a unifying force and framing tool in such a process (Westley and Mintzberg, 1989; Collin and Porras, 1991).

It has been discussed earlier in the literature that new ideas of organizing could be shaped and partly realized by visionary leaders, through processes of framing and sensegiving (Gioia and Chittipeddi, 1991; Gioia et al., 1994). To be legitimate, visions should contain elements of progressiveness and innovation and have the capacity to arouse enthusiasm and keep the organization together (Normann, 1977). Visions attempt to mobilize the organization to strive towards a desired future condition different from what is now prevailing, thereby linking the future with the present (Morris, 1987). Visions try to capture an entirety, that is, visions involve a holistic understanding of the organization and its stakeholders (Schoemaker, 1992; Morris, 1987). Then the role of a vision is to act as a common conceptual umbrella under which the organizational members gather (Mintzberg and Westley, 1992). This line of reasoning indicates that framing, for example, through visions, could be a way to influence the forming and transforming of strategic patterns in an organization through influencing the organizing processes.

The conceptualization of framing/sensegiving and sensemaking usually appears to be divided into two rather separate parts. First, the proactive and prospective framing would take place, followed by the reactive and retrospect sensemaking process. These two phases of the process are also attributed to different actors or groups of actors – the framing is done by a small group of top leaders, while the sensemaking is attributed to the remaining organizational members, or 'followers'. The relation between framing and sensemaking seems to be unidirectional, with the former influencing the latter. Thus, the usual notion of framing/sensegiving follows a clear hierarchical notion as it strives to influence others towards a specific meaning of organizational reality (Gioia and Chittipeddi, 1991). Feedback and opinions of the other organizational members are widely neglected, or top management decides what aspects to incorporate from occurring reactions, thereby maybe allowing for some bottom-up participation.

Even when assuming a clear distinction between 'leaders' and 'followers', a bottom-up perspective can complement this top-down view of leadership to enhance our understanding of how new ideas are developed in the organization (Ericson, 1998). In other words, leadership activities dealing with the formulation of new ideas and strategies, and followers' implementation activities could be viewed as activities that are inextricably linked, rather than being separated (Newton and Johnson, 1998). So, not only the framing in itself is important – the framing processes have yet to be made sense of by the organizational members (for example, Weick, 1995; Gioia and Chittipeddi, 1991).

To take this view one step further, we argue that new ideas are realized in a *translation process* (see Blomquist, 1996; Czarniawska and Sevon, 1996). Change ideas are not diffused but rather travel in an organizational field as narratives, which are successively transformed in social construction processes. Such a perspective would suggest that the mutual interplay between the framing by leaders and the sensemaking of all organizational members are at the core of the construction process (Ericson, 2001). Consequently, members of organizations would then be treated as active translators of the ideas framed by leaders.

Analysing these translation processes could enhance our understanding of the 'becoming' (Calori, 2002) of innovative forms of organizing, as these processes are crucial in strategizing and organizing processes. A central theme in this chapter is that new ideas and strategies developed in organizations undergo translation processes. A key question complementing the questions posed above then is: *how do translation processes in innovative forms of organizing take place and who are the key actors involved?*

Innovative organizing principles supplement the predominantly vertically oriented mode of managing with a more horizontal mode of interacting that requires the roles of managers and employees to go beyond the traditional relation of super-ordination and sub-ordination. Based on our empirical case studies, we thus argue for the need for an extended view on these sensegiving and sensemaking processes to understand leadership in innovative organizing modes. As Weick (1995: 175) states: 'The point is, we need to know what happens to sensemaking when it is organized horizontally rather than vertically.'

The framing concept in a traditional hierarchical organization can be criticized for being unidirectional. It describes the rhetoric used by leaders without noticing the translation processes that carry and change meaning in organizations or the roles attributed to different organizational actors. Instead, we argue for the need to develop a language that catches the 'dialogic' nature of these translation processes. Since we understand translation processes as being shared by a wide group of organizational actors, this implies that the sensemaking activities following the framing attempts are clearly reciprocal in character, requiring mutual relationships between the actors involved.

The arguments for moving beyond the unidirectional model are simple but convincing. Referring to Habermas' notion of communicative action, it can be argued that the growing complexity and dynamics of modern corporations necessitate a co-operative process of sensemaking (Habermas, 1981). In situations where participants initially cannot act in consensus, they need to engage in sensemaking processes to create a common horizon of understanding. Characterizing leadership as being related to the reciprocal sensemaking perspective has implications for leadership theory. Our general conclusion after having reviewed the pertinent literature in the field is that the notion of reciprocal sensemaking clearly adds to existing leadership theories, and, primarily, the charismatic, inspirational and transformational leadership styles.

*Charismatic leadership* describes the characteristics of both the leader and the followers in a special situation of devoted adherence to one leader. The charismatic leader, characterized by great self-confidence, dominance, a sense of purpose and the ability to articulate goals and ideas to the followers, can exert an extraordinary influence over his followers (Bass, 1990). Yet this theory overcomes the assumption of isolated traits responsible for effective leadership behaviour. The followers identify strongly with the charismatic leader. Even though the theory of charismatic leadership mainly emphasizes the relation between leader and followers, a number of authors have connected charismatic leadership to the leader's ability to formulate and articulate visions (Lawler, 1982) and to act as a symbol of the company (Mintzberg, 1973). During the 1980s and 1990s, there was a move towards regarding charismatic leadership as a way of understanding transformation and innovation (Conger and Konungo, 1987). However, writings on charismatic leadership usually assume a stable organizational frame in which charismatic leaders can influence their followers. Within the setting of innovative organizing modes, we cannot take these organizational prerequisites for exercising charismatic leadership as given. For example, in project-based organizations, sub- and super-ordination relationships might overlap and change from one project to the next, questioning the concept of stable leadership roles.

*Inspirational leadership* has been described as a 'weaker' form of charismatic leadership – weaker in the sense that the identification between leaders and followers might not be as strong (Downton, 1973). In the inspirational leadership model the followers are drawn to the goals and purposes of the leaders rather than to the leaders as such. Following Burns' (1978) definition of *transformational leadership*, Bass (1985) argues that transformational leaders would share the following four characteristics:

- charismatic leadership
- inspirational leadership
- intellectual stimulation
- individualised consideration.

All three theories are mostly based on a traditional hierarchical model of leadership, where the influencing process is largely unidirectional. They focus, in a sense, on the traditional sequence of framing and sensemaking, where the two groups of leaders and followers are firmly rooted in the hierarchy and not changed or redefined during organizing and strategizing processes. However, as introduced above, within the context of innovative forms of organizing we might instead need a model of leadership capturing the dynamics of reciprocal sensemaking, in which the two groups of leaders and followers interact and the boundaries between them blur to some extent.

Based on our empirical findings, we argue that the prevailing understanding of framing and sensegiving as the same process does not entirely capture the leadership processes occurring within innovative forms of organizing. Rather, we suggest a conceptual separation of the framing and the sensegiving processes. The framing process would still mostly remain in the hands of top management, setting the major strategic, future-oriented direction and the broad boundaries of organizing, while the sensegiving process might be opened up to extend the arena of potential sensegiving actors. Instead of employing a mainly unidirectional process of sensegiving, supported by other organizational members through their sensemaking, this new process is a reciprocal process of tight feedback loops, in which leaders and other organizational members jointly develop the direction of the organization, thus connecting the sensegiving and sensemaking processes in the form of an on-going dialogue.

Results of the INNFORM survey and case studies indicate that companies are adopting more open, democratic and project-oriented forms of organizing. This increases the demands on leadership – as captured in the separation of the concepts of framing and sensegiving. On the one hand, the framing activities from top management are important for building a coherent strategic direction and focusing the attention on core processes. On the other hand, top management is highly dependent on actors within and outside the organization to translate these ideas and develop more detailed strategizing and organizing practices. Although we can see a higher degree of democratic practices, the distribution of power remains asymmetric in favour of top management. It is up to top management to decide how much space for sensegiving and sensemaking activities to pass on to other organizational members, and top management also maintains the ultimate right to reduce this space. Asymmetric power relationships thus still remain a constituent factor of leadership processes. However, these appear to be exercised in a more subtle way, by influencing interpretation patterns and increasing the level of communication between the different actors involved. Yet, we might recognize political corrosion if followers comply with leaders for their own reasons and in pursuit of their own interests (cf. Grint, 2000: 18).

## THE PERSPECTIVE OF RECIPROCAL SENSEMAKING IN STRATEGIZING PROCESSES

Before presenting the two case studies, we will summarize the arguments developed in this chapter. Traditionally, framing and sensegiving have been considered as prospective, while sensemaking had a retrospective character. We argue that within innovative forms of organizing, framing and reciprocal sensemaking follow short feedback loops to allow for continuous change. Thus, the distinction between prospective and retrospective becomes blurred in continuous processes of strategizing and organizing.

While top management still plays a major role in the framing process, especially in the initial steps of strategic renewal initiatives, the translation process reduces the unidirectional character of followers making sense. Instead, the new role of employees allows them to expand their former role of following into a pre-set direction towards becoming active participants in the strategizing/organizing processes, by interacting with leaders and other actors in the organization. Thus, the process of translating becomes a mutual process, in which top managers not only receive feedback on their definition of the organizing/strategizing processes but also engage into more bidirectional processes of *reciprocal sensemaking*. Thus, top management allows the perceptions of other organizational actors to influence their views, and organizing/strategizing processes might rely on higher degrees of negotiation between different organizational actors. This interaction, including bottom-up sensegiving (in which managers take on perceptions formed by employees), has been largely ignored by earlier writings on leadership with its focus on the influence of leaders on followers. The power of leaders does not rest in themselves but on their followers, comprising a network of relationships. Extending the role of followers to more active participants of sensegiving and sensemaking processes goes beyond the deterministic view on leadership, that leaders could determine the future, and makes negotiable what used to be non-negotiable (cf. Grint, 2001: 419).

The *strategic arena* as the location in which strategizing processes take place is, thus, being broadened to include more actors. Consequently, the arena may have many appearances and unfolds at different layers of the organization. In more unidirectional organizations it would be rather common that the strategic arena is closed for actors beyond top management. But a closed arena might narrow down the possible variety of views and ideas potentially deriving from it. Then, the dialogue could be based on high levels of convergent, unitary thinking with the risk of unreflective acceptance of dominant positions regarding both the identification and outcome of strategic issues. Creating an open arena with a larger number of actors involved has the potential to counteract this problem of conformity (Ericson et al., 2000).

## STRATEGIZING AND ORGANIZING IN TWO INNOVATIVE FIRMS

In several of the case studies carried out within the INNFORM programme we have found clear evidence of the changes in leadership patterns discussed in this chapter. Here, two case studies will be presented and analysed to illustrate this discussion. These cases, that of the Östgöta Enskilda Bank in Sweden and of the construction tool manufacturer Hilti AG from the Principality of Liechtenstein, are examples of these new characteristics of leadership in companies experimenting with innovative forms of organizing. In order to understand the role of leadership played in the strategizing and organizing processes in these two cases, we will draw attention to how individuals and groups perceive and act in response to the framing activities of the central strategists. We will do so by analysing the cases in the context of sensegiving and sensemaking as established above.

In this chapter we can only present short studies of these two comprehensive cases, but our intention is to present enough empirical detail to the validity of our results.

## ÖSTGÖTA ENSKILDA BANK

This case analysis, based on twelve personal interviews (mainly with top and middle managers) conducted by two of the authors of this chapter, focuses on the successful development of a Swedish bank between 1994 and 2000. In the early 1990s, a major crisis took place within the banking industry in Sweden. In order to help Swedish banks to survive, the Swedish government felt obliged to intervene and back up several banks financially. However, the bank in focus here, Östgöta Enskilda Bank (ÖEB), a medium-sized bank operating mainly in one region in Sweden, was one of two Swedish banks able to survive the crisis without any help from the government. In 1994, after having handled the crisis, ÖEB made a challenging decision to adopt a new vision. The vision was to establish a number of local 'provincial banks' with strong local profiles and a focus on customized services, that is, a major geographical expansion through green field investments in different regions in Sweden. According to the CEO of ÖEB, the opportunity to be the sole provincial bank created an extremely interesting strategic position to reinvent the tradition of provincial banking.

### Strategizing and organizing within ÖEB

A leading idea behind this expansion was to grow in such a way that customers would not feel that they were dealing with a large bank, but rather with a bank where decisions were made quickly and where personal service was the guiding star. The bank took the opportunity to fill in the vacant strategic space that had arisen because of the demise of several competitors during the crisis in the banking industry. The expansion, in a sense, changed the appearance of the bank. From being a bank deeply rooted in the county of Östergötland, ÖEB incrementally became a national bank boosted by an increasing number of local provincial banks. However, even though the bank started to grow towards becoming a national bank, the idea of being a bank with a strong local touch permeated all subsequent strategizing activities.

Obviously, the framing of the central top managers – through providing the powerful vision of being a network of local banks close to the customers – set the further direction of the bank. But it is not possible to understand the result of the framing processes without focusing also on the sensemaking, and sensegiving of these framing activities by all other organizational members. Understanding the change journey in ÖEB from a sensemaking-based perspective means understanding how meaning is constructed and destructed (cf. Gray et al., 1985; Weick, 1995). In ÖEB this process certainly included the strategizing of the top management leading to the new vision for the bank, but also the emergence of local strategies and activities that took place through the involvement of a great number of actors.

The core of the strategizing processes lies in the organizing of the network of different local units. The following quotation from a vice-president at the centre of ÖEB elaborates on this idea:

> We shall be a network that consists of several local and independent banks. This means that each local bank has, to a great extent, the freedom to decide on its own way to go. We are not the Red Army. We are several guerrilla units. If the personnel in Värmland [a county in Sweden] wants to walk around in jacket and trousers, that's okay. If the personnel in Stockholm wants to walk around in suits, that's okay. If Värmland wants to have their own assortment of products, while Malmö [a city in Sweden] has another, then that's okay. If Värmland wants to have another fee policy than Malmö, then that's okay, too. (Vice-president)

The different guerilla units, though striving to carry out the overall vision, acted strategically in their own specific ways as a result of their local sense-making and translation of the ÖEB vision and in response to their local contexts. The activities taken by the local units partly reproduced the strategic pattern of the organization as a whole leading to incremental change. However, since the local provincial banks had the freedom to take strategic actions in somewhat different directions, the organizing of ÖEB implied the introduction of new patterns of activities that partly could also challenge old routines. The only strategic issue that was not negotiable was the level of risk-taking in granting credit, because the credit policy was the same all over.

> We want the customer to feel that all the decision power is in the local bank, even if the decision process on larger credits is standardized and centralized. Still, I think we are the fastest bank regarding credit decisions. (Local bank manager)

Furthermore, it should also be mentioned that during the first six to twelve months after the opening of each local bank, a so-called 'pilot' came from headquarters to help with the computer system. The role of the pilot was to help integrate the new provincial banks into the standardized information system within the bank network.

The evolution of shared meanings was the outcome of interactions between individuals (Langfield-Smith, 1992). In ÖEB this process started with a dialogue between the top management team and the newly recruited local bank manager. The evolution of shared meanings was initially strongly influenced by the framing of the CEO and his team. This framing, communicating the overall direction and leading values of the bank, was then translated into the company conducting more concrete strategizing activities.

Framing is a process that deliberately tries to influence the subsequent strategizing. However, as this case so evidently shows, the ongoing sense-making/sensegiving processes throughout the organization are critical for the strategic outcome. In ÖEB the vision was made sense of by the local bank managers and their recruited staff, and as a result of this sensemaking and sensegiving, assigned meanings might have differed from those thought of by the top leaders involved in the framing process. In fact, as the ÖEB case illustrates, a major characteristic of innovative forms of organizing is the openness towards the interpretation processes involving a great number of organizational actors.

Members of the top management of ÖEB also exerted some influence on local interpretation processes by being engaged in the strategizing processes in the different local banks through dialogues with local managers, both informal and more formal (such as regular meetings twice a year between all local managers and the top management team). But at the same time, the continuous feedback cycles also ensured that the views of top management were adapted to the shared meanings emerging in the network of local banks. Thus, the original vision was gradually translated through the interpretation and re-interpretation that took place in these reciprocal sensemaking activities.

Certainly, ÖEB is not a case that illustrates the traditional view of a grand vision formulated by the corporate headquarters followed by a process of implementing the 'framed' vision. On the contrary, the strategic development of the bank is greatly influenced by the strategic activities of key actors in all local provincial banks based on their respective sensemaking/ sensegiving. The local managers make sense of the vision in the context of the local market. Each local provincial bank has the freedom and responsibility to serve the customers in the specific region without intervention from the bank headquarters. Strategic actions taken locally include the name of each local bank, the location and design of the local premises, recruitment of local staff, range of bank products and bank rates.

The vision expresses the strategic intent to set up and define the boundaries for the subsequent local strategizing; this framing guides the further development of the strategy process. Since all local provincial banks have the freedom to form their own local strategies, these strategic activities together shape the strategic identity of ÖEB in a process of mutual feedback and interaction. Most strategic activities that were traditionally centralized in bank headquarters are here delegated to each local provincial bank, that is, the strategizing responsibility is located to where the customers are based. The central management of the bank supports the local provincial banks in specific issues and when needed. Accordingly, this bank is best described as a polycentric network of influential provincial banks, each with a local board and a local bank manager. In 1997 the bank was acquired by Den Danske Bank, one of the biggest bank corporations in Scandinavia, but without any subsequent changes regarding the strategizing and organizing philosophy of ÖEB.

The ÖEB case illustrates an organization that is in a process of becoming. At the same time as the bank is expanding its business, the vision is successively translated to new strategizing activities. The organizing idea is very much fostering the creation of new patterns of activities. Referring to the guerilla metaphor, this resembles the actions taken by guerilla units as they are conquering unknown domains. They are also introducing new paths and patterns which might then be either reproduced or challenged at a later stage.

The characteristics of ÖEB described here account for the whole organization. The freedom of each local provincial bank begins the day a new provincial bank opens, or rather when the search for a new bank manager starts.

> The starting point is the recruitment of a good local bank manager, a local 'hero', well-established in the specific region and a competent banker, who is given the task to create his 'own' bank. (Vice-president)

So, it is very much up to the local bank manager and the personnel at the newly started local office to create their own bank.

> As a local bank manager, responsible for this new provincial bank, I feel that we are given a free hand to form this business as we want. We have a large amount of trust from the headquarters, and they have the understanding that we know what is best in our local market. (Local bank manager)

The local bank managers recruited their staff from different competitors, which means that all recruited were both experienced in bank issues and had good relationships with a network of potential customers.

> They saw it as a big challenge to start working for a smaller bank where they saw the possibility to influence and take decisions, and where personal service is given priority. The main advantage of our decentralized form of organizing is that we all feel and can act as if this bank was our own company; we are a group of entrepreneurs... We are inspired by the vision to build our own bank. (Local bank manager)
> It is a tremendous strength in the entrepreneurship we aim for ... and we have created an organization that attracts more entrepreneurial people than any other Swedish bank. (CEO)

The bank's headquarters do not present any detailed strategies that are supposed to be implemented in the same way in every provincial bank. Instead, the idea is that each provincial bank has a strong local touch.

> No manager from the centre came down to tell us how to do it. Their view was that if they recruited the right local managers, we would then handle the process ... They [the top managers] were very supportive and interested, but they let us do things based on our own thinking. (Local bank manager)

The ÖEB case shows how the initial strategizing – after having successfully overcome the crisis in the banking sector – encompasses a proactive rethinking of the possible strategic direction for the future. However, this proactive rethinking process is not only taking place at the very top of ÖEB; each local bank in the ÖEB network is given the freedom to proactively strategize in their respective market context. Furthermore, in these processes feedback and horizontal sharing of experiences are regarded as very important. While many competitors in the banking sector are following the logic of becoming big through acquisitions, leading to more centralized strategizing, ÖEB reinvented the 'old' strategy of being local, realized through the idea of placing decision-making power close to the customer through a network of provincial banks. Strategizing by formulating the radical vision and organizing through gradually creating local bank units that are framed by the top management team, form an umbrella under which each local management team contributes to a further realization of this vision. What happens is localized strategizing – which means attributing concrete and partly new and different meaning to the initial vision, that is, sensemaking through concrete strategic actions/activities.

Finally, a comment must be made on the centrality of the top management in the ÖEB case. The central control consists of three dimensions. First, there are the framing activities established by the CEO and his team around the vision and business idea of the whole bank, continuously expressed by the CEO in different ways, for example, 'in a smaller bank you become a bigger customer'. Secondly, the predominant norm of having a strong profitability orientation is a common denominator. Thirdly, local managers must adapt to a common view on risk taking, combined with standardized routines for credit decisions.

> If we are successful in these regards, then we [at the centre] can allow almost any [degree of] local influence and freedom … We have really tried to stimulate our local bank managers to make use of the strategic flexibility that we allow, rather than telling them how to do it. (CEO)

The CEO does not feel he is giving up control in any negative sense. He and his top management team strongly believe in this way of building up the bank, or as one of the Vice-presidents expressed it: 'We are a network of local banks as autonomous as possible.'

In conclusion, the ÖEB case shows clear evidence of a company that through its innovative way of organizing the growing business – as a network of both very autonomous and vertically/horizontally interacting provincial banks with strong local identities, both internally and on the local market – has been fostering a high degree of local, proactive involvement in the strategizing process. This combination of organizing ideas and strategizing activities has its roots in the initial vision of the new ÖEB. In other words, this case illustrates a move from the traditional form of unidirectional sensegiving in strategy-making towards the successful combination of framing by the top leader and reciprocal sensegiving/sensemaking of numerous actors in the on-going strategizing.

## HILTI AG

This case illustrates the move from a more traditional company with a top-down framing/sensegiving approach towards an approach of framing combined with reciprocal sensemaking and shared organizing/strategizing processes.

### Strategizing and organizing within Hilti

The case of Hilti AG as a pioneer of innovative organizing modes has been presented in more detail in the preceding book (Ruigrok et al., 2000a). Empirically, this case study is based on 55 interviews, which were conducted with people from different positions within the company – ranging from members of the management board to logistics and manufacturing staff. The interviews had a duration of one to two hours each and were conducted by the same tandem-team of two researchers, one of them being one of the authors of this chapter. Hilti AG is a family-owned company, based in Schaan, Principality of Liechtenstein, which offers professional users in the construction industry a comprehensive programme of positioning systems, drilling and demolition, direct and screw fastening, anchoring systems, diamond, cutting and sanding, installation systems, firestop and construction fastening (<www.hilti.com>; April 2002). Hilti has experimented with its organizing modes for decades, as the company has always felt the pressure for product innovation – only innovation could justify the expensive direct sales force (consisting of two-thirds of its employees) needed to explain more complicated products to the customers on the construction sites.

The company and its culture have been heavily influenced by the founder Martin Hilti, who founded the company in 1941. By now, Hilti achieves sales of 3.1 billion Swiss Francs, and employs 14 390 people (as of December 2001). Around his 80th birthday, Martin Hilti was asked to reflect on his experiences as the business founder and he stated his view on leadership:

> Management means pioneering. And leadership means to direct an achieving community to a goal jointly decided upon, by giving the right information at the right time. It is not enough to just state the goal. It is decisive to jointly develop the goal. (Martin Hilti; interviewed by Rudolf Ciucci (1995: 30))

Though Martin Hilti cared for the social well-being of his employees, he ran the company alone for a long time. Only decades later, he created a board of managers around him to which he delegated more responsibilities; and the above statement must be seen in this light – jointly developing the strategy for him still meant within the top management group, though he greatly supported the involvement of employees into more strategic activities fostered by his successors.

In the early 1980s, a recession in the construction industry hit Europe and the USA. Experiences during this crisis taught the company that it needed to be more ready for change if it wanted to survive in changing markets. But change also meant that a more open way of co-operating in the company was needed, which included enhancing responsibilities of employees, fostering creativity and innovation, as well as establishing a willingness to steadily improve. It was felt that employees had to become more flexible in their thinking, willing to leave their comfort zones and search for new challenges. Communication was felt to be the crucial basic element. At the same time, it was realized that the initially strong corporate values were no longer widely shared throughout the company and that it had become necessary to focus on building a new corporate culture.

In 1985 a new programme was initiated with the slogan 'Leadership makes the difference – our corporate culture'. This new programme attempted to consciously steer cultural change. This programme included corporate-wide seminars in which thousands of employees participated. This stage focused on building the identification of the employees with the company; however, the framing and sensegiving process was clearly led by top management, and strong guidance in the sensemaking process was provided by the seminars in an attempt to direct interpretation along preferred directions. Employee feedback on the seminar content was not considered very important.

> Looking back, the leadership slogan was sometimes used as a weapon rather than as an active instrument; it was used to blame people for their performance rather than improve performance. We had to change that. (Member of the Executive Board)

Although the programme as such was quite successful, criticism arose around issues such as the lack of employee input in the development of different processes. In 1987 the strategic arena was broadened. In addition to the executive board, an extended Corporate Management Group was created to gain broader input into strategic decisions. All major market regions and product areas, as well as the crucial functions, were now represented in the top management board, facilitating the exchange of information as the basis for decision making.

Since 1979 the corporate policy and strategy had remained unchanged. Major changes in the business and environment now demanded their redefinition. In 1989, after three years of working on these issues, the *Strategy 2000* initiative was introduced, with a clear vision, mission and strategy and with the aim of focusing the company on its core competencies. New components were the market segmentation, specialization of the direct sales force, more standardized marketing practices, a new production strategy based on key technologies and key processes, a new form of division of labour and drastic outsourcing. To reduce interface problems, focus was put on jointly developing clear roles and responsibilities for interface tasks, as it was understood that with an increasing level of integration and interdependencies, these would be crucial. Regarding the employees, *Strategy 2000* focused on enhancing their identification with the products as well as increasing their involvement in the strategy-making process, thus leaving more room for the sensemaking processes of the individuals and the teams. However, the sensegiving process was still unidirectional – core values and directions were set by top management. The units received directions for the strategy they were to implement, and local differences were not taken into account.

For more than a decade Martin Hilti had prepared for his succession. At the end of 1989, Martin Hilti stepped down from the position of CEO in favour of his son Michael. In 1994 an external CEO took over, and Michael Hilti became Chairman of the Board of Advisors. Michael Hilti became a major driving force in extending the strategic arena beyond top management and in acknowledging the importance of the employees in the company's success by leaving them more space in the organizing/strategizing processes.

During the early 1990s it was, thus, realized that employee feedback needed to be taken seriously to ensure consistency and coherence through-out the company. At the same time, a new top management role was fostered, which explicitly stressed the involvement and coaching of employees in the corporate processes. At the same time the importance of feedback cycles in the sensemaking processes increased, supported by extensive training semi-nars for the employees, in which they could increasingly negotiate their views both with each other and also with top management. This new need to listen to what employees have to say can be emphasized by the statement of one executive board member: 'The fish starts smelling at the head' (cf. Werner and Hügli, 1995: 21). Over the following years, a strong emphasis was put on teams and on communication, with the intention of facilitating the development of shared meanings and interpretation patterns, as well as a joint understanding of the company's values and the direction into which it was moving. These ideas were more readily taken on by managers than by other employees, but Hilti showed endurance in providing the support needed for the new roles.

> The foremen had some problems to get rid of their old roles, and employees in manufacturing had problems to get used to the team focus. But we had trainings about teamwork and about the new roles, followed by supervision workshops to share experiences made with the new processes, and then again trainings about teamwork. (An Employee manufacturing metal anchors)

The basic ideas of the *Strategy 2000* concept were further developed in the *Champion 3C* strategy, which involved the different teams in the company in the strategizing process. Thus the sensegiving role was shared throughout the company, and, by incorporating ideas from throughout the company, a clear move towards reciprocal sensemaking can be seen. '3C' stands for customers, competences and concentration.

> *Champion 3C* can be adapted locally. Due to the intensive communication, it is widely accepted among employees; they are involved into the process and are trained in workshops for that. (Member of the Corporate Management Group)

The major framing action taken by top management in this period was to develop the distinction between the so-called 'accept it' and 'change it' categories. The former category comprises those issues at the base of the strategic direction, which should be accepted without much questioning, for example, the core business Hilti is in. The latter category consists of most other issues, and here the clear message to the organizational actors is that their involvement is wanted and asked for.

The new role of the employees was not easy to introduce into the company, as it was perceived that the awareness of what employees could achieve had to change first.

> *Champion 3C* increased the level of empowerment, for the first time we have real empowerment now. This is a challenge, and it's something that needs to be learned and practiced. The new processes need getting used to, but it's fun! (Head of business unit)

Instead of imposing a strategy on the business units, they are now asked to develop their strategy themselves, in alignment with all the other units involved. Thus, the responsibility for co-ordinating between interdependent units is also now decentralized. Top management just frames some very broad guidelines.

> *Champion 3C* is a new strategy review process to form a new strategy. Our old strategy was ten years old. At the moment, some pilot market organizations develop their strategy. They can strategically decide now what products to push. The strategic responsibility of the market organizations has been increased with *3C*, and country-specific strategies are developed. The only remaining frame is to maintain direct sales, but whether or not it wants to introduce certain products, the market organization is free to decide. (Head of region in Europe)
>
> The strategy development of the markets is an iterative process which now takes place together with the business units, and incorporates a number of feedback loops. We have formed a joint project for this for the first development, limited in time. Afterwards, we will have a periodic strategy update every three years. For implementing this strategy development concept, we have a dynamic personnel overlap for the rollout. In the first pilot, one manager participated, who then followed the process in his country. In that new project, other people participated, who could then transfer their experiences to their respective markets. That way, we can enhance the learning from the process, rather than reinventing the wheel. (Head of region in Europe)

In addition, reciprocal sensemaking in the form of sharing a set of values (tolerance, change, self-responsibility, freedom of choice and learning) throughout the organization was enhanced by corporate-wide seminars, in which these values were discussed, practised and further developed. An important aspect trained in these seminars is COTOYO, standing for *commitment to yourself*. This demands that the actors in the organization make up their minds whether they can and want to be part of such an organization, otherwise they must take the consequences and leave. The role of top management in the organizing and strategizing processes does not end with the framing role.

> I see my role as top manager in acting like yeast in a dough. I feel like a catalyst rather than a tool. We, as the executive board have to continuously question our own existence to provide credible guidance. (Member of the executive board)

Top management attempts to live reciprocal sensemaking. On the one hand, it is still important to maintain the overall strategic direction and the external responsibility for the business; on the other hand, it is considered important to understand how employees perceive crucial issues and to incorporate their feedback. One major way of achieving this aim is the participation of the top management team in all training courses and programmes offered by the company. This helps them to know what sort of formal knowledge they can expect from the employees and to make sure that top management shares the same values and does not make contradicting statements, thus enabling coherence and consistency in leadership. Secondly, top managers will often participate in on-going seminars to participate in discussions with the employees, to listen and respond to their feedback and to guage the 'mood' of the company.

As a further sign of this attempted coherence, the Strategic Management Development programme was renamed Strategic Manpower Development, as it was realized that otherwise the focus on developing people across the organization would be contradicted.

> Meaningful feedback and situational coaching are a must on all levels: to leverage existing and develop new potential, each person has to be coached and given feedback as a basis for his/her development. Each individual also has to give feedback to coaches as well as to team members. (Hilti People Strategy, *www.hilti.com*, April 2002)

In conclusion, the Hilti case offers a prime example of a company moving away from a more traditional approach of leadership, with a charismatic, paternalistic founder heading the company, towards leadership based on sharing the responsibility for the organizing/strategizing processes in the form of reciprocal sensemaking, while still setting the overall strategic direction.

> The new process gives us a say in the matter and thus increases motivation. Crucial was that the implementation was communicated well. (Employee, Logistics Sourcing, Plant 1)

The success of this approach is perceived to be the willingness to communicate and the effort spent on developing people so that they can, and want to, fulfil the roles they now take on.

## DISCUSSION – STRATEGIZING AND ORGANIZING PROCESSES WITHIN INNOVATIVE MODES OF ORGANIZING

In this section we return to the three questions raised at the beginning of this chapter. We first discuss which actors are involved in the translation processes in innovative forms of organizing. Then we characterize the new role of leadership in organizing/strategizing. Finally, we discuss sensemaking processes as dialogues on strategic arenas where new ideas are developed and shared.

### All actors in innovative forms of organizing are potential strategic actors

Both case studies underline how the framing, sensegiving and sensemaking processes change with the introduction of innovative organizing modes. One prerequisite for reciprocal sensemaking, including translation activities, appears to be the acknowledgment of 'mature employees'. This implies that the role of employees does not only grant greater freedom within the strategizing and organizing processes, but is explicitly 'to take charge' of them. Thus, besides a framing process, which is still mostly done by the top management, proactive feedback from other voices in the company is incorporated into the sensegiving process, so greatly extending the sensegiving and sensemaking roles to include a greater number of people in the company. The framing role remains that of 'setting the frame' of strategic activities – but the content of it changes. We see a transition from a decision-taking and informing role for (top) leaders to a role of setting the boundaries, or rather opening up the strategic arena, within which the members of the organization are enabled and motivated to act strategically. Establishing clearly defined 'accept it' issues within Hilti is a prime example of this. Sensemaking seems to evolve from a more individual to a reciprocally shared task, which in turn implies a move beyond the charismatic, inspirational and transformational models of leadership.

We now turn to the changing role of leadership in innovating forms of organizing in comparison with more traditional forms. The cases in this chapter show that there are a number of indicators of a change from the

TABLE 3.1   *The changing meaning of leadership in innovative modes of organizing*

| Traditional view | Emerging view |
| --- | --- |
| *Top managers:*<br>Framing, informing, persuading<br>– sensegiving | *Top managers:*<br>Framing, enabling, motivating<br>– reciprocal sensegiving/sensemaking |
| *Middle managers:*<br>Mediating<br>– sensegiving | *Leaders:*<br>Supporting/creating<br>– reciprocal sensegiving/sensemaking |
| *Followers:*<br>Accepting, implementing<br>– sensemaking | *Active employees:*<br>Creating/moving<br>– reciprocal sensegiving/sensemaking |

unidirectional towards the reciprocal perspective of sensegiving and sense-making, and this is particularly evident in the different roles leaders and employees take. In a stylized form, we can identify a number of typical key roles and their changes, which are summarized in Table 3.1 above.

### Top management roles

In both traditional organizations and more innovative organizations, the predominant role of top management is that of framers. However, in relation to the other employees in the company we can identify a change of content in these framing activities from informing employees about the strategic direction towards enabling and motivating employees to participate in strategizing and organizing processes. In the ÖEB case, the major meaning of the framing role is to set the strategic direction and regulate the movements regarding financial performance and risk taking. In the Hilti case, the focus of top management is more on setting strategic and behavioural boundaries, which are explained to the employees, who are now taking on an active role in the company. The purpose is to facilitate their sensemaking and translation processes by setting a frame. However, in both cases the role of top management changes towards acting as enablers of organizing/strategizing, for instance by giving input to strategic renewal. Here, we can see a parallel with the role of motivators, as discussed in the literature on transformational leadership (Burns, 1978).

### Middle management roles

In more traditional organizations middle managers often take on mediating and linking roles between top management and employees at lower levels of the hierarchy. This role is not passive, but managing is mainly unidirectional.

Within more innovative organizations, the middle-management role seems more proactive, creating meaning and momentum in the strategizing/organizing processes and being actively involved in moderating the reciprocal sensegiving/sensemaking processes. The following quote from the head of a business unit of Hilti underlines this reasoning:

> In my eyes, the important thing about *3C* is that we realize more that the market units and the product units are jointly responsible for how the business goes. The business units drive the product-oriented part of the strategy and the market organizations develop the strategy based on the business units' product ranges. We now have daily communication between the managers of each product and market organization and regular workshops for target setting. (Head of business unit)

## Roles of other employees

On the operative level, finally, the traditional role of employees is that of followers, who implement the signals from top and middle management levels. These signals are made sense of, but the interpretation takes place at a more individual level and remains rather unheard in the organization. Within innovative organizing modes, the role of employees is more active and challenging and can best be described as co-creating, or moving things. A member of the Hilti Corporate Management Group gives an example of this new employee role in the strategizing/organizing processes:

> *Champion 3C* sets the basic principles, but the strategy needs to be developed locally and differentiated. It is greatly accepted that, as intensive communication is taking place and employees are involved, lots of workshops with the employees involved take place. The aim is to communicate more about the strategy, and to achieve that all levels act in a more strategic way. Everybody shall be informed and participate. (Head of region in Europe)

Table 3.1 above could still give the impression that organizations were hierarchies with fixed boundaries, an assumption largely challenged by the INNFORM programme. Strategizing/organizing processes do not necessarily have to be determined by the hierarchical model of organization. Based on the two cases presented above we argue that the new perspective on leadership might be even more valid in the context of more flexible, loosely coupled forms of organizing. The case of Hilti clearly shows that a more communicative and dialogue-based approach of leadership can help to succeed in the competitive landscape of the new millennium. Similarly, the ÖEB case shows that in their networked form of organizing, combining hierarchical and horizontal interaction, fostering open dialogue is crucial.

However, the move towards a concept of leadership based on reciprocal sensemaking might have political implications. The change might take place in harmony, as power shifts could potentially open up space for political arguments about competences and opportunistic action to 'secure their own turf'. Also, organizations need to acknowledge that not every employee might want to become active in co-creating and moving the organization. Within Hilti, this problem has been clearly tackled by including some core values into the framing activities – among others, the willingness to take charge and be responsible for your own career, which might include leaving the company if unhappy about the demanded activities. Also in the context of the Hilti case we can see how the remaining framing role of leadership is based on the fact that these leaders control crucial information, which they do not share with the employees, even though the strategizing and organizing processes are to a large degree shared. We could thus agree with Grint (2000: 418) that controlling information is a *conditio sine qua non* of leadership.

Some central control also remains in ÖEB, combined with a strong consensus between top management and local managers on the local managers' relatively high degree of freedom of strategic action. Both groups agree that credit limits/decisions must be taken centrally, and that top management should control performance in each provincial bank through the shared information system. But regarding all other issues both groups agree that there should be strong local freedom to strategize, based on the basic idea that the organizing principles should foster the need for an entrepreneurial spirit in the local banks. In fact, both sides are of the opinion that local management should not have to obey any central campaigns for standardized strategic solutions. So far the bank headquarters have not intervened to reduce the degree of decentralizing and the discretion that the provincial banks have. As the success of the establishment and expansion of this bank is directly related to the innovative way of organizing and strategizing, there has been no reason to increase the central control.

### Ongoing processes of sensemaking as strategic dialogues on differant arenas

Sensemaking is usually described as being retrospective (Weick, 1995: 17), but Gioia and Mehra (1996: 1229) make a strong point of regarding sensemaking as an activity having a prospective orientation, that is, an attempt to make sense *for* the future. Correspondingly, we have shown in this chapter that companies engaging in innovative organizing modes tend to leave reactive strategy making in favour of more proactive strategizing.

Based on our empirical accounts, we argue that organizations might decide to support multiple appearances of the strategic arena by having several and simultaneous meeting places for strategic dialogues at and across different layers. These different appearances of strategic arenas could also be connected to each other in different ways (for example, through interlocking actors, and bottom-up sensegiving). In practice, dialogue takes place in different ways and in different social contexts within and around a focal organization and goes on more or less continuously, while issues and actors come and go, constructing and deconstructing meaning in change processes (Gray et al., 1985). This construction and deconstruction of meaning is going on in the dialogues between actors. Each dialogue implies processes of reciprocal sensegiving/sensemaking, where organizations are viewed to be constituted by systems of meanings and social processes of making sense. One way to further develop our proposed framework is to create a deeper understanding of how and why certain meanings are created among individuals. Here we should also consider the crucial dimension of sensemaking processes where the members of an organization spend considerable amounts of time negotiating an acceptable version of what is going on among themselves (Weick, 1979: 6).

To conclude, we can expect companies to increasingly rely on an efficient diffusion of important strategic dialogues throughout their organization, implying that a wider group of actors may have access to the strategic arena (Ericson et al., 2000) and take an active part in the reciprocal sensegiving/ sensemaking, including the development and translation of new ideas. Such an arena pattern fits with our earlier characterization of innovative modes of organizing, where the top-dominated pyramid is replaced or supplemented with more heterarchical, networking, team-based, project-based and horizontal forms of organizing (Pettigrew and Fenton, 2000a). The focus on communication and reciprocal sensegiving/sensemaking matches another growing trend in organizational analysis. Czarniawska (1997) explicitly connects the narrative perspective, with its focus on how we construct reality by means of narrative knowledge (Lyotard, 1984), to communication and argues that we use narratives whenever we communicate. The link between the narrative approach and the broader field of rhetoric is also obvious (with narration being one of the key concepts in rhetorical theory). The rhetorical skills of leaders receive more and more attention in literature, and particularly in the Aristotelian sense of a meeting 'among free men' (Müllern and Stein, 2000). The findings presented in this chapter are in line with this growing interest in communication, narratives and rhetoric as fruitful perspectives for understanding the new meaning of leadership in new forms of organizing.

# Chapter 4

# Learning and Continuous Change in Innovating Organizations

*Leona Achtenhagen, Leif Melin and Tomas Müllern*

## INTRODUCTION

It is frequently argued in the literature on new and innovative forms of organizing that organizations need to develop their capacity for rapid adaptation, flexibility and innovation (Nohria and Ghoshal, 1997; Volberda, 1998; Ghoshal and Bartlett, 1999). The challenge of building flexible, networked structures has been addressed from a variety of perspectives, for example structural (Volberda, 1998), processual (Handy, 1996) and knowledge management (Nonaka and Takeuchi, 1995), and a number of the indicators used in the INNFORM survey clearly show that intensive experiments to increase the capacity to adapt and learn are carried out in large companies all over the globe.

The INNFORM programme case studies also show that organizations are constantly engaged in processes of change through more or less deliberate attempts to change different aspects and elements of organizational practices. However, these attempts do not necessarily follow the same patterns. Sometimes the change efforts are radical and challenge an entire system of established ways of thinking, while in other cases they can be characterized as processes of incremental change. In the INNFORM case studies, we find numerous examples of both radical and incremental processes that are simultaneously changing both the forms of organizing and the activities and patterns of strategizing. In the continuous processes of change, *organizing* and *strategizing* are viewed as inextricably linked together in a single duality rather than as two separate processes.

In Chapter 2 of this volume Whittington and Melin argued for a changed perspective on organizations that would stress the continuous character of organizational change. The established field of organizational learning offers such a perspective on organizing by focusing on the ability of organizations to incorporate both exploitative forms of learning (single-loop in the terminology of Argyris and Schön, 1978) as well as more explorative (double-loop) forms (March, 1991).

Since change is increasingly becoming an integral part of the day-to-day functioning of a company, we need to learn more about how organizations incorporate change activities into their daily activities. More recent literature on organizational learning suggests that every organization can be described as a *learning culture*, with a specific set of characteristics influencing the ability to carry through change (Schein, 1992; Müllern and Östergren, 1997).

The basic proposition discussed and empirically analysed in this chapter is that organizations need to develop towards more flexible learning cultures in order to incorporate continuous change. The analytical framework theoretically identifies different forms of learning cultures, and three case studies are used to show both how organizations deliberately attempt to develop their capacity for continuous change and the problems and challenges encountered in on-going transformation processes.

The learning perspective developed in this chapter draws upon learning theory as well as cultural perspectives on organizations. By developing the concept of 'learning cultures' we emphasize the theoretical links between learning and culture: learning is always context-bound and has to be understood and described as social/cultural processes of sharing understanding between the members of the organization. Learning processes take place within the company as well as between the company and external actors. Two major activities in these learning processes are *internal sensemaking processes* and the *development of new ideas*. In other words, learning in organizations must build on two components: a social, interactive one, focusing on how meaning is created and spread in the organization (internal sensemaking), and another which focuses on the invention and apprehension of new ideas (that is, new to the actors in the organization). The concept of learning cultures, which forms the analytical core of this chapter, captures both of these aspects and attempts to integrate them in a more elaborate framework.

Thus, the continuous change perspective can be further elaborated by viewing change as a learning process, with a focus on the introduction and sharing of ideas among members of an organization. This perspective on learning is clearly in line with an emphasis on cultural processes. The organizing/strategizing concept takes a clear actor-oriented view of the development of organizations, which is a central ingredient in a processual view on culture.

This chapter further develops Dodgson's (1993: 375) argument that 'learning is a dynamic concept, and its use in theory emphasizes the continually changing nature of organizations'. With its focus on the learning culture in individual organizations it also complements the perspective of Nonaka and Takeuchi (1995) on the 'soft aspects' of knowledge creation from a national cultural perspective (in their case the Japanese culture).

Three cases are used to illustrate the theoretical points in the chapter. The presentation of the three cases aims to illustrate the theoretical line of reasoning rather than making a full process analysis. The case selection and analysis shows the usefulness of the theoretical frame of reference. Further research, however, needs to be done to fully understand the learning processes envisioned in this chapter. The analysis in the three case studies furthers our understanding of how learning cultures create the conditions for continuous change. The case studies, furthermore, illustrate how organizations deliberately try to develop a learning culture, to make them more flexible and alert to change. They also illustrate the different steps taken to build a more change-oriented organization.

More specifically, the following issues are addressed in the chapter:

- How learning relates to deliberate attempts at innovation. The notion of explorative learning is closely related to the discussion of flexible organizational arrangements (Volberda, 1998). The chapter discusses the normative idea that innovating organizations could be effective learning systems (Tushman and Nadler, 1986; Bouwen and Fry, 1991; Baldwin et al., 1997).
- How learning relates to attempts at reshaping processes in organizations. Learning characterized as an on-going interpretative game in organizations clearly relates to the notion of change as a continuous process. The chapter explores the view of organizing/strategizing as an on-going process from a learning perspective.
- How different learning styles occur in different institutional contexts. The chapter explores the idea of learning cultures, which might both enhance and restrict learning in specific cases. This part of the chapter builds on the distinction between exploitative and explorative learning.

## LEARNING AND CONTINUOUS CHANGE – AN OVERVIEW OF THE THEORETICAL FIELD

The literature on learning in general, and organizational learning in particular, is vast and draws on a number of disciplines. Reviews of the field usually conclude that there is a need for integrative approaches as well as for taking account of the context of learning (Huber, 1991; Dodgson, 1993). A number of theoretical dilemmas add to the complexity of the field (for example, individual vs. organizational learning; behavioural vs. cognitive approach; learning vs. change; learning processes vs. learning effects) and make it virtually impossible to summarize organizational learning in an integrated set of propositions. The complexity of the field thus makes it even more important to choose a theoretical perspective carefully for a particular study.

The continuous change perspective indicates that organizations are always in a state of flux, making change a high priority topic for top management. Organizations can be viewed as continuous and intertwined processes of organizing and strategizing, as dynamic entities, rather than just as static structures and strategic positions (Janssens and Steyaert, 1999). Studying organizing and strategizing implies a clear-cut focus on processual aspects of organizational life, with an aim to better understand these aspects through using processual labels (verbs or gerunds) instead of structural labels (nouns) and to regard processes as more fundamental than structures.

This dynamic perspective on intertwined processes of strategizing and organizing which unfold over time allows us to view changing organizations in their entirety; as a result, the old dichotomies of 'strategy-structure' and 'strategic-operational' dissolve. In this chapter, organizing will be described in terms of multiple processes of organizing activities. Furthermore, organizing implies strategizing, where strategizing means forming new strategic mindsets, activities and patterns. We use the phrase *organizing is strategizing* to capture the central argument that organizing and strategizing are parts of the same managerial processes, and that, therefore, they cannot be treated as separate managerial entities. Strategizing processes create the space for cycles of learning and evolution over time, based on more or less perpetual strategizing activities. In turn, organizational learning might facilitate the strategizing/organizing processes.

The theoretical links between a change perspective and learning are obvious if we take a closer look at the conceptual development of the organizational learning field. The incremental versus the radical change typology has its counterpart in learning theory, in the distinction between *exploitative* versus *explorative* learning (March, 1991; Levinthal and March, 1993). Exploitative learning refers to an organization's ability to evaluate and use internal and external knowledge (Cohen and Levinthal, 1990), while explorative learning is associated with complex search, basic research, innovation, variation, risk-taking and more relaxed controls (Clegg, 1999). The explorative learning style can also be, theoretically, connected to discussions in the field of entrepreneurship concerning creativity and innovation (Rickards, 1999). The concepts are similar to a number of well-known 'pairs' in the organizational learning literature, for example, single-loop and double-loop learning (Argyris and Schön, 1978), first-order and second-order learning (Lant and Mezias, 1992) as well as minor and major learning (Parkhe, 1991). We prefer the exploitative versus explorative distinction with its characterization of two broad categories of learning styles, as it reduces the terminological difficulties inherent in some of the other dichotomies in the literature. It is particularly appropriate for organizations using both styles to a certain degree at the same time, creating a duality rather than two endpoints on a continuum (on the discussion of dualities, see the chapters in Part 3 of this volume).

However, we must note that the apparent obsession with conceptual 'pairs' is unfortunate, since it obscures the processual nature of (both individual and organizational) learning. Recent attempts to develop a processual perspective on organizational learning clearly indicate that learning can be viewed as a social process in organizations, drawing from interpretative and social constructivist perspectives (Crossan et al., 1999; Hosking and Bouwen, 2000). If the learning perspective should fulfil the promise of adding to a continuous change perspective, we clearly need to break away from fixed dichotomies on learning. The learning perspective applied in this chapter rests on three propositions that are further developed below.

### Learning is an individual, cognitive act

Learning is a concept originally developed in individual psychology to describe the different mental processes aimed at facilitating interpretations of different situations, remembering things and acquiring knowledge through experience (Bower and Hilgard, 1981). Regarding *organizational learning*, two broad schools can be identified: the *behavioural* and the *cognitive school*. These schools focus on different aspects of the learning process. The *behavioural school* focuses on learning as a manifest change in behaviour of an individual, based primarily on classical or contiguous conditioning. The *cognitive school* focuses more on the mental processes connected to learning – cognitive structures help the individual to make sense and create meaning, and learning implies that these cognitive structures are changing (for example, Lindell, Ericson and Melin, 1998). Within the cognitive school we find the interpretative/ cultural approach as one distinct cognitive perspective with a broader focus on social processes of interpretation.

The learning perspective used in this chapter is based on the cognitive school; more specifically, ideas from the interpretative approach and Gestalt theory. Learning is viewed as the insight an individual gains when confronted with stimuli of different kinds that he or she is able to interpret. This perspective transcends the Gestalt ideas of perception by adding a linguistic focus on learning, arguing that organizational learning must be based on human communicative interaction (Dixon, 1994; Brown and Starkey, 2000). In fact, we argue that communication is a necessary ingredient in a theory on organizational learning. Similar ideas are put forward by Van Looy et al. (2000) on relational–constructionist approaches to organizational learning.

Characterizing learning as a cognitive act does not mean that behavioural aspects are rejected, but rather that the focus lies on cognitive aspects. From a managerial point of view the change of behaviour is crucial. It could be argued, though, that we need to understand the underlying cognitive processes which lead to changes in behaviour even though the desired result of learning is changed behaviour. From a theoretical point of view the causality assumption in the behavioural argument can be criticized, as changed behaviour is assumed to be an effect of learning (thus being an indicator of learning). Instead, other reasons for behavioural changes besides learning might prevail.

From a managerial point of view the cognitive perspective can add certain insights to the understanding of organizational learning. A key assumption of the cognitive perspective is that learning is a change of the mindset of managers (and others), which, in turn, reinforces the need for 'unlearning' (Hedberg, 1981) in organizations. The empirical evidence provided later in this chapter also shows how important cultural changes are, moving from adaptive learning cultures towards more reformative and generative learning cultures, reinforcing the ability to reflect upon culturally based habits in the organization (see the section Building Blocks for a Theory of Learning and continuous change below). It should also be stressed that the ability of any social system to learn and unlearn is closely linked to communication tools. A number of authors in the broad field of innovative forms of organizing stress the need for communication in flexible, boundary-less organizations. In their concept of the differentiated network Nohria and Ghoshal (1997) argue for the crucial role of communication in networked forms of organizing. A similar point is made by Eccles and Nohria (1992) in their 'rediscovery' of basic management tools, such as rhetoric.

## Learning is situated

The characterization of learning as an individual, cognitive act excludes the possibility of learning taking place on an inter-individual level, at least in the stricter sense of the word learning. The meaning of organizational learning must then differ from the meaning of individual learning. One useful way of describing organizational learning would be to view it metaphorically, as a way of characterizing different organizational processes (Dodgson, 1993). Then, we would compare organizational systems for storing knowledge with the human memory and we would compare the way of communicating in a company with individual sensemaking and flexible organizational arrangements with intuitive mental processes of imagination.

By combining these ideas from individual psychology with insights from social constructivism and neo-institutional theory, organizational learning can be compared to a language game taking place in an organized setting with certain rule-like conditions. Organizations can be described as learning cultures (Müllern and Östergren, 1997), forming distinct cultural patterns affecting the ability to innovate and spread ideas. Learning is thus situated in the cultural practices and shared understandings of the different actors or groups of actors in the company. The specific learning culture of an organization can be both a restriction and a condition for learning and continuous change. It can be a restriction if the cultural patterns make individuals risk-averse and if it promotes destructive group thinking. On the other hand, the cultural patterns can also promote invention or discovery of new ideas and the rapid spread of ideas among members of the organization.

Communication is essential to the understanding of organizational learning. Thus, the cognitive perspective must be complemented with a more social, communicative perspective. Based on the narrative approach of Czarniawska (1997) we argue that organizational learning can be described as a 'travel of ideas' – ideas that are interpreted and reinterpreted by members of the organization. Organizational learning can be described in terms of shared language and conceptions; for example, we use similar concepts, routines are institutionalized, things are written down and codified, and projects are noticed by mass-media. Not surprisingly, the literature on learning organizations also focuses heavily on the tools created to enhance learning and leans very much on ideas from knowledge management; more specifically, the distribution and transfer of knowledge (Stacey, 2001).

Of course, this language game differs depending on the specific conditions, in time and space, prevailing in an organization. These conditions can be described in terms of normative affiliation among members (DiMaggio and Powell, 1983), heterogeneity of interests (Clegg, 1999), distance between hierarchical levels, educational levels, external orientation and past experiences (Huber, 1991). Thus, from a continuous change perspective, the communicative aspects are crucial, and the ability to communicate in turn depends on the cultural characteristics of the organization.

### Learning is an interplay between the past and the future

The exploitation/exploration distinction of Levinthal and March (1993) can be further employed to describe the third basic assumption of this chapter. Referring to the cognitive school, we can identify two different styles of organizational learning. Learning can be described as *exploitative* (Levitt and March, 1988) – directed towards the past – and as *explorative* – directed to the future. To quote Levinthal and March (1993), organizations face the challenge of 'balancing the competing goals of developing new knowledge and exploiting current competencies in the face of dynamic tendencies to emphasize one or the other'. An effective learning system must, therefore, keep a dual time focus – learning from the past and exploring the future.

The skills, techniques and cultural processes needed to accomplish the two forms of learning are radically different. The exploitative style of learning is intimately connected to the current practices in the organization and the ability to effectively evaluate and reflect upon them. Exploitative learning is highly dependent on the control systems developed in the organization, and the ability to sense, interpret and react to signals and deviances. Thus, it is no coincidence that an information processing perspective has been highly influential in the cognitive vein of learning theory (Bower and Hilgard, 1981).

The explorative style of learning, on the other hand, draws on the innovative capacity of the organization, and, even though the ability to reflect upon current practices often is an important aspect of innovation, it requires different skills from exploitative learning. Different aspects of the innovative capacity in organizations have been stressed: wide distribution of slack resources (Nohria and Ghoshal, 1997), the constructive friction between managerial capabilities and organizational responsiveness (Volberda, 1998) or the interaction between tacit and explicit knowledge (Nonaka and Takeuchi, 1995).

From a theoretical perspective it is not contradictory to assume that organizations can accomplish both, that is, learn from experience at the same time as they free themselves from their history in order to be innovative. In fact, in the context of research on innovative forms of organizing, it can be argued that both forms of learning are needed in order to survive. Exploitative learning creates stability and enables the members of the organization to codify elements of knowledge, experiences and values. It also points in the direction of knowledge management, with its focus on building systems for collecting, storing and using knowledge. Explorative learning is the creative force that enables individuals and groups to innovate and thus to break away from established ways of thinking.

It should be stressed that we are discussing two forms of learning that can coexist in the same organizational setting. However, the challenge is to combine them to foster flexibility and efficiency. Previous studies on organizational learning show that organizations often excel in the exploitative form. There is also evidence that organizations might get stuck in 'unproductive' forms of learning (non-learning), being unable to use previous experience and facing obsolete world views. On the other hand, a one-sided focus on productive forms of learning could lead to a lack of exploiting innovative potential and disorientation of the employees.

## BUILDING BLOCKS FOR A THEORY OF LEARNING AND CONTINUOUS CHANGE

The characterization of learning above can be further refined by specifying two dimensions of learning: the introduction of new ideas and internal sensemaking. We use these two dimensions to characterize the learning styles found in the empirical case studies, which will be presented later in this chapter. They are, conceptually, described as two separate dimensions,

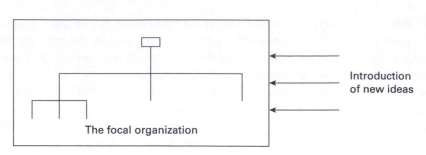

FIGURE 4.1   *Introducing new ideas*

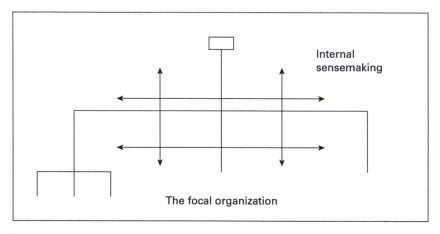

FIGURE 4.2   *Internal sensemaking*

even though the case evidence shows that they are intimately connected. As an analytical tool we identify four different types in each dimension, comprising 16 possible combinations. The introduction of new ideas has to do with the process of inventing and discovering ideas in the organizing/strategizing processes, and it answers the question 'where do ideas come from?' Internal sensemaking has to do with the internal diffusion/acceptance/sensemaking processes, and it corresponds to Crossan, Lane and White's (1999) group level integration, the creation of shared understandings and mutual adjustments. The two dimensions are illustrated in Figures 4.1 and 4.2 (where it should be noted that new ideas may not only come from outside but could be developed within the organization as well).

The interpretative perspective on learning stresses that ideas are important in the learning process – ideas being both the content and the 'fuel' of learning. We, therefore, argue that the process of introducing new ideas into the organization constitutes an important part of its learning and further strengthens the link between learning and continuous change (and innovation). This dimension has to do with the openness, ability, knowledge and willingness to find or invent new ideas (that is, which are new at least from the perspective of actors in the organization). The case studies in the INNFORM project were deliberately chosen to illustrate innovating organizations (in terms of experimenting with new forms of organizing). We would, therefore, expect that they score high marks on this dimension. In order to pinpoint how radical organizations perform in terms of introducing new ideas we need to identify different degrees of newness relative to previous conceptions in the organization. This means that the context of innovation is important in judging how radical a change effort is. Yet, change projects that are considered radical and frame-breaking in one institutional field could be considered as conventional wisdom in another field. The degree of newness is thus a relative concept.

There are four theoretical types of learning cultures, based on the introducing new ideas dimension: *conservative*, *adaptive*, *reformative* and *generative* learning cultures. An organization with a conservative learning culture is one that avoids change and uses an exploitative learning style to refine existing practices. Theoretical input to this category comes from social psychology and the phenomenon of *groupthink* (Janis, 1982), where the group develops a culture that prevents external information from influencing its decision making. The adaptive type corresponds to the single-loop learning of Argyris and Schön (1978) and describes an attitude to change focusing on adaptation within existing frames of reference in the organization. Whereas the conservative organization would usually be trying to avoid change, the adaptive organization is rather focused on incremental change, to react to disturbances by refining the system. The reformative and generative types both apply to explorative learning styles in the sense that the organizations explicitly try to further develop current practices and ways of thinking. We use two separate categories to describe the theoretical difference between organizations searching for inspiration and opportunities outside the organization, mainly learning from others (reformative) and organizations more devoted to genuine renewal/research, thus combining external and internal sources of inspiration (generative).

The introduction of new ideas can thus be described as the basic attitude towards new ideas in the organization. It ranges from an attitude that any challenge to existing frames of reference should be avoided (conservative), though a view that challenges should be incorporated into existing frames (adaptive) or be used to develop existing frames by inspiration received from others (reformative), to an attitude that challenges should be dealt with by taking the lead in finding new practices (generative).

Learning mechanisms and corresponding organizational processes obviously differ in the four types of learning cultures. In Table 4.1 below we

TABLE 4.1    *The introduction of new ideas – four ideal types*

| Introduction of new ideas – four ideal types | Style of learning | Typical organizational processes | Approach to change |
| --- | --- | --- | --- |
| Conservative | Exploitative learning | Safeguarding | Change avoidance |
| Adaptive | Exploitative learning | Internal control and feedback | Incremental/reactive |
| Reformative | Explorative learning | Environmental scanning | Major change efforts/proactive |
| Generative | Explorative learning | Research/innovation | Genuine renewal/proactive |

label the different learning mechanisms and corresponding types of change and examplify some typical organizational processes in each learning culture. It should be noted that both Table 4.1 and Table 4.2 are theoretical constructs and in a sense point at archetypical aspects of different learning cultures.

In Table 4.1, the degree to which an organization employs a continuous change perspective, as well as the organization's propensity for experimenting with innovative forms of organizing is likely to increase from the top to the bottom of the table.

Now, we look at the second major dimension of learning, internal sensemaking. As argued by Simon (1991), internal learning constitutes an important element of organizational learning. Simon defines internal learning as the transmission of information from one organizational member to another. Internal sensemaking is obviously affected by a number of structural and cultural factors. Following Mintzberg's (1979) distinction between horizontal and vertical decentralization, we argue that the functional/professional specialization/differentiation on a horizontal level, and the differentiation on a vertical level add to the heterogeneity or homogeneity of conceptions in an organization. A high degree of horizontal and vertical differentiation makes it, *ceteris paribus*, harder to diffuse ideas – at least from a top management perspective.

There are four types of internal sensemaking – *hegemonic, unified, split* and *anarchist*, in increasing order of heterogeneity – which are identified in Table 4.2. The hegemonic type of internal sensemaking is used to denote a centralized system of control, with a strong actor or set of actors dominating the sensemaking in the organization. It also denotes a system that resists change and uses a high degree of closure to protect the dominant view. The hegemonic type of sensemaking shares a homogeneous system of conceptions with the unified category. The major difference is that the unified type is characterized by more decentralized control and a more open attitude to change. It should be noted that the unified learning culture seems to foster two different types of change (cf. Table 4.1). On the one hand, unified learning

TABLE 4.2    *Internal sensemaking – four ideal types*

| Internal sensemaking – four ideal types | Homogeneity/ heterogeneity in conceptions | Typical organizational processes | Approach to change |
|---|---|---|---|
| Hegemonic | Homogeneous conceptions | Centralized control | Change avoidance |
| Unified | Homogeneous conceptions | Decentralized control | Incremental/ reactive or major change efforts |
| Split | Heterogeneous between levels | Distance between top management and employees | Major change efforts with a lot of resistance |
| Anarchist | Heterogeneous between levels and among groups of actors | Lack of control | Lack of change |

cultures are often connected to the adaptive approach to new ideas, with a focus on incremental or reactive change efforts, and with a conservative attitude to new ideas. On the other hand, the unified learning culture seems to be highly desirable from a top management perspective when striving to avoid change resistance. The challenge, then, is to combine the unified culture with a generative or reformative culture in the first dimension of introducing new ideas above.

The split type of sensemaking is characterized by heterogeneous conceptions, usually between hierarchical levels. Change efforts initiated by top management are often met by resistance from other levels (and/or other stakeholders of the organization). The split type differs from the anarchist, because the heterogeneity is based on differences between major stakeholders, and is therefore easier to identify. In the anarchist type the heterogeneity is based on both differences between major stakeholders and on individual differences. The approach to change also differs, with the split type characterized by major change efforts, whereas the anarchist type can rather be characterized by a lack of change.

The terminology chosen for the typologies deliberately differs from the learning concepts used above. The reproductive/experiential and productive/ entrepreneurial distinctions, as used in the organizational learning literature, do not notice the difference between our two dimensions, which means that we would find reproductive/productive aspects in both the first and the second dimension. In the first dimension – introducing new ideas – the conservative and adaptive learning cultures are more closely related to the reproductive/experiential learning style, and the reformative and generative learning cultures would correspond to the productive/entrepreneurial learning style, even though the ability to work with reproductive learning is highly important also in reformative and generative cases. The second dimension – internal sensemaking – adds a new element to the dichotomies in the sense that we can find the reproductive and the productive in all four learning cultures in Table 4.2 (with the possible exception of the hegemonic culture).

These two typologies can either be used for taking analytical snapshots of organizations or to describe trajectories, where the second alternative is more in line with the continuous change perspective developed here. In the empirical case vignettes below we focus on the change efforts to move towards more generative/reformative learning cultures, and to some extent on how organizations try to create unified systems for internal sensemaking. It should also be stressed that the tables, as they are constructed, do not evaluate the different learning cultures or the possible combinations between the two dimensions. It is not, for example, more desirable *per se* to have an adaptive or generative learning culture.

As proposed by Tushman and Nadler (1986), we see a strong connection between learning style and innovative behaviour in organizations. More radical change initiatives are connected to learning that resembles a productive form of learning. We would then expect a learning culture that adapts or is characterized by a reformative or generative approach to the introduction of new ideas. The theoretical link between learning culture and radical change efforts is complicated by the fact that the learning style (influenced by the learning culture) is both a dependent and independent variable. Organizations are, metaphorically, affected by both their past and their future: the past in the form of established ways of thinking in the organization and the future in the form of radical change attempts. Changing the culture is a common element in attempts at making the company more flexible, innovative and decentralized or delayered. The case evidence also shows that the companies attempt to reach a state of continuous change, trying to change their learning cultures by moving towards the generative/reformative style, at the same time as top management struggles to create a more unified internal sensemaking.

The move towards more flexible structures is complicated by the part of the learning culture which involves internal sensemaking. The implementation problems in radical change projects are often attributed to the internal sensemaking in organizations, and especially the internal heterogeneity of interests and conceptions (Ericson, 2001). Learning cultures can thus pose a problem for the implementation process, making it harder for top management to gain adherence for their views. Evidence from public sector organizations shows that they are often heterogeneous in terms of internal sensemaking, and in many cases could be characterized as split or anarchist (Müllern and Östergren, 1997). In much the same way a unified and hegemonic sensemaking can also be problematic if the proposed change ideas challenge deeply held conceptions in the organization.

## LEARNING AND ORGANIZING/STRATEGIZING

The learning culture typologies developed above will now be adapted to the continuous change perspective. We have argued that virtually all of the organizations in our INNFORM case sample are continuously involved in deliberate attempts at changing different aspects of the organization. Our focus on organizing and strategizing emphasizes the continuous change perspective. The learning culture typologies might give the impression that organizations are 'stuck' in one type of learning culture. In this section, we argue that our case study organizations are in a process of continuous change where the trajectory is of more interest than the actual positioning at one point in time. In order to illustrate the continuous change efforts, we analyse three case studies, with a special focus on the introduction of new ideas and internal sensemaking.

### Siemens Medical Engineering

Evidence from a number of the INNFORM case studies shows that companies are moving from learning cultures that focus on exploitative learning (that is, the conservative and adaptive types) towards reformative and generative learning cultures, thus focusing on explorative learning. Siemens is a good example of the move from a conservative type of learning culture towards a more open and proactive learning culture (cf. a more extensive case study in Achtenhagen, 2001). Siemens AG is a multinational player in electrical engineering and electronics, with firm roots in its home country, Germany. Over the past 150 years, Siemens has grown to become one of the largest electrical engineering companies in the world. In 1998, Siemens AG's 416 000 employees generated sales of DM117.7 billion, with new orders of DM119.6 billion. In the same year, the company spent DM9.1 billion on research and development. For a long time, Siemens image was that of a rather slow-moving, traditional company with a steep hierarchical structure. However, in 1993 the company-wide 'top' programme to enhance productivity started. At that time, a number of business units faced severe crises and turnarounds were attempted. This case study focuses on the business group Siemens Medical Engineering (S-Med), which was one of the groups to succeed with a fast turnaround. In 1998, S-Med achieved sales of DM7.994 billion, employing 18 300 people.[1]

Initially the strongest factor in influencing change for Siemens AG was the increasing external pressure from financial analysts. In Germany, pressure from shareholders had always been rather low. Increasingly, large German corporations are deciding to list their shares internationally and thus shareholders are becoming equally international. S-Med's move towards innovative modes organizing was triggered by the unit's crisis due to severe competitive pressure, US Food and Drug Administration (FDA) requirements for selling medical engineering equipment on the US market and the inability to adapt to these changing economic requirements.

Structural changes were the prerequisite for implementing a new process orientation, as the old structure scarcely allowed for cross-unit information flow or cooperation. Over the years of success and growth, Siemens had become an organization with a steep hierarchy, in which managerial positions were tenure-like, and cross-unit communication or cooperation was largely discouraged. While strategic decision-making responsibility had been decentralized to a large degree to the individual business areas, it was hardly passed on within those units. Thus, a slow-moving culture was created, in which performance mattered little and in which formal authority was not to be questioned: 'Once a manager, always a manager – no matter what you do wrong, no matter how you treat people – this was our Siemens culture' (Member of Corporate Development, Siemens AG). This split type of internal sensemaking led to high resistance towards change from managerial levels, while employees would often recognize the need for change. With the increasing crisis of the unit, and the enhancement of the corporate-wide programme to make the company more flexible, the number of hierarchical layers was reduced and 'managerial principalities' were broken up. The managerial roles, which used to be 'untouchable', changed dramatically. 'Much insecurity arose among the managers. … People in the lowest management layers were redundant. Before, we had eight layers, now we have five or less. The classic manager is now superfluous, what we need are coaches' (HR Manager, S-Med). By introducing obligatory feedback processes and eliminating hierarchical ranks, a new communication style was fostered and learning processes were initiated. Competence-based salaries, annual performance evaluation and feedback rounds were introduced by top management with the aim of breaking down old rules. People were instead encouraged to discuss weaknesses and failures, which had been avoided in the old culture. In addition, a number of different communication forums were established to reduce the conflict over resources between projects and core processes (for example, the product development process) and to increase cross-unit communication and cooperation: *'The need for joint decision-making has increased enormously, and people from different units realize they have the same problems'* (Manager Business Area, S-Med). It was also recognized that much of the cultural change had to take place on a discursive level, with the aim of changing the way people talked about the company and managers (for example, to label managers 'coaches' instead of 'superiors'), to enable change in organizational processes. The change processes were not easily managed, but the slow development of a more entrepreneurial spirit can be acknowledged (Achtenhagen, 2001). 'We did demand the entrepreneur, but we didn't provide the system in which the individual could act accordingly' (Member, 'top' programme). The new orientation also explicitly addresses the need (or desire) to establish a culture of continuous change. The Siemens case is a good illustration of the kind of cultural change needed to move towards a more reformative/generative learning culture, and thus create a flexible and learning organization. It also illustrates the importance of dealing with heterogeneous conceptions internally to reduce counter-productive conflicts between different functions and interests.

## Saab

Saab Training Systems is a wholly owned part of Saab AB. The company's special niche is computer-aided training equipment for military purposes, using visual simulations of different types of terrain and situations and laser-based systems. The laser-based systems are the firm's core competence (with a number of patents showing the high technological profile of the company and its employees). The business idea is to provide the customers with state-of-the-art training systems using experience-based learning. Saab Training Systems is a world leader in its area of simulation equipment based on laser technology for aimed weapons. The largest markets for its products are the UK, the USA and Germany. At the end of 2001, Saab Training Systems had close to 300 employees.

Saab Training Systems has a highly developed system for exploitative learning (especially on an individual basis). The company moved from a traditional factory organization with a functional and hierarchical structure to a team-based structure with an extremely flat hierarchy (each of around 50 teams reporting directly to the top management team), and a high degree of operational decentralization (and also a very high degree of strategic decentralization, even though the managing director maintains a great deal of control). These radical change efforts in the early 1990s were accompanied by a strong focus on individual and group-level learning in the teams.[2]

Each team is responsible for developing and refining both the end product and the processes, and they have proven to be very successful in accomplishing this goal, making the company very profitable in its industry. A major problem, though, has been the ability to innovate, which was also a responsibility assigned to the different teams. A highly adaptive learning culture was developed during the 1990s that, in a sense, shifted the emphasis from innovation (explorative learning) to refining present products and processes.

One important aspect of organizational learning is to create opportunities for the individual to learn by doing. An important arena for feedback is the direct contact with the customers, where different, functionally organized, teams often meet customers to discuss various issues concerning the product. The team itself is also an important factor in the feedback to individuals. The former Managing Director stressed that the teams should have access to all necessary information and that work results should be made visible and available to everybody. All interviewees also mentioned the weekly meeting between all team-leaders and the management team (including the Managing Director). The teams are organized to provide an environment for individual learning. One important aspect of this goal is the organization of teams around objects (subsystems of the products) rather than functions. The teams are in most cases cross-functional, bringing together people with different competences; they are thus specialized in terms of products, but not in terms of competence.

An important aspect of exploitative learning, with its focus on learning from experience, is how experience is stored and made available to others. The former Managing Director at Saab Training Systems emphasized the importance of trying to accumulate experience in the organization. This accumulation is achieved in a number of ways: the products in themselves are obviously an important factor, with a great deal of knowledge stored in the current line of products. The business process is also important with well-developed logistics in the three product areas (at least when it comes to production). A clear aim is also to accumulate experience not only in the individual, but also in the team and the company in general.

Saab Training Systems illustrates a move from an adaptive (and to some extent even conservative) learning culture with a low degree of organizational innovation, towards a generative (in its context, at least) culture with radical organizational and strategic renewal. The last years of the 1990s, though, showed a decrease in innovativeness, an issue that was addressed in a renewal effort launched in the year 2000 (the results of this effort were not yet clear when this chapter was written). It seemed that the organization had regressed to a more adaptive learning style. The internal sensemaking in the company can be clearly classified as unified with a strong degree of homogeneity in conceptions, which to some extent can be attributed to the small size of the company with its close to 300 employees.

## Trumpf

Trumpf GmbH + Co. is a German manufacturer of machine tools for punching, forming, laser machining, water jet cutting and bending for flexible material processing. As a world leader in laser technology, Trumpf offers solutions for special applications ranging from compact units to laser processing centres. The company is located in Ditzingen (near Stuttgart) and employed around 4500 people at the time of our study (late 1998), achieving a turnover of 1.7 billion DM.[3] The company was founded in 1923 and has since then brought a number of technological innovations to the market. Trumpf is headed by CEO Professor Leibinger, who also owns the majority of the company's shares. In 1992, Trumpf was hit by a severe crisis due to the recession in the machine tool industry. At this time, US and Japanese competitors had a competitive advantage, which could be attributed to cost-sensitive manufacturing, higher productivity and a more favourable environment. Between 1990 and 1994 around 40 per cent of all employees in the German machine tool manufacturing industry lost their jobs; often these were highly qualified technicians (Leibinger, 1997: 149). This crisis pressured Trumpf to quickly improve its learning processes – it was a question of company survival. In 1990, and thus before the crisis hit Trumpf hard, the company had realized that competitors were manufacturing at cost advantages of around 30 per cent. In that year, a group of managers had participated in a seminar on Japanese work processes. The managers were convinced that similar processes could – and should – be implemented within Trumpf, but they failed to persuade top management of this opportunity. We can interpret this effort as an attempt to move away from the hegemonic sensemaking types, at a point at which conceptions ceased to be homogenous. At this point, a conservative attitude towards accepting new ideas still prevailed – unless they were in the field of technological innovations.

In 1991, a pilot project was started to improve productivity and reduce costs. However, while the pilot project in itself was successful, acceptance within the rest of the company was rather low, as people in general felt too little informed about the aim and the scope of the changes. In response, the company introduced a number of regular meetings to increase the overall level of information. This can be seen as an initial move from conservative and adaptive towards generative learning, and a move away from the split type of internal sensemaking towards more homogeneous conceptions of the organizational learning needs. These learning processes facilitated the major change efforts carried out in response to the emerging company crisis. Once the crisis hit the company more severely, top management recalled the experiences of the group of managers at the Japanese-style management seminar and invited a workshop to take place within the company to find out whether and how processes could be changed accordingly within Trumpf.

In terms of the types introduced earlier, a leap from conservative to reformative learning by top management is evident here. Once the manufacturing process changes were initiated, Trumpf management realized that these changes would not be enough, but that the development of a new innovation process was needed as well. *'In response to the crisis, we managed to reduce delivery times from 12 to 3 months, but our old system couldn't handle that anymore – we had to reorganize'* (Head of Manufacturing). However, a different mentality and behaviour were needed from the employees. Formerly, people in manufacturing were hardly allowed to talk to each other, as they were expected to fulfil their tasks without actively engaging in improving processes. Therefore, any communication was considered not job-related and a waste of time. With the aim of increasing the involvement of the employees, a total of 15 events, each two days long, were held to discuss how to improve work procedures and to plan the implementation process. More than 250 suggestions for how to improve efficiency were developed, underlining the vast untapped internal potential for creativity and learning from each other. Employees were now expected to participate actively in improvement processes, and to be action-oriented and open for innovation and change – embarking on the path towards continuous change. A number of training courses were developed to support these changes in behaviour. Thus, we can see that, as a result of previous experiences, the Trumpf attitude changed increasingly from exploitative to explorative learning.

## COMPARATIVE CASE ANALYSIS

The three cases discussed above illustrate different approaches to continuous change and learning. Despite the differences in size, sector and organizational solutions, all three share the aim be innovative in organizing and strategizing. All three cases, S-Med, Saab Training Systems and Trumpf, illustrate a distinct move from a mainly adaptive culture towards a more reformative and/or generative culture.

In all three cases, competitive pressure is by far the most important driver for continuous change. All three companies have been able to change to highly flexible structures, driven by strong competitive and technological pressures. The renewal efforts in Saab, where the change in strategic focus (primarily towards a strong market orientation) went hand in hand with the introduction of a team-based form of organizing clearly show how intertwined strategizing and organizing are. In this case the strategizing process towards a stronger market view was a prerequisite for the team-based form of organizing at the same time as it was strongly dependent on it.

The combined efforts of market orientation and the team-based form of organizing led to an increased need to focus on internal processes within Saab Training Systems. This in turn forced the company to focus strongly on core competencies (in this case laser-based systems for military training). The late 1990s also posed new challenges to the company in terms of finding the means to innovate. Instrumental in the success of the company during the 1990s was the ability to create a reformative/generative learning culture, with a strong acceptance of new ideas, at the same time as the unified sensemaking facilitated the necessary changes internally.

Even though the S-Med case is more focused on the organizing aspects, it clearly shows how important it is to work with internal sensemaking in strategic change processes. The former organizational system with tenure-like positions clearly hindered a more entrepreneurial spirit and created resistance towards change. The company needed to change the forms of internal sensemaking before they were able to introduce more radical change efforts.

It is important to take notice of the size factor in analysing the internal sensemaking dimension. Large companies (for example, S-Med) obviously have more difficulties in creating a unified learning culture in the positive sense of a culture where the employees feel informed and accept ideas for change. However, top management in all three case study organizations have struggled hard to change the culture internally to pave the way for organizational renewal.

A number of observations can be made concerning the development and change of the learning culture in the three organizations. The first important observation which holds for all three cases is that trying to create a flexible, innovative organization is not a one-time event or effort; instead, it needs to be treated as a continuous process and given high priority by top management. Evidence from the three companies Trumpf, Saab and S-Med show that structural changes must be driven by more process-oriented moves in order to be successful.

In the case of Saab Training Systems, the new team-based form of organizing eventually turned out to be counter-productive when it came to innovation (the focus in the teams shifted from innovation to effectiveness) and much effort was spent in the late 1990s dealing with this problem. The Managing Director of the company also stressed the need for continuously working with corporate renewal, implying both on-going strategizing activities and new modes of organizing. In the case of S-Med, the old structure became a major problem for the internal sensemaking, with frequent conflicts between functional managers which demanded a new form of organizing representing another type of learning culture.

In Table 4.3 we see that all the companies in our case studies attempted to move from more exploitative towards more explorative learning styles. However, explorative learning could only take place once the more immanent problems had been tackled, overcoming a company crisis. These changes in attitudes towards accepting new ideas do not necessarily mean that a more homogeneous sensemaking would take place, but that a more conscious approach is taken towards sensemaking and actually allowing for different interpretations.

## CONCLUDING COMMENTS

The emerging efforts to understand continuous change in organizations through the perspective of strategizing and organizing is promising, but we need to specify the meaning of these two intertwined processes in order to further develop these theoretical constructs. In this chapter we have attempted this by regarding continuous change as learning, where two

TABLE 4.3  *Comparison of the case studies*

| | S-Med | Saab Training Systems | Trumpf |
|---|---|---|---|
| Drivers for change | External pressure by financial analysts, FDA requirement for US market | Internal: strive towards higher innovativeness | External: crisis in the machine tool industry, high costs and low productivity |
| Organizational characteristics and accompanied changes | From steep to delayered hierarchy and new project-oriented working modes | Team-based organization | Changes in work processes in response to competitive pressure, only then acknowledgement of importance of learning |
| Process of change in learning culture: introduction of new ideas | From exploitative (conservative and adaptive) toward reformative and generative learning | From adaptive to generative learning | From conservative to generative learning |
| Process of change in learning culture: sensemaking | From mainly hegemonic (however, conceptions were not necessarily homogeneous) to split sensemaking; trying hard to move towards unified sensemaking | Unified with a strong role played by the CEO, framing conceptions | From hegemonic sensemaking towards more unified sensemaking |
| Problems | Overcome feeling of 'safety' deriving from the Siemens group; replace seniority with performance and learning orientation | Eventually, the team-based form led to a strong focus on effectiveness in each team, and less focus on innovation | The change process involved laying off people for the first time, so moral issues became very important |

crucial activities have been in focus: the introduction of new ideas in order to change patterns of strategizing and/or forms of organizing, and the internal sensemaking that is needed facilitate the change. In order to qualify the type of change and degree of learning taking place we have used the dual concepts of exploitation and exploration.

A Chandlerian view on strategy driving the choice of organizational structure implies a more traditional view on organizational/strategic change, where the organization 'moves' between periods of relative stability and change (Chandler, 1962). A change effort is followed by a period of stability where the new structural solution is refrozen. The 'organizing is strategizing' concept radically challenges this view on strategic change, with change becoming an integral part of the strategic work in the company. The holistic view inherent in the 'organizing is strategizing' notion emphasizes that organizing is not just a consequence of the strategic decisions taken by top management (that is, strategy driving structure) but an inherent aspect of the strategic development of a company.

The basic view that organizing and strategizing are two aspects of the same managerial process creates a focus on continuous change in two respects. First, by emphasizing that organizing is more important than being just a consequence of strategizing – more complex and dynamic processes are stimulated, which, by themselves, create a stronger focus on constantly challenging old practices (Ghoshal and Bartlett, 1999). The Saab Training Systems case study clearly illustrates this increased complexity, with the strategizing being integrated in the highly decentralized team-based organization. The period from 1992 (when the team-based structure was introduced) to the present day is characterized by more rapid introductions of new products and a closer collaboration with customers. The dual focus on organizing and strategizing clearly developed the capacity to innovate and also created a need to constantly monitor and renew the organizational practices, thus making continuous change a top priority.

Secondly, the interconnectedness of organizing and strategizing fosters more flexible organizations, and puts a stronger focus on innovation and entrepreneurship. The process orientation in S-Med is a good illustration of this second point, where the new and more open way of communicating has transformed the company from a more conservative and adaptive learning culture towards a generative learning culture, with innovation as a key feature.

An important question is why this interconnectedness between organizing and strategizing has grown in importance. This part of the volume is in fact proposing that more integrated processes of organizing and strategizing are important characteristics of new and innovative forms of organizing. One evident answer is that competitive pressure forces companies to adopt more holistic and flexible ways of organizing, where the traditional causal relation between strategy and organization becomes obsolete. Flexible organizational arrangements are needed to respond to a variety of changes in the competitive environment (Volberda, 1998), and this tends to promote a more process-oriented view on organizing and strategizing. The Trumpf case is a clear illustration of this need for more holistic and flexible arrangements as a response to competitive pressure.

In both the Saab and the Trumpf case studies external pressure 'forced' the companies to move into a more explorative learning style. The triggering effect of a crisis marked the beginning of a new thinking, categorized as a generative learning culture, where change has been a top priority from the early 1990s onwards. This leads us to hypothesize that the generative learning culture is closely connected to change as a continuous effort in the organization, rather than a one-time event. And even though the generative learning in Siemens was not so clearly triggered by an external crisis it still illustrates the hypothesis. The move towards more generative learning forced all three companies to emphasize change as a continuous activity. In other words, to foster change-oriented strategizing activities, where new strategic ideas are adopted and/or invented, organizations might attempt to avoid a conservative learning culture and try to balance an adaptive learning culture with a more reformative and/or generative learning culture. When it comes to the other aspect of the learning culture – internal sensemaking – we can hypothesize that in order to facilitate the broad acceptance of change activities in the organization, forms of organizing could be developed that combine a unified type of sensemaking culture with a split type of sensemaking culture.

All three cases illustrate the need for a cultural change to create a more generative learning culture, and the Saab and Trumpf cases also illustrate that it often takes a crisis to mobilize support for this cultural change. The ability to create a more learning organization was clearly hindered by the conservative/adaptive attitudes towards new ideas prevalent in all three organizations before the radical change efforts of the early 1990s. The new generative attitude has clearly simplified the continuous efforts to develop the capacity to innovate and renew.

If we go back to the three issues brought up in the introductory section of the chapter we have observed, through the empirical analysis, a strong link between learning on the one hand and innovation and changing processes on the other hand. All three cases indicate that a more generative learning culture is needed to foster a more continuous and flexible approach to change. We believe there is a potential for further understanding of organizing and strategizing through the development of the exploration/ exploitation learning perspective to include an emphasis on new ideas, with a focus on learning cultures and sensemaking cultures.

## NOTES

[1]For this case, 20 interviews were conducted with different people within the S-Med and Siemens AG organizations.

[2]Empirically, this case is based on 15 interviews, which were conducted during 1998 by one of the authors.

[3]For this case study 15 interviews have been conducted with different people in the organization, mainly at the headquarters level and across all functions.

# Chapter 5

# A Cognitive Perspective on Strategizing/Organizing

*Marjolijn S. Dijksterhuis,*
*Frans A.J. van den Bosch and*
*Henk W. Volberda*

## INTRODUCTION

Well-known theories of organizational change rarely specify the behavior needed to achieve the intended consequences (Mezias, Grinyer and Guth, 2001). Recognizing the lack of insights into micro-level strategy processes, scholars have pushed strategizing and organizing forward as one of the themes that need to be explored (Chia, 1997; Weick, 1969; Eden and Ackermann, 1998; Whittington and Melin, Chapter 2 of this volume). Although it holds the promise of new lines of research, empirical studies on this theme are scarce. To fill part of this void, two *key questions* are addressed – both conceptually and empirically – in this chapter: (1) What type of activities do strategizing and organizing involve? (2) How are the two processes connected? We apply a cognitive perspective to answer the questions. This perspective is gaining considerable influence in micro-level strategy process research. In the area of managerial cognition, scholars have emphasized the role of decision makers' perceptions and beliefs in strategic decision processes and strategy renewal (Bettis and Prahalad, 1995; Barr, 1998; Papadakis et al., 1998). Interest in the role of organizational cognition in such processes has grown as well. Research on organizational cognition deals, for example, with routines and other recurrent patterns of organizational behavior as repositories of perceptions and beliefs (Ranson, Hinings and Greenwood, 1980; Heracleous and Barrett, 2001).

In their quest for a comprehensive view on the role of cognition in strategy processes, scholars have advocated a processual and multi-level approach (Meindl, Stubbart and Porac, 1994; Walsh, 1995). Several recent studies have used such an approach (Lyles and Schwenk, 1992; Schneider and Angelmar, 1993; Dijksterhuis et al., 1999). In this chapter, we build on insights from previous studies to examine how strategizing and organizing are connected over time and across levels. Four sets of strategizing and organizing activities are introduced which are essentially cognitive in nature. To study how these activities evolve, we focus on strategic reorientation as a particular type of strategy process. It involves a change in strategy accompanied by adaptation of other organizational dimensions such as structure, power distribution, and performance evaluation systems (Lant et al., 1992). Thus, new ways of organizing emerge alongside a new strategy which makes strategic reorientation a preeminent process for examining the connection between strategizing and organizing activities.

In this chapter, we present a framework which links strategizing and organizing to a set of key variables. We conducted a case study to provide insight into its application, which concerns a strategic reorientation at the home market banking division of Internationale Nederlanden Groep (ING), the largest financial services provider in the Netherlands. The reorientation project took place between 1994 and 1998. In a time of increasing environmental turbulence, divisional executives proclaimed their dedication to a segmentation strategy and initiated changes in structure for its support. The case study indicates the iterative character of the strategizing/organizing relationship over time and across levels. In this vein, the findings support the use of a processual and multi-level perspective in micro-level strategy process research (Pettigrew, 1992).

The chapter is structured as follows. In the next section, the different sets of activities are introduced; with the conceptualization of strategizing and organizing in place, the theoretical framework is discussed in the third section. Then, in the following section, the case study is presented to gain understanding of how the framework translates into practice before conclusions are drawn in the fifth and final section.

## STRATEGIZING/ORGANIZING: THEORY

Investigations of strategizing and organizing fall within the domain of micro-strategy research: the study of strategic issues in terms of processes at the level of individual and group interaction and their links to the organizational level and the level of organizational context (Johnson and Bowman, 1999). The complexity inherent in such research might explain the tendency of scholars studying strategizing/organizing to convey their thoughts in rather abstract terms. Various chapters in this volume represent attempts to generate a more fine-grained understanding. In the second chapter of this volume, Whittington and Melin depict strategizing and organizing as a 'single duality'. The authors argue that strategizing as the active processes of strategy creation converges with organizing to constitute a firm's competitive advantage.

As noted in the introduction, a perspective which has gained importance in studies of micro-organizational behavior is the managerial cognition perspective (Meindl et al., 1994; Walsh, 1995). Scholars adopting a cognitive stance have explained changes in strategy (Barr, 1998) and organizational structure (Ranson et al., 1980; Dijksterhuis et al., 1999) by referring to managers' cognition. Such research usually thrives on the assumption that their position within organizations allows managers to impose a particular set of beliefs, for example, through decision-making (Hambrick and Mason, 1984; Bettis and Prahalad, 1995). In decision-making processes, managers function as information workers (McCall and Kaplan, 1985). That is, they actively construct interpretations of organizational and environmental issues by linking received cues with their cognitive structures. Scholars who apply an interpretive view portray human activity 'as an ongoing input–output cycle in which subjective interpretations of externally situated information become themselves objectified via behaviour' (Porac et al., 1989: 398). Many previous studies in this area support the argument that decision-makers' perceptions of organization and environment are reflected in their decisions and actions. Research has yet to generate insight into the connection between thinking and action in a dynamic sense (Barr, 1998; Tripsas and Gavetti, 2000). In this vein, scholars have urged for going beyond decision-making to include the role of organizational cognition in the discussions. An organizational cognition perspective directs attention to stocks of knowledge which manifest themselves in organizational routines and competencies. This perspective is especially important when investigating organizing processes which are believed to fall at least partly within the organizational activity realm. In this chapter, a combined *managerial and organizational cognition perspective* is used to derive at a comprehensive account of strategizing/organizing.

Among theorists investigating the role of cognition in strategy processes, there is growing adherence to the conviction that fundamental changes in strategy, structure, and organization members' behavior are accompanied by the replacement of underlying belief systems (Ranson et al., 1980; Bartunek, 1984; Gioia and Chittipeddi, 1991; Mezias et al., 2001). As long as belief systems are an appropriate representation of the situation, they provide a frame of reference for directing effective actions (Weick, 1995; Barr, 1998). If such systems become obsolete and decision-makers start to act on 'impoverished views of the world' (Gioia, 1986: 346), it becomes difficult to respond promptly and effectively to external developments.

As a first step toward a cognition-based framework of strategizing/organizing, we build on these considerations to establish an understanding of the activities that comprise strategizing and organizing. Four conceptually distinct sets of activities are identified (see Figure 5.1). Strategizing is

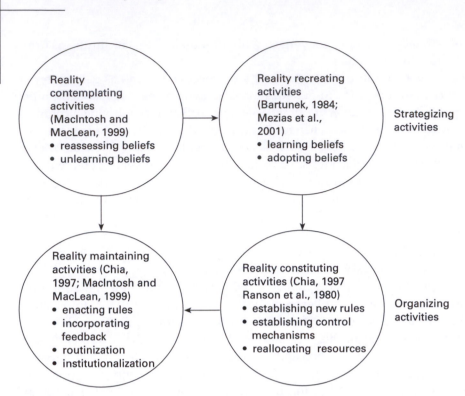

FIGURE 5.1    *Strategizing/organizing from a cognitive angle: four sets of activities*

associated with reality contemplating and recreating activities and organizing relates to reality constitution and maintenance. We argue that the different activities are closely linked, over time as well as across various levels of analysis.

## Strategizing: reality contemplating activities

Decision makers need to perceive and accept a need for change in order for any reorientation or change in collective beliefs to take place (Mezias et al., 2001). MacIntosh and MacLean (1999) have argued that a crisis brought about by the failure of an organization's systems to cope with an internal or external situation will trigger increasing questioning of taken-for-granted assumptions. Investigating the validity of existing 'provinces of meaning' (Ranson et al., 1980) in the light of the internal and external situation will be referred to as *reality contemplating* (see Figure 5.1).

A number of strategy studies have engaged in why and how provinces of meaning – often deeply ingrafted in the structure and working of organizations – are articulated and judged on their validity (Bartunek, 1984; Senge, 1990; Gioia and Chittipeddi, 1991; MacIntosh and MacLean, 1999; Mezias et al., 2001). Both MacIntosh and MacLean (1999) and Mezias et al. (2001) draw from their consultancy experiences to provide insight into conditions that nurture the contemplation process. In this vein, managers' commitment to the process is mentioned as it takes time to challenge and unlearn old beliefs, and develop a consensual understanding of the forces shaping the future. An open climate and the involvement of skilled facilitators have also proved to encourage individuals to articulate their assumptions about the business, their roles in it and their aspirations for both. Wide participation ensures the inclusion of a broad range of issues and viewpoints (Mezias et al., 2001).

The literature provides several examples of successful and not so successful contemplation efforts in organizations. MacIntosh and MacLean (1999) discuss a company-wide survey at the Rover Group undertaken in the late 1980s, which allowed executives to identify existing attitudes and rules. A less successful effort took place at Intel. Its top management failed to question the strategic rhetoric which undermined their strategy of being a major player in memory chips and microprocessors (Mezias et al., 2001). Finally, Tripsas and Gavetti (2000) confirmed the importance of 'deframing skills' – the ability to question existing strategic beliefs – in their discussion of Polaroid's inability to adapt to radical changes in the imaging business.

## Strategizing: reality recreating activities

Each of the aforementioned studies considers scrutiny of basic beliefs to be an important activity in an early stage of the strategy process, instigated by managers' perceptions of organizational and environmental conditions. What might have begun as mere intuition develops into a more thorough understanding of the appropriateness of existing beliefs. This announces a second set of activities giving substance to the strategy process: *recreating* the socially constructed reality (see Figure 5.1). It should be noted that contemplating activities might actually lead to the decision not to pursue strategic change. In this chapter, however, we leave this option out of consideration and focus on situations in which reality contemplating gives way to reality recreation.

Several academics have suggested that major changes in belief systems occur through dialectical processes in which old and new ways of understanding interact, resulting in a synthesis (Bartunek, 1984; Greenwood and Hinings, 1988; MacIntosh and MacLean, 1999). Others have emphasized the importance of unlearning old rationales before new worldviews can be adopted (Hedberg, 1981). Recreating a consensual belief system is generally considered a difficult and time-consuming task. Shared beliefs serve as a coordination mechanism (Bartunek, 1984), enabling the orderly production of roles and rules (Ranson et al., 1980). Second-order change in interpretive schemes is therefore likely to be experienced as threatening (Schein, 1980), leaving organization members disoriented and paralysed (Hedberg, 1981). Tripsas and Gavetti (2000) found that Polaroid's senior managers experienced great difficulty with developing new strategic beliefs, strongly discouraging search and development efforts that were not consistent with the traditional business model. According to MacIntosh and MacLean, old rules which are rejected are usually defensive routines 'which might impede any significant change and are outlawed by consensus.' (1999: 305).

### Organizing: reality constituting activities

In an essay on processual analysis, Chia describes organizing as 'an ongoing reality constituting and reality maintaining activity which enables us to act purposefully amidst a cacophony of competing, and attention-seeking inputs' (1997: 699). While this description directs attention to the continuity of organizing processes, we believe it is also helpful when exploring change episodes. To achieve a second-order change, in which a system itself changes (Fox-Wolfgramm et al., 1998), the new reality must be constituted and maintained.

We argue that strategizing conceptualized in terms of reality contemplating and recreating is primarily the domain of decision-makers. Because they dispose of the means to install new rules, *reality constituting* is partly a decision makers' responsibility as well (Ranson et al., 1980). Reality constitution refers to a set of activities through which decision makers secure their belief system within the very structure and working of the organization. For the new reality to settle, establishment of new rules does not suffice. They need to be enacted in daily practices (Barley and Tolbert, 1997; Ranson et al., 1980). In this vein, scholars have discussed the interpretational role of managers, which involves influencing the interpretations of various stakeholders (Daft and Weick, 1984; Isabella, 1990; Gioia and Chittipeddi, 1991). Creating a captivating vision which provides a symbolic foundation for the new set of beliefs has been labeled as a key feature in the initiation of strategic reorientation. Commitment to the new beliefs allows for proposed changes to become solidified (Gioia and Chittipeddi, 1991).

A stream of research has emerged which deals with the institutionalization of beliefs (Berger and Luckmann, 1967; Meyer and Rowan, 1977; Barley and Tolbert, 1997). Barley and Tolbert (1997) picture institutionalization as interactions between cognition and action. The process starts with the activation of new rules through behavioral regularities. Depending on the perceived desirability of the consequences, these rules are then replicated or revised. Representing their actual nesting in the organization, the new rules are externalized and objectified.

## Organizing: reality maintaining activities

The shift toward a new belief system needs to gain momentum to achieve second-order change in strategy and structure. *Reality maintaining activities* are managerial and organizational activities are aimed at reinforcing a constructed reality. Managerial activities involve application of positive and negative feedback (MacIntosh and MacLean, 1999). Confirmation of signals consistent with the new reality provides a multiplier effect, allowing it to take hold. Negative feedback helps to dampen actions and behaviors which belong to the old belief system. MacIntosh and MacLean (1999) use the term 'secondary rules' to indicate rules that determine how organizing principles should be maintained and updated. Their account of a strategic change program which was conducted with a Scottish food-manufacturing company serves to illustrate the role of feedback mechanisms. The managing director of this firm displayed new rules on the overalls he wore on the shopfloor as a clear signal to employees regarding the way the business would be run.

Reality maintenance is also achieved through more widespread organizational activities. Labianca et al. (2000) describe a stabilization phase in which organizational members increasingly rely on the new belief system – or consistently revert to old beliefs, in which case cognitive change has failed. Affirmation through repeated actions leads to maintenance of rules in the organization (Barley and Tolbert, 1997; Ranson et al., 1980). A belief system which is maintained over time offers a stable basis for organizational members' interpretations and actions. The shared background of mutual understandings constitutes the 'agreement' between members enabling the orderly production of roles and rules (Ranson et al., 1980). In the long run, especially when operating in volatile business environments, belief systems might, however, become cognitive rigidities. In other words, organizational inertia is rooted in the continuous affirmation of belief systems.

## The non-linear nature of strategizing/organizing

While we presented the strategizing and organizing activities sequentially in this section, in practice they are likely to take place in an iterative and to some extent reciprocal fashion. This proposition is grounded in findings from several studies on strategy processes (Bartunek, 1984; Gioia and Chittipeddi, 1991; Bettis and Prahalad, 1995; MacIntosh and MacLean, 1999). In a study of strategic change at a public university, Gioia and Chittipeddi (1991) portray the change process as iterations of sensemaking and sensegiving activities. These activities 'occurred essentially in a sequential and reciprocal fashion that encompassed progressively expanding audiences in the strategic change effort' (1991: 443). Bartunek (1984) reaches a similar conclusion in a study of a religious order whose belief system was undergoing

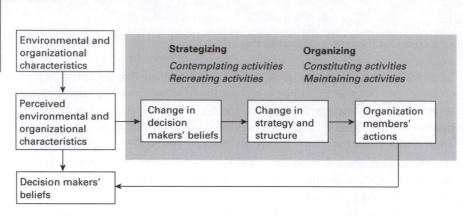

FIGURE 5.2    *A cognition-based fromework of strategic reorientation*

second-order change, which was eventually reflected in a major restructuring decision. During the period of second-order change in the belief system, structural properties entered into a reciprocal relationship with interpretive schemes and actions that was similar to the relationship between the interpretive schemes and actions.

To create insight into the dynamics of strategizing and organizing, the next step is to link the activities in Figure 5.1 to a set of variables which will be studied empirically. Besides contextual factors, the variables represent articulations of strategizing and organizing activities over time and across levels.

## CONCEPTUAL FRAMEWORK

Figure 5.2 displays the theoretical framework. Contextual factors are environmental and organizational characteristics. Changes in decision makers' beliefs, which are influenced by their perceptions, as well as changes in strategy, structure, and organizational members' actions, reflect underlying strategizing and organizing processes.

The framework builds on findings from previous studies. Several scholars have related a change in decision-makers' beliefs to a *perceived* mismatch between organization and environment (Barr et al., 1992; MacIntosh and MacLean, 1999; Gavetti and Levinthal, 2000). Which organizational and environmental characteristics are observed, and how they are interpreted, influences the magnitude and direction of such change (Mezias et al., 2001). The perceived mismatch confronts decision makers with the need to re-evaluate their existing belief set (*contemplation*) and develop a worldview that is consistent with the organizational and environmental context (*recreation*). As was noted before, studies on the role of cognition in strategy processes have signaled the importance of 'unlearning' beliefs that are no longer appropriate. Scholars investigating the role of decision makers' beliefs in strategy processes have focused on their effect on organizational outcomes such as strategy (Lant et al., 1992), structure (Bartunek, 1984), capabilities (Tripsas and Gavetti, 2000) and performance (Thomas et al., 1993). While evidence of this effect is substantial, *how* such beliefs translate into organizational belief systems which underlie a firm's strategy, structure and working is still an undernourished field of study. To investigate the evolvement of new beliefs across different levels, we look at how changes in decision makers' beliefs influence changes in formal *strategy* and *structure* as well as changes in *organization members' actions* (see Figure 5.2). If these actions change substantially and structurally, they reflect the emergence of new routines and capabilities, and thus of new organizational belief systems. The distinction between formal changes in strategy and structure and the enactment of formal rules in daily practices corresponds with Ranson et al. (1980)'s approach to structuring, which includes both formal configurations and interactive patterns to overcome the traditional opposition of structure to action. Reality *constitution* and *maintenance* are reflected in changes in these configurations and patterns.

When a new reality takes hold, it in turn influences decision makers' beliefs which indicates the reciprocal character of the relation between cognition and action (see Figure 5.2). Organization members' actions express cause-effect beliefs which are either confirmed when outcomes are as expected or contradicted when outcomes do not match the expectations. Confirmation strengthens the new belief system (Barr et al., 1992) which leads to the past shaping the template for understanding the future (Barr et al., 1992; Lyles and Schwenk, 1992; Bettis and Prahalad, 1995; Bate et al., 2000). Our argument is supported by McKinley and Scherer (2000) who suggest a positive relationship between organizational restructuring and the cognitive order experienced by managers engaged in the process. Managers are likely to embrace the belief system underlying the new structure, reinforcing the process they initiated in the first place. However, when performance is below the aspiration level and the current belief system is considered unable to provide an explanation, its re-evaluation is required (Barr et al., 1992) and a new cycle of strategizing and organizing begins.

Finally, the framework incorporates two key determinants of decision makers' perceptions. The impact of organizational and environmental stimuli has been widely acknowledged in strategy literature. In Figure 5.2, this determinant is labeled *Environmental & organizational characteristics*. The second factor is existing *decision makers' beliefs*. Beliefs develop over time through experience and vicarious learning and thus reflect past conditions rather than the current information environment. The two determinants represent different streams of research in information processing literature. The former is generally associated with bottom-up information processing, whereas the effect of beliefs on perceptions is key to top-down information processing (Walsh, 1995).

The second part of this chapter reports on a case study which was conducted to investigate how our framework might add to existing insights in

TABLE 5.1   *Profile of ING*

| Financial information | Ranking in Global 500 | Ranking in Global Life and health (stock) insurance industry |
|---|---|---|
| Revenues: 82 999.1 $ mil. | 20 | 1 |
| Profit: 4 098.7 $ mil. | N/A | 1 |
| Assets: 627 816.0 $ mil. | N/A | N/A |

**Number of employees**
113 143

*Source:* Fortune, 22 July 2002

strategizing/organizing. Three research questions deriving from Figure 5.2 guided the empirical exploration:

1  How do changes in decision makers' beliefs take place in strategic reorientations?
2  How do new beliefs of decision makers influence changes in strategy and structure?
3  How do new strategies and structures affect organization members' actions?

## STRATEGIZING/ORGANIZING: AN EMPIRICAL EXPLORATION

Searching for conditions under which we expect decision makers' perceptions and beliefs to matter to a firm's strategic behavior, the Dutch financial services sector was selected as a context for the case study. In recent years, this industry environment has experienced a transition from a relatively stable to a more volatile market, which has required decision makers to update their beliefs about the nature of the business and appropriate means of action (Bakker, 1994; Flier et al., 2001; Jurriëns and Jesse, 1996). The case material derives from an account of strategic reorientation at ING Bank Nederland; the home market banking business unit of Internationale Nederlanden Groep (ING). Table 5.1 provides some key information about the organization.

In 1991, a merger between NMB Postbank Group and Nationale-Nederlanden created ING, the first Dutch corporation to offer customers a full range of financial services. Its banking operations include consumer and business banking aimed at the European market. ING Bank Nederland (IBN) became the business unit responsible for banking services in the Dutch market. At the end of 1994, the division had a hybrid structure based on geography, products and functions with an extensive branch network at its core. The branches were relatively autonomous units, each governed by a manager who held decisional power over operational and tactical issues. ING's reputation as an innovative firm (Volberda et al., 2001) was a primary reason for selecting ING as a case study. The banking industry has been known for its members' reserved stance in customer orientation and product innovation: banks' strong position as financial intermediaries and a relatively low level of competition allowed this attitude to prevail. Over the past three decades, several developments have taken place which have fundamentally changed the position of the traditional financial institutions and have forced bankers to redefine their business. However, it has appeared to be difficult to change existing routines and rules. A clear example of this is ABN Amro, which has struggled to renew its organization to fit the new circumstances (*NRC Handelsblad*, August 2001, Rotterdam). Because we are interested in relating changes of managerial belief systems to changes in strategy and structure and organizational members' actions, we have chosen a case in which such changes are most likely to be present. In line with Pettigrew, a critical incident was chosen to 'provide a dramatic glimpse into the current workings of the social system' (1990: 275). Focusing on a particular strategic project is also consistent with Burgelman's (1983) and Quinn's (1980) observation that the logic of each trajectory is dealt with largely on its own merits and usually with a different subset of people. Dealing with a reorientation trajectory as a series of change events allows for the exploration of temporal and spatial contextual factors that shape these events (Pettigrew et al., 2001). The incident, a change initiative within the home banking division of ING which led to a new strategy and structure, was studied in relation to other critical events that took place within the division between 1985 and 1997, a period in which a foundation was laid for a more sales-orientated and cost-efficient organization. The project, called Segmentation, took place between 1994 and 1998. In essence, the trajectory involved a shift toward stronger customer orientation, which entailed radical changes in structure, performance measures and control systems. It was felt that such a reorientation was needed to cope with increased competition.

In the Fall of 1994, the Chairman of IBN presented the Management Board of ING with a vision for the business unit's strategic direction. Several key informants have labeled this speech as the first in a series of events that eventually led to a new strategy and new organizing principles within IBN.

## Methodology

The study of the Segmentation project aims at providing a better understanding of the patterns implied by the framework presented in Figure 5.2. We use a processual research approach to set the stage for a holistic and dynamic analysis of change (Pettigrew, 1997a). Besides consideration of phenomena over time, processual analysis often involves extension over

TABLE 5.2   *Sample profile*

| |
| --- |
| Interview sample: |
| Divisional board members (3) |
| Project managers (3) |
| Project team members (2) |
| Consultants (3) |
| Segment managers (2) |
| District managers (3) |
| Interview period: |
| January 2000 – July 2001 |
| Number of interviews: |
| 19 |
| Number of pages text yielded: |
| 223 (double-spaced) |

multiple levels. We focused on the decision-makers-group level of analysis, exploring changes in perceptions and beliefs over time. We focused, in addition, on the organizational level of analysis in terms of change actions and outcomes. Finally, a change effort should not be seen separately from the context in which it takes place. Processes by which firms retain, adopt and discard templates for organizing are considered a function of organizational (Pettigrew, 1985) and market and institutional pressures (Hinings and Greenwood, 1996). The concept of strategizing/organizing that emerges is one of coevolving cognitions and actions, constituting each other's context which, in turn, is embedded in a wider intra-organizational and external environment (Lewin and Volberda, 1999).

Presuming that decisions ultimately reflect decision makers' perceptions and beliefs (Porac et al., 1989), the investigation of cognitive patterns implies looking for manifestations of such processes in behavior or statements (Barr, 1998). Interviews with key actors and archival data analysis were conducted to create a detailed account of influential perceptions and beliefs over the period under investigation. Generating insights into cognition by means of interviews reflects the assumption that people are able to verbalize the content of perceptions and beliefs and the way in which these originated. Initial interviews with a project manager and the director of IBN's strategy department were conducted to reveal the key actors of the reorientation project. The interview sample is presented in Table 5.2.

The interviews, averaging between one and two hours in length, were transcribed verbatim from tape recordings. Interviewees were told their statements would be used anonymously. For accuracy, notes which indicated counter-intuitive or otherwise interesting information were reviewed immediately after the interviews and before transcription. The aim of the interviews was to capture strategizing and organizing activities, managerial perceptions and beliefs over time and the changes in formal and informal

TABLE 5.3  *Overview of additional sources of evidence, 1994–98*

| Source | Evidence |
| --- | --- |
| Visionary statement (Nov 1996) | New strategic direction and planned changes |
| Divisional board minutes (Jan 1995–June 1998) | Segmentation-related discussions; formal decision making |
| Work council reports | Planned and implemented changes in |
| Outlines of Segmentation (Nov 1996) | strategy and structure |
| Blueprint (May 1997) | |
| Market management HQ (May 1997) | |
| District organization (May 1997) | |
| Evaluation report (Nov 1999) | Post-reorientation evaluation |
| Organizational charts | Structure of ING and structure of IBN pre- and post-segmentation |
| Annual reports (1991–1998) | Financial standing Scope of activities Environmental perceptions at firm level |
| Banking textbooks | Strategic plans General information on industry developments between 1970–2000 |
| Banking journals (*The Banker, National Westminster Bank Quarterly Review*) | Real-time information on technological and regulatory developments |
| IMF reports | Real-time information on regional trends |
| BIS reports | Real-time information on industry trends |

rules as a result of the Segmentation trajectory. Two sets of principal questions were asked; one addressing change process issues and the other covering cognition contents. The questions were elaborated with follow-up questions.

Individual recollections are subject to retrospective rationalizing. To minimize a bias in the data, cross-checks for inconsistent findings were conducted and interview data was triangulated with information from internal documents and secondary industry data (see Table 5.3). The use of archival data is based on the assumption that decision makers exchange perceptions and beliefs which are objectified via decisions.

A total of 282 pages of archival material were collected within ING. In addition, we were successful in negotiating access to the minutes of business unit board meetings. Between January 1995 and June 1998, 90 regular board meetings and 10 strategy meetings resulted in 61 pages of double-spaced text on Segmentation.

Due to cognition's inherently abstract nature, construct validity is of special concern. Capturing theories-in-use rather than espoused theories

(Argyris and Schön, 1978), to allow us to establish the interrelationship between cognition and action, was achieved by:

1 comparing what was said in interviews with what was written down in milestone documents
2 asking follow-up questions that required interviewees to demonstrate what statements meant in practice
3 consulting two key informants to validate the project description once it was completed.

The type of perceptions and beliefs was not determined a priori; these emerged from informants' recollections of the trajectory's processing. Internal validity was increased by triangulation of data sources and by cross-checking interview findings to get to converging evidence.

Two analyses were critical for the purpose of this chapter: a reconstruction of the Segmentation project as depicted in decision makers' perceptions, beliefs and change actions between 1994 and 1998 – the period consistently identified by interviewees as the period of change – and an analysis of contextual factors that shaped the reorientation process. Both analyses derive from an identifiable set of steps. First, the central ideas and inferences were distilled from each interview and milestone document. Recurrent and salient topics were recorded on contact and document summary forms (Miles and Huberman, 1984). Second, the context of the strategic reorientation trajectory was delineated based on secondary industry and firm data. At the industry and country level, primary focus was on technological, socio-economic, competitive and regulatory developments. The firm's inner context was described in terms of strategic change episodes before and after Segmentation. The third step involved linking themes from interviews and documents to the spatial and temporal contextual factors to understand why and how strategy and structure and organization members' actions, via the application of a generative belief system and in their organizational and external context, changed considerably. From the analyses, a history emerged of how perceptions and beliefs coevolved with change actions leading to a strategic turnaround within IBN.

In reconstructing the strategic reorientation process, three sets of changes were looked for:

1 changes in decision-makers' perceptions and beliefs
2 changes in formal rules related to strategy and structure
3 changes in organization members' actions, reflected in changes in routines and competencies.

We started by identifying the cognitive central themes and eliciting the patterns of argumentation found in actions and texts. The interpretation of multiple texts, in context and over time, was also supported by a description of organizational and environmental conditions. The patterns of change were analysed in terms of the four sets of strategizing and organizing activities, both horizontally across time and vertically across levels. To get a better understanding of why things evolved the way they did, we first describe the environmental, organizational and temporal context in which the Segmentation trajectory took place. In the remainder of this section, the case will be presented.

## The environmental context: Dutch financial services in the 1990s

Due to modification of EEC legislative processes and national regulatory changes, technological progress and growing importance of shareholder value, historical relationships have become less important and price competition has slowly taken over in the financial services industry. New distribution channels have become available forcing bank managers to reconsider the role of branch networks in servicing customers. The traditional strength of branches – their embeddedness in local communities which provided a secure basis for business – has forcefully eroded since corporate clients have started looking for knowledge over social ties. Intensifying competition fueled by innovations in technology (Flier et al., 2001) and the entrance of unregulated non-banks in the financial services market (White, 1998; Hensmans, Van den Bosch and Volberda, 2001) have also demanded a radical change in management thinking. The three largest Dutch banks, ING, ABN Amro and Rabobank, have all responded to the changed conditions by rethinking their strategy and reorganizing their operations (Van Wijk and Van den Bosch, 2000). Efficiency improvement and a stronger sales focus have been key in these efforts.

In continental Europe, Dutch financial corporations have been at the forefront of rationalization and cost-cutting by reducing the number of branches and centralizing particular services (White, 1998). Major changes going on in Dutch society provide one explanation for their front-runner position. Flexibility, individualization and privatization have typified the societal environment in the 1990s (NNI, 1997). Technological advances in management information systems have allowed for managing on the basis of client segments rather than geography, a strategic approach adopted by many national and international financial services providers in the mid and late 1990s. Organizing business along client groups or product lines with support of specialized information technology systems, compensation systems and a strong sales force lies at the heart of new organizational models that have extended the range of performance measurement tools (White, 1998). Compared to, in particular, their Anglo-Saxon counterparts, Dutch banks have long applied a conservative marketing approach. Bank executives have been much less visible to clients and the relationship with employees, which reflects in the client–employee relationship, is still very hierarchical.

Only now have firms fully acknowledged the heterogeneity of clients' needs. Segmentation in line with customer needs was introduced into Dutch banks from the mid 1990s on, but even today insight into profitability of specific activities is poor (Deloitte Research, 1999). Strategy is still seldom carried out with the explicit purpose of giving a blow to the competition and reactions to each other's actions are rare (NNI, 1998). Alternative distribution processes have appeared, but a fundamental reconsideration of the role of branches has only just begun (White, 1998).

### The organizational context: ING and its home banking business unit

Amidst all the institutional and market changes, ING has developed into a financial conglomerate offering a wide range of banking, insurance and asset management services to retail and wholesale clients in the Netherlands and abroad. Since 1991 corporate-level and business unit-level structures have been redesigned several times to attain a structure which encourages exchange of knowledge and resources between geographies, expertise areas and subsidiaries. As a result of one such redesign effort in 1994, IBN is built around the bank branch network. Sales of life and non-life insurance through ING's branches in the Netherlands have been growing over the years, indicating ING's pursuit of a bancassurance strategy. Figure 5.3 shows ING's structure and the position of the home banking division, IBN, within that structure in 1998.

In 1998, IBN employed 10 000 people. The branch network consisted of 24 districts, each headed by a chairman who was supported by two vice-chairmen. Within each district, there were a number of area offices as well as some smaller, local branches. In total, ING's network comprised 150 area offices and 200 local branches. The structure of IBN constituted three hier-archical levels: the divisional board, geographic and functional managers and branch managers. Each board member (five in 1998) held responsibility for a particular portfolio of activities. However, strategic issues were decided collectively. Income from ING's banking operations increased from 2.849 million euros in 1991 to 8.687 million euros in 1998 (Annual Reports, 1991; 1998). Growth of home market banking activities was a primary contributor. Maintenance of a strong position in the Dutch banking market has always been an important goal for the business unit. Figure 5.4a gives a visual representation of IBN's structure before the strategic reorientation under consideration; Figure 5.4b shows the structure after its consequences had settled down.

### The temporal context: preceding strategic reorientations

Segmentation differed from previous strategic change projects in two ways. First, in the history of IBN there had not been a reorientation of such scale and

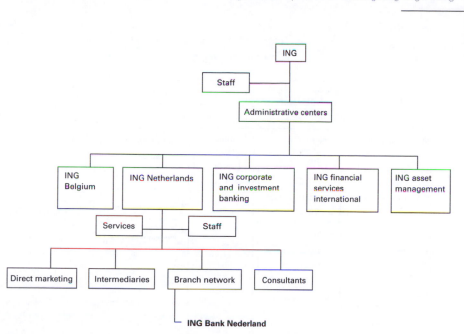

FIGURE 5.3    *Position of IBN within ING (1998)*

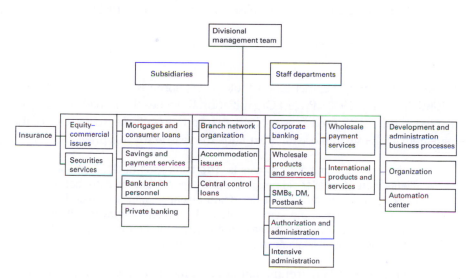

FIGURE 5.4a    *IBN's structure before the Segmentation project (1995)*

with such an impact on both the branch network and business unit headquarters. Second, preceding change processes were primarily aimed at cost reduction, whereas Segmentation was initated foremost to strengthen IBN's commercial orientation; it entailed an increase in number of employees.

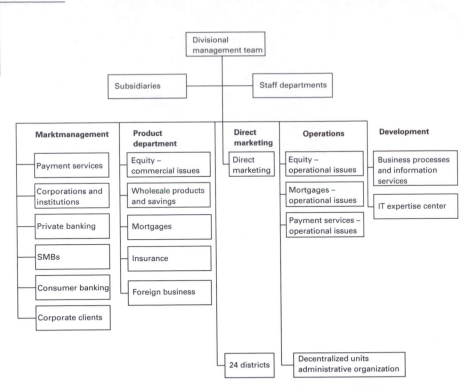

FIGURE 5.4b    *IBN's structure after the Segmentation project (1998)*

To understand why Segmentation took place, some historic information is helpful. In the late 1980s, Project Organization Branches (POB) had been implemented within IBN's predecessor, NMB, to improve customer focus. One of the managers in charge in those days explains the reason for this project:

> ...the bank did not have any clients. The bank itself decided who its clients were. A retailer did not go to ABN Amro. A branch manager of ABN Amro would never consider doing business with a retailer. For consumer business, the same applied. Many people knew that they had to ask in a very friendly manner if they needed a mortgage. ... It was obvious that this situation needed to change.

In addition to general environmental development, a downswing in performance as well as the announcement by a leading strategy consultancy firm that the future winners in financial services would be those firms *without* a branch network triggered strategic change. Technological developments were transforming the way business was done in banking, offering new delivery mechanisms and increasing transparency for customers. The branch network, for a long time a bank's most precious asset, suddenly seemed a heavy burden. The allocation of revenues and costs to clients became an important issue. How complicated this issue was and how radical the departure from existing practices was, can be seen from a recollection of one of the project managers:

> This is a terrible process, a terrible process – To find out how much is earned with particular products and why – because we were doing things which made us no money at all and we were doing other things which made us a lot of money. … We had a branch which delivered a bag of money. We did not know the various parts, we did not know the costs related to a cash transfer. The process is very complicated. All kinds of discussion about accountability emerged, especially about treasury.

Segmentation is rooted in the change processes of POB. The call for a stronger commercial orientation as a response to shifts in the societal and competitive environment was repeated in the mid 1990s when previous change efforts were thought to be insufficient for the bank to remain competitive in the long term. While the branches had been redesigned and a separation had been made between wholesale and retail, detailed knowledge of revenues and costs related to particular customer segments was still not available. Also, within the wholesale and retail segments, clients' needs were considered homogeneous.

### Applying the cognitive framework

Figure 5.5 shows four important time periods for changes in decision makers' perceptions and beliefs, formal strategy and structure, and organization members' actions. The different periods are marked by break points which represent shifts from one set of strategizing or organizing activities to another.

#### Contemplating activities: October 1994–October 1995

First was the *contemplation* period, October 1994–October 1995, in which the foundation was laid for strategic reorientation. In the light of technological advances, intensifying competition, and increasingly demanding customers, the CEO of ING encouraged the then Chairman of IBN to contemplate the existing business model and to create a vision which could be the foundation for the future strategy of the division. In his effort, the divisional Chairman was supported by a strategy consultancy firm, which had been involved in strategic reorientation trajectories in many other national and international financial services firms. During this stage, the consultants functioned mainly as sparring partners at both corporate and divisional level, encouraging managers to challenge the existing business model. When asked about the intervention by the CEO, the consultant directly involved in the Segmentation project noticed:

*Strategizing activities*

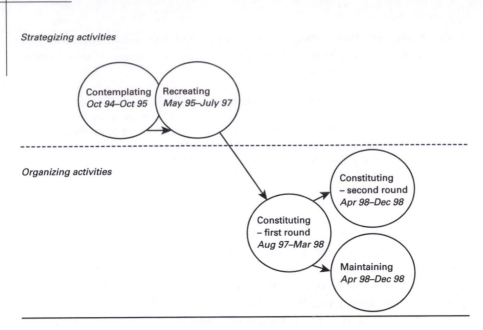

FIGURE 5.5    *Segmentation change process – summary*

> That is a normal procedure. I have noticed that within ING, there is a lot of pressure on all BU managers not only to come up with a plan for the next two years but especially to think about: where do you see yourself in about five to ten years from now. How can we make sure that we are not only dealing with daily business, but really think strategically about things; that is deeply embedded.

At the end of 1994, the Chairman of IBN gave a speech to the corporate management board in which he presented a vision on banking in the year 2005. As requested by the CEO, who considered technology an issue of primary interest for the efficiencies it promised to deliver, the opportunities of new technologies were a key topic. In terms of the model, managerial beliefs acted as a funnel, allocating attention to particular environmental elements (Gavetti and Levinthal, 2000). Soon after this event, the Chairman got promoted to the board of the Dutch business unit of ING. The newly appointed Chairman made some arrangements early in 1995 that set the stage for recreation. It was underlined that new business models were emerging in the financial services industry and that IBN applied a model which was relatively expensive. The Chairman appointed a project manager – someone from within the division – who was asked to investigate the alternatives. This manager generated insight into the way competitors were organizing themselves through company visits and by consulting the strategy consultancy firm. Formally a member of the project team, this consultancy firm was now actively involved in developing the new strategy.

The consultant who worked with the project manager describes his role as follows:

> My guess is that we have been the driving force in the beginning by saying: you really have to break through existing frames of mind and you need to get rid of the idea that everything is determined locally.

An analysis of costs per segment conducted by the same consultancy firm a few years prior was complemented by information on revenues, profits and product use to indicate deficiencies of the business model in place. As it turned out, there were several efficiencies to be gained.

### Recreating activities: May 1995–July 1997

This finding instigated *recreating* activities, marking the second key period of changing decision makers' perceptions and beliefs, May 1995–July 1997. The project team developed a segmentation strategy to increase revenues and market shares in the mass consumer and small- and medium-sized businesses segments (Final Report, October 1995). Implications would be far-reaching: transferring customer ownership from geographical units to segments; incorporating direct marketing and call centers to serve mass segments more efficiently and effectively; and building critical mass in the branch network to enhance expertise. Branches would become standardized service units. A counter-argument put forward in discussions about whether segmentation was the best strategy to pursue was concerned with the risk of following the herd rather than standing out. As appears from the divisional board meetings, the beliefs of board members strongly influenced the emerging strategy. Recreating was an iterative process; proposals moved back and forth between the project team and the divisional management board.

As the discussion now quickly started to revolve around the roles and responsibilities that segmentation might entail, the focus on the strategic implications of technology diminished. Evidence shows there was a preference for the more concrete tactical and operational issues over strategic matters, which are generally difficult to grasp. Finally approved by the divisional board, the proposal was then sent to the corporate management board. The management board considered the suggested changes too drastic. The project manager blames this reaction on the restraining effects of the existing business model: '[The new model] is difficult to imagine when you are thinking in terms of the model in place'.

While changing beliefs about the nature of banking and how IBN could succeed in this business triggered the development of a radically new business model, in the end some key organizing principles were kept in place in accordance with beliefs of corporate-level managers. In the opinion of management board members, it was essential to prevent the division from getting into a state of turmoil. It was decided that functional managers – so-called segment managers – would be appointed who would be responsible for the business in their segment. However, ultimate profit responsibility would remain with the geographic line – the district managers. The result was a matrix structure with a bias toward geography. The decisions in the Segmentation project were also influenced by practical considerations of decision makers at the business unit level. For example, while analysis had shown that a total of 13 districts would allow for minimalization of vulnerability, 24 districts were created. A smaller number would have forced the divisional management board to put managers at lower hierarchical levels; a decision that they felt would seriously undermine these people's motivation.

Formal approval was followed by the establishment of a project organization. Its aim was to elaborate on the approved strategy and overall structure, and to develop an organizational blueprint. The segmentation strategy entailed drastic changes in the branch network organization as well as at business unit headquarters. In the former, a new set of rules was developed which were primarily aimed at increasing the sales focus. For example, back office activities were removed from the task list of external account managers to increase sales capacity. The label 'external account manager' was replaced by 'relationship manager' to underline a customer orientation. Another example concerns the re-allocation of responsibilities to branch and district offices. In the new model, wholesale clients that had traditionally been serviced by local branches were transferred to district offices, eroding the branch managers' role as ING's figureheads in local communities. Decision makers had noticed an increased demand for product expertise and industry-specific knowledge and became convinced of the value of critical mass in this respect. Experts were brought together at district and divisional levels to service wholesale customers appropriately. When the blueprint of the new divisional structure was approved, it was sent to IBN's work council. In The Netherlands, work councils represent organizational employees; in strategic reorientation trajectories, these councils have an advisory role. Although they do not have the authority to block decisions, their interventions might well cause serious delays (Maassen and Van den Bosch, 1999).

With the basic building blocks in place, the next step was to fill in the processes that would give substance to the new strategy and structure. In the Fall of 1996, the project manager was replaced by a manager from the branch network who was made responsible for elaboration of the segmentation concept and a staff manager focusing mainly on design of the new administrative organization. Although customer segments had been defined, demarcation lines were still fuzzy. Segment managers were appointed to enable their involvement in the creation of segment strategies. They had considerable autonomy in developing a business plan, which was then approved by the divisional management board. In this stage, segment managers did not yet have formal responsibilities. As a former segment manager explains: 'We had to write all of it down ourselves – the authority and responsibilities we thought would be handy when operationalizing our plans.' In this situation, recreating activities preceded contemplation rather than the other way around. Developing a segment strategy, segment managers gathered insight into the responsibilities they should have to do their job. On the basis of the feedback that they provided, decision makers developed an understanding of the appropriate responsibilities, which were then formalized.

**First round of constituting activities: August 1997–March 1998**
In the third time period, August 1997–March 1998, a first round of *constituting* activities manifested in the execution of two pilots. According to the divisional chairman, knowing when to move from recreation to constitution is a matter of:

> … having the feeling that the risks you are taking are within certain limits. And assuming that you have the right people. At key positions you need people who can deal with that. This is just a matter of knowing the people. And you always pretend that everything has been taken care of toward outsiders. … Having the guts to stick out your neck.

The first pilot was executed on paper in one particular district. Translating the conceptual model into practice unleashed another round of recreating activities. This led to certain adjustments in the segmentation model. To speed up change, the divisional board hired an external interim manager who applied a militaristic approach to implementation. The divisional chairman explains the decision to involve this outsider in the implementation process as follows:

> At a certain point in time we say: 'this is what we want, this is where we go'. And everybody agrees. But then you have to make sure that everybody goes the same way. For this purpose, I hired the interim manager, to make sure everybody would go in the same direction. It is just a matter of knowing the organization. Everybody has his own interpretation and at that point it was important that we went in that direction.

The segmentation model was implemented in a second pilot district. Preparations by a steering committee consisting of district managers and staff from headquarters took place in the last few months of 1997. Implementation itself was done in the first half of 1998. Despite specifications for the new processes and structure, district management felt there was still considerable discretion in filling in the details:

> The actual implementation: How are the different segments going to
> be served? How do you deal with them? How are employees going to
> act?... This had not been specified. There was a conceptualization,
> but this had not yet been translated into practice.

The pilots fueled discussions about the new business model throughout the
particular districts. Experiences were communicated to the decision-makers
which allowed them to reconsider the appropriateness of the new rules.
While time consuming, these on-line search processes (Gavetti and
Levinthal, 2000) provided the means for refinement and adjustment.

### Second round of constituting activities and maintaining activities: April 1998–December 1998

After the new rules had been implemented, the divisional board approved
overall implementation. This marked the beginning of the second act of constitution, which took place between April and December 1998. Kick-off meetings
for the districts were scheduled sequentially. A former district manager recalls:

> ... this was completely conducted from the divisional headquarters. ...
> There was a complete schedule for this. So, at a certain point in time,
> there was the kick-off and large districts had to have two of such meet-
> ings. It was a kind of show and everybody got invited, all employees.

At the kick-off meetings, the plans were formally presented to employees for
the first time. Then, the new rules were implemented. A real and sustaining
change in organization members' actions necessitates the enactment of new
rules over time. In the Segmentation project, an actual and sustaining change
in behavior was hampered mainly by two factors. First, sales employees'
beliefs about their roles prevented them from willingly adopting the new
rules. A former district manager illustrates this as follows:

> Criteria had been established. ... A customer should meet this stan-
> dard. ... There was disbelief in the branch network organization about
> this: people felt very differently about it. Starting from the old situation,
> people had a completely different perception of the customer and had
> had that and were raised with this perception. ...

This was a time of long and recurrent discussions within districts. The new
rules were heavily criticized and opposed. Second, a complicating factor was
the lack of reward systems and performance evaluation systems which
could have been used as positive and negative feedback mechanisms. In the
Dutch banking industry, performance-based reward systems have only been
introduced recently. In 1997, when the segmentation strategy was implemented, regulatory agreements prohibited the use of such reward systems.
Performance evaluation systems were fragmented and organized along the

lines of products and geographies. Without the appropriate information, it was difficult to assess employees' performance. The voids in the information infrastructure also hindered segment managers' functioning. A segment manager describes how he built up his own customer relationship management (CRM) system to deal with the situation:

> ... we have built our own CRM system in which, from day one, every piece of information about customers could be stored. ... All non-financial information, but also all financial data, everything. Also the number of client visits, everything.

Over time, the new rules have largely settled in. Interviewees noted some differences in organization members' behavior between districts, which reflects the impact of local context on the enactment of new rules. Divergence has been reinforced by a culture of doing things your own way. Whereas learning effects *within* districts were evident in adjustments of the original business model over time, the exchange of experiences *between* divisions has been largely ad hoc.

To prevent organization members from reverting back into old habits, several *maintaining* efforts were made. Top-down corrections have strengthened the set of beliefs underlying the segmentation strategy. The divisional chairman illustrates the use of corrective action with the following example:

> We gave the districts more responsibilities. In a manner of speaking, they were given responsibilities that the regions had not had. If it became clear that these responsibilities had not been kept, they would lose them. We carefully watched the way in which people dealt with the responsibilities.

Another maintaining activity involved the use of performance-based rewards. Although the regulatory and information infrastructure conditions limited the range of possibilities, managers introduced team-based reward systems for particular commercial events. This stimulated employees to behave in line with the new rules. Besides being rooted in employee behavior, reality maintenance was manifested in how strategic reorientation influenced decision makers' perceptions and beliefs. Segmentation's perceived success confirmed their beliefs about the business and how to succeed in it. This is also illustrated in the initiation of several projects which hinge on its extension in the post-1998 period. In line with the original beliefs, the number of districts has been gradually reduced from 2000 onwards. Advances have been made in the information infrastructure; this has contributed to a shift away from the geographic line toward the business line. The matrix established in the Segmentation project has been taken a step further as executives' strive for an streamlined sales organization. Figure 5.6 summarizes key case study findings.

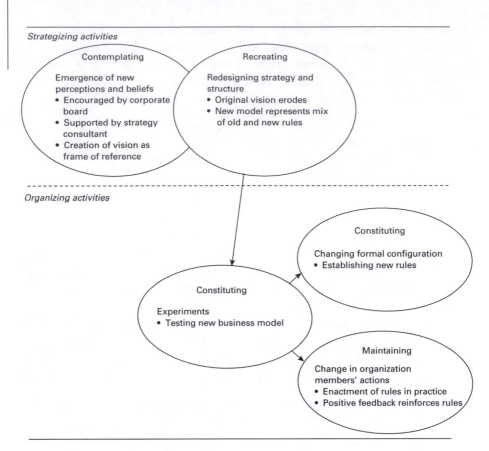

FIGURE 5.6  *Segmentation change process – elaboration*

## DISCUSSION AND CONCLUSION

In this chapter, strategizing and organizing have been represented as activities that are essentially cognitive in nature. To better understand these activities, we focused on strategic reorientation as a complex of strategizing and organizing activities, articulated in changing decision-makers' perceptions and beliefs, formal structure and structure, and organization members' actions (Figure 5.2). The case study which showed how our cognition-based framework translated into practice concerned reorientation at the home banking business unit of ING, INB. We used a processual and multi-level approach to track changes over time and across levels.

Tracking changes in cognition and action, a number of things become clear. Strategizing and organizing emerge from the evidence as complementary processes. However, they do not necessarily unfold sequentially. Multi-level analysis revealed that strategizing and organizing activities at one level of analysis can have spin off at other levels. These spin-offs influenced the overall change results by putting restraints on the magnitude and direction of change and, on other occasions, by stretching the initial change boundaries. A processual approach allowed for insight in mutual dependencies between strategizing and organizing. Although strategizing might be associated primarily with thinking and organizing with acting, our research indicates that constituting and maintaining activities unleash additional strategizing and that contemplating and recreating activities build on previous organizing efforts. Also, the success of a particular activity is influenced by the nature of other activities. For example, contemplation that has resulted in a clear vision might well add to a climate for change in which maintenance is easier to attain. Similarly, whether constituting activities include the establishment of maintenance mechanisms (reward systems, performance evaluation systems) is key to successful maintaining activities. The seeds for organizing are contained in strategizing. The opposite is valid as well. If constituting and maintaining activities are a source of sound feedback for decision makers, they may well fuel another round of contemplation and recreation.

Studying change efforts in their context helped to understand the dynamics of strategizing and organizing. The case shows, for example, how path dependencies and environmental constraints compromised decision makers' discretion. Furthermore, successive change projects have their roots in the Segmentation project's strategizing and organizing activities. Beliefs originally developed within the scope of the Segmentation project re-appear or are extended.

Some of the findings are counter-intuitive. The replacement of decision makers has been mentioned as a way to introduce new beliefs into an organization (Barr et al., 1992). However, in the Segmentation project, the arrival of a new chairman did not compromise the emerging belief set. The case study also showed that the belief system which influences decision makers' thinking and acting is not necessarily their own. Corporate-level managers' beliefs played a role in decision-making. The strategy consultancy firm which was hired also strongly influenced perceived environmental and organizational characteristics. Its expert knowledge provided the firm with the informal authority needed to have an impact on decision making. 'Borrowing' consultants' beliefs in constructing a view of the business landscape might be an effective way to avoid getting trapped in cognitive rigidities.

The research that underlies this chapter could be extended in a number of ways. First, it would be interesting to connect cognitive changes at the divisional level to changes at the firm and the industry level. The banking industry is an industry-in-transition. Industry recipes are questioned by managers across firms. In line with this, a second topic of interest for future research is the tendency of firms to copy each other's practices (*mimetic behavior*). Adopting formal rules applied by competitors or copying routines might work out negatively for a company if underlying beliefs are not well understood (Siggelkow, 2001). The research might also be extended to include other national and international banks. We are currently conducting a case study with a US financial conglomerate to deepen our understanding of the impact of context on strategizing and organizing dynamics. Finally, by choosing strategic reorientation as the main focus, we narrowed down the scope of the study. Deliberate attempts to drastically change strategy and structure are generally top-down driven. Future research should be explorations of change processes initiated outside the decision makers' domain to see whether strategizing and organizing evolve differently.

A primary advantage of the notion of strategizing/organizing is the comprehensive view on the strategy processes it entails. Based on a cognitive perspective, four sets of activities were defined and a theoretical framework was developed which allowed for the study of strategic reorientation over time and across various levels of analysis. The actual application of the framework through a case study, led to a better understanding of strategizing and organizing dynamics. We now have to take up the challenge of building on the findings.

# II

# Complementarities, Change and Performance

# Chapter 6

# Complementarities Thinking

*Richard Whittington and*
*Andrew M. Pettigrew*

## INTRODUCTION

The power of complementarities has already been touched on in this volume, but this chapter develops the complementarities notion as it will be drawn upon as the central theoretical idea of the following three chapters. These chapters will deal with a wide range of issues – from international performance, through innovative forms of organization in professional services to the transformation of large multinationals – yet each will share a theoretical base that requires more general grounding. The task here, therefore, is to ground these chapters in a broader understanding of complementarity theory's relationship to other theoretical traditions and to provide a general review of the kinds of predictions it makes for change and performance. This chapter also highlights complementarity theory's silence with regard to the processes of complementary change, an issue that the following chapters will pursue.

   Complementarity theory is essentially about 'fit', and so joins a long tradition within organization theory. We therefore start this chapter by drawing out the ways in which complementarity theory contradicts, reinforces and extends such traditions as contingency theory and the configurational perspective. We shall highlight particularly how complementarity theory and the configurational perspective share in a repudiation of contingency theory's reductionism and incrementalism, seeing performance as depending upon holistic systems whose integrated natures are antithetical to piecemeal change. However, complementarity theory differs from the configurational perspective in being more alive to uniqueness in organizational systems, and consequently to market power rather than simply internal efficiency as a possible source of performance advantage. Complementarity theory draws out the implications of internal integration more starkly than configurational theory and adds distinctive insights of its own.

The core section of this chapter, therefore, reviews complementarity theory's implications, drawing out the radical consequences of concepts such as the performance J-curve and 'complementarity traps'. Again and again, we shall reinforce the ambivalent nature of complementarity, its strengths in integration and complexity often being barriers in terms of change and diffusion. Moreover, while making much of the challenges of change, complementarity theory offers only quite simple prescriptions for managing the processes of change. We conclude, therefore, by making the case for more detailed attention to change processes than has so far been typical in complementarity studies and which shall be part of the endeavour of the following chapters.

## COMPLEMENTARITY AND FIT IN ORGANIZATION THEORY

The notion of 'fit' has a long pedigree in management thought. Contingency theory attributed strong performance consequences to appropriate matches between organizational structure and such variables as technology, strategy or environment (Chandler, 1962; Woodward, 1965; Lawrence and Lorsch, 1967a). Although a good deal of this early work was conceived of in static terms (Pettigrew and Whipp, 1991), contingency theory has begun recently to develop a more dynamic approach to describing continuous sequences of incremental adjustment from clear mismatch towards improving levels of fit (Donaldson, 1987; 2001). In what Donaldson (2001) terms neo-contingency theory, performance is not simply a dependent variable, but a stimulus to change itself. Contingency theory can thus now claim a dynamic view of organizations in which performance has a central role. But this is a partial view. The expectation of near-automatic correction towards performance-maximizing fit allows contingency theory to detach itself from the messy business of actually managing change. Contingency theory does not bother much with action and process (Whittington, 2002).

Another complaint against contingency theory is its reductionist propensity to disaggregate organizations into distinct, mutually independent dimensions – technology, strategy, structure and so on. These are seen as varying according to a range of factors in a manner that is largely indifferent to variations in other dimensions. From the 1970s onwards, management theory has developed a more holistic appreciation of how these dimensions interrelate and how 'coherence' between them may be critical to success (Pettigrew and Whipp, 1991). This holistic kind of thinking was early represented by the Seven Ss of Waterman et al. (1980), the archetypes developed by Miller and Friesen (1978) and Miles and Snow's (1978) three coherent strategy types of analysers, prospectors and defenders.

The most developed form of this kind of holistic perspective is the configurational perspective (Miller, 1986, 1992; Meyer et al., 1993; Ketchen et al., 1997). Configurations consist of multidimensional constellations of organizational characteristics that commonly occur together – these characteristics might range from strategy, through structure, to culture and technology. Configurations are seen as tightly-coupled; in other words their dimensions hold together in a mutual dependence that is at once hard and risky to disturb. The self-reinforcing effects of this kind of mutual dependence have positive performance consequences (Ketchen et al., 1997). Indeed, internal fit among organizational dimensions is typically more important than external fit with environmental variables (Miller, 1992).

This emphasis on internal rather than external fit has important implications. By contrast with contingency theory, configuration theory is prepared to allow for several effective solutions to a given set of environmental challenges. The well-oiled internal meshing of alternative configurations deliver equifinal outcomes. Tight internal fit implies another contrast with contingency theory and its disaggregated view of organizations. The configurational view of change is as something that is typically episodic and revolutionary, rather than continuous and incremental (Romanelli and Tushman, 1994). Tight integration means that incremental adjustments will only spoil the smooth internal workings of the configuration; better to rip everything apart at one go. This presumption in favour of explosive transformations leads to one similarity with contingency theory, however. The explosive view lets configurational researchers off the same hook of exploring carefully the processes of change. They fail to address the challenge of managing coherence through holding together interrelated changes over extended periods of time (Pettigrew and Whipp, 1991).

Configuration theory anticipates a good deal of the economic theory of complementarity, even to the extent of using the same language of complementarities (Miller, 1986; 1992). There is a similar emphasis on holism, the importance of mutual reinforcement and the problem of change. There is also an equivalent neglect of change processes (Pettigrew et al., 2001). Where complementarity theory differs most is in its focus on competitive advantage, leading both to a concern for the non-inimitability advantages of complementarities and a focus on uniqueness rather than the general types ('analysers', 'prospectors' and so on) that are common in configurational research. Complementarities researchers have also developed different econometric techniques for exploring performance effects, particularly in distinguishing the impact of dimensions individually from their impact collectively as complementary systems (Ichniowski et al., 1997; Whittington et al., 1999). The next section will develop the economics of complementarities more fully, pulling out some of the key implications for performance and change.

## THE ECONOMICS OF COMPLEMENTARITIES

The notion of complementarities is another way of approaching the benefits of fit. Paul Milgrom and John Roberts (1995: 181), the pioneers of complementarity theory within economics, define complementarities as existing when 'doing *more* of one thing *increases* the returns to doing *more* of another' (emphases in original). Applied to the strategic, structural and technological variables of the firm, this amounts to a notion of internal synergy. Investing in one variable makes more profitable investing in another, setting off a potential virtuous circle of high performance. The key implication is that choice variables should not be thought of discretely, but as belonging to potentially integrated systems of mutually reinforcing elements. Everything in the business should fit smoothly together. Thus Milgrom and Roberts (1995) analyse in detail how the long-run success of Lincoln Electric relies upon a coherent system bringing together the interdependent elements of low-cost strategy, piece rates, permanent employment, high earnings, internal promotion, firm-specific training and old plant and equipment. None of these elements would necessarily make business sense taken individually and the absence of any one would damage substantially the benefits of the remainder.

Milgrom and Roberts (1990; 1995) provide a detailed exposition of the mathematics of complementarities, drawing on notions of lattice theory and supermodularity. But complementarities can also be visualized fairly simply as nets of inter-relationships. Thus Michael Porter (1996) maps out complementarities in terms of interconnected 'activity systems'. In the case of furniture retailer Ikea, the key elements of limited customer service, self-selection by customers, modular furniture design and low manufacturing cost are placed at the centre and highlighted, with their mutually reinforcing nature emphasized by bold connecting lines. Limited service relies upon customer self-selection; low costs depend upon modular designs. These central elements are in turn reinforced by a whole set of relatively minor elements, such as ample inventories and in-house design, that are shown as less densely interconnected and placed on the periphery. The point is that Ikea's success does not stem from any one element on its own; competitive advantage grows out of the system of activities as a whole.

The complementarities notion is intuitively attractive and strongly consistent with established traditions in organization theory. It also has powerful managerial implications, some extending, some adding to those of earlier traditions. The remainder of this section will spell these out, paying particular attention to issues of change and performance.

Fundamental to the practical implications of complementarities is understanding the downside of system effects between complementary elements. Milgrom and Roberts (1995: 191) warn: 'Changing only a few of the system elements at a time to their optimal values may not come at all close to achieving all the benefits that are available through a fully co-ordinated move, and may even have negative payoffs.' This is not just to restate the importance of full systems for attaining desirable outcomes; it is to point to the possibility that initiatives that would be beneficial if taken alongside other complementary initiatives might easily be damaging either on their own or in company with different kinds of initiative. A managerial action that is good in one context will likely be indifferent to bad in most others.

A first implication here is fairly direct. Milgrom and Roberts (1995) emphasize the importance of strong central direction for achieving effective change. Decentralized, bottom-up approaches are handicapped in delivering complementary change. Local experiments and piecemeal initiatives are liable to be abandoned as they fail to find their fit within the rest of the organization. Only once initiatives are cumulated into complementary packages are they to likely to deliver their payoffs. Complementarities therefore favour strong central leadership, capable of imposing and maintaining coherence between complementary elements. An example of this is the leadership provided by Percy Barnevik in the early years of ABB, when he quickly acted on many dimensions to construct a new engineering multinational in which strategy, structure and systems all fitted into place (Whittington et al., 2000; Ruigrok et al., 2000b).

A close corollary of the dangers of incoherent change is the problem of transition. Change on many dimensions cannot be completed in an instant. The challenge for managers, therefore, is to manage the steps between untangling one complementary system and bedding down the new complementary system. With no new system in place, and with some of its building blocks potentially dysfunctional as they await their complements, organizations in transition are likely to suffer severe performance penalties, possibly worse than the original status quo. During transition, moreover, people can look back to a past when things more or less worked, even if less well than they could; meanwhile the better future for which they are struggling is still unclear and uncertain. Here arises what we have called elsewhere 'the perils of the J-curve' (Whittington et al., 2000). Even in the best co-ordinated systems of complementary initiatives, performance during transition is likely to follow a J-curve: movement from the unsatisfactory performance that first triggers change, through a period of still worse performance as the old system is disrupted, and then finally into a period of higher performance as the superior new system gets into gear. Another implication of complementarities, therefore, is that things tend to get worse before they get better. It takes strong leaders indeed to survive these kinds of change processes.

The J-curve effect of complementarities warns also that it is easy – and in the short-term safer – for organizations to get stuck at suboptimal levels of performance. Siggelkow (2001) describes how the American women's clothing company Liz Claiborne went from spectacular success in the 1980s to negative growth and falling margins in the early to mid 1990s. The old complementary system – based on fashion apparel for professional women – no longer worked, but the company could not envision a new system with which to replace it. Existing management spent several years in piecemeal initiatives that had no effect or even made things worse. These initiatives were doomed because unsupported by complementary initiatives; they exacerbated the situation because putting even more strain on what was still fairly effective in the old system. It was not until the appointment of a complete outsider as Chief Operating Officer in 1994, followed by his promotion in successive years to Chief Executive and then Chairman, that a new full system based on a wide range of women's clothing could finally be implemented. Sales and margins then gradually began to improve. Implementing full system change took courage and vision. It would have been easy for Liz Claiborne to have continued fiddling at marginal change, with each disappointing initiative only reinforcing a belief that on the whole it was better to leave things intact. In the same way as there is a 'competence trap' (Levitt and March, 1988), in which firms stick rigidly to what they do best, so there is a 'complementarities trap', according to which firms persist with what once fitted best because incomplete initiatives seem only to make things worse (Pettigrew and Whittington, 2001).

Complementarities traps and fear of the J-curve also help to explain the slow diffusion of best practice across industries and nations. Obviously some of the system benefits may depend upon elements that may be absent or weaker in some contexts than others. But even allowing for this, pioneers are few, laggards many. In a careful comparison of the effects of complementary human resource management practices in American and Japanese steel plants, Ichniowski and Shaw (1999) found that only 10 per cent of American plants had adopted the innovative practices of the Japanese. This was despite the facts both that Japanese plants were significantly more productive and that the American plants adopting these practices equally outperformed their more traditional local rivals. In a similar fashion, we have observed that, during the 1990s, only about one in twenty European firms were adopting the full set of complementary changes associated with innovative organizing, but that these few enjoyed very substantial performance premia (Whittington et al., 1999). As Ichniowski and Shaw (1999) put it, complementarities imply substantial 'switching costs' in moving from one complete system to another entirely different system. There is a high up-front price to pay for change.

Another part of the explanation of slow diffusion is the opacity of complementary systems. As Milgrom and Roberts (1995) say of their successful Lincoln Electric company, it was easy to spot the more spectacularly distinctive characteristics, much harder to understand how these characteristics interacted with the more humdrum to form such an effective whole. Despite television documentaries, press articles and business school case studies, nobody managed to imitate the company. This is, of course, an up side to complementarity's complexity. Complementary systems are hard to understand, hard to implement and so hard to imitate (Porter, 1996; Rivkin, 2000). Unlike configurational approaches with their concern for types, complementarity theorists therefore emphasize uniqueness in the marketplace. The monopolistic rents of unique positionings, as well as the internal efficiencies of well-integrated systems, drive performance. In short, once an effective complementary system is in place, it should become a powerful source of inimitable advantage. It may be difficult and costly getting there, but complementarities can be well worth the trouble.

However, the advantages of inimitability are double-edged, in a way that is typical of the complementarities notion. Inimitability relies upon a tightness of system integration that is liable to statis and rigidity. Loosening the elements of the system, as Rivkin (2000) describes IBM doing in the personal computer market, makes a company more flexible but also more prone to imitation. IBM introduced its personal computers from outside the core system that was its mainframe business and accordingly faced at once a wave of imitative entrants into its market. Rivkin (2000: 843) sums up the dilemma acutely: 'Loosely coupled organizations, it appears, are responsive to change, but vulnerable to imitation. ... Designers of organizations must decide which they fear more: inertia or imitation.' Hard to imitate is also hard to change.

As we review these implications of the complementarity notion, we are surely struck by how repeatedly it emphasizes the challenges of change. But we must acknowledge too that its prescriptions for managing this change have a simplicity that fails to meet the mark – strong leadership and completed systems can only be a start. Here organization theory in general, and complementarity theory in particular, are handicapped by undue predilections for the analysis of comparative statics (Pettigrew et al., 2001). If comprehensive, complementary change is not to be completed in the explosive, revolutionary moments implied by configuration theory, we shall need a great deal more attention to change over time. Assembling comprehensive visions, sequencing steps while projecting coherence, negotiating J-curves and breaking free of complementarity traps are not instantaneous achievements to be passed over with the glib assurance that economic logics will quickly prevail. They require skills of timing and sequence, capacities to project forwards while linking backwards, resources for endurance and the will to persist about which we still know far too little. To make complementarity theory practical in a positive sense we need to add to the warnings of complexity, helpful guidelines for management action. Completing complementarity theory requires a much stronger sense of managerial process.

## CONCLUSIONS

This chapter has situated the complementarities notion within a long theoretical tradition emphasizing the importance of 'fit'. Unlike earlier contingency theory approaches, complementarity theory takes a holistic view of organizations, conceiving them as potentially integrated, self-reinforcing systems. As we remarked in Chapter 2's discussion of the 'Organizing/ Strategizing' concept, this holistic view is fully consistent with several theoretical endeavours within the contemporary social sciences. The complementarities notion is also closely aligned with the recent interest in configurations within organization theory. Complementarity and configurational notions share not just an emphasis on holism, but also an appreciation of mutual reinforcement and the difficulties of change. Complementarity theory is additive, however, both in the starkness of its formulations and in introducing a stronger sense of market as well as internal sources of advantage.

There are strong and distinctive implications from complementarity theory. Integration is both a source of strength and a source of weakness. There is the potential for internal synergy but, without the right context, good initiatives can easily turn bad. Organizations can easily sink into complementarity traps, in which piecemeal initiatives disappoint because unsupported and the low point of the J-curve is prematurely interpreted as failure. Leadership must be strong, not just to assemble comprehensive programmes, but to survive the long gap before the positive effects of completed systems finally kick in. Successful systems are hard to accomplish and slowly diffused through organizational populations. Once established, however, they can be a double source of advantage: smooth internal mechanisms deliver efficiency, while inimitability endows market power. The more inimitability rests on complex integration, of course, the more difficult such systems will be to change when – as it must – that time finally comes.

The chapters that follow will explore these notions of complementarity more fully. As well as demonstrating the performance benefits of complementarities, they will explore the central, hanging question raised by complementarity theory: what are the effective processes involved in managing complementary change?

Chapter 7

# Complementarities in Organizational Innovation and Performance:

## Empirical Evidence from the INNFORM Survey

*Silvia Massini and Andrew M. Pettigrew*

## INTRODUCTION

Recent theoretical and empirical literature on organizational change has analysed the implementation of organizational practices in sets and clusters. The evidence on clusters or systems of organizational practices suggests that they are correlated across firms and appear to be adopted consistently together, although not always immediately coherently. For example, firms are introducing practices for knowledge sharing, information technology (IT) systems and strategies, and new human resources (HR) practices. They are also managing hierarchies and developing networks: structuring the organization by projects, decentralizing operations and developing horizontal linkages (Pettigrew and Fenton, 2000a).

The notion of innovating in sets has been captured in organization and industrial economics by the idea of complementarities. This builds on the notion of Edgerworth complements and defines complementarities between activities as existing when 'doing *more* of one thing *increases* the returns to doing *more* of another' (emphases in original) (Milgrom and Roberts, 1995: 181).

Intuitively, the notion of complementarities can be conceptualized with the notion of synergy, that is, investing in one resource makes more profitable investing in another. Formally, complementarities correspond to positive mixed partial derivatives of some payoff functions, which indicate that the marginal returns to one variable are increasing in the levels of another variable. However, Milgrom and Roberts develop the mathematics of complementarities without referring to the standard assumptions of the payoff function, such as concavity and divisibility, typical of neo-classical economics. Instead, they define complementarities by drawing on the notions of lattice theory and supermodularity (Milgrom and Roberts, 1990; 1995).

As illustrated in Chapter 6, complementarities in organization theory share with configuration theory the view of organizations as holistic systems of integrated elements. The self-reinforcing effects of these interrelated dimensions may have important positive consequences on performance. The managerial challenge is therefore to co-ordinate coherent change of mutually dependent dimensions. Indeed, the importance of coherent rather than piecemeal change is well accepted in organization theory (Pettigrew and Whipp, 1991). Complementarities theory suggests that well designed systemic changes may generate higher than average returns, yet the uniqueness and complexity of complementary changes make their imitation highly problematic (Rivkin, 2000). Even if it is possible to observe some spectacular characteristics of successful companies, the underlying mechanisms which make some interactions outstandingly successful and profitable are much more hidden and difficult to identify and even more difficult to implement.

The notion of complementarities can support diversification strategies: firms may find profitable new activities in areas that are complementary to areas that are being improved. Complementarities may also support the development of path dependency, or cumulative change (Milgrom et al., 1991), and suggest the co-evolution of the elements constituting a system, because once the movement of a whole system of complementary variables begins, it tends to continue (Milgrom and Roberts, 1995).

Empirical research on complementarities has provided a range of qualitative and quantitative work, from case studies which analyse exemplary execution of coherent systemic change (see for example Milgrom and Roberts (1995) on Lincoln Electric; Porter (1996) on Southwest and IKEA; Bartlett and Ghoshal (1993) on ABB), to econometric analyses which investigate the effect of specific practices, often ranges of (new) human resource practices (Ichnioswki et al., 1997) and their interaction with IT (Bresnahan et al., 2002). The econometric research on complementarities explores performance effects isolating the impact of individual elements and the combined effect of systems of managerial practices and organizational changes.

This chapter represents a contribution to the empirical, quantitative evidence on complementarities using the INNFORM survey. As we described in Chapter 1, this survey has the rare merit to encompass a high number of organizational dimensions in large and medium firms, and to relate them to two points in time, 1992 and 1996. It also includes companies from a number of different countries, Europe, the US and Japan, thus allowing regional comparisons. These characteristics of the survey design of the INNFORM programme make the database a unique source for empirical exploration of complementarities. Previous analysis from the INNFORM survey has provided supportive evidence on the relation between complementarities and performance (Whittington et al., 1999). However, in that study, the analysis was focusing on the extent of adoption of new organizational practices, and explored the existence of complementarities among the high adopters of new managerial and organizational practices. Consequently, like most empirical research in this area, the analysis was mainly static.

Building on the previous analysis from the INNFORM survey, we make full use of the time dimension and analyse the effect of multiple, interrelated organizational *changes* on corporate performance *changes* in a large set of large and medium Western firms in the period 1992–96. To the best of our knowledge there are no other published studies of this kind in the literature.

We define three main dimensions of organizations, structure, processes and boundaries, and build combinations of these composite, multiple indicators of change. We find that the companies introducing the full system of change enjoy a performance premium. We also distinguish between emerging regional patterns that may indicate the effect of different institutional settings in defining, implementing and rewarding alternative systems of changes.

We find dissimilarities in the complementarities–performance relation in the UK, German-speaking countries and the USA, with different combinations of organizational changes showing higher rewards in performance in different regions. However, our analysis also suggests that partial systems or piecemeal change have negative effects on performance and that complementarities can reward strong leaders able to envision and guide the implementation of coherent systems of change.

The regional analysis indicates that some systems are more likely to increase performance in a region than in others. Policy makers may want to learn about the crucial components of performance enhancing systems and define interventions that facilitate their implementation to improve the international competitiveness of their national champions.

Our analysis reveals that some individual changes and systemic changes can improve performance (with the effect of the full system exceeding the effect of a set of individual practices) but piecemeal changes can have detrimental effects on performance. This finding is consistent with the J-curve effect found in Whittington et al. (1999) for the high adopters of organizational innovations. Since the several organizational dimensions constituting systems cannot necessarily be implemented simultaneously, managers introducing complementary changes must be ready to observe a reduction in performance before enjoying the full benefits of the systemic changes. Further evidence of the causes and consequences of the J-curve effects are provided in Chapter 8 of this volume.

In the next section we describe the notion of complementarities as defined by Milgrom and Roberts (1990 and 1995) and report on some empirical work which uses this notion. In Chapter 1 we described and discussed the number of relevant organizational elements identified in the literature and investigated in the INNFORM survey; in the third section of this chapter we use those elements to define multiple and systemic changes and map their adoption in different regions to compare and discuss regional differences of their frequencies. But how widespread are systems of organizational changes in large companies? Are there regional variations in the adoption of bundles of changes? These questions are investigated in the fourth section. Having found a number of regional contrasts in the incidence of adoption of systems of organizational changes, we undertake the econometric analysis of the complementarities–performance relation for the whole sample and in different regions to test the contribution of the aggregate as well as individual elements to corporate performance. We present these results in the fifth section of this chapter. Finally, in the last section, we summarize and discuss the findings.

## COMPLEMENTARITIES AND PERFORMANCE

The notion of complementarities has been developed by Paul Milgrom and John Roberts (1990, 1995) to understand the revolutionary changes in modern manufacturing which involved changes in technological production and organizational strategy. They refer to the emergence of flexible manufacturing as an example of successful and substantial, closely co-ordinated changes in a range of firm's activities. Even if the changes occur over a period of time, the full benefits are only enjoyed by an eventual radical restructuring.

The notion of complementarities as defined by Milgrom and Roberts refers to the multiple interactions and interdependencies between technological factors and organizational variables. Milgrom and Roberts use complements in a broad sense, as a relation among groups of activities with the characteristic that 'if the levels of any subset of activities are increased, then the marginal return to increases in any or all remaining activities rises' (Milgrom and Roberts, 1990: 514). As a consequence, if the marginal cost of some activities in the group falls, it may be optimal to increase the level of all the activities in the group. The notion of complementarities refers to the adoption of existing practices, but, in general, a firm adapting to environmental change will find it more profitable to start new activities in areas which are complementary to the newly increased activities (Milgrom and Roberts, 1995: 186).

They define complementarities between activities as existing when 'doing *more* of one thing increases the returns to doing *more* of another' (emphases in original) (Milgrom and Roberts, 1995: 181). They define complementarities drawing on the notions of lattice theory and supermodularity (Milgrom and Roberts, 1995).

A lattice $(X, \geq)$ is a set $X$ with a partial order $\geq$ with the property that for any $x$ and $y$ in $X$, $X$ also contains a smallest element under the order that is larger than both $x$ and $y$ and a largest element that is smaller than $x$ and $y$. If $x \vee y$ ($x$ join $y$) denotes the smallest element larger than $x$ and $y$, and $x \wedge y$ ($x$ meet $y$) denotes the largest element smaller than $x$ and $y$, then $f$ is supermodular and its arguments are (Edgeworth) complements if and only if for any $x$ and $y$ in $X$ $f(x) - f(x \wedge y) \leq f(x \vee y) - f(y)$.

Among other interesting properties, supermodularity provides a way to formalize the idea of synergy and system effects, that the whole is more than the sum of its parts. If $x$ and $y$ are two points in $R^n$ and $x$ is strictly larger than $y$, supermodularity is mathematically equivalent to the statement that for every $x$ and $y$, the payoff of increasing every component from $y_i$ to $x_i$ is larger than the payoff of individual increases (Milgrom and Roberts, 1995: 185):

$$f(x) - f(y) \geq \left[ \sum_{i-1}^{n} f(x_j - y_{-i}) - f(y) \right]$$

From an operational point of view, supermodularity and complementarities imply that when strong complementarities exist it is more likely that individual adaptation will fail to produce superior results, the distance from the team's equilibrium to its optimum can be large, and central strategic direction is valuable. Complementarities can be a source of non-convexities, in addition to indivisibilities normally associated with modern manufacturing, which make it impossible to reach a global optimum. The existence of complementarities makes it relatively unprofitable to only partially adopt the modern manufacturing strategy. However, strategic direction can be effective in achieving improvements without detailed knowledge of the individual elements to reach the optimum of the payoff function, but only needs to identify the relevant elements where complementarities exist. On the other hand, systematic errors associated with centrally directed change could be less costly than unco-ordinated errors of independent operating units. Therefore, the numerous interactions and interdependencies of complementary changes give rise to non-convexities that make optimal decision making unattainable and require co-ordinated choice among a number of decision variables.

Among the examples of complementary changes provided by Milgrom and Roberts (1990) there is the fall in the cost of computer aided design (CAD) equipment and software, which is likely to lead to their increasing adoption. Associated with that is adopting a broader product line and updating products more frequently. Short production runs imply economizing on inventory costs and quicker response to customer demand. Indirect effects of a fall in the cost of CAD and software are adoption, and therefore falling costs, of data communication, and marketing and engineering changes.

Empirical evidence on the effect of complementarities on performance is provided by Milgrom and Roberts (1995) in their analysis of the long-run success of Lincoln Electric. This relies upon a coherent system which brings together a number of interdependent organizational and strategic elements: low-cost strategy, piece rates, permanent employment, high earnings, internal promotion, firm-specific training and old plant and equipment. None of these elements would necessarily make business sense taken individually and the absence of any one would substantially damage the benefits of the remainder. The example of GM is used to illustrate how heavy investments in equipment associated with the new methods of mass production, like robotics, during the early 1980s failed to bring the expected returns because of lack of related, complementary adjustments in human resources practices, decision systems and product development processes.

In general, empirical studies with evidence supporting complementarities tend to refer to the interaction of technological adoption (like robotics, and other improved capital equipment or IT) and organizational practices (like relationship with suppliers, or interaction between manufacturing and marketing divisions), with the introduction of a range of HR practices or adjustments to existing ones.

Most of the other research on complementarities which have followed Milgrom and Roberts' (1990, 1995) seminal works and provided additional supportive evidence on the complementarities–performance relationships have focused on human resource management (HRM) practices, or new work practices and IT. However, rich quantitative evidence in such studies is still rare, as the effect of complementarities thinking requires information on a high number of organizational and technological dimensions, for a large number of firms, possibly over time.

Ichnioswski et al. (1997) have investigated the effect of innovative work practice systems on productivity in 36 steel finishing lines owned by 17 different steel companies in the USA over time. They compared disaggregated and aggregate, systemic organizational changes to identify the contribution of the individual element to performance. Based on 15 HRM practices they built four alternative systemic changes with different degrees of innovativeness, from a traditional system to a system that incorporates all new HRM practices. The high number of observations, more than 2000, allows estimating the effect of their adoption on productivity using panel data models and a number of control variables. Their evidence shows that systems of innovative HRM practices have a positive impact on productivity and quality, while adopting individual work practices have little or negative effect.

Breshnaham et al. (2002) have estimated complementarities between IT, work organization and performance in 300 large US firms in the period

1987–94. They collected data on workplace organization, labour force characteristics, and installation of IT equipment, and explored complementarity effects in firms' production functions as represented by interaction terms of pairs of elements and the effect of individual elements. Their findings also support the existence of some complementarity between pairs of (composite) elements, although they do not investigate the effect of the full system constituted by the three elements considered in their research.

Mendelson and Pillai (1999) have investigated something similar to complementarities in what they call the Information Age organization, which they define around three elements: decentralization, information practices and an inter-organizational network structure. Mendelson and Pillai argue that the Information Age organization is better equipped to cope with fast-changing, dynamic and information-rich environments. Their study of 90 computer and electronics firms in California in 1992–93 shows that the Information Age organization, characterized by decentralization, information practices and an inter-organizational network structure, improves business success, as measured by a number of variables, such as profitability and growth, returns on sales, returns on value added, sales growth. They suggest that their results would apply to any other dynamic and information-rich industry. They built a composite variable to measure the adoption of the three elements, but unlike Ichnioswski et al. (1997) and Breshnaham et al. (2002), they did not investigate the case when only one of these elements is introduced.

In the organizational and managerial literature, the understanding that organizational changes tend to occur in systems is reported in a number of studies, for example the 'integrated set' of practices of the N-form (Hedlund, 1994), or the systemic character of new organizational forms (Miles and Snow, 1992). More recently, qualitative evidence has been published by Siggelkov (2001) who presents a longitudinal study of internal changes in organizations as a response to external environmental changes. His study of Liz Claiborne analyses individual choices and their tight interconnection as a system as Liz Claiborne adjusted to major environmental changes in the 1990s.

Following and integrating both lines of investigations, the multi-dimensional changes in organizations and the existence of complementarities, the INNFORM survey included a wide range of questions to investigate the relationship between organizational changes and performance. Using the INNFORM survey, Whittington et al. (1999) have researched the complementarities–performance relationship in Western organizations, referring to a number of organizational dimensions which captures three main aspects of the firm: structure, processes and boundaries (see also Chapter 1). Their findings suggest positive returns to system-wide rather than piecemeal changes. In particular, they found that the most comprehensive system of organizational innovation gives the highest premium in terms of performance. Consistently with the notion of complementarities they found the adoption of partial systems might be associated with negative performance.

These empirical studies provide valuable and interesting contributions of the effect of organizational change on business performance, but most of them present *static* analyses. A rare exception is the work by Ichnioswski et al. (1997). As Milgrom and Roberts (1990) acknowledge, they also present a static model which, however, is suggestive about the nature of the path of the modern manufacturing strategy, but captures the notion of *change* underlying the definition of complementarities only partially.

This chapter provides a new exploration of the INNFORM survey, which, building on the results by Whittington et al. (1999), develops the analysis of the systems of complementary organizational innovations and performance by considering the *changes* of the variables over the period 1992–96. Moreover, it estimates the models for the whole sample and then for different (regions the UK, German-speaking countries and the USA) to find country-region-specific results where the globally widespread new organizational practices are mediated by specific institutional contexts.

## THE ORGANIZATIONAL VARIABLES FOR THE ANALYSIS OF COMPLEMENTARITIES: BUILDING SYSTEMS OF ORGANIZATIONAL CHANGE

The INNFORM survey covered a wide range of organizational aspects. In order to synthesize coherently the rich information gathered with the survey instrument, individual elements have been combined into new, composite variables. These represent three organizational dimensions, Structure, Processes and Boundaries, and capture the main dimensions of contemporary change. The composite variables have been combined in *systems* of organizational changes. The systems are used in the exploration of complementarities in organizational changes in large organizations and for the empirical investigation of their effect on performance.

These dimensions follow the same criteria and headings as in the previous analysis of the complementarities and performance relationship by Whittington et al. (1999) using the INNFORM survey. However, in the present study we are interested in investigating the dynamic relationship between organizational changes and performance. The individual elements are transformed into a series of binary variables, where 1 represents increase in the extent of a certain organizational aspect or managerial practice. The three composite dimensions are defined as binary variables corresponding to *changes* in the individual components of the composite variable. Thus the composite variables are defined as follows. Structure includes Delayering, increase in the importance of a Project-based structure, increase of Strategic decentralization of decision making and increase of Operation decentralization of decision making. The composite variable Processes includes increase in Vertical networking, increase in Horizontal networking, increase in new HR practices, and increase in IT. Vertical and Horizontal networking, HR practices and IT are composite variables themselves as they synthesize several items included in the questions (see the INNFORM questionnaire in the Appendix to this volume at www.sagepub.co.uk/resources/pettigrew.htm). The variable Boundaries includes increase of Outsourcing, increase in Strategic alliances, and reduction of Range of business (or Downscoping).

A company takes a value of 1 if it passes the change conditions according the following rules. A company takes the value 1 for Changing Structure if it passes three out of the four conditions and zero otherwise. It takes the value 1 for Changing Processes if it passes three out of the four conditions and zero otherwise. It takes the value 1 for Changing Boundaries if it passes two out of the three conditions and zero otherwise.

Finally, the three composite variables, Structure, Processes and Boundaries, have been used to build the four possible variables for systemic changes. System 1 includes changes in all the three dimensions: Structure, Processes and Boundaries. System 2 combines changes in Structure and Processes. System 3 combines changes in Processes and Boundaries and System 4 combines changes in Structure and Boundaries. Similar to the composite variables, these systems are built as binary variables, but this time the new system variables takes the value 1 if the sum of the components is three in the case of System 1, and zero otherwise, or value 1 if the sum of the composite variables is 2 in the case of Systems 2, 3 and 4.

Table 7.1 summarizes the nature of the individual, composite and systemic variables.

## HOW WIDESPREAD ARE SYSTEMS OF ORGANIZATIONAL CHANGE?

We built the multiple indicators and compared the adoption of composite and systemic changes in different geographical regions, Europe, Japan and the USA. As discussed in Chapter 1, we found country/regional differences in the adoption of individual organizational aspects. For example, Japanese companies introduced fewer or more incremental organizational changes. In general, certain organizational changes appear more likely in some regions than in others due to regional-country-specific historical, institutional and cultural constraints (this point is discussed more extensively in Chapter 12). But do regional differences emerge also for combinations of individual elements? Since the composite variables are built on individual elements that differ across regions we would expect to find differences also in the composite and systemic variables. Table 7.2 reports the distribution of the composite and the systemic indicators of changes by geographical region. Overall, the distributions of these variables are statistically different across

TABLE 7.1   *Defining the individual, composite and systemic variables*

| Composite Variable | Construction (variables coded 1 if true; 0 otherwise) |
| --- | --- |
| Changing Structure | A.  Delayering: reduction in organizational levels<br>B.  Project-based structure: increasing use of project-based structure<br>C.  Higher Operational decentralized decision making<br>D.  Higher Strategic decentralized decision making<br>Changing Structure = 1 if $A + B + C + D \geq 3$ |
| Changing Processes | A.  IT: Higher use of IT systems, IT strategy and EDI<br>B.  Horizontal Networking: company scores increase on Horizontal linkages<br>C.  Vertical Networking: company scores increase on Vertical linkages<br>D.  Human Resource Innovations: company increase lateral HR networking & integrating HR practices<br>Changing Processes = 1 if $A + B + C + D \geq 3$ |
| Changing Boundaries | A.  Outsourcing: High<br>B.  Strategic Alliances: firm engaged in any alliance during the four years<br>C.  Downscoping: Firm reduces the number of businesses it operates in<br>Changing Boundaries = 1 if $A + B + C \geq 2$ |

| System Variable | Construction (variables coded 1 if true; 0 otherwise) |
| --- | --- |
| System 1 | Changing Structure + Changing Processes + Changing Boundaries = 3 |
| System 2 | Changing Structure + Changing Processes = 2 |
| System 3 | Changing Processes + Changing Boundaries = 2 |
| System 4 | Changing Structure + Changing Boundaries = 2 |

the three regions, as indicated by the first column of statistical tests. The Japanese frequencies of changes in the multiple indicators and the systems variables are always significantly lower than in Europe and in the USA. The European sample shows significantly higher frequencies for Structure and System 2 (Structure and Processes) compared to the US sample. Significantly more US companies introduce changes in Processes and Boundaries and their combination (System 3) compared to the European ones. However, the frequencies of changes in System 1 (Structure, Processes and Boundaries) and System 4 (Structure and Boundaries) do not appear statistically different between the USA and Europe.

Table 7.3 reports the same distributions as in Table 7.2 but with a regional breakdown of European firms, for the UK and German-speaking countries (Germany, Switzerland and Austria), and their comparisons with Japan and US. The distributions of multiple indicators and systems variables in UK and German-speaking countries only differ in the case of Structure, with 40 per cent of companies in German-speaking countries compared to 28 per cent in the UK. All the other indicators do not differ between the UK

TABLE 7.2   *Changes in the composite indicators and system variables, Europe, Japan and the US, 1992–96*

| | Europe (%) | Japan (%) | USA (%) | Chi-2 (prob.) | Chi-2 (prob.) EUR–JP | Chi-2 (prob.) EUR–US | Chi-2 (prob.) JP–US |
|---|---|---|---|---|---|---|---|
| INT1 | 30.3 | 6.2 | 16.5 | 57.857 | 55.822 | 7.004 | 76.654 |
| Structure | | | | (0.000) | (0.000) | (0.008) | (0.000) |
| INT2 | 74.9 | 53.7 | 82.3 | 41.594 | 33.146 | 3.950 | 94.293 |
| Processes | | | | (0.000) | (0.000) | (0.047) | (0.000) |
| EXT | 44.9 | 30.7 | 57.0 | 22.107 | 13.535 | 6.144 | 39.668 |
| Boundaries | | | | (0.000) | (0.000) | (0.013) | (0.000) |
| System 1 | 13.0 | 1.2 | 8.9 | 28.665 | 28.734 | 1.230 | 28.673 |
| S + P + B | | | | (0.000) | (0.000) | (0.267) | (0.000) |
| System 2 | 25.1 | 4.7 | 12.7 | 48.872 | 46.609 | 5.791 | 54.079 |
| S + P | | | | (0.000) | (0.000) | (0.006) | (0.000) |
| System 3 | 34.2 | 18.7 | 46.8 | 29.766 | 19.112 | 7.420 | 49.436 |
| P + B | | | | (0.000) | (0.000) | (0.006) | (0.000) |
| System 4 | 16.4 | 1.6 | 11.4 | 36.597 | 36.722 | 1.277 | 39.525 |
| S + B | | | | (0.000) | (0.000) | (0.258) | (0.000) |

*Source*: INNFORM programme survey

and German-speaking countries. Companies in the UK and German-speaking countries introduced more changes in all the multiple indicators and systems variables than their Japanese comparators. The comparisons between the European regions and the USA provide a more varied pattern. In the case of changes in Processes, the European sample differed significantly from the USA, with more US companies introducing Processual changes than European firms. However, the breakdown of European regions shows that the UK and German-speaking countries do not differ from the USA, indicating that lower percentages of changes in Processes would be found in the other European countries in Northern and Southern Europe. The results for the other variables are similar to those for Europe as a whole, except for the weaker differences between UK and USA for Boundaries and System 3 (Processes and Boundaries) where UK companies do not fall too far behind the USA. Finally, more German-speaking companies appear to have introduced Structural changes, by themselves and in combination with Processes and Boundaries, that is, System 2 and System 4.

These results raise an important question: are these systemic changes introduced simply as a result of simultaneous but independent adoption of individual dimensions of the organization, or are they introduced in systems because changing one dimension requires changes in other dimensions of the organization? In other words, is there evidence that the organizational elements considered in this study are perceived as being complementary?

We can test whether these multiple organizational changes are undertaken independently, or 'randomly', or if they have been introduced in systems as the result of a holistic view of the organization, which implies

TABLE 7.3  Changes in the composite indicators and system variables, UK, German-speaking countries, Japan and the US, 1992–96

| | UK 1992–96 (%) | Germany 1992–96 (%) | Japan 1992–96 (%) | USA 1993–97 (%) | Chi-2 (prob.) UK–Ger | Chi-2 (prob.) UK–JP | Chi-2 (prob.) UK–US | Chi-2 (prob.) Ger–JP | Chi-2 (prob.) Ger–US |
|---|---|---|---|---|---|---|---|---|---|
| Structure | 27.9 | 40.2 | 6.2 | 16.5 | **4.583** (0.032) | **38.702** (0.000) | **3.912** (0.048) | **64.155** (0.000) | **12.163** (0.000) |
| Processes | 78.2 | 75.7 | 53.7 | 82.3 | 0.240 (0.624) | **27.445** (0.000) | 0.555 (0.456) | **15.263** (0.000) | 1.165 (0.280) |
| Boundaries | 46.4 | 44.9 | 30.7 | 57.0 | 0.061 (0.804) | **11.038** (0.001) | 2.460 (0.117) | **6.631** (0.010) | **2.662** (0.103) |
| System 1 S + P + B | 14.0 | 14.0 | 1.2 | 8.9 | 0.000 (0.990) | **28.762** (0.000) | 1.315 (0.251) | **26.544** (0.000) | 1.159 (0.282) |
| System 2 S + P | 25.7 | 30.8 | 4.7 | 12.7 | 0.886 (0.347) | **40.457** (0.000) | **5.484** (0.019) | **47.762** (0.000) | **8.454** (0.004) |
| System 3 P + B | 36.3 | 34.6 | 18.7 | 46.8 | 0.088 (0.767) | **17.092** (0.000) | 2.539 (0.111) | **10.674** (0.001) | **2.850** (0.091) |
| System 4 S + B | 16.2 | 18.7 | 1.6 | 11.4 | 0.293 (0.589) | **32.346** (0.000) | 1.009 (0.315) | **36.017** (0.000) | 1.840 (0.175) |

*Source:* INNFORM programme survey

that changes in one dimension must be accompanied by changes in other aspects. The probability of independent events law states that if multiple events occur (organizational changes were introduced) randomly their frequency would correspond to the product of the frequencies of the individual elements. If the frequency of a systemic change is higher than the product of the frequencies of its components and exhibits a higher frequency than the theoretical case of independent adoption, then we find evidence that the components of the systemic variables are not independent. Perhaps managers in those companies realized that changes in some aspects or dimensions of the organization must be introduced in bundles and complemented by changes in other dimensions. We can statistically test the hypothesis of independence of organizational changes in multiple dimensions, by comparing the actual frequencies of the Systems with the hypothetical, expected frequencies obtained by multiplying the frequencies of the multiple indicators that constitute the systems.

The top of Table 7.4 presents the results for Europe, Japan and the USA and the bottom for the UK and German-speaking countries. We find that in Europe the frequencies of System 1 (Structure, Processes and Boundaries) and System 4 (Structure and Boundaries) are significantly higher than the corresponding theoretical frequencies of independent joint adoption of their components. This is not the case in Japan and in the USA where the differences between actual and expected frequencies are not statistically different from zero for all the four possible systems.

We should remember the presence of some systematic differences between the samples that might affect systemic and holistic change, but which we are not able to control. The companies in the samples were drawn from the population of medium and large organizations in all the regional surveys. However, US firms are much larger than UK ones, with firms in Continental Europe being somewhere in between (Table 7.5). We do not have access to the size of Japanese companies.

Does large size impede systemic organizational changes? Should we expect more or less holistic changes in companies which are considerably larger? Do the highly integrated organizational structures in Japan make them more likely to introduce holistic changes? In the bottom part of Table 7.4 only the UK presents statistical differences between observed and theoretical changes in System 1, and, with a smaller level of significance (10–11 per cent) in Systems 2 and 4. No System variable in German-speaking countries shows a significant difference with the theoretical frequency. These findings suggest that very large firms, like the US ones, are less likely to adopt systems of organizational changes, compared to relatively smaller firms.

The analysis in this section has provided further evidence of the nature and extent of regional differences in the adoption of organizational changes. Consistent with the descriptive results on adoption of individual organizational changes between 1992 and 1996 reported in Chapter 1, we have found

TABLE 7.4  *Test on independence of organizational changes, 1992–93 to 1996–97*

| | Europe | | | Japan | | | USA | | |
|---|---|---|---|---|---|---|---|---|---|
| | Freq. | Exp. Freq. | z (prob.) | Freq. | Exp. Freq. | z (prob.) | Freq. | Exp. Freq. | z (prob.) |
| System 1 S + P + B | 13.0 | 10.2 | **1.936** (0.026) | 1.2 | 1.0 | 0.222 (0.412) | 8.9 | 7.7 | 0.383 (0.351) |
| System 2 S + P | 25.1 | 22.7 | 1.176 (0.120) | 4.7 | 3.3 | 1.183 (0.118) | 12.7 | 13.5 | −0.229 (0.591) |
| System 3 P + B | 34.0 | 33.6 | 0.239 (0.406) | 18.7 | 16.5 | 0.938 (0.174) | 46.8 | 46.9 | −0.006 (0.502) |
| System 4 S + B | 16.4 | 13.6 | **1.715** (0.043) | 1.6 | 1.9 | −0.418 (0.662) | 11.4 | 9.4 | 0.616 (0.269) |

| | Europe | | | UK | | | German-speaking countries | | |
|---|---|---|---|---|---|---|---|---|---|
| | Freq. | Exp. freq. | z (prob.) | Freq. | Exp. freq. | z (prob.) | Freq. | Exp. freq. | z (prob.) |
| System 1 S + P + B | 13.0 | 10.2 | **1.936** (0.026) | 14.0 | 10.1 | **1.701** (0.044) | 14.0 | 13.6 | 0.112 (0.455) |
| System 2 S + P | 25.1 | 22.7 | 1.176 (0.120) | 25.7 | 21.8 | 1.247 (0.106) | 30.8 | 30.4 | 0.094 (0.462) |
| System 3 P + B | 34.0 | 33.6 | 0.239 (0.406) | 36.3 | 36.3 | 0.013 (0.495) | 34.6 | 34.0 | 0.135 (0.446) |
| System 4 S + B | 16.4 | 13.6 | **1.715** (0.043) | 16.2 | 12.9 | **1.295** (0.098) | 18.7 | 18.0 | 0.179 (0.429) |

*Source:* INNFORM programme survey

TABLE 7.5 *Company size across regions*

| Employees (thousands) | US N = 73 | Europe N = 315 | UK N = 162 | Continental Europe N = 153 |
|---|---|---|---|---|
| Average | 20.79 | 11.08 | 6.51 | 15.95 |
| Median | 5.66 | 1.16 | 0.96 | 1.50 |

*Source*: INNFORM programme

here strong regional differences in the adoption of multiple and systemic changes. We found overall diversity in the frequencies of multiple and systemic indicators across the three regions. The proportion of Japanese companies adopting multiple and systemic changes are always significantly lower than Western companies, confirming the lower degree of change not only in individual organizational dimensions but also in multiple dimensions. The higher proportions found in Europe are related to firms introducing changes in Structure and their combinations with Processes and Boundaries, that is, System 1, the most comprehensive system combination, and the combination with Processes (System 2).

The second important finding from this section is that in Europe higher than expected percentages of companies introduce systemic changes within organizations compared to the USA and Japan. The smaller size of European companies compared to US organizations might be behind this finding. We found stronger evidence in the regional breakdown of Europe, especially in the UK where firms are relatively smaller. It seems plausible to relate this finding to the size of the organizations: medium sized organizations are more likely to change in multiple dimensions compared to very large firms. However, there may be other institutional factors which affect the adoption of bundles or systems of organizational and managerial changes (see Chapter 12 for a discussion of these issues).

## COMPLEMENTARITIES IN ORGANIZATIONAL CHANGES AND CORPORATE PERFORMANCE: MODELS AND RESULTS

In the previous section we found that the majority of the firms in our samples introduced organizational changes in their structure and boundaries. We also found that the biggest changes were in processes. Previous analysis using the INNFORM survey data showed that partial implementation of the full set of organizational innovations can have little or even a negative effect on performance and only the complete set has clear positive performance effects. In that analysis, however, the focus was on the high adopters of new organizational practices, and, like most empirical work on complementarities and performance, the analysis was carried out at one point in time. Also Milgrom and Roberts (1990) acknowledge that their analysis, which is suggestive about the nature of the path of the modern manufacturing strategy, is static and only partially captures the notion of change underlying the definition of complementarities.

The aim of the present analysis is to develop models to test the *dynamic* relation between complementarities and performance. In particular, are firms introducing multiple or systemic *changes* more likely to *improve* their performance? And is introducing partial or piecemeal change associated with decreasing returns?

The previous section also reports evidence on different regional patterns of systemic changes. Can we expect different effects of complementarities on company performance across regions, or is this relationship typically invariant across regions? We have argued that national institutional features might favour some combinations of organizational changes. Although we do not measure these factors, do institutions and cultural setting affect also the impact of systems of organizational changes on corporate performance, or do systemic organizational changes offer the same premium in performance in different regions? We have not found any previous research comparing the complementarities and performance relationship in different regions. However, given the discrepancies in the percentages of adoption we expect varied patterns in the regional analysis.

We first estimate models of the effect of complementary organizational changes on corporate performance for the whole sample and then we explore regional effects with specific models for each region. We can only test this effect in the Western sample because we do not have information of the performance of Japanese firms. The general model we estimate is:

$$\Delta \text{ Performance} = f(\Delta \text{Organizational Innovations})$$

where the symbol delta indicates we are dealing with the differences between 1992 and 1996. Among the organizational innovations variables we have individual components, the multiple, composite indicators and the system variables.

Since most available performance data derives from the survey and are mainly categorical, in a 1 to 5 Likert scale, we use ordered Probit models. These models are used to estimate a relationship between an ordinal-dependent variable and a set of independent variables. Standard Least Square techniques require a continuous dependent variable and therefore are not suitable for our data.

In Ordered Probit models an underlying score is estimated as a linear function of the independent variables and a set of cut points. The probability of observing outcome *i* corresponds to the probability that the estimated linear function, plus random error, is within the range of the cut points estimates for the outcome:

$$\Pr(outcome_j = i) = \Pr\left(k_{i-1} < \beta_1 x_{1j} + \beta_1 x_{1j} + \cdots + \beta_1 x_{1j} + u_j \leq \kappa_i\right)$$

where the random error $u_j$ is assumed to be normally distributed. The model estimates the $k$ coefficients $\beta$s along with the *I-1* cut points, where *I* is the number of possible outcomes, in our case five. Ordered Probit models are a generalization of ordinary binary probit models. The actual values taken on by the dependent variables are irrelevant except that larger values are assumed to correspond to a higher outcome. An alternative to the (ordered) Probit model would be the (ordered) Logit model. They differ in the assumption on the error term, normally distributed in the former, logistically in the latter. They are similar distributions, except in the tails, which are thicker in the logistic. In most applications they do not differ (Greene, 1993). Probit, and Logit, models test the effect of the impact of changes in x on the probability of the dependent variable. Note that in Probit and Logit models higher significance levels (10–20 per cent) can be considered as evidence of a relationship between the variables.

In addition to the organizational innovations which represent the internal organizational strategy we included external environmental factors, captured by the firm's market share, as a control term for changes in performance (Hay and Morris, 1991).

The performance data for the UK were collected from the CD-Database Onesource. We used changes in the return of capital employed between 1992 and 1996. However, the measure for performance for the rest of the sample is derived from the questionnaire. It is a 1 to 5 scale of self-reported changes in performance in the four-year period between 1992 and 1996. This information was used for Continental European firms because of the difficulty of obtaining reliable and comparable published financial performance data in Continental Europe. Therefore the survey instrument for Continental European firms included two additional questions on the relative financial performance compared to other companies in the same industry/sector, and changes in performance over the period under analysis. These questions were also included in the US survey.

In order to undertake a general analysis on the effect of organizational changes on performance in the pooled sample, and use the same models as in the rest of the sample, British companies have been ranked, divided in quintiles and given the corresponding value from 1 to 5 to provide measures consistent with the 1 to 5 Likert scale in the rest of the sample. Although the use of self-reported scales could introduce a bias, this allows a more comprehensive analysis than would otherwise be possible. Previous research has shown high levels of convergence between such subjective estimates of performance and more objective measures (Dess and Robinson, 1984; Hart and Banbury, 1994).

Tables 7.6 to 7.9 summarize the estimates of the ordered probit models respectively for the whole sample of Western companies, the UK, German-speaking countries, and the USA. For each region, we estimate a set of models to test the effect on performance of the individual organizational changes;

the composite variables; individual and composite variables; the four systems; systems and individual; systems and composite; and all variables systems, composite and individual variables. The analysis of the pooled sample also allows comparisons with the static analysis from the INNFORM survey (Whittington et al., 1999).

Some models, generally those with the individual organizational change variables, include a high number of variables. We follow a general to specific process to derive a reduced model with significant variables. We start with a complete, general model where we include all the organizational variables that we assume affect corporate performance according to the theory, then we delete non-significant variables, one by one, starting from the least significant, to obtain a more parsimonious model. In some cases, when we have a limited number of observations (German-speaking countries and the USA) this becomes necessary to obtain robust estimations of significant variables. In Tables 7.6 to 7.9 we report the results for the general, starting models and the reduced models. The diagnostics reported at the bottom of the tables indicate that the variables in the analysis are jointly significant. In some cases, when a large number of variables are entered in the model, the Chi-square test for the joint significance of the included explanatory variables is not significant, and we only obtain significant diagnostics after deleting some of the non-significant variables. In these cases, the general model illustrated in the table is the first reduced model with jointly significant variables. The reduced models reported have been carefully selected by checking the changes of the significance levels in the coefficients and diagnostics at each step of the deletion process and, when necessary, investigating alternative deletion routes.

Table 7.6 provides the results for the models estimated in the entire sample of Western companies. The first two columns are for the model with individual variables: Column 1 presents the model with the full set of individual variables and Column 2 the reduced model. After the deletion process the only significant variables are changes in Project-based structure, New HR practices, and Outsourcing. New HR practices and Outsourcing have positive coefficients and are consistent with the recent evidence on the complementarities between organizational change and corporate performance. However, increasing Project-based structure has a negative effect on changes in performance, and this seems to contrast with the relatively widespread practice of structuring organizations by projects. In this model, changes in market shares have only a weak positive effect on changes in performance, indicating that external factors like a stronger position in the market over the four-year period can increase corporate performance. This result emerges in most models for the pooled sample reported in Table 7.6.

Column 3 reports the model with the three composite variables, Structure, Processes and Boundaries. None of them is significant and none increases in significance with the deletion process, therefore the reduced model is not reported here. This result is not inconsistent with the previous model where we found one significant variable per composite variable, Project-based structure for Structure, New HR practices for Processes, and Outsourcing for Boundaries. A significant composite variable would already signal some complementary effects between the components of the multiple indicator of a particular organizational dimension, Structure, Processes and Boundaries.

As we expected from the previous results, the model with individual and composite variables (columns 4 and 5) provides similar results to columns 1 and 2, but, in addition to Project-based structure, New HR practices, and Outsourcing, Vertical networking shows a positive effect on changes in performance. This finding is also consistent with the literature on the importance of enhancing vertical linkages communication and relationships while increasing horizontal flexibility and autonomy. However, here only increasing Vertical networking is likely to increase returns to the organization.

The rest of the table shows models with the system variables by themselves, with individual variables, with the composite variable, and all together. Columns 6 and 7 illustrate the estimations of the model with the System variables, respectively the general model and the reduced one. Both columns show that only the full set of organizational changes (System 1) has a positive effect on corporate performance. However, the diagnostics indicate the result is not strong. This emerges also when the model includes also individual variables (columns 8 and 9), composite variables (columns 10 and 11), and all variables, system, composite and individual (columns 12 and 13), and the diagnostics improve when individual variables are included. The positive effect of the adoption of systemic organizational changes is obtained invariably in all these models. We also find confirmation of the effect of the individual variables which were significant in the previous model specifications, HR practices and Outsourcing, with a positive effect on changes in performance and Project-based structure with negative effect (columns 2 and 13). The reduced model with systemic and composite variables (column 11) is similar to the model with only systems (column 7) and shows the improvement in the diagnostic after dropping market share.

However, the model with system and individual variables (column 9) also reveals a negative effect of Systems 2 and 3 on the changes of corporate performance. Therefore the results in the dynamic models are similar to the static analysis of complementarities from the INNFORM survey: changes in corporate performance are reduced by the adoption of partial systems of organizational changes, while the adoption of the whole system of changes in Structure, Processes and Boundaries (System 1) increases company performance. In these models we also find a milder effect of introducing stronger Vertical and Horizontal networking in addition to New HR practices and Outsourcing on performance (column 9).

These findings represent an important addition to the empirical analysis of complementarities and performance, because of the *dynamic* nature of the present analysis which relates *changes* in systems of organizational changes to *changes* in corporate performance.

This evidence refers to the pooled sample of large organizations in Europe and the USA. However, given the differences in the adoption of organizational changes across regions, discussed above, we investigate the complementarities–performance relationship in three regions, the UK, German-speaking countries and the USA.

Table 7.7 reports the results of the ordered Probit models for the UK. Columns 1 and 2 show the estimations of the model with the full set of individual variables, respectively the general model and the reduced model obtained through the deletion process of insignificant variables. We observe clear differences from the pooled analysis. Here we find that changes in Vertical networking, Strategic decentralization, and Strategic alliances have a positive effect on changes in corporate performance. Differently from the previous analysis, Project-based structure and Outsourcing are not significant, and, surprisingly, New HR practices are likely to reduce performance. This last finding contrasts with some empirical literature on complementarities, which is focused on the adoption of a range of HR practices. Surprisingly Market share also has a negative effect on corporate performance. The negative sign of changes in Market share appears in other models in Table 7.7, and tends not to be significant in the models with system variables.

Columns 3 and 4 report the models with the composite variables. The reduced model (column 4) indicates that, in the UK, changing Boundaries by Outsourcing, engaging in Strategic Alliances or refocusing the range of business have a significant positive effect on performance. We know from Table 7.3 that almost 50 per cent of UK companies are introducing changes in Boundaries. However, when both individual and composite variables are included in the same model (columns 5 and 6) Boundaries are only weakly significant in the general model (column 5), and Structure and Processes are significant, but negative. In the reduced model (column 6), the negative effect of Structure and Processes on changes on performance is accompanied by changes in their individual components. We found a negative effect of Delayering and a positive effect of Strategic decentralization, which constitute Structure, and a positive effect of Vertical networking and a negative effect of New HR practices, which are elements of Changing Processes, but the net effect of the individual components of both Structure and Processes is positive.

The remaining part of Table 7.7 reports estimates of the models with the systems variables and their variations. Column 7 is for the general model with the four systems, and columns 8 and 9 report the results of two reduced models, derived from two alternative deletion processes. The general model with the system variables (column 7) indicates that System 1 (Structure, Processes and Boundaries) and 4 (Structure and Boundaries) have a positive

TABLE 7.6 Ordered Probit estimates of the relationship between changes in company performance and changes in organizational Design system. Dependent variable is changes in firm performance in the period 1992–93 to 1996–97 – whole sample of Western firms

| | Individual | | Composite | Indiv. + Comp. | | System | | System + Individ. | | Sys + Comp. | | All variables | |
|---|---|---|---|---|---|---|---|---|---|---|---|---|---|
| | | Reduced | | | Reduced | | Reduced | | Reduced | | Reduced | | Reduced |
| Variable | (1) | (2) | (3) | (4) | (5) | (6) | (7) | (8) | (9) | (10) | (11) | (12) | (13) |
| Market share | 0.071 | 0.091 | 0.063 | 0.074 | 0.077 | 0.067 | 0.064 | 0.079 | 0.087 | 0.066 | | 0.080 | 0.092 |
| | [0.254] | [0.134] | [0.284] | [0.235] | [0.205] | [0.258] | [0.275] | [0.209] | [0.159] | [0.260] | | [0.200] | [0.133] |
| System 1 | | | | | | 0.501 | 0.253 | 0.528 | 0.540 | 0.829 | 0.223 | 0.469 | 0.243 |
| | | | | | | [0.188] | [0.116] | [0.059] | [0.050] | [0.147] | [0.136] | [0.084] | [0.182] |
| System 2 | | | | | | −0.138 | | −0.389 | −0.344 | −0.507 | | −0.330 | |
| | | | | | | [0.397] | | [0.071] | [0.099] | [0.246] | | [0.124] | |
| System 3 | | | | | | −0.039 | | −0.203 | −0.236 | −0.085 | | | |
| | | | | | | [0.763] | | [0.222] | [0.132] | [0.749] | | | |
| System 4 | | | | | | −0.102 | | | | −0.406 | | | |
| | | | | | | [0.708] | | | | [0.426] | | | |
| Structure | | | 0.044 | | | | | | | 0.346 | | | |
| | | | [0.696] | | | | | | | [0.388] | | | |
| Processes | | | 0.045 | −0.152 | | | | | | 0.087 | | | |
| | | | [0.694] | [0.349] | | | | | | [0.599] | | | |
| Boundaries | | | 0.039 | | | | | | | 0.087 | | | |
| | | | [0.704] | | | | | | | [0.599] | | | |
| Delayering | | | | | | | | | | | | | |
| Project-based structure | −0.107 | −0.079 | | −0.106 | −0.081 | | | −0.087 | −0.085 | | | −0.090 | −0.095 |
| | [0.067] | [0.153] | | [0.068] | [0.148] | | | [0.152] | [0.160] | | | [0.138] | [0.091] |
| Operational decentr. | 0.023 | | | 0.021 | | | | 0.033 | | | | | |
| | [0.741] | | | [0.753] | | | | [0.648] | | | | | |
| Strategic decentr. | 0.035 | | | 0.034 | | | | 0.055 | 0.064 | | | 0.081 | |
| | [0.676] | | | [0.678] | | | | [0.509] | [0.342] | | | [0.240] | |

(Continued)

TABLE 7.6 (Continued)

| | Individual | | Composite | Indiv. + Comp. | | System | | System + Individ. | | Sys + Comp. | | All variables | |
|---|---|---|---|---|---|---|---|---|---|---|---|---|---|
| Variable | (1) | Reduced (2) | (3) | (4) | Reduced (5) | (6) | Reduced (7) | (8) | Reduced (9) | (10) | Reduced (11) | (12) | Reduced (13) |
| Vertical networking | 0.081 [0.514] | | | 0.104 [0.397] | 0.139 [0.101] | | | 0.106 [0.392] | 0.184 [0.043] | | | 0.122 [0.309] | 0.130 [0.155] |
| Horizontal networking | 0.115 [0.362] | | | 0.155 [0.239] | | | | 0.130 [0.311] | 0.153 [0.122] | | | 0.131 [0.322] | |
| IT | 0.017 [0.830] | | | | | | | 0.016 [0.836] | | | | | |
| New HR practices | 0.111 [0.284] | 0.139 [0.125] | | 0.147 [0.164] | 0.121 [0.199] | | | 0.150 [0.159] | | | | 0.142 [0.166] | 0.130 [0.155] |
| Downscoping | −0.144 [0.405] | | | −0.141 [0.416] | | | | −0.138 [0.464] | | | | −0.152 [0.422] | |
| Strat. alliances Outsourcing | 0.244 [0.039] | 0.219 [0.052] | | 0.248 [0.034] | 0.230 [0.043] | | | 0.272 [0.039] | 0.280 [0.027] | | | 0.261 [0.061] | 0.188 [0.103] |
| Observations | 377 | 402 | 449 | 377 | 395 | 449 | 449 | 377 | 382 | 449 | 495 | 379 | 402 |
| Test of incl. variables $\chi^2$ (d.f.) | $\chi^2(10) =$ 15.87 | $\chi^2(4) =$ 9.54 | $\chi^2(4) =$ 1.75 | $\chi^2(10) =$ 16.70 | $\chi^2(5) =$ 12.33 | $\chi^2(5) =$ 4.52 | $\chi^2(2) =$ 3.71 | $\chi^2(13) =$ 20.41 | $\chi^2(9) =$ 18.42 | $\chi^2(8) =$ 5.41 | $\chi^2(1) =$ 2.23 | $\chi^2(12) =$ 19.48 | $\chi^2(5) =$ 11.33 |
| (prob.) | (0.104) | (0.049) | (0.781) | (0.081) | (0.031) | (0.478) | (0.157) | (0.086) | (0.031) | (0.713) | (0.135) | (0.078) | (0.045) |
| Pseudo $R^2$ | 0.014 | 0.008 | 0.001 | 0.015 | 0.010 | 0.003 | 0.003 | 0.018 | 0.016 | 0.004 | 0.002 | 0.017 | 0.009 |
| $\theta_1$ | −0.787 (0.398) | −0.737 (0.366) | −1.311 (0.129) | −0.740 (0.397) | −0.739 (0.370) | −1.379 (0.099) | −1.347 (0.088) | −0.665 (0.408) | −0.692 (0.388) | −1.317 (0.155) | −1.376 (0.083) | −0.800 (0.387) | −0.783 (0.367) |
| $\theta_2$ | −0.127 (0.396) | −0.116 (0.363) | −0.664 (0.116) | −0.077 (0.396) | −0.114 (0.368) | −0.730 (0.082) | −0.699 (0.069) | 0.002 (0.407) | −0.029 (0.386) | −0.667 (0.145) | −0.720 (0.065) | −0.133 (0.385) | −0.162 (0.365) |
| $\theta_3$ | 0.420 (0.396) | 0.406 (0.363) | −0.174 (0.113) | 0.471 (0.396) | 0.416 (0.368) | −0.239 (0.077) | −0.209 (0.064) | 0.552 (0.408) | 0.516 (0.387) | −0.175 (0.142) | −0.239 (0.060) | 0.415 (0.385) | 0.361 (0.364) |
| $\theta_4$ | 1.269 (0.398) | 1.249 (0.365) | 0.628 (0.115) | 1.320 (0.398) | 1.263 (0.370) | 0.566 (0.079) | 0.596 (0.067) | 1.405 (0.410) | 1.382 (0.389) | 0.631 (0.145) | 0.578 (0.062) | 1.275 (0.387) | 1.207 (0.367) |

In square brackets: probabilities for independent variables; in round brackets: standard errors for ancillary parameters.

effect, and Systems 2 (Structure and Processes) and 3 (Processes and Boundaries) have a negative effect, but System 3 is not significant. The reduction process brings two alternative models, one with Systems 1 and 2 (column 8) and a model with Systems 2 and 4 (column 9), both with very similar diagnostics and net effect of changes in the systems. This might be due to high correlation between Systems 1 and 4 (see the Appendix to this chapter). The model with Systems 1 and 2 (column 8) clearly indicates that introducing only changes in Structure and Processes has a negative effect on firm performance, whereas adopting the full set of systemic changes, Structure, Processes and Boundaries has a positive effect on the likelihood of increasing performance. This result supports the complementarities and performance relation that piecemeal changes in organizations tend to reduce returns, whereas changing a set of complementary dimensions at the same time seems to improve financial performance.

The models with individual and system variables provide very similar reduced models (columns 10 to 17). The significant individual variables are the same as in the reduced model with individual and composite variables, mainly Delayering and New HR practices, with a negative sign, and Strategic decentralization and Vertical networking with a positive sign. Continuing the reduction process we obtain models where only Strategic decentralization among the individual variables is significant, System 2 is negative and System 1 (column 12) and System 4 (column 16) have a positive sign.

The intermediate models obtained during the reduction process (columns 11 and 14) signal other weak, but interesting effects underlying the relationship between organizational changes and performance in our UK sample. Thus in the columns we see the negative effects of Delayering, of New HR practices, Horizontal networking and Downscoping. Meanwhile, positive performance effects are associated with the introduction of Vertical networking, Strategic alliances and Outsourcing.

The final model with composite and system variables (column 17) only has System 4 (Structure and Boundaries) and Structure. System 4 exhibits a positive coefficient and Structure a negative coefficient indicating that changing only Structure is likely to reduce company performance, but the combination of Structure with Boundaries is likely to increase performance. This again is consistent with complementarities theory.

Overall the findings for the UK indicate that among the structural changes Strategic decentralization and Vertical networking have positive effects on changes in performance, and Delayering and New HR practices have a negative effect. When these individual changes are introduced with other elements which have no effect on performance if introduced in isolation, only changes in Boundaries have a positive effect on performance, whereas changes in Structure and Processes have negative effects. However, when UK firms introduce changes in Structure and Boundaries by themselves, or jointly with Processes, these combinations provide higher effects on Performance than Structure and Processes individually.

The regression results for German-speaking countries are described in Table 7.8. Columns 1 and 2 report the estimations of the model with individual organizational elements. The reduced model (column 2) presents the same results as the pooled analysis (Table 7.6), positive effect of New HR practices and a negative effect of introducing a project-based structure. Also Changes in market share have a significant, positive effect on Changes in performance. This result appears in all models for German-speaking countries, and often the significance improves in the more parsimonious models. The negative effect of introducing a Project-based structure is somehow surprising because organizing by projects seems to be widely adopted in this region compared with the other regions, and we would expect to find a positive effect on corporate performance. It could be, however, that the short-run effect of implementing such new organizational structures is a reduction of performance; or it could be that the implementation of such practice in isolation is likely to reduce performance, but if introduced with other, complementary organizational changes can improve firm performance. We can test this hypothesis in the next models with composite and systemic variables. The model with the composite variables (columns 3 and 4) supports the hypothesis of complementarity effects. Although weakly, Changes in structure, which includes Delayering, Project-based structure, Strategic and Operational decentralization, is the only significant variable among the three dimensions. Therefore, when a Project-based structure is adopted with other structural elements we found a positive effect on corporate performance. When the composite variables are entered in the model with the individual elements (columns 5 and 6), the significance of Changes in structure improves and its coefficient increases. In addition to the individual elements found in Column 2, positive New HR practices and negative Project-based structure, we also find that Operational decentralization and Strategic decentralization have a weak negative effect on performance. The three elements with the negative coefficient are components of Changes in structure and the sum of their coefficients is lower than the coefficient of Changes in structure, which indicate that introducing organizational changes in bundles can yield a premium, whereas introducing isolated changes can be detrimental to performance.

Similar findings emerge from the models with systemic changes, in the various versions, without other variables and with individual and composite elements. In the model with the systemic variables (columns 7 and 8) only System 2 (Structure and Processes) and System 4 (Structure and Boundaries) are significant, the former with a positive coefficient, the latter with a negative, but lower coefficient. This result is in clear contrast with those for the pooled analysis and the analysis for the UK. In the former, the full set of changes (System 1) has a positive effect on changes in performance; in the UK analysis the combination of changes in Structure and Processes

**TABLE 7.7** Ordered Probit estimates of the relationship between changes in company performance and changes in organizational design system; dependent variable is Changes in firm performance in the period 1992–93 to 1996–97 – UK

| Variable | Individual | | Composite | | Indiv. + Comp. | | System | | | System Individual A | | | System Individual B | | | Sys. + Comp. | |
|---|---|---|---|---|---|---|---|---|---|---|---|---|---|---|---|---|---|
| | | Reduc. | | Reduc. | | Reduc. | | Reduc. A | Reduc. B | | Reduc. | RERed. | | Reduc. | RERed. | | Reduc. |
| | (1) | (2) | (3) | (4) | (5) | (6) | (7) | (8) | (9) | (10) | (11) | (12) | (13) | (14) | (15) | (16) | (17) |
| Market share | -0.178 [0.184] | -0.210 [0.103] | -0.166 [0.182] | | -0.158 [0.239] | | -0.139 [0.269] | | | -0.054 [0.705] | | | -0.052 [0.716] | | | 0.119 [0.872] | |
| System 1 | | | | | | | 0.553 [0.480] | 1.110 [0.001] | | 1.327 [0.009] | 1.176 [0.009] | 1.089 [0.003] | | | | | |
| System 2 | | | | | | | -0.494 [0.074] | -0.572 [0.023] | -0.485 [0.040] | -1.307 [0.002] | -1.067 [0.002] | -0.755 [0.008] | -1.262 [0.003] | -1.055 [0.002] | -0.702 [0.009] | | |
| System 3 | | | | | | | -0.050 [0.827] | | | -0.509 [0.208] | -0.483 [0.102] | | -0.468 [0.244] | -0.125 [0.654] | | -0.055 [0.899] | |
| System 4 | | | | | | | 0.537 [0.394] | | 0.985 [0.001] | | | | 1.358 [0.006] | 1.256 [0.003] | 1.073 [0.001] | 0.914 [0.211] | 1.107 [0.001] |
| Structure | | | 0.034 [0.869] | | -0.533 [0.085] | -0.417 [0.144] | | | | | | | | | | -0.511 [0.066] | -0.560 [0.027] |
| Processes | | | -0.077 [0.724] | | -0.500 [0.106] | -0.460 [0.091] | | | | | | | | | | -0.034 [0.902] | |
| Boundaries | | | 0.287 [0.110] | 0.376 [0.024] | 0.330 [0.187] | | | | | | | | | | | 0.134 [0.714] | |
| Delayering | -0.074 [0.416] | | | | -0.145 [0.168] | -0.170 [0.073] | | | | -0.181 [0.101] | -0.163 [0.096] | | -0.163 [0.146] | -0.158 [0.111] | | | |
| Project-based structure | | | | | | | | | | 0.090 [0.520] | | | 0.073 [0.605] | | | | |
| Operation decentr. | | | | | | | | | | -0.038 [0.786] | | | -0.050 [0.725] | | | | |
| Strategic decentr. | 0.133 [0.235] | 0.146 [0.177] | | | 0.237 [0.061] | 0.228 [0.044] | | | | 0.295 [0.075] | 0.246 [0.032] | 0.216 [0.040] | 0.289 [0.081] | 0.231 [0.047] | 0.189 [0.073] | | |

(Continued)

TABLE 7.7 (Continued)

| Variable | Individual | | Composite | | Indiv. + Comp. | | | System | | System Individual A | | | System Individual B | | | Sys. + Comp. | |
| | Reduc. | | Reduc. | | Reduc. | | | Reduc A | Reduc B | | Reduc. | RERed. | | Reduc. | RERed. | | Reduc. |
| | (1) | (2) | (3) | (4) | (5) | (6) | (7) | (8) | (9) | (10) | (11) | (12) | (13) | (14) | (15) | (16) | (17) |
|---|---|---|---|---|---|---|---|---|---|---|---|---|---|---|---|---|---|
| Vertical networks | 0.379 [0.038] | 0.282 [0.060] | | | 0.470 [0.009] | 0.326 [0.044] | | | | 0.540 [0.015] | 0.243 [0.122] | | 0.527 [0.018] | 0.357 [0.065] | | | |
| Horizontal networks | | | | | | | | | | -0.156 [0.536] | | | -0.138 [0.584] | -0.208 [0.345] | | | |
| IT | -0.215 [0.143] | | | | | | | | | -0.098 [0.532] | | | -0.086 [0.583] | | | | |
| New HR practices | -0.241 [0.146] | -0.274 [0.081] | | | -0.241 [0.153] | -0.201 [0.207] | | | | -0.182 [0.290] | -0.199 [0.207] | | -0.187 [0.278] | -0.201 [0.206] | | | |
| Downscope | | | | | -0.441 [0.144] | | | | | -0.169 [0.596] | | | -0.173 [0.586] | -0.296 [0.272] | | | |
| Strategic alliances | 0.283 [0.165] | 0.269 [0.170] | | | | | | | | 0.276 [0.297] | 0.248 [0.279] | | 0.239 [0.372] | | | | |
| Outsourcing | 0.192 [0.357] | | | | | | | | | 0.318 [0.236] | 0.232 [0.289] | | 0.276 [0.310] | | | | |
| Observation | 118 | 123 | 144 | 164 | 118 | 133 | 144 | 164 | 164 | 110 | 133 | 149 | 110 | 132 | 149 | 164 | 164 |
| Test of incl. vrbles χ²(d.f.) | χ²(8)= 13.19 | χ²(5)= 11.93 | χ²(4)= 4.71 | χ²(1)= 5.10 | χ²(9)= 17.10 | χ²(6)= 12.28 | χ²(5)= 11.01 | χ²(2)= 11.46 | χ²(2)= 11.47 | χ²(15)= 23.09 | χ²(9)= 20.30 | χ²(3)= 14.39 | χ²(15)= 23.99 | χ²(9)= 21.85 | χ²(3)= 15.68 | χ²(6)= 12.49 | χ²(2)= 12.17 |
| (prob.) | (0.105) | (0.036) | (0.318) | (0.024) | (0.047) | (0.056) | (0.051) | (0.003) | (0.003) | (0.082) | (0.016) | (0.002) | (0.065) | (0.009) | (0.001) | (0.052) | (0.002) |
| Pseudo R² | 0.035 | 0.030 | 0.010 | 0.010 | 0.045 | 0.029 | 0.024 | 0.022 | 0.022 | 0.066 | 0.048 | 0.030 | 0.068 | 0.052 | 0.033 | 0.024 | 0.023 |

(Continued)

TABLE 7.7 (Continued)

| Variable | Individual | | Composite | | Indiv. + Comp. | | System | | | System Individual A | | | System Individual B | | | Sys. + Comp. | |
|---|---|---|---|---|---|---|---|---|---|---|---|---|---|---|---|---|---|
| | Reduc. | | Reduc. | | Reduc. | | Reduc. | Reduc A | Reduc B | Reduc. | Reduc. | RERed. | Reduc. | Reduc. | RERed. | Reduc. | Reduc. |
| | (1) | (2) | (3) | (4) | (5) | (6) | (7) | (8) | (9) | (10) | (11) | (12) | (13) | (14) | (15) | (16) | (17) |
| $\theta_1$ | −1.513 | −1.589 | −0.820 | −0.700 | −1.88 | −1.771 | −0.906 | −0.891 | −0.867 | −1.392 | −1.374 | −0.928 | −1.431 | −1.65 | −0.918 | −0.866 | −0.880 |
| | (0.653) | (0.612) | (0.225) | (0.133) | (0.638) | (0.613) | (0.152) | (0.125) | (0.125) | (0.702) | (0.635) | (0.133) | (0.703) | (0.615) | (0.133) | (0.250) | (0.126) |
| $\theta_2$ | −0.970 | −1.025 | −0.218 | −0.099 | −1.33 | −1.200 | −0.298 | −0.281 | −0.256 | −0.796 | −0.793 | −0.286 | −0.834 | −1.067 | −0.276 | −0.254 | −0.269 |
| | (0.651) | (0.609) | (0.217) | (0.123) | (0.634) | (0.610) | (0.139) | (0.112) | (0.112) | (0.700) | (0.633) | (0.118) | (0.701) | (0.612) | (0.118) | (0.244) | (0.113) |
| $\theta_3$ | −0.388 | −0.443 | 0.300 | 0.401 | −0.725 | −0.615 | 0.234 | 0.233 | 0.257 | −0.126 | −0.194 | 0.270 | −0.162 | −0.460 | 0.284 | 0.261 | 0.246 |
| | (0.645) | (0.604) | (0.214) | (0.124) | (0.628) | (0.606) | (0.136) | (0.110) | (0.111) | (0.696) | (0.629) | (0.117) | (0.696) | (0.609) | (0.117) | (0.242) | (0.111) |
| $\theta_4$ | 0.206 | 0.158 | 0.858 | 1.000 | −0.116 | 0.009 | 0.813 | 0.850 | 0.874 | 0.532 | 0.460 | 0.915 | 0.499 | 0.182 | 0.935 | 0.882 | 0.865 |
| | (0.643) | (0.601) | (0.220) | (0.138) | (0.624) | (0.603) | (0.147) | (0.123) | (0.124) | (0.694) | (0.627) | (0.131) | (0.693) | (0.606) | (0.132) | (0.247) | (0.125) |

In square brackets: probabilities for independent variables; in round brackets: standard errors for ancillary parameters

(System 2) is negative, and this effect is counter-balanced by either System 1 or System 4.

When systemic and individual variables are entered in the same model (columns 9 and 10), only System 2 is significant; System 4 is no longer significant and, among the individual elements, New HR practices has a positive effect on performance, Project-based structure is negative, Operational decentralization and Strategic decentralization are both weakly significant and negative (columns 11 and 12) as in the previous case (columns 5 and 6). In this model a new element, Horizontal networking, is significant and negative. Like Project-based structure, this practice is widely adopted by German-speaking firms and therefore this result is somewhat unexpected. However, as in the case of Project-based structure, we find that when this element is combined with other structural and procedural practices constituting System 2, the joint adoption brings a higher performance premium compared to the individual adoption. This again is consistent with complementarities theory. This is also supported by the models with systemic and composite variables (columns 13 and 14) where Structure and Processes have a negative effect on performance if introduced separately, but their combined adoption as System 2 offers a premium increasing the probability of positive changes in firm performance. We do not report the model with the entire set of variables, individual, composite and systemic, because it provides a reduced model identical to the model with systems and individual variables (columns 10, 11 and 12). Moreover, given the low number of observations, the estimates of the complete model would not be robust.

Finally, Table 7.9 reports the results of the models for US firms. We do not find any individual negative effect in the US. The model with individual variables (columns 1 and 2) reports a positive effect for Operational decentralization and Horizontal networking. Between the two variables, Horizontal networking exhibits a higher coefficient with a higher level of significance. These variables did not emerge as affecting corporate performance in other regions, or in the pooled analysis. Compared to the other regions, more companies in the US have introduced stronger Horizontal networking. We should remember that US companies are also larger than European companies and might require a stronger implementation of horizontal links which connect distant and peripheral units. Our models show that reinforcing Horizontal networking in larger organizations has a positive effect on performance. Higher degrees of operational discretionality, which could be particularly important to increase flexibility in larger organizations, also have a positive effect on the likelihood of higher corporate performance. Increased Market share is significant in all models and clearly illustrates the impact of such external factors in the corporate performance of US companies. This clear, strong effect of market shares on performance only emerges in this region.

**TABLE 7.8** Ordered Probit estimates of the relationship between changes in company performance and changes in organizational design system. Dependent variable is Changes in firm performance in the period 1992–93 to 1996–97 – German-speaking countries

| Variable | Individual | | Composite | | Individual + Comp. | | System | | System + Individual | | | | Sys. + Comp. | |
|---|---|---|---|---|---|---|---|---|---|---|---|---|---|---|
| | | Reduc. | | Reduc. | | Reduc. | | Reduc. | | Reduc. | Reduc. | Reduc. | | Reduc. |
| | (1) | (2) | (3) | (4) | (5) | (6) | (7) | (8) | (9) | (10) | (11) | (12) | (13) | (14) |
| Market share | 0.511 [0.109] | 0.439 [0.111] | 0.293 [0.175] | 0.311 [0.172] | 0.343 [0.224] | 0.409 [0.148] | 0.267 [0.184] | 0.299 [0.169] | 0.408 [0.192] | 0.479 [0.109] | 0.447 [0.131] | 0.503 [0.091] | 0.312 [0.230] | 0.302 [0.221] |
| System 1 | | | | | | | 0.740 [0.343] | | 0.273 [0.777] | | | | 0.283 [0.801] | |
| System 2 | | | | | | | 0.620 [0.057] | 0.778 [0.005] | 1.187 [0.010] | 1.190 [0.002] | 1.105 [0.003] | 1.055 [0.004] | 1.363 [0.078] | 1.590 [0.004] |
| System 3 | | | | | | | -0.056 [0.847] | | -0.071 [0.841] | | | | 0.368 [0.610] | |
| System 4 | | | | | | | -0.915 [0.072] | -0.525 [0.109] | -0.289 [0.718] | | | | -0.682 [0.479] | |
| Structure | | | 0.258 [0.266] | 0.258 [0.266] | 1.166 [0.015] | 1.041 [0.013] | | | | | | | -0.523 [0.441] | -0.926 [0.052] |
| Processes | | | 0.124 [0.641] | | -0.215 [0.615] | | | | | | | | -0.710 [0.140] | -0.539 [0.132] |
| Boundaries | | | -0.169 [0.456] | | | | | | | | | | -0.211 [0.743] | |
| Delayering | -0.131 [0.309] | | | | | | | | | | | | | |
| Project-based structure | -0.337 [0.011] | -0.327 [0.007] | | | -0.406 [0.008] | -0.422 [0.001] | | | -0.338 [0.016] | -0.327 [0.010] | -0.334 [0.008] | -0.322 [0.011] | | |
| Operational. decentr | -0.337 [0.524] | | | | -0.312 [0.129] | -0.226 [0.236] | | | -0.197 [0.319] | -0.164 [0.362] | | -0.279 [0.056] | | |
| Strategic Decentr. | 0.053 [0.798] | | | | -0.298 [0.204] | -0.241 [0.258] | | | -0.208 [0.361] | -0.233 [0.270] | -0.345 [0.045] | | | |

(Continued)

TABLE 7.8 (Continued)

|  | Individual | | Composite | | Individual + Comp. | | System | | System + Individual | | | | Sys. + Comp. | |
|---|---|---|---|---|---|---|---|---|---|---|---|---|---|---|
|  |  | Reduc. |  | Reduc. |  | Reduc. |  | Reduc. |  | Reduc. | Reduc. | Reduc. |  | Reduc. |
| Variable | (1) | (2) | (3) | (4) | (5) | (6) | (7) | (8) | (9) | (10) | (11) | (12) | (13) | (14) |
| Vertical networking |  |  |  |  | -0.068 [0.334] |  |  |  |  |  |  |  |  |  |
| Horizontal networking | -0.297 [0.218] |  |  |  |  |  |  |  | -0.486 [0.051] | -0.382 [0.089] | -0.344 [0.119] | -0.328 [0.135] |  |  |
| IT | 0.144 [0.414] |  |  |  | 0.184 [0.334] |  |  |  | 0.095 [0.594] |  |  |  |  |  |
| New HR practices | 0.637 [0.017] | 0.595 [0.013] |  |  | 0.654 [0.017] | 0.632 [0.009] |  |  | 0.482 [0.095] | 0.518 [0.046] | 0.523 [0.043] | 0.513 [0.047] |  |  |
| Outsourcing | 0.180 [0.562] |  |  |  | 0.191 [0.532] |  |  |  | 0.309 [0.358] |  |  |  |  |  |
| Strategic alliances | -0.008 [0.977] |  |  |  | 0.049 [0.852] |  |  |  |  |  |  |  |  |  |
| Downscoping | 0.410 [0.435] |  |  |  | 0.395 [0.447] |  |  |  | 0.452 [0.403] |  |  |  |  |  |
| Observations | 80 | 87 | 92 | 92 | 83 | 86 | 92 | 92 | 83 | 83 | 83 | 83 | 92 | 92 |
| Test of included variables $\chi^2$(d.f.) | $\chi^2(11) =$ 18.16 | $\chi^2(3) =$ 15.84 | $\chi^2(4) =$ 5.67 | $\chi^2(2) =$ 4.88 | $\chi^2(12) =$ 20.27 | $\chi^2(6) =$ 22.11 | $\chi^2(5) =$ 13.02 | $\chi^2(3)=$ 12.00 | $\chi^2(13) =$ 27.45 | $\chi^2(7) =$ 25.71 | $\chi^2(7)=$ 24.88 | $\chi^2(6) =$ 24.49 | $\chi^2(8) =$ 15.65 | $\chi^2(4) =$ 13.44 |
| (prob.) | (0.078) | (0.001) | (0.225) | (0.087) | (0.062) | (0.001) | (0.023) | (0.007) | (0.011) | (0.001) | (0.000) | (0.000) | (0.048) | (0.009) |
| Pseudo $R_2$ | 0.082 | 0.067 | 0.023 | 0.019 | 0.091 | 0.094 | 0.052 | 0.048 | 0.120 | 0.112 | 0.109 | 0.107 | 0.062 | 0.053 |
| $\theta_1$ | 0.286 (1.089) | -0.065 (0.959) | -1.869 (0.387) | -1.869 (0.307) | -0.424 (1.108) | -0.022 (0.971) | -2.039 (0.353) | -1.951 (0.320) | -0.591 (1.184) | -0.694 (1.042) | -0.595 (1.033) | -0.658 (1.039) | -2.564 (0.531) | -2.436 (0.448) |
| $\theta_2$ | 1.281 (1.078) | 0.872 (0.949) | -1.014 (0.303) | -1.024 (0.307) | 1.318 (1.071) | -0.022 (0.971) | -1.096 (0.224) | -1.034 (0.189) | 0.533 (1.152) | 0.417 (1.017) | 0.479 (1.013) | 0.438 (1.014) | -1.597 (0.444) | -1.499 (0.350) |
| $\theta_3$ | 2.124 (1.077) | 1.672 (0.949) | -0.271 (0.289) | -0.286 (0.168) | 2.206 (1.072) | 1.860 (0.957) | -0.313 (0.195) | -0.260 (0.162) | 1.427 (1.150) | 1.306 (1.009) | 1.362 (1.006) | 1.318 (1.007) | -0.804 (0.424) | -0.710 (0.325) |
| $\theta_4$ | 3.061 (1.094) | 2.758 (0.966) | 0.696 (0.295) | 0.678 (0.177) | 3.271 (1.091) | 2.959 (0.977) | 0.689 (0.204) | 0.739 (0.172) | 2.493 (1.163) | 2.356 (1.023) | 2.412 (1.020) | 2.363 (1.022) | 0.213 (0.422) | 0.292 (0.325) |

In square brackets: probabilities for independent variables; in round brackets: standard errors for ancillary parameters

The model with the composite variables shows that only changes in Processes are significant (columns 3 and 4), however, when we regress individual and composite variables (columns 5 and 6) we obtain a different result: the same individual elements as in the first model, Operational decentralization and Horizontal networking, are significant and positive, but among the composite variables, Structure is significant and negative. When introduced individually Operational decentralization brings a positive premium to companies' performance, but its association with other structural changes (delayering, project structure or strategic decentralization) has a detrimental effect on performance. If complementarities exist in US organizations we would expect to find that the implementation of the full set of changes as systems has a positive effect on performance and overall we would find the J-curve effect of organizational change on performance, as found in the static analysis (Whittington et al., 1999).

All the remaining columns report results for models with systemic changes. Columns 7 and 8 show the models with the systemic variables. The reduced model (column 8) shows that System 1 and System 2 are significant, System 1 with a positive effect on performance changes, although not very strong, and System 2 with a negative effect. Firms that jointly introduce changes in the three dimensions, Structure, Processes and Boundaries, are likely to increase their performance. On the contrary, the adoption of the partial System 2 (Structure and Processes) has a high negative effect on performance, consistent with the complementarities theory. However, the dramatic reduction in the coefficient of System 2 when System 1 is dropped (column 10) indicates multicollinearity between these variables (see the correlation table) in the Appendix to this chapter). This is quite common when there is insufficient information (number of observations) in the sample to estimate the parameters in the model.

The results obtained in the present study corroborate the importance of organizational complementarities and their effect on corporate performance. When companies consider changes in their structure and processes, they should also consider the introduction of other organizational practices such as Boundary changes, like outsourcing activities, refocusing the range of businesses and possibly engaging in strategic alliances.

The estimates of the model with system and individual variables (columns 9, 10 and 11) and the model with system and composite variables (columns 12, 13 and 14) are consistent with the previous results. System 2 is significant and negative. Operational decentralization and Horizontal networking are also significant but positive, and there is some evidence for a positive effect of increasing IT (IT strategy, IT systems and electronic data exchange (EDI)). In the second model (column 13), System 1 and Processes have a positive effect on changes in performance, while System 2 has a negative effect.

Finally, the model with all the variables, individual, composite and systems (columns 15 and 16), replicates the findings of the model with system and individual variables (column 11) where System 2 (Structure and Processes) is negative and individual components of both Structure and Processes, Operational decentralization and Horizontal networking increase corporate performance. Clearly the whole model had far too many variables for the number of observations in the US sample and the reduced model reported has been carefully selected between alternative deletion paths.

## DISCUSSION AND CONCLUSIONS

This chapter has explored the existence of complementarities among organizational changes and their effect on corporate performance. Previous empirical studies represent interesting contributions and provide valuable evidence of the effect of organizational change on business performance, however they mainly present *static* analyses, or empirical evidence based on a low number of exemplar cases of adoption of complementary systems of organizational changes. Also the model presented by Milgrom and Roberts (1990) is essentially static, however, they argue, it is suggestive about the nature of the path of the modern manufacturing strategy. Therefore they only partially capture the notion of *change* underlying the definition of complementarities.

In this chapter we have considered a wide range of organizational changes adopted by large firms in the period 1992–96. Using a sample of 538 Western firms we have identified multiple dimensions of organizational changes and analysed the impact of the individual and systemic changes on their financial performance.

The idea that isolated organizational changes may require additional complementary changes and therefore convey negative or lower returns than if introduced with other organizational innovations is increasingly accepted; however, the existing empirical econometric literature on complementarities has only provided limited dynamic analyses of changes, probably because of data limitations. Gathering an appropriate database for such analysis is a strenuous and challenging task.

Using the data from the INNFORM survey we have tested the notion of complementarities, that, due to the complex interaction of complementary organizational dimensions and managerial practices, changing only a few of the system elements may not be enough to achieve the benefits of implementing a fully co-ordinated change.

First we investigated the incidence of adoption of bundles and systems of organizational changes across regions; then we estimated ordered Probit regression models with individual and systemic changes to find supporting

TABLE 7.9  Ordered Probit estimates of the relationship between changes in company performance and changes in organizational design system; dependent variable is Changes in firm performance in the period 1992–93 to 1996–97 – US Firms

| Variable | Individual (1) | Individual Reduc. (2) | Composite (3) | Composite Reduc. (4) | Individual + Comp. (5) | Individual + Comp. Reduc. (6) | System (7) | System Reduc. (8) | System + Individual (9) | System + Individual Reduc. (10) | System + Individual Reduc. (10) | System + Composite (11) | System + Composite Reduc. (12) | System + Composite Composite Reduc. (12) | All (13) | All Reduc. (14) |
|---|---|---|---|---|---|---|---|---|---|---|---|---|---|---|---|---|
| Market share | 0.457 [0.051] | 0.462 [0.035] | 0.538 [0.009] | 0.522 [0.011] | 0.505 [0.029] | 0.522 [0.021] | 0.543 [0.010] | 0.534 [0.010] | 0.464 [0.070] | 0.501 [0.030] | 0.532 [0.020] | 0.483 [0.022] | 0.499 [0.017] | 0.542 [0.009] | 0.508 [0.041] | 0.529 [0.020] |
| System 1 | | | | | | | 0.856 [0.475] | 0.984 [0.186] | 0.971 [0.411] | | | 1.078 [0.149] | 1.056 [0.157] | | 1.479 [0.239] | |
| System 2 | | | | | | | −0.975 [0.117] | −1.023 [0.097] | −2.358 [0.043] | −1.224 [0.021] | −1.119 [0.032] | −2.198 [0.029] | −1.315 [0.039] | −0.605 [0.120] | −2.870 [0.018] | −1.119 [0.032] |
| System 3 | | | | | | | 0.201 [0.538] | | 0.338 [0.319] | | | | | | | |
| System 4 | | | | | | | −0.074 [0.931] | | | | | | | | | |
| Structure | | | −0.285 [0.410] | | −0.928 [0.064] | −0.817 [0.086] | | | | | | 0.865 [0.258] | | | | |
| Processes | | | 0.467 [0.094] | 0.436 [0.115] | 0.268 [0.454] | | | | | | | 0.689 [0.023] | 0.594 [0.042] | 0.575 [0.049] | | |
| Boundaries | | | 0.008 [0.976] | | −0.166 [0.648] | | | | | | | | | | −0.627 [0.135] | |
| Delayering | | | | | | | | | | | | | | | | |
| Project-based structure | | | | | | | | | | | | | | | 0.460 [0.168] | |
| Operational decentr. | 0.192 [0.243] | 0.166 [0.162] | | | 0.391 [0.014] | 0.298 [0.037] | | | 0.365 [0.011] | 0.319 [0.021] | 0.297 [0.030] | | | | 0.391 [0.006] | 0.298 [0.030] |
| Strategic decentr. | 0.090 [0.591] | | | | | | | | | | | | | | | |
| Vertical networking | −0.349 [0.336] | | | | −0.458 [0.205] | | | | | | | | | | | |

(Continued)

TABLE 7.9 (Continued)

| Variable | Individual | | Composite | | Individual + Comp. | | System | | System + Individual | | | System + Composite | | | All | |
|---|---|---|---|---|---|---|---|---|---|---|---|---|---|---|---|---|
| | | Reduc. | | Reduc. | | Reduc. | | Reduc. | | Reduc. | Reduc. | | Reduc. | Reduc. | | Reduc. |
| | (1) | (2) | (3) | (4) | (5) | (6) | (7) | (8) | (9) | (10) | (10) | (11) | (12) | (12) | (13) | (14) |
| Horizontal networking | 0.569 [0.079] | 0.425 [0.051] | | | 0.622 [0.063] | 0.519 [0.023] | | | 0.543 [0.043] | 0.498 [0.044] | 0.581 [0.014] | | | | 0.380 [0.194] | 0.581 [0.014] |
| IT | 0.237 [0.212] | | | | 0.191 [0.326] | | | | 0.259 [0.201] | 0.241 [0.188] | | | | | | |
| New HR practices Downscoping | -0.151 [0.706] | | | | | | | | | | | | | | | |
| Strategic alliances Outsourcing | | | | | 0.305 [0.422] | | | | 0.329 [0.305] | | | | | | 0.757 [0.066] | |
| Observations | 69 | 70 | 74 | 74 | 70 | 70 | 74 | 74 | 62 | 70 | 70 | 74 | 74 | 74 | 62 | 70 |
| Test of incl. vrbles $\chi^2$ (d.f.) | $\chi^2(7)=14.83$ | $\chi^2(3)=13.31$ | $\chi^2(4)=11.03$ | $\chi^2(2)=10.34$ | $\chi^2(9)=19.60$ | $\chi^2(4)=16.27$ | $\chi^2(5)=11.03$ | $\chi^2(3)=10.63$ | $\chi^2(8)=22.78$ | $\chi^2(5)=19.68$ | $\chi^2(4)=17.93$ | $\chi^2(5)=16.11$ | $\chi^2(4)=14.76$ | $\chi^2(3)=12.75$ | $\chi^2(9)=25.81$ | $\chi^2(4)=17.93$ |
| (prob.) | (0.038) | (0.004) | (0.026) | (0.006) | (0.021) | (0.003) | (0.051) | (0.014) | (0.004) | (0.001) | (0.001) | (0.006) | (0.005) | (0.005) | (0.002) | (0.001) |
| Pseudo $R_2$ | 0.078 | 0.069 | 0.053 | 0.050 | 0.102 | 0.085 | 0.054 | 0.052 | 0.133 | 0.102 | 0.093 | 0.078 | 0.072 | 0.062 | 0.151 | 0.093 |
| $\theta_1$ | -1.155 | -1.325 | -1.344 | -1.314 | -1.129 | -1.368 | -1.591 | -1.640 | -0.782 | -1.123 | -1.351 | -1.305 | -1.371 | -1.336 | -0.914 | -1.351 |
| | (0.341) | (0.278) | (0.319) | (0.295) | (0.367) | (0.281) | (0.276) | (0.262) | (0.381) | (0.333) | (0.282) | (0.306) | (0.299) | (0.297) | (0.378) | (0.281) |
| $\theta_2$ | -0.453 | -0.652 | -0.572 | -0.542 | -0.425 | -0.687 | -0.836 | -0.884 | -0.096 | -0.418 | -0.659 | -0.496 | -0.576 | -0.551 | -0.166 | -0.659 |
| | (0.301) | (0.221) | (0.271) | (0.246) | (0.329) | (0.224) | (0.213) | (0.195) | (0.349) | (0.290) | (0.224) | (0.259) | (0.249) | (0.247) | (0.340) | (0.224) |
| $\theta_3$ | 0.263 | 0.089 | 0.094 | 0.117 | 0.365 | 0.069 | -0.170 | -0.220 | 0.762 | 0.361 | 0.104 | 0.221 | 0.131 | 0.129 | 0.740 | 0.104 |
| | (0.298) | (0.210) | (0.268) | (0.244) | (0.333) | (0.213) | (0.194) | (0.173) | (0.357) | (0.290) | (0.213) | (0.258) | (0.246) | (0.245) | (0.348) | (0.213) |
| $\theta_4$ | 0.761 | 0.576 | 0.576 | 0.595 | 0.364 | 0.572 | 0.316 | 0.262 | 1.280 | 0.876 | 0.611 | 0.724 | 0.631 | 0.617 | 1.267 | 0.611 |
| | (0.302) | (0.215) | (0.272) | (0.248) | (0.333) | (0.217) | (0.194) | (0.171) | (0.371) | (0.297) | (0.218) | (0.262) | (0.249) | (0.250) | (0.360) | (0.218) |

In square brackets: probabilities for independent variables; in round brackets: standard errors for ancillary parameters

TABLE 7.10   *Summary table of the regression results*

| Variable | Pooled sample of western firms | UK | German-speaking | USA |
|---|---|---|---|---|
| System 1: S + P + B | ++ | + | | + |
| System 2: S + P | − | − | ++ | − |
| System 3: P + B | − | | | |
| System 4: S + B | | + | − | |
| Structure | | − | +/− | |
| Processes | | | /− | ++ |
| Boundaries | | + | | |
| Delayering | | − | | |
| Project-based structure | − | | − | |
| Operational decentralization | | | − | ++ |
| Strategic decentralization | | ++ | | |
| Vertical networking | + | ++ | | |
| Horizontal networking | + | | − | ++ |
| IT | | | | |
| New HR practices | | − | ++ | |
| Downscoping | | − | | |
| Strategic alliances | | + | | |
| Outsourcing | ++ | | | + |

One symbol, + or − , indicates weak positive or negative significance or only in some models; two symbols, ++ or −, indicate strong positive or negative significance often across all models.

evidence of complementary effects of organizational *changes* in large firms as measured by the positive effect on *changes* in corporate performance.

Table 7.10 summarizes the main findings in the full sample of Western firms.

The pooled analysis indicates that the adoption of a full set of changes in organizational Structure, Processes and Boundaries (System 1) increases the probability of improving corporate performance. However, on the other hand, the adoption of partial systems, Structure and Processes, or Processes and Boundaries, is likely to reduce performance. We found that, in general, in Western companies, some individual organizational innovations like Outsourcing and, less strongly, Vertical and Horizontal networking, can have a positive effect on corporate performance. We also found that increasing Project-based structure has a clear, negative impact on performance. This last finding is wholly consistent with the theory of complementarities: piecemeal organizational changes may not be enough to obtain full benefits, and they can even have detrimental performance effects. Increasing organizing by projects has been adopted widely by Western firms in the period investigated, and therefore we expected to find a clear increase in performance. Here we find that this organizational structure may not reward if introduced in isolation within organizations. Introducing innovative practices involving all organizational dimensions appears more likely to reward daring managers.

The regional analyses identify specific patterns of complementarities. In the UK we find strong evidence of the harmful performance effect of introducing partial systems of structural and processual changes. On the other hand, redefining organizational boundaries appears particularly beneficial to UK companies. For example, engaging in strategic alliances is likely to improve corporate financial performance, but refocusing the range of business does not appear to be helpful. When changes in these boundary-defining elements are introduced contemporaneously the effect on performance is unequivocally positive. This is also the case when composite boundary changes are implemented with structural and process changes. It is also interesting that in the case of structural and processual changes some components, Strategic decentralization and Vertical networking, have positive effects on performance if adopted by themselves, but other elements, like Delayering and New HR practices, are likely to reduce performance if introduced in isolation. A similar effect is observed if structural changes have been introduced without changes in other dimensions, or if associated with changes in processes.

We should note that we do not have the self-reported measure of relative performance and changes in performance for the UK sample, as we do have in the case of Continental European and US firms. The changes in performance in the UK are measured by changes in return of capital employed between 1992 and 1996, collected from Onesource. Using an objective measure of performance here might explain specific results for the UK, like the positive effect of enhanced strategic decentralization and vertical networking. But the result on HR practices is somehow unexpected and in contrast with the existing evidence in the UK.

The findings for German-speaking countries are in contrast with those for the UK. Among the systemic changes System 2, Structure and Processes, has a clear positive impact on performance, whereas the combination of structural and boundary changes, System 4, has a negative effect. Among the individual elements, Project structure has a negative effect. As in the pooled analysis, we find that Operational decentralization has a mild negative effect on performance, however the composite variable for Structure has a positive sign in the models where composite variables are entered, alone or with the individual elements. Structural elements have negative effects on performance, but are positive if introduced in bundles. At the same time, structural and process changes have a negative effect on performance if introduced independently, but positive if they are adopted as a system.

Among the Process elements there is another strong contrast with the UK: increasing the extent of New HR practices increases the probability of improved performance, but reinforcing Horizontal networking decreases it. This finding is opposite to the pooled analysis and supports the existence of complementarities because, as we have remarked, changing organizational structures and processes as a system in the German-speaking region has an overall positive effect on corporate performance.

US companies present some common patterns with the pooled analysis and with the UK. The first, important common result is about the existence of complementarities, as illustrated by the positive effect of the adoption of the full set of organizational changes (System 1) on performance, and the negative effect of the 'partial' system with changes in Structure and Processes and without changes in Boundaries. We also find a positive coefficient for Outsourcing, as in the pooled analysis. The other findings for US companies, positive effects of Operational decentralization and Horizontal networking, and Processes, are also very interesting because they are elements of System 2 which overall has a negative effect on performance.

Although the INNFORM survey has offered a rare, rich database for the empirical analysis of complementarities, it does have some limitations. The variables from the survey range between 1 and 5 and innovative companies that were already adopting high degrees of new organizational practices in the first period are not allowed to move further to higher levels. Therefore the analysis presented in this chapter, which is concerned with changes, essentially refers to companies who had the possibility to change. However, the INNFORM survey was retrospective, carried out in 1997 with enquiries about 1992 and 1996, therefore managers who have experienced positive changes during the period might have answered 4 in 1992 and 5 in 1996.

If the 'static' analysis from the INNFORM survey in Whittington et al., 1999 was about the 'high adopters' or innovating companies, our study is more concerned about the companies in the middle of the population, which can implement strategies to reach the firms at the frontier. This group represents a substantial proportion of the population compared to the innovators (see Massini et al., 2002, where we mapped the evolutionary dynamics of changes in organizational routines in the population).

Furthermore we do not distinguish companies according to the starting point or take into account the extent of adoption of new managerial practice in the first year. A change of one unit in an organizational element, if starting from a low or very low level, may not be sufficient to improve performance; the same change of one unit if starting from a higher level might be more effective. On the other hand, a small change when already adopting some organizational practices at a high level might not make a strong impact. Ideally we would have liked to include the 'starting point' and an interaction term between the starting level and the extent of change. Unfortunately this would have introduced too many variables. Moreover, the intrinsic collinearity among organizational and managerial practices limits our ability to distinguish between the impact of individual and systemic change. These considerations indicate that there are still interesting issues to be investigated in the empirical analysis of the relationship between complementarities in organizational change and corporate performance.

When we explored the existence of mutually dependent organizational changes, attempts were made to define systems as emerging from the data, using multivariate statistical techniques (factor analysis and principal components analysis). This would have allowed letting the data indicate and discover systems, instead of building them from theoretical considerations, which superimpose interrelations between organizational aspects. Although theoretically satisfactory, these empirically derived systems did not appear to perform well in regression models.

On the contrary, the systems defined on the basis of theoretical assumptions have shown interesting effects on corporate performance. Changing the full set of elements offers a premium that cannot be enjoyed if only piecemeal or isolated changes are introduced. Some individual elements can also award positive performance benefits, but can also undermine performance if they interact with other practices.

Our finding that systems of organizational changes increase performance, while marginal changes in individual organizational dimensions have little or negative impact are consistent with the J-curve effect of organizational changes on corporate performance described in Whittington et al. (1999). Individual components can improve the probability of higher performance, and this probability also increases if the changes are introduced in systems, but piecemeal change can make performance worse. Because of the intrinsic difficulty of changing a number of elements at the same time, companies should be prepared to experience transition penalties before enjoying the performance benefits of changing organizational practices.

The difficulty of identifying and implementing systemic changes may also support the development of path dependency, or cumulative change (Milgrom et al., 1991), and suggest the co-evolution of the elements constituting a system, because once the movement of a whole system of complementary variables begins, it tends to continue (Milgrom and Roberts, 1995). When this path dependence locks organizations into partial systems which weaken performance and impede the introduction of innovative practices to enhance profitability, companies find themselves trapped in their organizational systems. Firms characterized by tightly coupled interactive systems of activities will find it difficult to adapt to environmental changes and may be exposed to the rigours of a complementarities trap.

Complementarities traps and the fear of the J-curve help to explain the slow diffusion of best practice across industries and nations. System benefits might depend on elements that may be absent or weaker in some national contexts than in others. Policy makers should learn about what elements are more likely to bring superior performance in their national environment and define interventions which facilitate their implementation to improve the international competitiveness of their national champions.

Including industry variables in the analysis of complementarities and performance would add an extra dimension to explaining observed sectoral differences in performance and control for some heterogeneity, but unfortunately this information was not available for our Continental European firms.

At a more micro-level, performance differentials can be explained by the difficulty of identifying non-obvious internal connections between organizational elements. Rivkin (2000) discusses how the complexity of complementarity implies difficulties to imitate successful strategies. When choices and options are interconnected it is more difficult to understand, implement and thereby imitate the systems of organizational practices held by competitors.

Managers face computational difficulties in exploring all the possible combinations of alternative configurations and their possible outcomes (Rivkin, 2000). It appears easier to explore changes in the neighbourhood of the existing and firm specific organizational landscape rather than trying to move from a local peak to a global one. Consistent with a 'satisficing' approach to decision making (March and Simon, 1958; Cyert and March, 1963; Nelson and Winter, 1982), managers are more likely to employ not-optimizing heuristics for decision making. Companies might be constrained to consider only incremental changes because they are trapped in their highly interactive and complex systems and unable to execute more adventurous alterations to the current configuration. Strong leadership is required to build coherent systems of complementary elements that are hard to implement. In Chapter 8, which follows, we offer a detailed process analysis of the *what*, *why* and *how* of building complementary changes in BP and Unilever. In these long-term change processes intergenerational leader effects were crucial in delivering performance improvement through complementary change.

## APPENDIX 7.1

### Whole sample

|  | Structure | Processes | Boundaries | System 1 | System 2 | System 3 | System 4 |
|---|---|---|---|---|---|---|---|
| Structure | 1.0000 | | | | | | |
| Processes | 0.1178* | 1.0000 | | | | | |
| Boundaries | 0.1322* | 0.0241 | 1.0000 | | | | |
| System 1 | 0.5993** | 0.2229** | 0.4152** | 1.0000 | | | |
| System 2 | 0.8765** | 0.3260** | 0.0922 | 0.6838** | 1.0000 | | |
| System 3 | 0.1331* | 0.4241** | 0.7900** | 0.5256** | 0.2270** | 1.0000 | |
| System 4 | 0.6872** | 0.0498 | 0.4762** | 0.8721** | 0.5699** | 0.4117** | 1.0000 |

### UK

|  | Structure | Processes | Boundaries | System 1 | System 2 | System 3 | System 4 |
|---|---|---|---|---|---|---|---|
| Structure | 1.0000 | | | | | | |
| Processes | 0.2079* | 1.0000 | | | | | |
| Boundaries | 0.1452 | 0.0023 | 1.0000 | | | | |
| System 1 | 0.6472** | 0.2127* | 0.4333** | 1.0000 | | | |
| System 2 | 0.9466** | 0.3104** | 0.0941 | 0.6851** | 1.0000 | | |
| System 3 | 0.1772 | 0.3985** | 0.8121** | 0.5336** | 0.2206* | 1.0000 | |
| System 4 | 0.7063** | 0.0852 | 0.4729** | 0.9163** | 0.6089** | 0.4562** | 1.0000 |

### German-speaking countries

|  | Structure | Processes | Boundaries | System 1 | System 2 | System 3 | System 4 |
|---|---|---|---|---|---|---|---|
| Structure | 1.0000 | | | | | | |
| Processes | 0.0199 | 1.0000 | | | | | |
| Boundaries | 0.0272 | 0.0291 | 1.0000 | | | | |
| System 1 | 0.4926** | 0.2288 | 0.4477** | 1.0000 | | | |
| System 2 | 0.8147** | 0.3783** | 0.0080 | 0.6047** | 1.0000 | | |
| System 3 | 0.0052 | 0.4119** | 0.8060** | 0.5554** | 0.1527 | 1.0000 | |
| System 4 | 0.5849** | −0.0078 | 0.5316** | 0.8422** | 0.4584** | 0.4075** | 1.0000 |

### USA

|  | Structure | Processes | Boundaries | System 1 | System 2 | System 3 | System 4 |
|---|---|---|---|---|---|---|---|
| Structure | 1.0000 | | | | | | |
| Processes | 0.1039 | 1.0000 | | | | | |
| Boundaries | 0.2109 | 0.0699 | 1.0000 | | | | |
| System 1 | 0.7026** | 0.2247 | 0.3408* | 1.0000 | | | |
| System 2 | 0.8578** | 0.2743 | 0.1867 | 0.8190** | 1.0000 | | |
| System 3 | 0.2118 | 0.4903** | 0.7436** | 0.4583** | 0.3139* | 1.0000 | |
| System 4 | 0.8079** | 0.0904 | 0.3919** | 0.8696** | 0.7022** | 0.3557* | 1.0000 |

*:significance at 0.01;**: significance at 0.001

**Chapter 8**

# Complementarities in Action:

## Organizational Change and Performance in BP and Unilever 1985–2002

*Andrew M. Pettigrew and
Richard Whittington*

In Chapter 7 we showed how apparently foresightful and daring leaders who introduce coherent systems of organizational change are likely to be rewarded by significant performance improvements. Our pooled analysis of 538 Western firms revealed that the adoption of a full set of organizational changes (Structures, Processes and Boundaries) increased the probability of improving corporate financial performance. On the other hand, the adoption of partial systems of change (Structures and Processes or Processes and Boundaries) is likely to reduce financial performance. Interesting and significant as these results are, they leave many unanswered questions about the management processes of delivering performance improvement in organizational settings. The process scholar, curious about the character, sequencing, dynamics and outcomes of change journeys is likely to be concerned about the *what*, *why* and *how* of turning possibly high-risk complementary change into a virtual cycle of performance improvement. Why do organizations commit themselves to complementary change, and how do they manage over time the complexities and risks of such holistic change processes in order to deliver performance gains? These questions represent the central focus of this chapter on complementarities in action.

This chapter has six parts. In the first part we discuss some of the latent assumptions in existing literature on complementarities and change and offer our own conjecture on the *what, why, when* and *how* of complementarities in action. We then pose some of the main questions which have guided our case study investigations. The second part provides a brief profile of our two case studies, BP and Unilever, and gives a broad overview of the change journeys in both organizations from the mid 1980s to 2002. In the third and fourth parts we offer a more detailed analysis of the sequence, phases and cycles of change in both companies and chronicle the external and internal factors which triggered change and the links between the building of complementarities and performance enhancement. The fifth part compares and contrasts the patterns in the process of delivering change in our two case study firms. In this part of the chapter we draw upon the additional insights of the March (1991) and Levinthal and March (1993) theory of exploratory and exploitation adaptation and combine this with complementarities theorizing about change and performance. In the concluding sixth section we pinpoint some of the core points of learning from the BP and Unilever experiences about the practicalities of leading and managing complementary change.

## INTRODUCTION

In spite of the obvious theoretical, empirical and practical appeal of the question, we as management researchers seem to have been curiously uncurious about why and how certain organizations consistently outperform their competitors (Pettigrew et al., 1999; Pettigrew, 2000). Where such studies exist they are often found wanting, sometimes because of disputes about the chosen method of performance measurement and, in other cases, because of a tendency to use either univariate or unithematic explanations of performance differences. In spite of a real metamorphosis in its theoretical and empirical development since the mid 1980s, the research literature on organizational change continues to be weak on linking change processes to performance outcomes. There are now many studies revealing the complexities of organizational change processes, even more evaluating change interventions, and still others trying to disentangle the interrelated set of factors contributing to the success of change initiatives. However, in very few empirical studies do researchers seek to link change capacity and action to organizational performance. By now process analysts of change should have been interested not just in the results of change processes or the processes that lead to those results, but also in the dynamic and holistic appreciation of both process and outcomes (Pettigrew et al., 2001).

The tradition of theoretical development associated with Milgrom and Roberts (1990, 1995) and their followers has so far been explicit about the *what* of the relationship between complementarities and performance, but largely silent on the *how* of creating the complements and linking them to performance. However, the complementarities tradition is not the only one contributing to our understanding of performance determinants. Earlier work by Pettigrew and Whipp (1991) examined comparatively and longitudinally the *what*, *why* and *how* of the determinants of performance in matched pairs of firms in four mature industry and service sectors in the UK. The well-known study by Collins and Porras (1994) builds a strong analysis of the factors that created and sustained so-called visionary companies, but their analysis stops short of explicitly linking change with financial performance. Recently the longitudinal case study work of Siggelkow (2001, 2002b) has begun to treat the fit between organizational practices and activities as a dynamic concept. Fit is not just the static interlocking of a set of variables but is better appreciated as a continuous co-evolution of a complex whole. Siggelkow's (2002b) paper is sensitive to 'evolution towards fit' and part of his contribution is to begin to identify patterns in the developmental pathway to fit between configurations of core, elaborating and other elements in the organization. Sigglekow's earlier paper (2001) on the Liz Claiborne fashion company used environmental challenge as the disturbance element to internal and external fit leading to the danger of what Whittington and Pettigrew characterize in Chapter 6 as 'complementarity traps'. This temporal turn in writing about complementarities has now been enriched by writing on contextuality and activity systems (Porter and Siggelkow, 2002). These authors note that competitive advantage 'is more likely created by sets of strategy-specific activities that interact contextually than by sets of generic activities that interact in generic ways' (Porter and Siggelkow, 2002: 2).

Our own work on complementarities in action is based on a theory of method which is avowedly contextual and temporal (Pettigrew, 1990, 1997a, 2001; Whittington et al., 2002). The building of sets of complementary innovations and their subsequent exploitation and adaptation can only be revealed with time series data, and that building process is likely to be customized to the particularities of certain internal and external contextual features of the firm. It is, of course, the highly complex, variable and particular nature of the processes and outcomes of building complementarities which makes the resultant systems so hard to imitate even when the elements appear to be visible (Rivkin, 2000; Winter and Szulanski, 2001).

In the introductory chapter to Part 2, the complementarities part of this volume, we offered some informed conjecture about the challenge of building, sustaining and adapting complements. We also noted that complementarity theory offers only quite simple prescriptions for managing the processes of change. Implicit in the earlier work on the Lincoln Electric Company by Milgrom and Roberts (1990) was the view that complementarities favoured, indeed required, strong central leadership. But, of course, Milgrom and Roberts were silent on the processes and characteristics of that central leadership and how the centre related to the periphery. Milgrom and

Roberts were also silent on the challenges of transitions. We noted that, in the transition between the old and new complements, things may get worse before they get better, what we labelled as the performance J-curve. We also noted the likelihood that organizations might be attracted by the political and emotional comfort of incremental change which might lead to sub-optimal performance. We also raised the prospect of organizations driving up performance and then becoming locked into a suboptimal success recipe, or a complementarities trap. As the external and internal contexts of the firm change there may also be demands to keep the virtuous circle of change turning. Complementarities may need to be renewed and reinforced constantly.

These broad areas of conjecture about the management of complementary change have been operationalized in a series of analytical questions which have guided the data collection and analysis of our two case study firms. So, we have been interested in whether complementary change was intended or emerged from a process of learning-by-doing. If the process was intendedly holistic, what were the initial set of complements and why were they chosen? What combination of context and action, leadership intent and 'muddling through with a purpose' created the desire for this degree of change? What role did history, culture and performance crises play in the timing and extent of the complementary changes? What were the sequence of changes over time and, indeed, was the change process as much sequential and overlapping as simultaneous? Was there any evidence of the cycling and recycling of change attempts to build complements over the long term? Did we observe performance declines before performance improvements and, if so, how did the leadership system cope with such problems of transition? If, as we expected, building complements and driving up performance was a long-term process, how was that process enabled or disabled by leadership succession? How was any evident performance improvement explained and turned back to reinforce the continuing pursuit of holistic change? Looking at the overall process of change in BP and Unilever, what were the similarities and differences in the change journeys in the two companies? Did we observe a common change journey in both companies or variation in the content, process and pace of change as each company sought to drive up performance through a complementary system of change?

### BP AND UNILEVER: PROFILES OF PERFORMANCE 1985–2002

In the Summer of 2002, the consistently high performance of BP and Unilever was verging on the superlative. Even the informed and sceptical heavyweight press in the UK could not contain its enthusiasm. Inevitably BP and Unilever's star status was wrapped around the persona of their chief executives. In the case of BP, the attribution was singular – Lord Browne was fêted. In the case of Unilever, the Anglo-Dutch company, there are the traditional, joint senior corporate officers: Niall FitzGerald is Chairman of Unilever Plc and Vice-chairman of Unilever NV and his Dutch compatriot, Anthony Burgmans, is Chairman NV and Vice-chairman, Unilever Plc. But Niall FitzGerald has been in post since 1996 and is often seen (at least in the UK) as the first among equals at the top of Unilever.

The *Financial Times*, in a hagiography of Browne (*Financial Times*, 1 August 2002 and 2 August 2002) cited fellow oil executives describing him as 'a renaissance man, the Sun King of the oil industry' and, when referring to corporate scandals and boardroom disgraces, 'one Titan who remains untoppled' (cited in *The Guardian*, 4 October 2002). Some CEOs achieve prominence by transforming the fortunes of a large company but Browne's actions in the late 1990s could be said not just to have transformed BP but also the energy industry of which BP was now a critical player.

Niall FitzGerald does not quite yet have the visibility of Browne, but his claims to prominence as a successful chief executive are equally clear. 'He has built a reputation as one of the world's most powerful marketeers at a group that employs 265 000 people in 100 countries' (*Sunday Times*, 9 June 2002). In this article FitzGerald was portrayed as a celebrated leader of change in a sprawling company noted for its conservatism. The *Sunday Times* headline was 'Unilever anarchist fights status quo'.

The adulation heaped on Browne and FitzGerald may be warranted in the Summer of 2002, but it is also precarious; the fortunes of great companies can fall as well as rise and their chief executives can and do fall from grace. Look at what has happened to the reputations of Percy Barnevik, lately of ABB, and Jack Welch, lately of GE. And are the performance improvements of companies just to be explained by the actions of single leaders, or must we explore the cumulative actions of a set of leaders over time? This we will explore in our case analysis of BP and Unilever from the mid 1980s to the early part of the twenty-first century.

But what of a summary profile of our two giants? In 2002, BP was number 2 in its sector by market capitalization (at $200 billion), number 8 in the *Financial Times* global ranking and number 1 in the UK. Using the same measure of market capitalization (number of shares issued multiplied by the market price of those shares in March 2002) Unilever was number 62 in the *Financial Times* global ranking (at $23 billion) and number 16 in the UK. (*Financial Times* 500, 10 May 2002). BP's turnover in 2002 was $175 billion and Unilever had a turnover of $48 billion. BP employed 110 000 people worldwide in 2001 and Unilever 279 000.

In 2002, BP had four main businesses, a reduction from the eleven business of the 1980s. The four are exploration and production; gas, power and renewables; refining and marketing; and chemicals. Of these four businesses, exploration and production is by far the most important financially and politically. BP made a massive $8 billion replacement cost profit in 2001, a far cry from the low point of 1992, when only a $352 million profit was

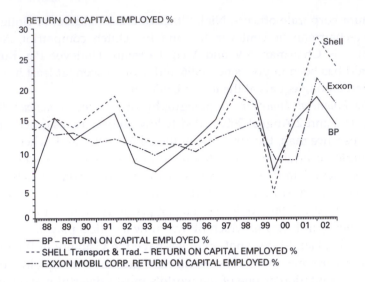

RETURN ON CAPITAL EMPLOYED %

— BP – RETURN ON CAPITAL EMPLOYED %
- - - SHELL Transport & Trad. – RETURN ON CAPITAL EMPLOYED %
—·· EXXON MOBIL CORP. RETURN ON CAPITAL EMPLOYED %

FIGURE 8.1   *BP's performance against its competitors*

made. Over that same period, 1992 to 2001, BP's share price rose nearly year-on-year from $11.44 in 1992 to $46.51$ in 2001. BP's key comparators and competitors are Exxon Mobil and Shell. Their relative positioning with these competitors was fundamentally changed in 1998 when BP acquired Amoco for $110 billion and Arco in 2000 for $30 billion.

Unilever are, of course, engaged in the manufacture and marketing of branded consumer goods, primarily foods, detergents and personal products. These activities were finally consolidated in 2002 into two global divisions, Foods and Personal Care. Like BP, Unilever had long been pursuing a programme to divest non-core businesses and to grow and strengthen an increasingly smaller range of global brands. Unilever's key competitors in 2002 were L'Oréal in home and personal products, Nestlé and Kraft in food and Procter & Gamble in both sectors.

Figures 8.1 and 8.2 reveal BP and Unilever's returns on capital employed compared with their two most immediate competitors over the period 1988–2002.

Figure 8.1 indicates that over the complete time series there are three points, 1992–93 and 1998–99, when the performance of all three oil majors took a hammering. These are points when the world price of oil took substantial drops, in 1992–94 from $19 to $15 per barrel and from 1998–99 from $19 to $10 per barrel (Brent prices, *BP Amoco Statistical Review of World Energy*, June 1999).

Notwithstanding the crucial performance determinants of world oil prices, Figure 8.1 shows that for most of the period between 1988 and 1995 BP was performing below its major competitors. It is not until 1995 that BP began to overtake its major European-based competitor Shell and then in

1996–98 overlook Exxon. But why? The two most crucial determinants of BP's performance are oil and gas prices. Beyond these two determinants there are three controllables over which BP executives have some discretion: costs, tax policy and capital expenditure. Alongside these three controllables BP executives can position their businesses to mirror or change the rules of the game in their industry. This they have done not just by their mergers with Amoco, Arco and Burmah Castrol between 1998 and 2000, but with a major European downstream alliance with Mobil in 1996 and a variety of upstream alliances and joint ventures with other oil companies such as Statoil. These changes in organizational boundaries not only affect market share and power, they also represent crucial opportunities for cost-driven efficiencies. A senior BP Executive commented:

> The industry was due for a shake-up (in 1996). We cosied up to Mobil…that was the first big signal that times were changing. There was a predicted cost saving of £400 million a year, from that we did £500 million. That is massive – enormous.

Similar cost savings were made with dramatic speed and efficiency with the acquisition of Amoco and Arco. By the end of 2000, two years after the Amoco deal and only 12 months into the Arco acquisition, BP had reduced operating costs for the new group by $6 billion.

But the account of BP's relative performance improvement in the 1990s is not just a chronicle of boundary/strategy changes and changing the rules of the game in the industry, it is also much to do with drives to refashion organizational structures and processes. BP is an excellent contemporary example of complementary change where there is considerable evidence of a link between organizational change and improved company performance. We discuss below the pathway in developing these complementary changes.

Figure 8.1 also shows that towards the very end of our time period of analysis Shell appears to out-perform both BP and Exxon-Mobil, at least on return on capital employed. One explanation for this relates to the fact that both BP and Exxon had acquired new capital assets which appeared on the balance sheets as premium market value while their old assets (and those of Shell, who had made no big acquisitions at that time) appear on the balance sheet as current value. This, of course, inflates Shell's return on capital. But the performance record of companies is not just about numbers, it is also a reflection of perceptions, and by the Summer of 2002 Shell's failure to engage in the previous three years of industry consolidation had left them with an image of being leaden footed:

> It (Shell) has lost its reputation as a mover and shaker, an even worse fate than losing the top spot (to BP) as the UK's biggest oil company … BP has the tremendous advantage of being seen as a mean, aggressive company, while Shell just plods on, Shell-like. ('Shell trails BP's lead', BBC on-line news 2 April 2002)

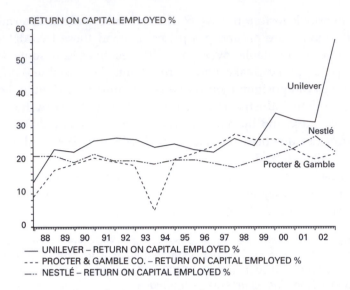

FIGURE 8.2  *Unilever's performance against its competitors*

Turning to Unilever, Figure 8.2 clearly indicates that, on the measure of return on capital employed, Unilever outperformed its major competitors Procter & Gamble and Nestlé from around 1987–88 to 1997 and then leapt ahead again of Proctor & Gamble for the last three to four years of our time series.

Unilever's relative performance is in some ways more complex to analyse than BP's. While the oil majors share a concern with oil and gas prices, Unilever is involved in two different kinds of business, foods and home and personal care. Its major competitors do not have closely similar profiles. For example, L'Oréal is a key competitor in personal care products, but absent in foods and home care. Nestlé competes strongly in food products, but not in home and personal care. At the beginning of this period at least, Procter & Gamble was much more heavily dependent on the US market, while Unilever – and Nestlé – were relatively strong in Europe.

Nevertheless, across both the two main sectors of food and home and personal care, Unilever shared a common customer in terms of the major retailers. How to deal with the growing power of the major retailers was a common strategic challenge to both it and its key comparators here, Procter & Gamble and Nestlé. The pressure on margins exerted by the retailers to a large extent explains the similar patterns of performance the three companies achieved throughout most of this period. The relatively weak performance of Procter & Gamble in the earlier period can be partly attributed to its exposure to Wal-Mart in the USA, before Wal-Mart expanded substantially overseas and European retailers woke up to their full potential. The sharp dip in Procter & Gamble results in 1993 was attributable to a one-off mistake with financial derivatives. Procter & Gamble's subsequent overtaking of Unilever was partly the reward for victory in the 'soap wars', when Unilever's innovative soap powder was discovered to damage materials. Unilever subsequently climbed back ahead when, as we shall see later, its Restructuring for Outstanding Performance finally completed the package of complementary change begun in the 1980s. Unilever's subsequent Path to Growth programme turbocharged performance in the following years, while Procter & Gamble stumbled with overambitious growth targets and restructuring, leading to the firing of its new chief executive, Durk Jager, in 2000.

We now move on to consider the change journeys of BP and Unilever from the mid 1980s to 2002. In examining these changes we will focus on the elements of change identified and defined in Figure 1.1 of Chapter 1 of this volume. From time to time we will also broaden our category of boundary change (defined in Chapter 1 to include downscoping, alliance formation and outsourcing) to include a wider set of strategic changes involving, for example, the repositioning of both firms through mergers and acquisitions.

## THE BP CHANGE JOURNEY: 1985–2002

Faced with the complexities of history, the great danger is to make it tidier than it was. Stage and phase models are classic ordering devices which without some self reflective criticism can indeed over-tidy and over-structure. This danger is, of course, amplified when the phases are then personalized into eras of the tenure of different chief executives. However, in seeking to open up and simplify a complex account, the most productive way for us to start is to think of the Walters, Horton, Simon and Browne eras in BP's recent history. Sir Peter Walters was Executive Chairman (and de facto CEO) from November 1981 until March 1990. Sir Robert Horton was Chairman and CEO from March 1990 until being asked to resign in June 1992. Sir David Simon (now Lord Simon) was first Chief Operating Officer, March 1990 until June 1992, then CEO on Robert Horton's resignation in June 1992 until June 1995 and finally he was Non-Executive Chairman from July 1995 until he entered the Blair Government in May 1997. John Browne has been CEO of BP since July 1995.

Across the tenure of these four CEOs it is possible to think of four phases of corporate development which in time led to substantial performance improvement. In the first phase, which covered the latter part of the Walters era and the two years of Horton's leadership, BP began to face up to the excesses of a decade of more of diversification and of an industry in long-term decline. BP, like its peers, was challenged by the long-term redistribution of profits and shift in market power in the oil industry. All the oil majors lost share of crude oil production in the 1980s and the effects of this are reflected in Figure 8.1. In addition, the oil majors were also threatened by the commoditization of major technologies, increasingly efficient global spot markets for oil, and the rise of national oil companies and growth of service companies.

In response to these pressures, BP, like many of its oil company peers, pursued a conventional performance turnaround strategy. So across the end of the Walters era and into the Horton era BP divested assets totalling over $4 billion, began to shrink head count and repurchase debt and started the process of generating cash flow from setting and reaching performance targets. But when Robert Horton took over in March 1990 he completely re-conceived this traditional turnaround strategy and launched Project 1990 on BP. This was an attempt at comprehensive and holistic change which in the short term faltered and contributed to Horton's resignation in June 1992, but in the medium and long term led to the delivery of complementary change and performance improvement by the mid to late 1990s.

Phase 2 between 1993 and 1996 was led by Simon and supported by Browne, who for most of the time led the powerful exploration and production part of the company. This was the era of PRT: performance, reputation and teamwork. Simon drove BP's performance up from the 1992 low point, started the process of entering alliances and joint ventures to achieve economies of scale and share risk and reinforced those parts of Project 1990 which supported decentralization, performance management and cross-company teamworking and learning. BP was moving rapidly to be a twenty-first century company in structures, processes and boundaries.

Phases 3 and 4 have been driven uncompromisingly by John Browne. Phase 3 dates roughly from 1996 to 2000. This is the period of the great strategic moves to acquire Amoco and Arco and BP's leap to be number 2 in the industry after the reconstituted Exxon Mobil. These acquisitions not only gave BP economies of scale, but also a distinctive set of assets with a re-balancing of the portfolio from oil to gas and a much stronger retail base in the USA. This is also the period when the complements began to fit together and BP's new organizing capabilities matched its new confidence and capabilities in strategizing.

But what could be possible after phase 3? The message so far is one of organic growth combined with further cycles of exploitative performance improvement using by now an organizational machine which had not only rejuvenated the old BP assets, but had dissected and integrated the new assets accruing from the three big acquisitions of 1998–2000. BP was also re-branded in 2000 as 'Beyond Petroleum' and was now a world leader in thinking and action about corporate governance and corporate social responsibility.

The starting point for our account of BP's complementarities in action is Robert Horton's return from the USA in March 1989 to become first Deputy Chairman and then Chairman and CEO of BP. By this time Robert

Horton had a reputation as a hard-driving, no-nonsense executive who had in turn rationalized BP's chemicals operations, sought unsuccessfully to downscope BP's 1970s diversifications in minerals, coal and nutrition and then had been sent out to the USA in the mid 1980s to sort out BP's acquisition of Standard Oil. With the acquiescence of Peter Walters, and before he was formally appointed Chairman, Robert Horton set in train the strategic thinking and action which led to the launch in March 1990 of Project 1990 on BP's 'sleepy' institutional form. Project 1990 aimed to:

1  reduce complexity throughout the corporation
2  redesign the central organization
3  reposition the corporation in approach and style for the 1990s.

Project 1990 was driven from the top by Horton (aided by a specially chosen group of high-flying middle managers) and designed to reduce the structural complexity of BP. Of the corporation's three-dimensional matrix organisation – the business streams were to be strengthened and the functional and regional–national streams reduced in size and influence. The purpose and size of the group and HQ in London was to be reduced by cutting back large functional departments, transferring the remnants into the business streams (at that time four: exploration, oil, chemicals and nutrition) and the rest of the HQ staff were formed into specially constructed teams. There was to be a devolution of responsibility and decision making to the four business areas and the number of central committees was to be drastically reduced. Horizontal networking through a team-based structure was to replace the slow cascading of information up and down the previously extended hierarchy and the new more open flows of information were to be enabled by large investments in the IT infrastructure.

Alongside the above structure changes BP also attempted to make process changes. Doing things with the new BP style involved first signalling and encouraging new behaviours encapsulated in the slogan OPEN: Open thinking, Personal impact, Empowering and Networking. After the top 300 executives in BP had all been through a 'Leadership in Change' programme, a series of cultural change workshops were then rolled out through BP's international presence in 70 countries. This central plank of human resource change was to be reinforced by a new performance review and reward system tied to soft (values-drive) criteria as well as hard. Personal development plans were introduced for all staff and all this was tied to the first explicit statement of corporate vision and values.

Boundary changes were also part of the strategic intent. BP's vast central information systems section of 1000 plus employees was outsourced and renewed attention was given to downscoping the business to take out non-core businesses such as minerals, coal and nutrition. Horton aimed to 'reduce the cost of complexity, yet maintain an integrated corporation' that he hoped would as a result become 'the most successful oil company of the 1990s'.

Here was the grandest, most aspirational programme of complementary change involving significant alterations in structure, process and boundaries yet attempted in UK business. Yet in the short term it was all to end in tears. In June 1992 Robert Horton was asked to resign by the BP board. His successors, David Simon and John Browne, were able to build upon and reformulate Horton's vision and eventually bring about the complementary changes Horton could intellectually envisage but not strategically and operationally deliver.

Why was Robert Horton intellectually and intuitively right and why did he fail to deliver while his successors did? The fact that they did is not just evident from the outcomes specified in Figure 8.1, but also from the essential means summarized in Table 8.1. This table is based upon the content analysis of BP archives over the period 1988–1998[1]. At the top we see the last two years of the Walters era, all of the Horton era, the period when Simon was CEO, his overlap with Browne as Non-Executive Chairman and the first three and a half years of Browne's tenure as CEO. The main content areas of change are summarized on the left in the three working dimensions of the INNFORM programme of Structures, Processes and Boundaries, plus a critical additional category in the BP chronicle – that of changes to further simplify and integrate the business. The bottom four columns of the figure show, in turn, BP's average staff numbers worldwide and the UK replacement cost profit and the fluctuations over this period in the Brent oil price per barrel.

The numbers in the columns and rows represent change initiatives recorded year by year, indicator by indicator. All change initiatives are weighted the same – thus the massive boundary change in 1998 as BP merged with Amoco would be counted as one, just as a much smaller joint venture between BP exploration and Statoil in 1993. Even with this signal limitation, Table 8.1 gives a very clear picture of the distribution, sequencing and intensity of the organizational changes in BP over the chosen time period. The coding of the change initiatives into the categories was checked by a second coder; any discrepancies were then discussed and final allocations were then agreed between the two coders. Table 8.1 represents a reliable picture of change in BP from documentary sources which have, in turn, been confirmed and interpreted by personal interviews.

Table 8.1 is an adaptation and development of the nine indicators of change detailed in Figure 1.1 in Chapter 1 of this volume. The three indicators in process and boundary change are the same but two further indicators have been added to the structure changes to reflect the BP context, and a fourth major category of simplification integration has been added to capture sustained change in those areas during the period late 1992 until 1998. The two additional structural indicators – downsizing and co-location/

TABLE 8.1  *BP organizational change, staff numbers and performance: 1988–1998*

| Chairman/Chief Executive Officer | Walters | | | Horton | | Simon | | | Browne | | | Total |
|---|---|---|---|---|---|---|---|---|---|---|---|---|
| Year | 1988 | 1989 | 1990 | 1991 | 1992 | 1993 | 1994 | 1995 | 1996 | 1997 | 1998 | Total |
| Decentralizing | 3 | 2 | 1 | 2 | – | 1 | 1 | 1 | 1 | 1 | – | 13 |
| Downsizing | – | 1 | 1 | 1 | 3 | 8 | 2 | – | – | 1 | – | 17 |
| Co-location/ Centralization | – | – | – | – | – | – | – | – | 4 | 2 | – | 6 |
| Delayering | – | 1 | 1 | – | – | 1 | 1 | – | – | 1 | 1 | 6 |
| Project Forms of Organizing | 3 | 2 | 12 | 2 | 2 | 2 | 6 | 2 | 1 | 1 | – | 33 |
| Structural Change | 6 | 6 | 15 | 5 | 5 | 12 | 10 | 3 | 6 | 6 | 1 | 75 |
| Horizontal and vertical communication | 1 | 1 | 5 | – | – | – | 1 | 2 | 2 | 1 | 1 | 14 |
| Changes in IT | 1 | 1 | 2 | – | – | 1 | 2 | 1 | 1 | – | 1 | 10 |
| New Human Resources | – | – | 4 | 1 | – | 1 | 4 | 4 | 3 | 1 | 2 | 20 |
| Process changes | 2 | 2 | 11 | 1 | – | 2 | 7 | 7 | 6 | 2 | 4 | 44 |
| Downscoping | 1 | 2 | 4 | 1 | 2 | 6 | 2 | – | 1 | – | – | 19 |
| Outsourcing | 1 | – | – | – | 2 | 1 | 2 | 1 | 1 | – | – | 8 |
| Developing strategic alliances | – | – | 1 | – | 1 | – | 2 | – | 1 | 2 | 2 | 9 |
| Boundary changes | 2 | 2 | 5 | 1 | 5 | 7 | 6 | 1 | 3 | 2 | 2 | 36 |
| Simplification/ integration | 7 | 5 | 3 | 2 | 5 | 8 | 5 | 5 | 10 | 1 | 3 | 54 |
| Total | 17 | 15 | 34 | 9 | 15 | 29 | 28 | 16 | 25 | 11 | 10 | 209 |
| Av. Staff Numbers Worldwide | 125450 | 119850 | 118050 | 115250 | 105750 | 84500 | 66550 | 58150 | 53700 | 55650 | 98900** | |

*(Continued)*

TABLE 8.1  (Continued)

| Chairman/Chief Executive Officer | Walters | | Horton | | | Simon | | Browne | | | | |
|---|---|---|---|---|---|---|---|---|---|---|---|---|
| Year | 1988 | 1989 | 1990 | 1991 | 1992 | 1993 | 1994 | 1995 | 1996 | 1997 | 1998 | Total |
| Av. Staff Numbers UK | 28950 | 30700 | 30850 | 30450 | 28300 | 21900 | 17900 | 16800 | 15950 | 18050 | 19950** | |
| Replacement Cost Profit (£million)* | 1437 | 1361 | 1204 | 1035 | 352 | 896 | 1515 | 1120 | 2150 | 2787 | 4651*** | |
| Brent Oil Price per Barrel ($) | 14.96 | 18.20 | 23.81 | 20.05 | 19.37 | 17.07 | 15.98 | 17.18 | 20.81 | 19.30 | 13.11 | |

Notes
*Replacement cost profit excludes stock profits and losses before extraordinary items such as less related taxation and minority interests. It reflects the average cost of supply incurred during the year and thus provides insight into underlying trading results. It is acknowledged by BP as the clearest indicator of the company's performance and is used by them as such in annual accounts and results bulletins.
**These figures are inflated against the others as they include extra staff brought within the group as a result of both the merger with Amoco, and BP's downstream merger with Mobil in Europe that took place in 1996.
***This figure is in US$ as a result of the merger between BP and Amoco on 31 December 1998.

centralization represent, in turn, sustained attempts during the Simon era to drive down costs and in the Browne era to balance off tendencies to decentralize and empower with a desire to re-centralize some of BP's activities. Co-location, emphasizing the need for the centre to be strengthened while simultaneously engaging with the businesses – was felt to be a better turn-of-phrase than centralizing.

Simplification integration was a constant theme in the whole period but was given additional emphasis in the aftermath of Project 1990. A crucial feature of Project 1990 was the formation of scores of teams whose objectives were to problem solve rather than prevaricate in the newly delayered and empowered organization. A key part of the company's subsequent organizational strategy between 1992 and 1998 was the rationalization and integration of these teams and the standardization of activities across the group as a whole. This integration and rationalization thereby produced simplification and a considerable on-going reduction in costs. These cost reductions are clearly indicated in the big employee reductions between late 1992 and into 1997. Downsizing and downscoping were the main vehicles of employment reduction in the period late 1992 to 1994. It was these complementary change actions which substantially explain the great improvements in BP's relative return on capital employed in the same period.

Table 8.1 irrevocably establishes the presence of complementary change in BP over the period 1988–98. There is evidence of substantial intended change in all four broad areas. 1990 and 1993 reveal the greatest number of change initiatives followed by 1996, the first year also of a new CEO, John Browne. Throughout the period the greatest number of change initiatives were structural, followed by simplification integration (itself highly structural) with processes and boundaries the least in number (though in the case of boundaries, sometimes of massive scale). It is noteworthy that many of the changes signalled in 1990 by the high-profile Project 1990 were already in train by 1988 and 1989. The end of the Horton era in mid Summer 1992 is associated with great performance and governance crises. These crises precipitated massive structural and simplification changes and, for a time, a withering of process change. However, these process changes were reactivated between 1994 and 1996. The years 1990 and 1994 are the two peak years of holistic change when there is evidence of intended change in 10 and 11 of the 12 change indicators.

Table 8.1 demonstrates that for complementary change to begin to take effect substantial time, patience and persistence is necessary. Holistic change means not just doing lots of things but doing them consistently and staying the course. As we shall also see, complementary changes not only requires great vision, as in Project 1990, but also great delivery. Maintaining success in such a process is itself about delivering successes. Robert Horton was the visionary who got the new BP on the road in the early 1990s but the concept was not enough. Simon and Browne delivered.

But why in the short term did Horton fail, if indeed the case is now clear that he prepared the ground for future success? Big outcomes are rarely explained by single causes. When Robert Horton was asked to resign in June 1992 it was not just because of any doubts about the appropriateness of Project 1990, or because of his hubris, or because of accumulating weaknesses in BP's performance and reputation; it was because of a volatile mixture of all these factors. Additionally there was the process and tenor with which Project 1990 was introduced and justified to a BP that was at that time ill-equipped to handle large-scale holistic change.

BP entered the 1990s with considerable debt problems. A combination of the Standard Oil and Britoil acquisitions of 1987, plus the buy back of the BP shares from the Kuwait Investment Office in 1989, had left the company financially stretched. A former CEO takes up the story:

> We were bumping up against any reasonable sort of debt limits. With the early 90s recession we had a dreadful dilemma, to cut the capital expenditure in exploration, to a lesser extent to rationalize downstream or whether to go against falling oil prices and growth rates. We soldiered on for about a year. I was very much in favour of cutting capital expenditure but the Board wanted to cut the dividend... It was only when the recession started to bite in a big way and demand fell off and downstream margins collapsed, the oil price weakened – but it was basically the downstream business that created the additional tension in the balance sheet.

So the business context in which Project 1990 was launched started off as constraining and then became visibly punishing.

Robert Horton attempted to parry the short-term pressures and argue.

> ...we need this Project 1990 even more now. But, of course, the flip-side of that coin was that people were saying. I have the day job and do I really have to come to this culture change workshop? I got furious about the defections – there was that sort of disciplinary thing.

The gathering pressures drew out the sceptics and opponents of Project 1990. A fellow director commented:

> I found it academically interesting but only up to a point ... You could see some cutting edge stuff, but all those meetings? They were nothing to do with the business of the company – they were to do with bonding, an awful lot of management mystique.

But the group directly threatened by Project 1990 were what Horton christened 'the Brigadier Belt', the middle- to senior-level managers, many in the now doomed big HQ departments who had been the protectors and facilitators of the old BP structure and culture.

> He called them the Brigadiers. They were the middle managers who were in a very difficult position. They were on the one hand the main

line of communication downwards and therefore absolutely essential to the culture change programme, but they were also the most threatened people in the whole process.

A former CEO echoed this view:

We realized to work in this new way in this new head office you didn't need 2000 people. You didn't need the message carriers – the brigadiers who, of course, hated this because it destroyed their power base.

But Project 1990 was most exposed when it was most needed in the long term. Project 1990 was a long march designed to alter the old BP culture, cryptically portrayed by managers 'as like managing in treacle'. This was not to be achieved overnight.

I had always said it was a marathon. I had in my mind's eye that it would take four or five years.

Project 1990 foundered on Robert Horton's hubris and the problems of legitimating what was undoubtedly the right thing to do in a context increasingly intolerant of actions which did not appear to deliver business results. A senior head office specialist commented:

It was not portrayed in terms of we have to do this to get costs down or even to do this for enhanced business performance. It was the expounding of a vision. BP will be the most successful oil company in the 1990s. But the link between these organizational and cultural changes and the vision about success and performance – that link was not there and that I think is a real weakness.

A senior director also remarked:

I think the learning was that this is all very well but we have a business to run and you had better not take your eye off the ball. You can do these things, but only on the back of a horse!

Having been persuaded by a number of US business leaders that 'this had to be a crusade', Robert Horton could not and would not disengage. Increasingly his sceptics and opponents saw the contradiction between the authoritative crusade and the cultural messages about openness and empowerment:

It is curious, Bob made it on culture change when it was a new expression – and he was right in principle. But he was the wrong person to deliver it.

But when Robert Horton fell on his sword in June 1992 his successor shrewdly judged this was a moment not just for change but also for continuity. A fellow director described the changeover in these terms:

> There was a big reaction around Bob's call to resign … his demise
> was a signal for us to go into penury mood. The six of us sat down and
> we went through it all down to the pictures on the wall saying we can't
> afford this – we can't afford that. And that lasted ferociously – it is still
> around – but it lasted to the exclusion of almost any strategic sensible
> long-term debate for about 2–3 years. We got profitability up and we
> benefited from a lot of the pluses that Bob brought in because of
> Project 1990. It still lives: nobody talks about it anymore, of course, but
> he was way ahead of his time in a lot of his thinking. And he was right
> about many of the organizational things.

The message now was encapsulated in the simple slogan from David Simon – PRT: performance, reputation and team work. There was to be no growth without performance, and no survival without performance. A senior manager described David Simons' first large meeting as CEO with an anxious London office immediately after Robert Horton resigned. 'The stylistic differences were apparent immediately. Here was "the great communicator"' Mr Everyman. There was no nuclear science – just a series of simple messages, conceptually easy but hard to deliver.' David Simon, jacket off, microphone in hand, left the platform and walked through the tense and troubled audience trying to deal with questions about why and where next. He relaxed his audience, but only as a prelude to an orgy of blood on the carpet.

But the wise folk at this and subsequent gatherings noticed that there was a T in PRT. Team work was the symbol of continuity in among the impending change. A head office specialist commented:

> The word was, out with the exit of Horton we can forget about that
> stuff. But David Simon was taking pains to say no – this cultural stuff
> is important and it remains and it's right. So although the actual formal
> process of culture change was by then pretty well ended in most of BP –
> it was getting this extra boost from the top.

This picture is confirmed by one of David Simon's immediate colleagues:

> We stepped back from it and said we have got to change some jargon,
> but some of the messages are right and we should retain it and that
> was quite conscious. But there was a short-term crisis and we must
> use that to get the costs down – quickly and ruthlessly and we did.

In 1995 David Simon stepped down as CEO and John Browne succeeded him. Simon in turn succeeded Lord Ashburton as Non-executive Chairman. But the changing of the guard was more than just continuity of top personnel, there was more telling evidence of continuity in underlying philosophy alongside, again, a change in direction, this time to strategically reposition BP in the world oil industry and begin to change the rules of the game in that industry. But before the big strategic changes came the structure, systems and to a lesser extent the process changes. John Browne turned BP's three big businesses – oil, exploration and chemicals – into 91 business units, all focusing relentlessly on performance. The idea was to break BP into smaller, more accountable and responsible performance centres, while simultaneously obtaining the benefits of scale and knowledge transfer by building corporate group leadership meetings and problem solving through peer groups. So there is some fragmentation and glue: 'That is the logic – to have your cake and eat it.'

While John Browne was simultaneously fragmenting and complicating BP, he was also integrating and simplifying it. After several years of decentralizing, this emphasis was maintained in the context of a drive to create a stronger strategic centre. All this was focused on the organizational obsession with performance. Hierarchy had disappeared in the layered status sense, but had massively increased in the immediacy of the performance targets and the incentive systems which buttressed them. Further evidence of the centralizing tendencies in BP was Browne's imposition of a common operating environment for IT – a signal weakness until then in the company's IT infrastructure. In 1997 there was nowhere to hide among BPs slimmed-down staff of 55 000, but the message was underlying continuity and building up the complements:

> I think (Browne) tried very hard to follow in the footsteps of Simon – deliberately so. The two seemed to work well together – so things started in the Simon era largely were continued into the Browne era and were maybe Browne's ideas in the first place. So the performance culture was embedded in everybody and the quarterly performance reviews were embedded everywhere.

A colleague who knows Simon and Browne well, captured this picture of the two CEOs:

> He (John) did many of the same things as David and he spends as much time in the City as David did. But he looked to a broader pattern. David is not great in my view as a strategist. John brings that as well and he is terrifyingly efficient for the company and for himself through the company.

So the strategic thinking and acting of Browne was now harnessed to repositioning BP in the industry and then applying the fiercesome organizational capabilities to drive performance in an enterprise of even greater scale:

> Once we got our own costs in order then we made the massive jump with Amoco. We are able to apply these well-honed processes to a bigger aspect … John was able to look at the whole industry picture and went through the strategy in great detail and started positioning the company to take advantage of its new-found respectability in financial markets.

BP in 1998 was now a very long way in scale, performance and respectability from what it had been at the low point of the Summer of 1992. A former

CEO had this to say about the underling continuities and changes that delivered that performance improvement:

> If you look at the personal characteristics of the three of us, we are very different people. But there is continuity of philosophy, but with widely different personal characteristics.

By 1997 BP had honed, developed and added to Horton's 1990 view of holistic change. The difference between 1990–92 and 1997 was that the company was not just thinking holistically but was thinking and acting holistically. It was not just that elements of complementary change were together, but that they were made to work together by a CEO with as finely grained strategic as operational capabilities, by decentralized business units held together by a clear central strategic framework and performance targets and incentives, but also by the residue of commitment from the old BP culture. All this was energized by the tangible improvements in relative business performance and by the confidence of success. The complements had come together and delivered the performance improvement but would this mean organizational machine be reinforced or destabilized by the impending massive mergers with Amoco and Arco and then the smaller boundary changes which were to follow?

It seems the BP organizational performance machine has triumphed, although, as we saw in Figure 8.1, BP's relative return on capital dimmed in the short term relative to Shell. The organizational and strategic capabilities honed through Phase 2 and into Phase 3 of the BP journey were applied with energy and skill in integrating the three acquisitions into BP. Clear principles and expectations were set for the integration process and then clear actions taken to drive forward on the targets. The executive expectations were set in advance of the merger and communicated immediately. Rapid pace was decreed the key to success. Non-negotiable targets were set and the message was 'communicate, communicate, communicate'. The principles for the new company were agreed and communicated early. There was to be a single organization, early definition of the structural building blocks and those who would occupy them, with clear roles for leaders and expectations for continuous change. As a result of these and other activities, the performance targets of $5.8 billion pre tax measured against the 1998 cost base were met by February 2002. But by this time we were well into Phase 4 of the BP change journey and there was now an appeal to performance improvement beyond cost and efficiency means. This broader, growth-oriented strategy was first announced in July 2000 and entailed targets of 5.5 per cent production growth and growing financial returns based on what BP call mid-cycle operating conditions.

For the two years 2000 to 2002, BP successfully met the output growth target of 5.5 per cent, but in the third quarter of 2002 BP announced a 13 per cent drop in earnings and forecast that 3 per cent growth was a more realistic target. As Lord Browne put it at the third quarter announcement meeting:

> We have expected to grow by 5.5 per cent, but we have failed … we expect to grow by 3 per cent, this is disappointing … There are no excuses, we just haven't delivered.

Two days later Shell's third quarter results displayed a 17 per cent fall in profits. Shell blamed the downturn on tough trading conditions in refining and marketing. Despite booming oil prices following fears of an attack on Iraq, Lord Browne had said at his third quarter meeting 'the current environment has little upside and significant downside risks'. Early signs at BP are that this may be the moment to announce a big cost-cutting drive at Sullom Voe the largest oil and gas terminal in Europe. For some, the virtuous circle of complementary change in BP has to keep turning.

## THE UNILEVER CHANGE JOURNEY: 1985–2002

Unilever was created in 1929 by the merging of the British-based soap and detergent businesses of William Lever and the Dutch margarine and edible oil activities of the Van den Bergh and Jurgen families. Since then, brands have been at the heart of the business which has now coalesced around the two global divisions of Foods and Home and Personal Care. Since 1929, the two parent companies have been operating as a singly unit: Unilever NV is based in the Netherlands and Unilever Plc is located in London. Unilever also has the governance complication of co-CEOs, but they are both 'chairmen' of the combined Unilever Group and not CEOs of the two separate companies. The pattern of governance in recent times has been for these two chairmen roles to be occupied by a Dutch and British passport holder and for these two to be joined by the next chairman in a special committee of three. This pattern afforded a stable alliance across the two original constituent parts and orderly succession and strategic continuity between generations of top leaders. Over the period of our interest the chairmen have been Maljers (1984–94) and Angus (1985–91); Tabaksblat (1994–99) and Perry (1992–96), and now FitzGerald 1996–present and Burgmans 1999–present. Niall FitzGerald, an Irish citizen, is the first non-Britain to take the London chairman position. He has also broken the Unilever mould in the directness and depth of change he has stimulated in the Unilever Group.

For most of the past 20 years Unilever has participated in a stable, but unremarkable success (see Figure 8.2). Unlike BP there have been no great business crises or financial traumas to propel Unilever into revolutionary change. The pace and atmosphere of change has accelerated since FitzGerald came on the scene in the mid 1990s, but even in that era the drivers for change were more internally generated than externally imposed. The style of change pre-1996 in Unilever has been incremental, cumulative and progressive, but always cautious and controlled. This might be explained by a number of features of the group's governance, leadership systems and culture. The dual chairmen provided checks and balances, control and collegiality at the top. The strong tradition of decentralization to national and regional organizations provided with it a historical reticence to impose a strong strategic framework from the centre. The traditional glue which has held Unilever together has been like-minded recruitment and a strong socialization process among the far flung Unilever executive cadre. A common set of business principles and culture held Unilever together, not an explicitly articulated and enforced set of corporate goals (Lorenz, 1996; Goffee and Jones, 1996).

The realization in the mid 1990s that this historical strength had become a contemporary weakness was part of the inner and outer context which made FitzGerald's centralizing tendencies more acceptable. By then it was clear to all that Procter & Gamble and L'Oréal's greater corporate strength was producing a faster rate of exploitation of market opportunities and more accelerated product development processes than seemed possible in Unilever. The structural, process and systems changes engineered by FitzGerald in the mid 1990 were not only consistent with the continuous pattern of strategic changes which preceded them (the core strategy and its derivatives) but now essential to harvest the benefits of a more focused organization. The complementarities came together in the early part of the FitzGerald era, were reinforced by improving business results (until 1999) and then took off again with the now more explicit complementarities change logic which was driven forward in the path to growth holistic change process of 2000.

Looking back to order history we can see two eras of transformation in Unilever since the early to mid 1980s. The first era, roughly stretching from 1980 to 1994, encapsulated the leadership of Maljers, Angus and Perry and was much about the so-called 'core strategy' of breaking up the old Unilever conglomerate and through the Starfish programme building the new legs of the more focused and performance-driven business. This was an era of divestment of older businesses, which were either peripheral to the emerging sense of the core or acquisitive in building the new elements of that core. Perry's 1992 strategy review consolidated these tendencies, but also led to some organizational process changes to complement and enable the business strategy and boundary changes. Chief among these were Project Crystal, which reviewed the purpose and style of the corporate centre, and some important process changes, which encouraged network building across the global corporation and a greater sense of the economic and social value of learning and knowledge transfer to the increasingly product-dominated form of organizing. With elements of the strategy and process changes now in place, it was left to FitzGerald and Tabaksblat to deliver the missing structural and systems complements and keep the strategy and process changes in motion. Era two can be personalized around FitzGerald and below we sketch its essential purpose and potential.

## The first era of change: 1980–92

What did Unilever look like at the beginning of the 1980s as our first era of change was being contemplated? In the 1960s and 1970s Unilever expanded through the pursuit of vertical and horizontal integration. In the context of a light-touch corporate centre and a tradition of decentralization to very strong national organizations, the company proliferated brands of uneven quality and profitability and service companies that were encouraged and supported by the national managers who drove a great deal of the product development process. In the 1970s Unilever had evolved as much as planned its own advertising agency, market research agency and packaging, transport and chemicals businesses. FitzGerald (2002) has recently characterized this period as one when Unilever strayed from its original corporate purpose and essentially became a conglomerate.

By the mid 1960s Unilever could see that more product co-ordination was necessary and product co-ordination groups grew slowly from three in 1962 to six in 1969 and ten by 1977. Little by little, management increased the product co-ordinators groups' role in Europe until they had direct line responsibility for all operating companies in their businesses. So product-based organizations with different degrees of central influence in varying regions were formed and there was a fundamental tilting of the matrix away from the formerly powerful national companies and the previously sole-supplier service companies. These moves were stimulated by a complex mixture of competitor pressure (Procter & Gamble were displaying greater agility from a more centralized product-development process); management fashion in re-thinking organization design; and a sense that 'the conglomerate' was becoming unmanageable (Bartlett and Ghoshal, 1987; Foster, 1988).

The struggle to improve co-ordination combined with unspectacular performance to precipitate the strategic re-think which emerged publicly in 1984 as the core strategy. While still respectful of the cultural totem of decentralization it seems the top and centre of Unilever was now ready to impose. The impositions were a new concern for strategic focus around the recently labelled core businesses of foods, detergent, personal products and chemicals. From 1984 to 1988, Unilever disposed of £2 billion of non-performing brands and non-essential supply companies and acquired £4 billion of new businesses. The biggest of these was the US Chesebrough–Ponds group which began the strong move into personal care and the UK Brook Bond portfolio which strengthened foods. But this was just the beginning of a massive and continuing programme of acquisitions and disposals which continue to this day. The mid 1980s refocusing was taken further by the Starfish programme of 1988, which began to emphasize particular geographical areas and sub-categories within the four core businesses. The underlying rationale was a need to globalize beyond the European base and with this a need to identify priorities. The organizational structure which had evolved somewhat in the 1960s and 1970s remained essentially stable, based on the traditional three-man 'special committee' at the top, still powerful national operating companies, and in the middle a board made up of individuals with international (typically Europe plus US) product co-ordination roles, or with regional responsibilities. Processes were governed by the principle of devolution and the famously collegial managerial networks. Maljers et al. (1996: 560) later looked back on this period as 'measured progress': 'Successful change has to be anchored in stability, else it runs the danger of provoking chaos.' Continuity with moderate change was the message and the style in Unilever at that time.

In time the keyword 'core' itself became contestable and eventually in the 1990s it disappeared from Unilever's organizational lexicon. In 1988 Angus was defining core as 'those businesses that we properly understand, in which we have critical mass, and where we believe we have a strong competitive future'. But at the same time, FitzGerald was already prepared to be heretical in suggesting their 'core' could 'entrap': 'we must examine the peripheries of core continuously so that we can see how we can push those borders out' (quoted in Foster, 1988: 67).

The 1990s changes (and the end of the first era in our analysis) began with the 1992 strategy review, coinciding with Perry's arrival as one of the two chairmen. This review extended the logic of the earlier strategy reviews to identify still more strongly the necessary geographical focus (Asia and emerging markets) and the need to eliminate underperforming businesses within the whole portfolio. In a classic portfolio sense, 'star' categories and products began to be defined. At this stage, there was no crisis in Unilever, only a variety of frustrations. The 1992 review heralded new opportunities in Asia, in Eastern Europe and arising from increasing progress to economic integration in the European Union. There was also a heightened sense of the challenges posed in these conditions by more globally-centralized rivals such as L'Oréal and Procter & Gamble.

The 1992 strategy review went in tandem with a number of other changes, concentrated on processes. Perry was particularly associated with the slogan 'If only Unilever knew what Unilever knows' and the notion of 'Unileverage'. He was keen on networking, improving innovation and presided over the massive extension of e-mail networks (UNISON). The Innovation Centre concept spread around the company, concentrating research and development and marketing resources on a regional and global basis and bringing them together within the same units. Early steps towards the Innovation Funnel (a standardized methodology for screening innovation projects) were begun. Perry established a central corporate planning unit properly for the first time, and the Hax strategy development process was introduced and began to diffuse. Acquisitions and divestments continued along the lines of developing the star businesses and regions. At the same time, there was major rationalization of capacity, especially within the new regional unit of Lever Europe, which allowed the elimination of unnecessary national manufacturing and other facilities.

## The second era of change: 1993–

This second era of change picks up the aftermath and some of the disappointments of the period 1983 to 1993, the preparation and launch of the 'Restructuring for Outstanding Performance' proposition in 1996 and its enhancement and continuity by the rolling out of 'Path to Growth' in 2000. Behind all these organizational and business developments was the vision and energy of Niall FitzGerald who became co-chairman designate in 1994 and assumed the role and the power in 1996. But in between the public announcement of succession in 1994 and taking up the role in 1996 FitzGerald had to survive the public humiliation of the Persil Power Fiasco. This relaunch of one of Unilever's star brands fell apart as it became clear an undetected flaw in its accelerator was destroying the garments being washed. As head of the Detergents product group at the time FitzGerald had a lot of explaining to do, but his close relationship with the Dutch co-Chairman Maurice Tabaksblat carried him through to his promotion. FitzGerald later said:

> If I had come to the view that the affair had mortally wounded me ... I would have taken the decision to leave. But there was quite a strong view that we were at a point in our history where we were making great efforts to make the business less risk averse, and if the moment a risk was taken which went wrong, that person had to leave, then in a sense that would have been more damaging. (quoted in Davidson, 1997: 54)

Having survived the Persil Fiasco, FitzGerald returned to his part-time task of leading the working party constituted in 1993 to recommend reorganization of the Unilever Group. Some have argued the Persil humiliation helped FitzGerald by creating a mini crisis in a Heartland product, which helped to build a more receptive context for change (Davidson, 1997). But there were other even more tangible drivers of change at the time. Return on capital had peaked at 17.2 per cent in 1992 and by 1995 was down to 14.2 per cent and operating profit margins had peaked even earlier in 1990. Some of the Unilever non-executives had been mumbling about 'performance drift' and there was a feeling beyond FitzGerald that Unilever was showing classic signs of organizational fatigue. 'Extra levels of complexity on an already convoluted structure with confused accountabilities, constipated decision making and frustrated de-motivated staff' (Lang quoted in Lorenz, 1996: 46).

FitzGerald's diagnosis was broadly based, but this quotation captures part of the problem he saw in Unilever at the mid 1990s.

> I saw that the unique strength of Unilever should be to send a clear set of objectives from the centre and then give maximum freedom within that framework for people to operate in, but the organization to facilitate that wasn't in place.

Instead of this, FitzGerald wanted a form of organizing where:

> There was a clear setting of principles and a strategic framework at the centre and then we say 'you go and do it', we won't interfere unless you move outside the framework or you are not meeting your plans.

This view, of course, captures the classic duality of simultaneously centralizing and decentralizing. Hold the ring and empower, one of the characteristics we discuss more fully in Part 3 of this volume. FitzGerald drove a coherent set of organizational changes through Unilever, which began to fit with its strategy and business model.

The 'Restructuring for Outstanding Performance' change initiative removed the confusion between co-ordinations with profit responsibility and local companies with operating responsibilities. It also abolished the traditional Special Committee at the very top of Unilever. The driver was the need to prioritize still further, especially on five 'priority regions' (emerging markets) and seven 'star' categories out of a newly defined thirteen. The principle was classically Chandlerian in its separation of strategy from operations (Whittington and Meyer, 2000). The new Executive Committee of seven members had clear policy responsibility and a corporate view, but no direct profit responsibility. The seven were a mixture of category directors (Foods, Home and Personal Care, Industrial) plus the two chairmen and functional directors. Although the category directors had no profit responsibility, unlike the previous co-ordinators, they had global scope beyond Europe and the USA. The set of Business Group directors below them had operating and profit responsibilities generally on a regional basis: for example, Home and Personal Care, Europe; Foods, North America. Country operating companies were clearly integrated within the Regional Business Groups. Executive Committee and Business Groups would be brought together by the Unilever Executive Council. The advantages of this new structure lay in establishing a clear corporate view, disentangling profit and operating responsibilities from policy and rendering corporate debate less territorially defensive. The structure instituted more global ownership of key categories, brands and strategies, but played to Unilever's established strengths of decentralization by comparison with L'Oréal and Procter & Gamble. The 1996 Annual Report (the first with FitzGerald as co-Chairman) insisted: 'Our deep roots in local cultures and markets around the world are our unparalleled inheritance and the foundation for future growth. We will bring our wealth of knowledge and international expertise to the service of local consumers – a truly multi-local multinational.'

Other changes moved in parallel with this reorganization. The notion of organizing around processes (rather than functions) reinforced the innovation emphasis (thus the company defined the 'innovation process' as combining research and development and marketing), and also helped rationalize across borders, again relegating national operating companies (thus the 'supply chain process' might not be integrated within one country, but deliberately draw on other factories within a region). A new performance system was introduced based on trading contributions and economic value added and with a Business Group (rather than solely national operating company) performance-related element. The performance commitments of Business Group Presidents were described in the new terms of a 'contract'. In some parts of Unilever, balanced score card notions were introduced.

Language was standardized around common worldwide 'professional skills' and notions of 'organizational effectiveness'. Product and functional networks, formal and informal, were developed as a deliberate mechanism to support the new category directors and increase functional integration. Relatively formal networks such as Human Resources could spin-off project networks such as Recruitment or development networks such as Organizational Effectiveness. The International Category Boards, which provided the formal global framework for categories, had quasi-networks in the forms of International Business Terms around particular brands with typically much more loosely defined and fluctuating memberships and tasks. A new Innovation Process Management system based on the Funnel, but supported by Lotus Notes, provided standarized and integrated means of supporting innovation, especially category, on a global basis. Divestments of peripheral businesses continued (notably Speciality Chemicals in 1997) as did reinforcing acquisitions (for example, Helen Curtis in 1996 reinforcing the personal products business in the USA).

By 1997 and 1998 the above sets of structure changes seemed to be the missing elements in the complementary picture that drove up Unilever's relative business performance (see Figure 8.2). Picking up a basket of measures of performance change from 1985 to 1999, operating margins within Unilever went from below 6 per cent to over 11 per cent; return on capital employed more than doubled from less than 11 per cent to over 22 per cent and net cash flow from operating activities totalled over 50 billion Euros. But Unilever's fourth 'lever' of value creation – underlying sales growth – was still lagging behind its immediate competitors in 1999. This deficiency plus the sharp fall in their share price in 1999 (explained by FitzGerald largely as a result of the rush of money to new economy stocks, FitzGerald, 2002) were all part of the background to the announcement of Path to Growth in February, 2000.

'Path to Growth' was this time explicitly acknowledged as a broadly based and integrated programme of change. By 2002 FitzGerald was describing

Unilever's overall change philosophy in terms of 'waves of change'. 'A single initiative is not enough – it needs to be reinforced again and again, and each initiative needs to be part of an integrated whole' (FitzGerald, 2002: 8). The portfolio message about concentrating on a smaller and smaller number of highly profitable and growing world-class brands was reinforced at the top structure level by breaking the company into the two global divisions of Foods and Home and Personal Care. Further emphasis was given to the disciplines of the targeted performance system, but this time an additional emphasis was given to cultural change 'to increase the degree of stretch … and increase the speed of action' (FitzGerald, 2002). FitzGerald also took this opportunity to 're-direct, renew and revitalize' his leadership team. This was achieved by a combination of exiting of lesser performers, 'enrichment of the gene pool' through acquisitions and through mid-career recruitment. 'As a consequence 40 per cent of the top 100 are different from the team of 2 years ago, 80 per cent are different from 5 years ago (in 1997) and the average age has come down by 10 years' FitzGerald (2002). Unilever was in 2000 now driving for sales growth from its ever shrinking portfolio of brands which were being refreshed by acquisitions and disposals. By the third quarter of 2002 (and after a series of strong results) Unilever announced a 33 per cent rise in pre-tax profits. Its leading brands had showed sales growth for the previous 12 months of 4.5 per cent and 5.4 per cent for the third quarter of 2002. Unilever was now achieving substantial performance improvement from its trajectory of complementary change.

## PATTERNS IN THE PROCESS OF DELIVERING CHANGE AND PERFORMANCE IN BP AND UNILEVER

The BP and Unilever cases illustrate some of the virtues of investigating change journeys over significant periods of time and within a historical context. Such analyses are capable of exposing the interplay between context and action over multiple levels of analysis and the way factors external and internal to the firm shape patterns of continuity and change. Leader effects in the short term can be linked to performance consequences in the longer term as different generations and styles of leadership interpret and adjust to the strengths and limitations of any particular generation and any beneficial continuities between generations over time.

But what are some of the patterns in the process of adaptation in BP and Unilever over time, and how are we to account for such patterns and link them to our goal of explaining the links between organizational change and firm performance? In a series of papers, March (1991, 1995), Levinthal and March (1993), and Lewin, et al. (1999) have developed a theory of the adaptation of firms and populations of firms which explains firm performance and survival as a balancing act between exploratory and exploitative activity. March (1991) portrays organizational adaptation as a duality of exploration of new possibilities and exploitation of old certainties. Exploration is characterized as involving risk taking and innovation, sustained search for novelty, and the combining together of possibly previously unrelated strategies and knowledge in order to deliver superior outcomes. In contrast, exploitation involves less risk, is more closely justified in terms of short-term means–ends behaviour, is efficiency driven and cost related and is designed to take advantage of existing bundles of skill and knowledge. Levinthal and March (1993) argue that the returns associated with exploration are distant in time and are highly volatile while the gains from exploitation are likely to be proximal in time and more certain. Both authors contend that long-term evolution and superior performance are likely to be dependent on an appropriate mix of exploratory and exploitative adaptations. They argue that too much exploration will imperil short-term success and too much exploitation will imperil long-term survival.

This is an appealing and elegant theory of adaptation and performance which as we shall see can be profitably linked to the BP and Unilever pathways of change. However, dichotomies reveal and conceal; simplify and distort. The March and Levinthal work is as yet substantially empirically untested and it is remarkably silent on the micro-processes of choice and change as firms struggle to both exploit and forget their histories and invent their futures. We shall seek, therefore, to account for the BP and Unilever pathways by a judicious mixture of theoretical approaches which are, in turn, sensitive to the dualities of exploration and exploitation, economic theories of complementarities and a process view of changing.

One way of interpreting the Walters, Horton , Simon and Browne eras in BP's recent history is to see them in turn as eras of exploitation and relatively unexceptional success; of exploration and signal failure; of exploitation and developing success; and combined exploitation and exploration and an era of relatively conspicuous high performance. Project 1990 was, without doubt, a time of maverick leadership and high personal and corporate risk. The Horton era ended with the exit of Robert Horton in the gloom of personal failure, but with the seeds of future success yet to be exploited by the next generation of leaders. An immediate associate of Robert Horton commented:

> There comes a time in the tide of history of the corporation when a maverick like me comes to the top. I remember him saying that.

Horton himself several years later acknowledged the risks of exploratory activity:

> The lessons I draw are these are essential exercises but they are personally very dangerous. My wife said to me it is the bravest thing you have ever done in your life … that one recognizes that occasionally

> you have got to have changes, that it is fraught with danger. But if I had
> my time again I would do it again … it unquestionably had to be done …
> And whether I am there or not did not matter, it just continues on and
> I think everyone as an impartial observer would say it has been very
> much the motor that has driven the rest of the company along into the
> successful position that it is in now.

This is a reasonable, but a partial view. The Horton era of exploration and risk needed, in turn, the Simon era of exploitation and the current Browne era of exploitation and exploration. The Browne capacity to build on the Simon exploitation pattern, which he (Browne) had been engaging in continuously since the late 1980s, combined with his big exploratory strategic moves, not only ensured a further step-wise change in BP's performance but also stimulated the change in the competitive rules of the game in the world oil and gas sector. Since Browne became CEO of BP in July 1995, the corporation has, in turn, produced a massive downstream refining and marketing partnership with Mobil (1996); built a ground-breaking partnership with Bovis construction to extend and improve its European service network (1997); formed a strategic partnership with one of Russia's leading oil and gas companies, A.O. Sidanco (1997); and merged with Amoco, Arco and Burmah Castrol between 1998 and 2000. This is exploration with a vengeance which affords the dual performance benefit of market leadership for the long term and the opportunity to harness the, by now, well-practised BP exploitation routines of driving down costs to deliver performance in the short term.

Unilever's trajectory of change and performance shows some similarities and some differences with BP. Sticking for the moment with the language of exploration and exploitation, it is clear that Unilever's pathway to performance change was more evolutionary and for a long time less intendedly holistic. One very senior manager reflected afterwards:

> One certainly did not have a grand vision in which all of these
> changes had a clear place which one then spooled out one at a time.
> No … They were clearly all things that were subjects of enormous
> frustration to us at the top of the business. We knew we had to tackle
> them simultaneously … But I can't say it was the product of some
> master plan.

The Maljers and Angus era (1984–94) and the Tabaksblat and Perry era (1992–96) were periods of purposeful change with strong evidence of sequential and overlapping initiatives all directed to the strategic repositioning of the business, but the tone was measured and careful and the net effect largely exploitative in character. It wasn't until FitzGerald took over in 1996 that an era of more expansive exploratory change began, but balanced with some targeted exploitative behaviour to reduce costs and sharpen up performance management systems *and* outcomes. So, in BP the pattern post-1990 was exploration followed by exploitation and then the combined exploration and exploitation of the Browne era. In Unilever, the pattern of the three generations of leaders was exploitation, followed by more exploration culminating in the joint exploration and exploitation of the FitzGerald era.

There were also differences in the sequencing of changes in the two companies. In Unilever, the sequence was almost continuous strategy and boundary changes throughout the whole period 1984 to 2002, overlapping with some modest process changes in the early 1990s, and with the major structural, governance and systems changes not occurring until 1996 onwards. In BP, however, we saw the beginnings of the boundary/strategy changes in the late 1980s and early 1990 as BP sought to divest itself of peripheral parts of its portfolio. These modest boundary changes then overlapped with the aspirational structure and culture changes of Project 1990. Process changes then followed in the mid 1990s and the very big strategy changes (to acquire Amoco, Arco and Burmah Castrol) occurred in the late 1990s.

As we have seen, there were also differences in the explicitness with which holistic and complementary change was attempted in each company. Project 1990 in BP was intendedly holistic, but did not deliver on its intentions until the mid to late 1990s. By that time BP had been energized towards large-scale complementary change by a number of factors external and internal to the company. These included the crisis circumstances and governance traumas of 1992; the learning by doing from the organizational changes of Project 1990; Simon's shrewd realization that elements of the Horton vision had to be carried through, even though the architect of change was no longer there; and then the changing priorities and style occasioned by Browne's rise to the very top of BP in 1995. The intellectual logic and vocabulary of complementarities was also brought into BP in the mid 1990s by Browne. He had graduated with a Masters degree from Stanford University and the close and continuing links between BP and Stanford meant that the Stanford-based academics (Milgrom and Roberts) were personally able to shape BP thinking. The fact that McKinsey were regular advisers to BP in that era and they were also linked to Roberts added to the intellectual imprinting of complementarities thinking at the highest levels of BP.

The Unilever pattern of change was certainly not intendedly holistic, but could be characterized as emergent holism by the end of the 1990s. FitzGerald's speech to Goldman Sachs in 2002 contained very explicitly holistic forms of change language and since the Path to Growth change programme of 2000 Unilever had, in thought and action, realized the payoff from leading change as an integrated system of mutually reinforcing elements. But for most of the period of investigation in Unilever, their change pathway is better portrayed as an exercise in sequential, overlapping change episodes rather than the explicit simultaneous orchestration of a range of change practices. In among these overlapping change initiatives, the critical moment for Unilever was Restructuring for Outstanding Performance in 1996. This change completed the circle of strategy and boundary, structure and process changes. Since 1997, Unilever's performance has taken off, beating almost all its competitors on the main measures. It was not the structural changes by themselves that achieved this. The structural changes relied on better processes and a more forward strategy with a better portfolio of brands. The Unilever story thereby emphasizes that higher performance requires the full set of complements, but that putting them together can take years of careful foundation building.

Even though BP started the process of change differently and harnessed their complements more quickly, the most obvious similarity between the two cases is the time it took to build the complements and harvest the performance benefits from them. There is no sign or symptom of the quick fix in either of these two cases.

Building the complementarity pieces into the organizational jigsaw takes time and requires considerable energy, persistence and patience. In these processes we obviously have to give due weight to a number of factors. Sustained change requires a cocktail of pressure from the outer and inner context of the firm. Unilever were stimulated by the performance drift of the 1980s and early 90s and the constant adverse benchmarking with their key competitors, Procter & Gamble and L'Oréal. The Persil crisis of 1994 could have ended FitzGelrad's career, but instead it was used to help justify the key structural and governance changes of 1996. The 1992 crisis in BP was also a great enabler of a faster rate of change. But changes in outer context have to be seen and acted upon by the leadership system; leader effects cannot be ignored in explaining the links between change and performance. The big and shared message from the BP and Unilever cases is that leader effects need to be understood across generations of leaders and not just within generations. For the time being, Browne and FitzGerald are receiving the acclaim and this may have some justification. Compared with their peer groups they may be somewhat exceptional in their qualities of holistic thought and action and in their abilities to master the strategic and the operational. But Horton took the big risk in BP and Simon carried elements of his message forward, while taking the necessary short-term actions to turn the company around. Browne built on this legacy. FitzGerald also inherited a system that was moving in the direction, if not at the speed, he desired. Many of the foundational blocks for change had by that time been put in place by Maljers, Angus, Perry and Tabaksblat. Indeed, if it had not been for Tabaksblat's support, FitzGerald would not have survived the public loss of face from his role in the Persil crisis of 1994. Leader effects can be important, but as of much else in organizational life they need to be assessed in their holistic context.

## LEADING COMPLEMENTARY CHANGE

What are some of the lessons for the practice of leading complementary change deriveable from the BP and Unilever case histories? The first lesson is wrapped up in the capacities now demanded of leaders in the innovating organization. The theory and logic of complementarities requires special qualities of holistic thinking and holistic action from leaders. This means conceptual ability of a high order to grasp trends early and to think through a pattern of response which can deliver mutually reinforcing effects. The move to action recognizes the importance of building organizational capabilities as a competitive weapon. These more strategic imperatives have to coalesce with a concern for targeting and delivery that in turn requires a great facility for operational detail. Part of the Browne and FitzGerald capacities and accomplishments was that they could straddle and exploit a range of dualities. They helped to build organizations which explored and exploited the strategic and the operational, hierarchies and networks, and tendencies to centralizing and decentralizing.

But complementarities theory does not just proclaim the virtues of building linked systems of innovations such that two plus two produces more than four; it also has the additional insight – the potential for negative synergies. A particular practice not only depends on its complements to yield its full benefits, but it may also have negative effects if those complements are absent. Our statistical analyses in Chapter 7 confirmed both the positive and negative propositions of complementarities theory.

The importance of systems of synergistic relationships and the dangers of negative synergies produce some powerful predictions which have been clearly revealed in the BP and Unilever cases. Because the payoffs to change depend on a complete system of complementary practices, successful change is likely to require strong leadership from the top to achieve system-wide transformation. A necessary condition for complementary change is the kind of strong, aware and engaged central direction practised by Simon and Browne in BP and FitzGerald in Unilever. This does not mean, of course, that local experiments and piecemeal initiatives have no part to play in the foundational processes of building complements. The road to complementary change in BP and Unilever required a long haul of exploration and exploitation and in that long haul there were important and large pockets of innovation in constituent parts of the business, which were then brought to the centre and rolled out across the corporation. Thus in BP, Exploration and Production was the great innovation centre for building organizational capability. When Browne moved from CEO of Exploration and Production to CEO of BP he then brought the learning from his previous job to the centre. Perry did the same thing in Unilever. Prior to taking up the joint chairman role in 1992, Perry had been co-ordinator for Personal Products. In that role he had successfully experimented with the regional and global innovation centre idea and other process changes which post-1992 were rolled out across the corporation. So, in building complementary change, there is bound to be variation in the pace of change across the corporation and collecting and connecting the learning from the change leaders becomes a crucial part of energizing the whole from its parts. The politics of envy associated with such dynamics often requires the leader of the fast change localities to move into power positions at the top and centre for the rollout of the learning to take place.

Our proposition about the perils of the J-curve were well illustrated in the BP case. The J-curve effect is the risk of performance decline as one system of complements is dismantled, while the next system is still expensively being put in place with partial changes leading to declining performance, and only comprehensive change yielding high payoffs. The fact that things may get worse before they get better means that strong leaders are needed to survive transition processes, something Horton failed to do in BP. There is comfort in partial changes. They are politically and emotionally easier to contemplate, but encourage long-term declines. But the inertia of suboptimal systems, the comfort of partial moves, and the initial penalties of changes which disrupt the old complements and which cannot yet put in place the new complements, all conspire to create the great leadership challenges – how to bring forward a leadership system capable of the degree of risk which will break complementary traps. Even allowing for Browne's current difficulties, there is no question about his track record in delivering change and performance improvement in BP and FitzGerald can make similar claims in Unilever. Individual differences do matter in organizational life.

Alongside the capacity to lead, complementary change journeys also need an attuned capacity for learning. Early in his tenure as CEO of BP, Browne articulated at length his view that 'learning is at the heart of a company's ability to adapt to a rapidly changing environment' (Browne in Prokesch, 1997: 148). The logic behind the examples in the Prokesch article and in subsequent analyses by Griffiths et al. (1998) and Hansen and von Oetinger (2001) all indicate the sophisticated use of learning theory and learning mechanisms as practical tools of organizational capability-building in BP. Both Unilever and BP have recognized that learning starts at the top, 'a clear purpose allows a company to focus its learning' (Browne in Prokesch, 1997: 150). 'We have a clear strategy, but crystal clear communication' FitzGerald (2002: 3). But clarity in terms of purpose and strategic framework is nothing without the redesign of organizational processes to collect and connect knowledge and this has been a clear part of the package of interdependent changes created in BP and Unilever.

In part one of this book we emphasized the new importance of the duality of organizing/strategizing. BP and Unilever are exemplars in recognizing and managing this duality. They are also both mindful of our other related idea that the virtual cycle of complementary change needs to stay in motion. The time and persistence needed to build the complements is itself a spur to leading change as a continuous process. But the dangers of complementary traps (well evidenced in the Liz Claiborne case, Siggelkow, 2001) is a further strong reason for the active and continuous nature of complementary change processes. FitzGerald has captured this well.

> Setting change in motion is only the beginning. The task now is to make sure the whole company is mobilized and that we maintain or indeed accelerate momentum. This means introducing 'waves of change' to keep the process moving forward – and introducing them in the right sequence. A single initiative is not enough – it needs to be reinforced again and again, and each initiative needs to be part of an integrated whole. (FitzGerald, 2002: 8)

We doubt if there is a universal 'right sequence' to introduce complements, since the logic, timing, and form of change is so much a feature of local company circumstances. But the crucial notion is that, whatever the sequence, the complements and the capabilities that underpin them must be fully assembled before performance benefits really come through. This takes time, and the virtuous circle must be kept in motion even once assembled. Here inter-generational leadership is crucial. Duration of leader in post and the careful management of leader succession are at the heart of leading continuity and change and the skilful management of continuity and change is at the core of the relationship between leadership, change and performance.

## NOTE

[1]We are grateful to William Pettigrew for this archival analysis.

**Chapter 9**

# Complementary: Change towards Global Integration in Four Professional Service Organizations

*Evelyn Fenton and Andrew M. Pettigrew*

## INTRODUCTION

This chapter explores the transformation process in four professional service organizations (PSOs) as they seek to strengthen the ties between their international subunits and thereby integrate more effectively their global service provision to customers. This transformation process is of interest to our study as it displays common characteristics in terms of content and sequencing shared by all of our case studies. Moreover the process of global integration in our PSOs has been approached by a strategy of comprehensive change across a wide range of organizational dimensions.

Our interest in PSOs is part of a wider study of new forms of organizing and company performance in Europe, Japan and the USA (Fenton and Pettigrew, 2000a). Drawing on case study evidence from PSOs in the construction and business advisory sectors, we argue that these PSOs are already well advanced in the process of internationalization. Global integration represents a logical strategic response to complex environmental and demanding customer requirements for these firms. Further, that organizing around sectors or specialist networks enables these professional service firms to transfer knowledge more effectively across loosely coupled subunits and to provide a more innovative service to clients.

Our empirical research will demonstrate evidence of complementary change in four PSOs towards global integration. Here complementary change has an aggregated connotation and thereby bears similarities to Greenwood and Hinings's (1993) archetypes. But our emphasis differs in that we do not focus on the underlying interpretative scheme of the change process. Rather, our aim here is to highlight the different elements of the change process and the way in which they interconnect to provide coherence. In this way our analysis is closer to that of managerial logic (Rumelt and Stopford, 1996) than the more diffuse cultural interpretations given by organizational members to change. In other words, we have looked at actions and their consequences more than their underlying meanings to the professionals involved. To this end we examine commonalties in the process and sequencing of organizational change. We then go on to discuss the management of this new form of organizing and highlight some unresolved management challenges.

This chapter is structured in seven parts. Our literature review looks at the importance of studying PSOs and the challenges they face in becoming globally integrated organizations. It then goes on to outline the theoretical basis for complementarities underlying the change process in our PSOs. After a discussion of the research questions and methods employed, we present our results on the content and sequencing of change in four global PSOs. Then we go on to discuss our findings on the consequent management challenges. This is followed by discussion and conclusion sections.

## LITERATURE REVIEW

In this section we analyse the character and significance of PSOs, to demonstrate the importance of knowledge management in the context of growing a globalizing firm. Managing the change to globally integrated services would appear to occur at a later phase of internationalization, at which point firms have identified the need to go beyond the capacity for global reach to be competitive. This approach to knowledge management, we argue, is exemplified in high performing firms, which take a complementarities approach (Milgrom and Roberts, 1995) to managing change.

Sharma (1997) has noted that the importance of PSOs in society is due to the high degree of specialization and the division of labour in the modern economy. He goes so far as to say that 'business as we know it would come to a grinding halt' (1997: 758) without these knowledge-intensive firms. PSOs are of particular interest in the context of new forms of organizing, because they exhibit precisely those characteristics which larger, more hierarchical organizations are seeking to adopt in the new competitive environment. Liedtka et al. (1997: 47) single out their flat structures, service-oriented workforces, participative decision processes and, in particular, their representation as a pure form of 'knowledge-based' business, as characteristics which appeal to more mainstream business organizations as the critical competencies to acquire for the future.

The definition of a PSO has occupied a significant place in the literature (Bartol, 1979; Abbott, 1988; Maister, 1993; Lowendahl, 1997). Sharma (1997) has outlined the extreme positions on this theme as ranging from the notion of professions as different from other occupations in degree but not in kind (Hughes, 1956), to the key distinguishing characteristic being a basis on abstract bodies of knowledge (Abbott, 1988). This last definition is more loose and inclusive of all occupations where there is a routine application of abstract knowledge to particular cases. Along with Sharma, we take Abbott's definition to include all those who undertake their occupations by the use of expert knowledge acquired through training and experience, have a service orientation, distinctive ethics and a great deal of autonomy and prestige in the modern economy (Sharma, 1997).

These characteristics present PSOs with unique challenges around managing human resources and intangible assets. Not least of these, for the current study, concern the efficient and effective capture and dissemination of knowledge in the context of a growing global business. Our case study evidence reveals a common approach to managing global services, which has given rise to the identification of the requirement for integrated knowledge management in our PSOs.

One important theme running through studies of the professions has been the scale and impact of the changes, which they have undergone. (c.f. *Organization Studies*, 1996: 17 (4) given over to this debate and Greenwood and Lachman, 1996). This is an important theme for the study of new organizational forms because dramatic changes in the business environment are important drivers of organizational change. The dramatic changes both documented and forecast in recent management literature (Handy, 1990; D'Aveni, 1994; Hamel and Prahalad, 1996) suggest that organizational change is now a permanent feature of economic life. It is therefore of interest to know, more than ever, how best to manage continuous organizational change. Professional firms, despite their differences from other firms, are not immune to competitive pressures, particularly the larger firms with a global reach. The very nature of these firms as knowledge based has made them especially sensitive to changes in IT with their requirement to capture and disseminate knowledge efficiently and effectively.

A number of recent articles have looked at changes in forms of organizing and managing professionals. For instance Cooper et al. (1996) have adopted a dialectical view of change in their analysis of two law firms undergoing shifts from one organizational archetype to another. Their focus is upon interpretations of ideas around professionalism and partnership, which underlie the P2 (traditional) and Managerial Professional Business (new) archetypes of these firms. Their key finding is that one archetype does not replace the other, but is layered over the other, resulting in an archetypal mix of interpretative schemas within these professional firms. The role of strategic leadership is highlighted by Hinings et al. (1991) and Denis et al. (1996) as crucial during periods of major change. Denis et al. (1996) provide evidence which demonstrates the need for collaborative leadership between a tightly knit group of professionals to perform specialized, differentiated and complementary roles in the change process. Further, they show that radical transformations tend to occur in a cyclical pattern, whereby substantive change is interspersed with periods of political realignment. It is the symbolic, substantive and political effects of various leadership tactics, which drive these cycles. The focused nature of these writings on cultural or leadership attributes of change, neglects a wider analysis of the content of major change. There is also a lack of clarity concerning the sequencing of change initiatives and the way in which different organizational factors might fit together in an overall programme of change. It is this content and its sequencing which we have sought to capture in our PSO case studies.

## Patterns of internationalization in PSOs

It has been noted that customization and client–supplier interaction are fundamentally inherent in business service transactions (O'Farrell et al., 1998), thereby influencing both the mode and scale of international market entry for PSOs. In particular, management and technical consultancies which are information intensive display high levels of internationalization. Roberts (1999) has isolated some common characteristics which act as constraints on the methods of internationalization utilized, including the need for personal contact between product and client, the importance of quality and reputation, a long term buyer–seller relationship, human capital and information intensiveness and the need for cultural sensitivity.

The drivers for the internationalization of PSOs are the result of both supply- and demand-driven forces (Roberts, 1999). On the demand side, the increasing globalization of economic activity has prompted PSOs to mirror their clients; while on the supply side, economies of scope and scale can be achieved by providing services to a larger market, necessitating a global reach. Roberts (1999) reports on findings that business firms supply foreign markets primarily through affiliates because of the embedded relationship between client and producer, the need for personnel to be deployed in the marketplace to maintain quality and the desire to protect reputations and intangible assets. A typical pattern is for a PSO to buy a foreign office or establish a small office abroad on the back of a local project. As Roberts (1999) notes, the requirement for an overseas presence means that most PSOs progress rapidly from a national firm to an international firm without a period of exportation (Sharma and Johanson, 1987). As the level of market commitment required for a business service firm to establish a presence can be expected to be less than that required for manufacturing firms, PSOs jump from national to overseas subsidiary without the intermediate stage of export activities, or the use of independent representatives, such as agents. Thus the process of internationalization for PSOs may be less incremental than manufacturing.

Vandermerwe and Chadwick (1989) have attempted a useful classification system for the internationalization of services along the axes of relative involvement of goods and the degree of consumer–producer interaction. Our case study PSOs are located in the sector providing 'pure' services (low on goods) and higher consumer–producer interaction, and such labour-intensive business services principally involve people in the internationalization process. Given that capabilities are in the heads of employees and interaction is fundamental to the business process, the essence of an international strategy will be to gain as much control over the delivery process as possible. This is obtained through direct investment in branches, and subsidiaries, or through mergers or acquisitions.

The distinctive character of PSOs already referred to above means that historically there has been less of a focus on minimizing transaction costs than on concerns for quality and reputation. Our case study evidence shows that increasing market knowledge and commitment in the establishment of overseas offices leads to a gradual spread into foreign markets. Further, that having attained an international presence, our PSOs are facing challenges around maintaining consistent quality standards in service delivery.

The network perspective is also relevant to understanding the behaviour of PSOs, such that PSOs are very much embedded in the context of a network of interorganizational and interpersonal relationships (Axelsson and Easton, 1992). For PSOs this involves close and sustained contact with customers, suppliers and competitors. Here the influence of social relationships is the key to business transactions (Granovetter, 1985) and particularly those relationships between the subunits and the parent company. One may therefore see the process of internationalization in PSOs as having elements of both the stage approach and the network perspective (Coviello and McAuley, 1999).

Our case study PSOs found that over time they have entered into multiple foreign markets through either foreign direct investment or merger and acquisition, and grown considerably in terms of personnel to include foreign nationals as well as a larger parent body due to enhanced reputation at home. The internationalization literature is somewhat less developed theoretically in explaining this 'advanced' stage of internationalization for service firms. The focus on modes of market entry has not gone beyond mergers and acquisition, nor have they discussed the managerial implications of increasing scale and complexity, particularly where mergers and acquisitions are not the preferred options. Edvardsson et al. (1993) go some way to remedy this with a typology of stages in the internationalization process, which is concerned with management issues and organizational development. These four stages are: prospecting, introduction, consolidation and reorientation. The first two stages are the initial and early internationalization strategies whereby the organization is still learning about new markets and establishing customer and partner relationships. The consolidation phase sees the firms well established in foreign markets, with contacts and routines more fixed. Reorientation involves firms adjusting to local conditions or seeking new opportunities to renew technological or knowledge competencies. In this last phase there is a need to reconsider prior modes of working and seek organizational and marketing creativity.

Globalization has been very influential in driving large professional firms into different forms of organizing (Greenwood and Lachman, 1996). Having to follow clients into new markets has provided challenges to existing ways of organizing internationally and to the ability to capture and disseminate knowledge (Baden-Fuller, 1993; Ferner et al., 1995). Within business advisory firms the most significant response to competitive challenges has been the spate of mega-mergers, which has transformed the Big Eight into the Big Six (Greenwood et al., 1990) and more recently to the Big Four or Five. The strategic responses to environmental discontinuity have included the restructuring of strategic management and HR processes (Ferner, et al., 1995) and the changing relationships of accountants with other professionals and managers (Armstrong, 1985; Galanter and Palay, 1991). Our findings highlight another common strategic response, that of creating global service integration.

Our case study PSOs may be seen to be between the stages of consolidation and reorientation in their strategic response to globalization. The significance of this stage for our PSOs was the recognition by all of them that global reach was not enough to be competitive. All agreed that they had to leverage their global presence to provide both a standardized quality and customized service globally. To achieve this goal requires personnel of high calibre to maintain an international quality and reputation. In addition there is the requirement to maintain internal and external organizational networks for knowledge generation and transfer. It is the means by which these PSOs sought to leverage their global presence through global integration that is the focus of this chapter.

In terms of our case study PSOs, a globally integrated organization is shown to have a number of interlocking features within three broad organizational variables[1]:

1 **Strategic Boundaries**: a strategic intent to harness the benefits from a global presence into a coherent operation. This involved delineating the sharper boundaries created by moving from a diversified strategy to a focus on developing either markets or regions. Very often one region may be used initially as a launch pad for the diffusion of wider global change.

1(a)  Standardization: in order to offer a more integrated and coherent quality of service worldwide, business processes and procedures had to be standardized.

1(b)  Specialization: firms are finding the competitive environment is forcing them to  specialize in order to add value to the services which they provide.

2  **Structure**: in order to manage the dualities of standardization and specialization, PSOs must co-ordinate a new range and configuration of services. To this end structures have changed with the addition of layers of hierarchy, the decentralization and focusing of operations and an increase in the scope of project-based working.

3  **Processes**: new process changes are very much intertwined with structural change, including an overall increase in both vertical and horizontal communication.

3(a)  IT and knowledge management: in order to support and increase the efficiency of horizontal networks extensive investments have been made in IT and knowledge management systems.

3(b)  HR: behavioural support and incentives for networking have had to be realized through the adoption of new HR policies and practices. For instance, task forces, cross-functional and cross-boundary teams and firm-wide mission building.

The move to a reorientation stage by our PSOs is therefore associated with widespread change focused upon developing a greater capacity to provide a high-quality standard of services globally. The adoption of these changes by our PSOs is shown to have their own pattern of progression (see Figure 9.2 later in this chapter) in the order of strategic boundary changes followed by structure and process changes. The internationalization literature is less explicit on the detailed content and sequencing of organizational change in the later stages of the internationalization process. Therefore we have attempted to conceptualize the common change patterns found in our case studies from alternative theoretical perspectives. It is the diversity and range of organizational factors implicated in the change to global integration which suggests a holistic perspective on change. Thus we have adopted a complementarities approach to studying change in our case study PSOs.

### Transformation in global PSOs: a complementarities perspective

So far the literature lacks a comprehensive account of change across a number of firms which might provide a more generalizable picture of successful organizational transformation for global PSOs. This type of analysis poses challenges for the researcher who must grapple with a high degree of complexity in understanding whole system change. One approach is the archetype development route adopted by Hinings and Greenwood (1988b), Greenwood and Hinings (1993), Laughlin (1991) and Cooper et al. (1996). This is a useful way of characterizing the shifts in modes of organizing and provides rich data on internal processes, most notably systems and structure which are linked within a coherent interpretative scheme. What is less clear from these analyses is the sequencing and pattern of the individual changes and the generalizable nature of these findings to other firms. To this end we have adopted a complementarities approach as a form of analysis for understanding organizational change within our case studies toward globally integrated PSOs.

The concept of complementarities is an important theoretical development from the industrial economics field. It has application to a wide variety of industries, not just professional services and develops the thinking from contingency through to configuration theory. The contingency perspective sees performance as dependent on the 'fit' between key organizational variables such as size and structure (Donaldson, 1996). However, it develops contingency further by seeking to address the multilateral kinds of fit required for organizational effectiveness (Drazin and Van de Ven, 1985; Meyer et al., 1993). In this way it resembles configurational theory (Miller, 1986, 1996) with its emphasis on the more holistic and systemic nature of organizations. In their study of modern manufacturing, Milgrom and Roberts (1995) describe the basic notion of complementarity as 'doing *more* of one thing increases the returns of doing *more* of another'. Performance is therefore dependent upon a set of complementary changes within organizations. They use the example of the introduction of CAD technology to show that it paid best when associated with complementary inventory, production, marketing and management policies. In this way Milgrom and Roberts go beyond the simple one-to-one associations governing performance relationships in contingency theory. These complex interaction effects develop the configurational notion that changing any variables must be in association with others that are complementary to it; otherwise the returns will be negative.

However, the complementarities approach goes beyond configurational analysis by suggesting the requirement for a disaggregated approach to performance testing. In this way, complementarities suggests a simultaneously aggregated and disaggregated approach that compares the contributions of individual organizational practices, with the performance payoff being an expression of their combined effort. Thus the reverse effect is expected, where piecemeal change (that is, without the full complement of practices) results in negative performance. Moreover, as Ichniowski et al. (1997) argue from their study of HR practices, complementarity among practices implies that the magnitude of the performance effects of the full system is larger than the sum of the marginal effects from adopting each practice individually. When analysed together, the full system effects should exhaust the individual effects on performance. The study by Ichniowski, et al. (1997) forms part of a wider literature on bundles of HR practices and organizational performance that is one of the key areas of management within which PSOs have not deliberately, until recently, sought to excel themselves[2]. A similar finding has been demonstrated in a recent empirical study on the adoption of new modes of organizing in European and UK firms (Whittington et al., 1999) which showed that the adoption of all nine modes identified in the study resulted in exceptional performance payoffs. See also Chapter 7 of this volume by Massini and Pettigrew for an update and extension of this analysis.

Similar conclusions on complementary effects have been posited from qualitative case study work. For instance, Starbuck's (1993) case study of a high-performing New York law firm (Wachtell) uncovered an ambiguous and contradictory organization, brought about by complexity, internal inconsistencies and incoherence. Starbuck discovered that to explain this firm's success he needed to resort to the metaphor of a house of cards:

> Wachtell contains many elements that fit together and reinforce each other. Each element is individually a flimsy component with which to build an institution, and some elements are individually farfetched. Yet, they fit together so well that removing one element might undermine the whole structure. (1993: 916)

While this is an account of an exceptional firm located in one site in New York, it retains many of the features we uncovered in our own study, not least of which is the importance of synergistic sets of practices. The importance of alignment in organizational initiatives has also been emphasized by the work of Liedtka et al. (1997) on professional services, who note that piecemeal attempts at imitating value-driven initiatives will ultimately fail.

Similarly, Pettigrew (1999b) has attempted to capture complementarities in action with his case study account of BP Amoco over a 10-year period of change to the structures, processes and boundaries of the firm. This account seeks to go beneath the generalities of statistical analysis to expose the micro-level processes of continuity and change which can explain the long-term history and consequences of complementary change. See Chapter 8 of this volume by Pettigrew for a development and extension of this work comparing complementarities in action in BP and Unilever. The work on complementarities therefore shows fruitful signs of activity in both qualitative and quantitative methodologies.

## RESEARCH QUESTIONS

The current literature is poorly developed on the management and change processes involved in transforming global PSOs into globally integrated organizations. We have few insights into the *what* and the *how* of change in global firms in this sector. Also, the complementarities approach of Milgrom and Roberts (1995) is essentially static and aprocessual in character. We know little of the *what*, *why* and *how* of the creation and recreation of complementary changes in firms over time and of how managerial choices and change processes may deliver the performance effects identified from the European survey results of the INNFORM programme. This leaves us with key questions as to the form, conduct and sequencing of global transformational change. To this end we have analysed our case study PSOs with the following questions in mind:

1   What combination of internal and external context created the desire for change towards integrated global networks?
2   What was the content and sequencing of the change programme?
3   What were the benefits and disbenefits from the change process?

This chapter reports findings from four professional service organizations where there is evidence of complementary action in organizational change over the time period from the late 1980s to the late 1990s. These four cases together illustrate the sequencing and development of complementary change in action and pose challenges for their management and sustainability. The following section of this chapter will discuss our methods and the data sources we used to try and get answers to our questions.

## METHOD

Our methodology is rooted in the tradition of process research in strategy (Chakravarthy and Doz, 1992; Pettigrew, 1992, 1997a). In particular, we have adopted a longitudinal perspective on change, which has meant exploring the antecedents of organizational change initiatives as well as the interlocking organizational events which comprise a history. This perspective is driven by a contextualist theory of method, advocated by Pettigrew (1985, 1990) and the innovation studies of Van de Ven et al. (1989). This has meant being concerned with both horizontal (time) and vertical (for example, internal and external) levels of analysis. In this way we have sought to capture the holistic and processual character of organizational transformations over time. Thus an inductive research strategy was employed which was both iterative and developmental. Rather than imposing a theoretical framework from the start, being open to what the sites had to say was deemed as most important (Glaser and Strauss, 1967). This did not mean operating in a vacuum; rather, a tentative framework around complementary change was created with propositions which informed the initial research strategy. This type of inductive approach demands flexibility (Silverman, 1985) and a level of objectivity to be able to change direction with the emerging data. In this way a cyclical pattern of research is undertaken, from data to analysis, and back to the data again.

## Data collection

Four case studies are the focus of this analysis, originally chosen as matched pairs from two different industry sectors: construction and management consultancy. Our choice of successful global PSOs has provided commonalities within the data set such that these might be analysed together in a meaningful way, while our choice of two different sectors has shown sector not to be a confounding variable.

A systematic collection of evidence along our nine indicators of change underpinned our processual study. Here we aimed for pluralist accounts of historical and contextual organizational reality (Pettigrew, 1990). The case studies developed from chronological accounts of the context and content of change to develop analytic themes. These themes indicated links between our nine indicators of change and to the organizational context and history. A meta-analysis across our case studies confirmed the emergence of a pattern of transformation towards global integration through complementary practices. To this end we collected evidence from those responsible for the implementation of these changes as well as those who had to work within them.

## Data types

The time period for data collection was between 1996 and 1999. This research involved two main types of data: in-depth interviews and documentary data. Initially a chronology needed to be established from documents and in-depth interviews, in order to extend the first proforma, which then had to be tested in further interviews. The companies were very helpful in providing a number of documents, including internal publications, books on company history and internal memos.

A total of 68 professionals were interviewed in the four firms, in interviews lasting from one to two hours. These interviewees included functional heads of department, such as finance, human resources, legal, research and development, marketing and professionals at junior and partner levels. Most respondents had been with their firms for a considerable period of time. Those who were relatively new had status and responsibilities within their organization, which meant that they provided a fresh but informed perspective on organizational developments.

The following section of the chapter will introduce our case study firms and present our results along the nine multiple indicators indicated by our survey (see Figure 9.1 below).

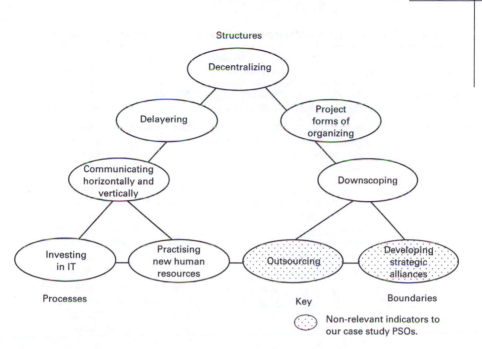

Structures

Decentralizing

Delayering

Project forms of organizing

Communicating horizontally and vertically

Downscoping

Investing in IT

Practising new human resources

Outsourcing

Developing strategic alliances

Processes

Key

Boundaries

Non-relevant indicators to our case study PSOs.

FIGURE 9.1    *New forms of organizing: the multiple indicators*

## FOUR GLOBAL PROFESSIONAL SERVICE ORGANIZATIONS

Our case study PSOs are broadly from two different sectors: Ove Arup and Davis Langdon and Everest from the construction industry and Coopers & Lybrand and Spencer Stuart from management consulting (albeit that Spencer Stuart specialize in search and selection consultancy). All are among the top three to five companies in their sector and may therefore be considered high performers. Three of the four are partnerships, while Ove Arup is a limited company. However, all have and do exhibit the unique characteristics of professional services and partnership organizations: high levels of individualism, operational freedom, few lines of authority and organizational members with esoteric expertise.

All our cases comprised a loose federation of offices which were undergoing a transformation toward global integration. A summary of the firm characteristics of our case study firms is given in Table 9.1.

During the time of data collection all our case studies had embarked upon a change programme within the last two to five years and therefore had differing rates of progression (see Table 9.2 later in this section). Ove Arup and Coopers & Lybrand Europe (CLE) were the most advanced, with change programmes fairly comprehensively implemented in one region which would provide the platform for future global changes. Davis Langdon & Everest (DLE) and Spencer Stuart were still grappling with changes in one

TABLE 9.1    *Firm characteristics of four case study professional services organizations*

| Firm characteristics | Arup | Davis Langdon & Everest | Coopers & Lybrand Europe | Spencer Stuart |
|---|---|---|---|---|
| Size (employees) | 2000 UK 6000 worldwide | 2000 UK 6000 worldwide | 2000 Europe | 114 UK 960 worldwide |
| Business | Consulting engineers to the construction industry | Quantity surveyors to the construction industry | Management consultancy | Search and selection services for business |
| Business areas | Building engineering Civil engineering Services engineering Specialist fields | Survey work and legal services | Telecoms Retail and consumer Pharmaceuticals Financial services | Financial services Industrial and life sciences Consumer Media/ communications and high tech |
| Change strategy | 'Reformation' to restructure UK firm; 'One Arup' to integrate global firm | Move to a unified global enterprise via a Swiss Verein | Move to global integration on a theatre (continental) basis; CLE was a test bed for future theatre operations | Move to global integration Explored initial developments towards this goal in Europe and the US |

or more regions which although not as advanced, were also providing the impetus for thinking about further global change. Ultimately, the strategic aim of all our case studies is to leverage intellectual capital on a global scale in the most efficient and effective manner.

### Environmental and competitive drivers

Major changes in the consulting industry are affecting not only how firms conduct their business but also their long-term viability (Higgins and Ferguson, 1991; Suryanarayanan, 1989). The recession of the late 1980s and early 1990s had left these organizations with the recognition that they needed to become more competitive and in particular more globally integrated. All four PSOs already had a global presence, but without an explicit strategy of globalization. By the end of the 1980s or early 1990s all had similar intentions to integrate what, up until then, had been disparate and autonomous offices around the world. This was in response to the globalization of clients and the need to provide them with a standardized quality of service.

Additionally, customers were becoming more discriminating and demanding. Prices had become very competitive at the same time that customers were looking for added value. All the firms had identified new competitors, some of which were previous employees, as well as diversification by practitioners of other related service sectors. As a result of these pressures all our case study PSOs felt that they needed to become more customer aware, responsive and flexible while delivering a value added service (Suryanarayanan, 1989). As a senior partner at Spencer Stuart explained: 'We are beginning now to look much more thoughtfully at client needs as a driver for how we organize ourselves … there are more clients today … who are demanding services from us in more than one geography'. The competitive environment had led these firms to rethink their strategies and become globally integrated. More specifically, the intention was to harness the benefits from a global presence into a coherent operation. This could only be implemented by complementary changes in organizational strategic boundaries, structure and process.

## Changing strategic boundaries

Only one boundary indicator had changed for our case study firms, that of increased downscoping to focus their service to clients. Unlike our survey firms, outsourcing and creating strategic alliances were of little or no significance, hence the prefix of 'strategic' to 'boundaries'. Given the requirement by competitive forces to both provide specialized services and standardize their delivery, our PSOs managed this duality by undertaking a more focused strategy in developing either markets or regions. All the firms have an explicit strategy to develop competencies along either or both of these lines. For instance, Arup have divided the UK into sector and geographic boards and created worldwide market specialisms in energy and transport. DLE are the least well developed in specialization, but have started in areas such as hospitals, hotels and schools. They are anticipating economies of scope by using the knowledge from hotels to build hospitals when, as they predict, the market for hotels goes into decline. As a partner at DLE explained the change in thinking within the firm:

> I think we are much, much sharper in 1998, we are having discussions now that we could not even have dreamt of having in 1990 … a lot of it has been due to specialization, of having probes out there in the sectors and subsectors of the market that are telling us these things are changing.

Both CLE and Spencer Stuart have developed significantly in specialization by each targeting four industry sectors, thereby developing specialized industry knowledge in the context of sector requirements (see Table 9.2 at the end of this section). In this way their consultants develop deep specialisms and are able to be responsive to clients.

An example of downscoping in CLE, which has been an important strategic move linked to global integration, has been the carrying out of larger and more multi-disciplinary projects and specifically focusing more strongly on technical solutions while reducing the 'tail' of smaller projects for smaller clients.

A crucial ingredient in the strategic process has been the influence of a powerful leader driving the change process and providing the vision within these PSOs. A DLE equity partner spoke about the senior managing partner who was leading the change programme:

> He had the vision in terms of we need to specialize to survive and we need to have a core service with things wrapped around and make an overall service … We needed to sell something different and we have almost led the way to some extent in radical thinking about what the services are.

In order to standardize globally and offer a more integrated service, these PSOs have had to realign their structures, particularly in terms of hierarchy and centralization.

### Structural reconfiguration

All of our case study firms have altered their structures in the last five years and continue to do so, primarily to manage the dualities of standardization and specialization. Structural changes have served to co-ordinate the new range and configuration of services while integrating both the services and the member firms. The immediate effect of these new arrangements has been to add layers of hierarchy, decentralize and focus operations and increase the scope of project-based working.

All of our PSOs added layers to their organizations, either with the creation of divisions or an overlay of networks across autonomous subunits. Arup, because it is not a partnership, was able to create the most traditional structure by forming divisions, or boards, on the basis of sectors and geography. Previously all the UK offices had reported to the policy board individually, now they were all assigned to one of four boards reporting to a policy board. A fifth board was reserved for the overseas subunits while networks were created to integrate independent but affiliated subunits. These boards had chairmen to which the offices were accountable financially and operationally. Similarly, in DLE, firms were assigned to a region with profit accountability overseen by lead partners.

The other two firms created industry-sector networks which added a virtual layer between the executive and the subunits. This is a virtual layer because lines of accountability between the individual consultant and his or her subunit leader remained equally as strong as those between the individual consultant and the network leader; thus a very similar configuration to the matrix structure with dual lines of reporting. CLE and Spencer Stuart have formalized their networks by assigning budgets and leaders. They have also introduced more complexity into their firms in that individuals belong to both sector networks (which are not profit responsible) and member firms (which are profit and loss accountable). In this sense this arrangement amounts to a network overlaying member firms.

The effect of the new structural arrangements has been to create strategic centralization and operational decentralization at the subunit level. For instance, Arup's new structure allowed the policy board to concentrate on firm-wide strategic decisions and to devolve operational and market matters to the five operational boards, rather than allow this to reside at local office level. Similarly, DLE's regionalization aimed to shift the focus from the member firms to the region, enabling a more strategic view of the region while the executive concentrated on global policy, although change here is less developed than the other firms, as the regions are not yet well integrated. This effect was mirrored in both CLE and Spencer Stuart, who injected a more strategic view of the individual industry sectors into their industry network participants while strengthening the strategic overview of their executive boards. In general then, specialized strategic issues have been decentralized to an intermediate level within these firms, such as operational boards and regions, or network sectors and practices. The intention has been to shift individual motivations and allegiances from the level of the local office to the sector or region.

All of our cases except Spencer Stuart have historically been project-based organizations due to the nature of their work. More recently Spencer Stuart began operating on a project basis for global clients in order to provide a comprehensive service in worldwide search and selection. They have seen the necessity of working in multi-country teams to be more customer responsive. Even so, all our PSOs are now spending more time in groups. Not just in work teams, but in teams to develop skills or markets and business planning.

The pattern of structural reconfiguration usually began with the notion of linking people together to leverage expertise and these initiatives have initially been piloted in a regional area such as Europe for CLE, USA and UK for Spencer Stuart and UK for Arup and DLE. These networks are next expected to extend internationally, by which time they will have started to make an impact on people's daily lives. A Spencer Stuart partner found that within 12 to 18 months it was tangible in terms of hiring programmes and the commercial dynamics of the business. In this way the process changes follow on closely to support and reinforce structural change.

## Process changes

At the same time as structures have been changing, so internal processes have had to change to support these new structures. Thus new process changes are very much intertwined with structural change; for instance, IT systems implemented with structural change are often found to require subsequent alteration as the new structure takes hold. The first effect of changing processes has been an overall increase in both vertical and horizontal communication as a result of greater strategic centralization and networking to facilitate the exchange of knowledge. In order to support and increase the efficiency of horizontal networks, extensive investments have had to be made in IT. Also, behavioural support and incentives for networking have had to be realized through the adoption of new HR practices.

Internal communications within our PSOs have intensified as a result of the new structural configurations. The creation of layers has increased vertical communications and accountability. Also the centres of these organizations have become more strategic and demanding of their subunits. At the same time, horizontal communications have increased between subunits with the creation of market and geographical groups or divisions. These horizontal linkages have been created in addition to those informal networks which existed historically within these firms. Thus it can be inferred that greater complexity has been introduced into the working patterns of these firms, at the same time as there has been an introduction of greater strategic clarity.

The requirement to become globally integrated and provide a wider range of skills has led our PSOs to seek the benefits of IT and knowledge management systems. Therefore enormous investments have had to be made in IT to support the increased complexity generated by intensive communications as well as the requirement for knowledge retrieval, capacity and dissemination. All our PSOs had invested in a common architecture for IT, e-mail or Lotus Notes and a knowledge management or database system. DLE were the least advanced in this respect, as their IT strategy was only just being implemented at the time of this research. All four firms have an explicit IT strategy and recognized that IT would remain an on-going investment for the firm. A Spencer Stuart partner explained the implications of a coherent IT programme:

> It was decided that a fundamental plank in achieving a business where the whole was greater than the sum of its parts, was a cohesive universal technology plan and an investment plan. So at that point the freedom to invest in technology was taken out of the hands of country managers and it was the first bite at country managers' almost total authority which caused some ructions.

In the five years prior to this research Spencer Stuart spent 20 per cent of turnover on IT and employed over 100 people worldwide on systems development, systems support and knowledge and information management.

PSOs are culturally attuned to networking and now find that this has become more formalized with new HR practices designed to make these interactions more standardized and efficient. In this way, horizontal and vertical linkages now become more an object of scrutiny in order to leverage the capacity of the firm's intellectual capital. To this end all our firms had adopted new HR practices such as task forces, cross-functional and cross-boundary teams. Additionally the fact that these practices were more sustained, intensive and geographically integrated was important in bringing about the changes described. Indeed, the two firms in the construction sector had formalized their HR function for the first time with the recruitment of an HR professional and the standardization of HR policy and procedures. Arup is the most advanced in this respect and may be said to have adopted HR complementarities due to the breadth of HR initiatives undertaken. To this end they have a comprehensive personnel strategy dealing with issues such as resourcing, development and training, reward, personnel support and international mobility.

Indeed, as stated previously, recruitment is now aligned with the new organizational configurations, for instance both DLE and Spencer Stuart are recruiting people for specialist posts. The recognition that professional services is about adding value has meant that training has been a central initiative in DLE, as a partner explained: 'The whole basis of the way that we operate is that we are trying to give clients something else, and that way you have to broaden your skill base and that of your staff'.

## The sequencing of the change process

We took a disaggregated approach to our case studies by analysing the PSOs along the nine multiple indicators shown in Figure 9.1. A qualitative case study methodology has enabled us to extend the depth of the INNFORM survey results by revealing the *why* and the *how* alongside the *what* of our survey. More importantly, we were able to look beyond the discrete initiatives to ascertain their impact on one another. As our case study work progressed and deepened, there emerged a very similar pattern of initiatives or managerial logic (Rumelt and Stopford, 1996) underlying the organizational transformations. This pattern fell into the system changes identified from our survey and were found to be driven by similar environmental and competitive changes. From our analysis of interviews and documents we were able to identify the sequencing of the system changes as shown in Figure 9.2.

It is important to stress at this stage that the sequencing of these systems was not entirely discrete, and, in line with our thinking about complementarities, showed considerable overlap at both the individual and systemic level of change. For the purposes of narrative clarity, however, we have ordered the changes according to the predominant tendency within our firms. There may have been minor incursions into this order of change, where for instance one aspect of the process changes preceded an element of structural change. But on the whole this was the order in which the majority of the organizational indicators underwent change. Moreover, it must be

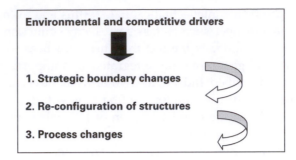

FIGURE 9.2   *Sequencing of organizational change processes in PSOs*

remembered that competitive pressures are always evolving and that these firms recognize this and are prepared for continuous change.

Table 9.2 illustrates the changes which took place within our four PSOs along the nine indicators. Only Spencer Stuart shows a move to project-based organizing, because the others have all historically been project based. Search and selection firms differ in that most assignments are handled by a single consultant. The attribution of medium change to the other three firms reflects the adoption of different types of project working such as multi-disciplinary teams and cross-boundary task forces. It will be seen further that boundary changes within PSOs are somewhat different from other sectors. For instance, outsourcing has only been significant for CLE and this in terms of administrative functions. The other firms have not outsourced in this manner. Similarly, the resort to strategic alliances is only a recent activity for CLE, which has allowed them to bid for and deliver large projects. Where this occurs in Arup and DLE's strong external links with architects, this is not a new phenomenon. It is only in redefining strategic boundaries that PSOs exhibit similar initiatives to other firms and for this reason we have relabelled the boundary changes to reflect a strategic change in focus. Specifically, we have defined these changes in terms of the dual requirement for PSOs to provide specialized services and standardize delivery through the geographic integration of firm knowledge.

### Summary of complementary change

Taken individually, the changes undertaken within these firms are not remarkable or new. Indeed some appear positively traditional, such as the addition of hierarchy to previously flat organizations. What is of importance is not their individual character but what they collectively bring to the change programme. The scale and comprehensive nature of the whole pack-age of changes which have an internal coherence is the innovation for these firms. It is this very underlying logic of the whole pattern of change which makes these change programmes both viable and innovative. We have not attempted in our analysis to establish the link between complementary change and performance with these firms, although all may be seen to be high performers within their industry sectors. But our view is, that these firms are special in terms of their professionalism and the desire to be the best in their industry.

Our notion of complementary change is whole system organizational change where each part reinforces the benefits of the others, thereby giving a logical coherence to a whole package of change initiatives. In this way we concur with Whittington and Melin (see Chapter 2 of this volume) when they argue for dissolving the distinction between strategy and structure by reconceptualizing organization or 'organizing' as the strategy. Similarly, Rivkin (2000) includes entire organizational configurations in his simulation model of complex strategies. In this way, it is the particular logic of organizational configuration which is deemed strategic.

All four case studies reported similar environmental and competitive drivers and responded with a similar sequence of change initiatives: strategic change, followed by structural and then process change initiatives (see Figure 9.2). Overlaps were seen to occur largely between structure and process changes, with strategic boundaries establishing the lead in the change pattern. It is the strategic intent to become globally integrated organizations which drives these subsequent change patterns. Our evidence shows these complementary change patterns to be both emergent and intentional. So that for instance, environmental imperatives dictated to all the importance of global integration with the necessity for a standard service worldwide. This led to the formation of specialized groups and networks, followed by changes in IT and changes in the direction of communications and knowledge flows. Only later were these initiatives followed by changes in HR practices.

It would appear that the lag in process changes behind strategic boundaries and structure created subsequent management challenges for our PSOs. These challenges demonstrate the heterogeneous nature of global PSOs, both culturally and in their capabilities. They also demonstrate the importance of history for these firms, in the way that perceptions are built up over time to condition behaviour. Process changes may prove to be the most challenging to bring into alignment with strategic boundaries and structure.

We now examine the experiences and central issues in the management of these global professional firms as they undergo complementary changes.

## MANAGING THE NEW PROFESSIONAL SERVICE ORGANIZATION

Our PSOs may be seen to be in between the stages of consolidation and reorientation of Edvardsson et al. (1993) as they seek new ways to integrate their

TABLE 9.2  *Complementary changes in four professional services organizations*

| Change dimensions | Arup | DLE | CLE | Spencer Stuart |
|---|---|---|---|---|
| Structure Boundaries<br>SPECIALIZATION<br>Integrated global strategy | Development of world wide market specialisms in energy and transport.<br>Sector concentration<br>Global geographic board<br><br>HIGH CHANGE | Development of market specialisms in hospitals, schools and hotels<br><br>MEDIUM CHANGE | Focus on four industry sectors:<br>• Financial services<br>• Retail and consumer<br>• Pharmaceuticals<br>• Telecoms<br>HIGH CHANGE | Focus on four practices:<br>• Financial services<br>• Industrial and life sciences<br>• Consumer<br>• Media/communications and high technology<br>HIGH CHANGE |
| Structure<br>Layers | Added layers with creation of five boards<br>HIGH CHANGE | Added layers with creation of regions<br>MEDIUM CHANGE | Added layers with creation of European office (MCS)<br>HIGH CHANGE | Added layers with creation of practice networks<br>HIGH CHANGE |
| Centralization | Boards<br>HIGH CHANGE | Regions<br>MEDIUM CHANGE | Industry sectors<br>HIGH CHANGE | Practice networks<br>HIGH CHANGE |
| Projects | More involvement in groups of all kinds to develop networks not just for work activities. | | | |
| | MEDIUM CHANGE | | | Becoming more project based<br>MEDIUM CHANGE |
| INTERNAL COMMUNICATION<br>Processes | Divisional structure increasing vertical communication. Market and skills networks increasing horizontal communications<br>HIGH CHANGE | Regional structure including vertical communications with centre and horizontal communications within regions<br>MEDIUM CHANGE | Sector networks increasing horizontal communications between offices and vertical communications to MCS executives<br>HIGH CHANGE | Practice networks increase horizontal networks with practices and vertical networks to sector heads and executive board<br>MEDIUM CHANGE |

*(Continued)*

TABLE 9.2 *(Continued)*

| Change dimensions | | Arup | DLE | CLE | Spencer Stuart |
|---|---|---|---|---|---|
| **P r o c e s s** | IT INVESTMENT | Common IT architecture: HIGH CHANGE | Common IT architecture: LOW CHANGE | Common IT architecture: HIGH CHANGE | Common IT architecture: HIGH CHANGE |
| | HR PRACTICES | Professional HR Director appointed Whole package of initiatives launched HIGH CHANGE | HR initiatives MEDIUM CHANGE | HR initiatives HIGH CHANGE | HR initiatives MEDIUM – HIGH CHANGE |

services globally and provide a standard quality service. Professional service organizations are traditionally based on informal networking. The move toward more integrated network structures in our case studies had formalized this networking while continuing to rely on traditional social mechanisms of control to co-ordinate business activities and interpersonal interactions. It was these processual aspects of our PSOs which lagged somewhat behind the other complementary changes and impacted upon the degree of integration achieved so far, although here too change was evident in parts.

As partners own the firm as well as being managers within it they are subject to different management controls from senior managers in a large company. Where collaboration is required between different partner-led groups, behaviour has to be regulated by norms and mutual co-operation. The utilization of these social mechanisms was modified both as an emergent result of the complementary changes undertaken by our PSOs and deliberately to reflect the new strategic intent of becoming globally integrated. We now turn to a discussion of some of the challenges experienced by our PSOs from continuing to utilize traditional social control mechanisms within the new strategic boundaries, structure and processes.

## Management issues and challenges

Our probing within the PSOs revealed a discernible system-wide imbalance in the degree of integration within their networks and subunits because of a variety of confounding factors. This has led to a situation where some member firms or subunits are actively involved in the specialist networks or groups while others are less able or resistant and hence do not feel well integrated. This lack of integration has become compounded when these PSOs moved into creating global networks and raised a number of critical management issues. Integration problems may be seen as a result of a variety of factors operating singly and together. Three sets of factors: contextual, historical and social, were identified as contributing to behavioural outcomes which undermined integration.

### Context

The contextual factors concern the different market conditions and internal capabilities of individual practices. Individual country partnerships experience variations in their external markets, either because of market maturity or market structure. As a Spencer Stuart partner noted:

> Europe is a brilliant tapestry of differentials ... the economic opportunity for them in Spain is very different to the economic opportunities for us here in New York or Germany. They resent the cost of participation but would be equally resentful if given a choice to participate differentially as a tier two business.

So, for example, country practices with few multinational clients, or who are positioned in a national market, will exhibit parochial behaviour. The task here is to make sure that the essential ingredients of the organizational formula are subscribed to while at the same time respecting the cultural nuances of the country practices. This is a difficult challenge for these firms as a Spencer Stuart partner outlined:

> There is this issue of global businesses, that are trying to be globally effective and have tried to pursue a one-speed approach, a common aspiration and we are not operating in a one-speed world. And that is a very difficult issue to deal with. Working at what you can allow to be legislated at a local level and what is sacrosanct, are different issues.

Differences in success could also be due to different growth rates or critical mass in one's market. For instance, DLE exhibited marked regional differences in the buoyancy of the construction market which contributed to differential profitability in their UK offices. These differentials are in many cases a matter of time, until a country or region develops its full potential. Such market differences in work orientation create incompatible goals between individual practices and the network. This issue remains an on-going debate within PSOs and a barrier to optimal integration unless they can cope with the duality of standardization and customization of rules.

Incompatible goals are also evident where network members do not share the same level of expertise or experience of networking. As a Spencer Stuart partner explained the dilemma in their firm: 'For many people in reality, we are converting geocentric, non-specialized people and putting them for the sake of convenience into these groupings which they did not drive or help in the most part'. Skill differences are also an issue when working with different national partners. So, for instance, some country practices have a lower skills profile which leads to selecting out from the network or specialist group. To resolve this problem, Spencer Stuart are focused on filling the skill gaps within their various practices: 'And we have now been using that premise to drive our hiring plan for three years in earnest ... the practices are a meaningful component and have come into the firm'.

### Historical factors
Key historical factors impinging on the management of change which have developed over the years include: perceptions of inequality and cultural fragmentation within firms. All of our PSOs had developed successful offices where there was a critical mass of people and where decision making and hence power resided. This inevitably led to perceptions of inequality by outlying member firms which saw themselves at a disadvantage politically within the firm. These sorts of tensions can undermine the trust required for co-operative behaviour, while encouraging opportunism.

Along with perceptions of inequality which have developed over the years among member firms, there has also been a fragmenting of the firm culture. For instance, some regional Arup offices have better links than others, either through choice or historical development of associations (Fenton and Pettigrew, 2000c). Subcultures inevitably develop within geographically distant firms, which detract from efforts towards global integration.

In addition, Arup and DLE both had independent firms within their umbrella organization. This creates additional complexity because the priorities of the independent firms are often different from the goals of the owned practices. They are motivated by profits and need to be convinced about spending money on building up new structures like networks and specialist groups.

Convincing the independents to join a globally integrated firm with the same goals, vision and standards is the most challenging part of the integration exercise for these firms.

### Social factors

None of the PSOs had developed effective sanctions beyond peer group pressure, similarly, there was little in the way of reward and recognition systems in place to encourage positive behaviour in the changed firms. For instance, no firm could give examples of rewards for co-operative behaviour in their networks or specialist groups. Rewards usually operated for the benefit of individualistic behaviour, or the member firm. The lack of incentives appeared to reduce the motivation of some network members to co-operate, particularly where competing allegiances between the network and the local office were already present. For instance, Spencer Stuart had 19 different reward modes around the firm five years previous to this study and could not use compensation to influence behaviour. The first thing they had to do was break that tradition: '… which was huge because it was a real bastion to local independence to say to the office managers, "sorry this is not the system we are using"' (Partner).

They still only reward their practice networks obliquely but acknowledge that they will have to implement a number of changes to encourage new behaviours:

> One of the things we are going to have to do to be consistent with our strategy is, we have got to find a way of rewarding people for creating value for the firm, as opposed to value for themselves. We are also going to have to look, where it is appropriate, at evaluating the reward groups have as groups, as opposed to individuals … we are going to have to spend a huge amount more time in evaluating and appraisal of people. Country managers or office managers will actually be paid according to whether they are running a successful knowledge business or not. (Partner)

As Jones, Hesterly and Borgatti (1997) point out, congruent co-ordination mechanisms reinforce one another to promote co-operation. However, the content of some social mechanisms may undermine others and create incoherence in the system (Jones et al., 1997: 923–4). So, the ineffectiveness of peer pressure in certain circumstances combined with a lack of authority, juxtaposes uneasily with inappropriate reward systems in these PSOs. Additionally, different elements of their cultures undermine specialist practice co-ordination, such as the importance of individualism, which is so strong in these firms. For instance, the culture of Spencer Stuart has traditionally been decentralized, individualistic and entrepreneurial. This legacy can detract from the ability to pull people together in teams. As a senior partner noted: 'So we are looking for a rather perverse make up, which is independence of mind and spirit, but an appetite for teamwork and collective engagement and enterprise. It's tough to find'. However, the evidence suggests that there are additional problems of a contextual and historical nature in integrating their organizations, giving rise to a legacy of mistrust and opportunistic behaviour in some quarters. Long-established relationship patterns may be incongruous with more recent initiatives and require adjustment, elimination or compensatory measures. Indeed, the passage of time and new contingencies may require on-going adjustments if our PSOs are to remain adaptable.

Our case study evidence seems to suggest that these and other PSOs will require much inventiveness and creativity in managing structures, processes and strategic boundaries to overcome the deep-rooted traditions of informal networking and relationship modes of working. Global integration requires individuals to forsake old established patterns and adopt a more standardized, company-wide approach. The payoffs for such sacrifices need to be appreciable, not least in convincing professional service staff that their talents will be enhanced and more creative as a result.

## DISCUSSION

Our analysis of the transformation to global integration within four professional service organizations has shown that for transformational change to work there needs to be a new conceptualization of the way in which organizational variables are aligned with each other. The current climate of business signals profound competitive changes, which are forcing companies to experiment with new forms of organizing. Our PSOs have developed ambitious strategic goals in response to business pressures. These are foremost to become globally integrated, providing a uniformly high standard of service, which is sufficiently specialized to add value for their clients. For these PSOs, this means moving from federal, informally networked organizations, towards more formal network structures and specialist groups, with corresponding systems and management styles.

It is noticeable that our PSOs are variable in the degree to which they have advanced along the transformation process towards global integration. DLE being at the earliest stage of development (low to medium change on all dimensions), followed by Spencer Stuart with moderate to high change and CLE and Arup demonstrating the most advanced transformation. A number of factors account for this heterogeneity. First, there are the historical antecedents, such as position in the market and prior experience of change, which have led some PSOs to move later. For instance, it was not until the merger between Davis & Belfield and Langdon & Everest had settled that DLE could consider the next move towards specialization and global integration; so it demonstrates more moderate change in these dimensions. Second, there is the issue of leadership, and that key individuals within the organization recognize the need for change (Pettigrew, 1985). Arup's previous chairman had attempted change initiatives in the early 1990s but these were nationally based. It was not until a new chairman with a global vision undertook a wider strategic change programme that the process toward global integration could begin. Third, size is an issue when resources are needed for wholesale organizational change. Spencer Stuart as the smallest PSO had to harness resources for dedicated management and training programmes to effect global change.

Nonetheless our PSO case studies show remarkable homogeneity in the type of change which they undertook, along the dimensions of strategic boundaries, structure and processes. All recognized the same environmental and competitive pressures and adopted a similar strategic response. It is noticeable that three of the four firms were explicit that their adoption of global integration was in preference to merger or acquisition which marked their competitors. This preference was chosen for a variety of reasons. Arup and Spencer Stuart have a history of growing organically and regard their expertise and way of working as superior in their industry. DLE, as the product of a merger 10 years previously, had a new senior partner with a preference for global integration.

Change on this scale, which is both geographically and organizationally transformational, requires a new mode of changing. New forms of organizing demand a more comprehensive and dynamic concept of fit. Structure is no longer the simple dependent variable of strategy (Chandler, 1962) they are equal partners. Also, it is more than just strategy and structure that must fit together; it is the corporation as a whole. Fit involves not a static interlocking of variables, but rather a continuous co-evolution of a complex whole. This emphasis on the continuous processes involved in moving strategic boundaries to achieve global integration acknowledges the single duality of 'organizing' and 'strategizing' as a holistic process (Whittington and Melin, Chapter 2 of this volume). From this we can infer that our PSOs are in the process of continual 're-accomplishment' (to use Whittington and Melin's word) and given the dynamic nature of their competitive environment, part of the successful execution of their re-accomplishment will be the execution or conduct of strategizing within these organizations. It is this process of strategizing which must be in concert with the other organizing processes.

The new notion of fit is in part captured by the notion of complementarities developed by Milgrom and Roberts (1995). Complementarities refer to the potential for mutually reinforcing effects between particular business practices when joined together. Practices are complementary when doing more of one increases the returns to doing more of another. Here the practices are synergistic: two plus two produces more than four. We have demonstrated how the competitive environment has acted as a catalyst for sequential change initiatives in three key system variables. The choice of change initiatives by these PSOs demonstrates a coherent firm logic, whereby the strategic response to the competitive environment signals the structural and process changes which follow. This gives a new sense to synergy, that of synergies between systems of many practices. Successful business models – Japanese manufacturing in the 1980s, the flexible specialization of Italian craft manufacturers, the high-tech ventures of Silicon Valley – all involve complete and coherent systems of practices. In these cases, it is not just strategic boundaries and structure, but process, culture and context that contribute to performance. In our work, we have concentrated on the complementarities between strategy, structure and processes.

This has implications for creating and sustaining competitive advantage, as Rivkin's (2000) simulated model of strategic complexity demonstrates. Good strategies are difficult to imitate when decisions are numerous and intertwined. Therefore high performing firms will be successful for longer when strategic complexity is high.

This emphasis on coherent systems takes us to the second additional insight from the notion of complementarities – the potential for negative synergies. Synergy traditionally emphasizes positive effects; the complementarities notion warns of negative outcomes. Milgrom and Roberts' (1995) modelling underlines the likelihood, not only that a particular practice depends on its complements to yield the full benefits, but also that in the absence of its complements, the particular practice can produce negative effects. Just-in-time delivery works wonderfully as part of a coherent system, but without matching manufacturing, information and HR practices, the result is chaos. This is the downside of complements, particularly when managers fail to perceive interaction effects. Siggelkow (2002a) warns that misperceptions by managers of complementary interactions tend to be more detrimental than misperceptions of substitute interactions, that is, where the marginal benefit of an activity decreases in the level of the other activity.

Similarly, our PSOs demonstrate lags in the management processes used to control and co-ordinate complex business activities. Many of the co-ordination mechanisms used by these firms, such as culture, peer pressure, incentive systems, reputation and trust, are unchanged from their previous organization. In this sense they resemble the law firms of Cooper, et al. (1996), whose sedimented structures coexisted with different competitive commitments, or the outdated managerial models found in Siggelkow's (2001) account of Liz Claiborne. We see from our case studies that the coexistence of old management processes with the new organizational arrangements make an uneasy mix and detract from complementary change on a global scale. In this way we might conceptualize our PSOs as going through a process of linear progression, as described by Siggelkow (2002a), whereby a change from one configuration to another configuration nevertheless retains business activities (or core elements in Siggelkow's (2002a) and archetypes in Greenwood and Hinings' (1988) terminologies) from the previous period which are not well aligned with the new configuration.

Our PSOs would seem to be grappling with issues of formalizing co-ordination mechanisms, of dealing with the historical fragmentation of cultures and perceptions in the global firm. Moreover, they are having to align incentive systems, a strong bastion of professional independence, with performance based on networking and group behaviour. These PSOs are recognizing that to make the leap into full global integration they may need to close this gap in global process initiatives. For the prime message from complementary change is that holistic change is key while piecemeal initiatives are unlikely to succeed.

We have seen how traditional incentive systems are not commanding co-operative behaviour because they are not aligned with the system-wide changes undertaken by these firms. Increasingly our PSOs are considering incentives to reward networking, group behaviour and the increased sharing of information and knowledge. Moreover, incentive schemes are being constructed so that they are able to reward for adding value to the firm.

There is also the issue of inequalities in the network, due to the external contexts of member firms or their internal abilities to conform to the new organizational arrangements. Here it may be necessary for PSOs to subsidize these parts of the organization until they have 'caught up' with the majority. They may need to consider establishing rule mechanisms to ensure that both individuals and subunits are motivated to network; by, for instance, additional incentives for those parts of the organization which are more parochial. Thus the whole issue of incentive systems for global heterogeneous firms seems to demand innovation and flexibility in process management.

There are thus significant consequences from attempts to conduct complementary change for our PSOs. The major effect of system-wide change would seem to be the creation of greater organizational complexity. For instance, drawing strategy boundaries around regional integration and specialization, with subsequent additional layers of management, internal networking, knowledge management and performance indicators, have increased the heterogeneity of these firms.

Additionally these change programmes have created or reinforced a number of dualities which themselves have added to this complexity (Pettigrew and Fenton, 2000a). For instance, firms are having to live with and manage both hierarchies and networks. This is evidenced by an increase in the number of vertical relationships with the addition of layers to the hierarchy, as well as an increase in horizontal relationships created by the greater formalization of peer networking through, for instance, cross functional teams, sector networks and conferences.

Our PSOs also show signs of having to deal with greater performance accountability upwards as well as greater horizontal integration sideways. Specialist networks and groups are accountable to the managing board and are also simultaneously required to network over wide geographical distances.

There has been a greater centralization of global strategy and a decentralization of regional and specialist strategy along with operations. Both effects may need to be monitored in order for the whole to remain congruent with strategic boundaries.

Additionally, our PSOs have seen the need to orchestrate the global standardization of their services while continuing to customize and develop their specialist offerings.

These organizations have also seen the necessity to identify knowledge and make systems and routines available for its codification, as well as the good citizenship to share such knowledge. This may require the alignment of both cultural and incentive systems for integrated knowledge management to work on a global scale.

A complex pattern of interlocking dualities emerges, presenting an overall complementary configuration of organizational activities. This requires understanding by management of their interaction effects in order to avoid costly misperceptions (Siggelkow, 2002b). Consequently our PSOs should be willing to invest more to reduce uncertainty about the pattern of interactions between these activities. More generally, our PSOs may need to balance a sense of continuity and change for their personnel if they are to retain them. Continuous innovation may still require some platforms of stability, gained for instance by shared values and organizational goals, underpinned by a strong culture.

These cycles of complexity creation may also need to be associated with attempts at complexity reduction. For instance, a stronger and more direct strategic leadership which can clarify and provide coherence and a sense of purpose for the firm may achieve this. Most successful attempts at eliciting top team co-operation have been helped by creating a simplifying corporate language and one which emphasizes the internal coherence of the change programme (Pettigrew, 1999b). Leaders must also be able to grasp some of the big challenges to do with incentives and disincentives for collaboration. Here size is a crucial issue as our PSOs have recognized. Large and geographically dispersed networks lead to greater complexity which our PSOs have tackled through more formal mechanisms of control, including their subdivision into more manageable work units. The role of leaders in these new integrated global PSOs is a potentially fruitful area of further study.

## CONCLUSION

Our analysis of transformation in four PSOs has revealed the emergence of a pattern of complementary change over time. While each firm began with a different starting point and exhibited a different pace of change, all could be said to demonstrate complementary changes in strategic boundaries, structure and processes. Driven by the environmental imperatives of global competitiveness, these firms have all adopted an integration strategy in order to ensure global quality standards and efficient knowledge exchange across borders. Strategic boundary change must be supported by structural change, evidenced in the move to specialization and networks which, in turn, must be underpinned by process changes involving greater communication, new HR practices and IT strategies.

The congruence between these change factors gives rise to complementarities, whereby the whole programme of change provides greater returns to the organization than any individual change element alone. Previous research has not dealt with the sequencing of complementary change factors, or their timing. What this study begins to demonstrate is that congruent sequencing in change is not enough. Lags in process change within our PSOs served to seriously undermine these ambitious programmes towards global integration. The management of our PSOs is evolving from traditional social control mechanisms to more formal modes and incentives, which must in turn be aligned with the specialisms, networks and integrative structures, to co-ordinate and reward the subunit, group and individual levels of the organization.

This research has only studied four organizations in two sectors. Future research could usefully verify (thereby increasing generalizability) or refute our findings by studying global PSOs in other sectors such as law, accounting and advertising, and in larger populations, through, for instance, survey research. It could also be argued that comparability is weak, given the difference in size between our four firms, to which we reply that employee size is not a confounding factor, but that a global presence is significant in driving this complement of organizational changes. Additionally we have not made any links between complementary change and performance; thus the benefits over time remain to be proven. Finally, we have uncovered three sets of management challenges as these PSOs move towards global integration. No doubt there are others to be discovered, reflecting different sectors and/or stage of organization development.

## NOTES

[1] A theoretical background to this framework may be found in Whittington et al. (1999).

[2] We are grateful to an anonymous reviewer of an earlier draft of this chapter for this insight.

# Managing Dualities in the Innovating Organization

# Chapter 10

# Managing Dualities

*Carlos J. Sánchez-Runde*
*and Andrew M. Pettigrew*

## INTRODUCTION

Organizations show many faces and perform multiple functions. Often tensions arise in aligning actions in mutually reinforcing modes. Organizations have always needed to be understood and managed in complementary and systemic ways.

The notion of competing and apparently contradictory tendencies is well embedded in the writing on complex organizations. As far back as the early 1960s, Burns and Stalker (1961) developed the theme of mechanistic and organic systems in firms. Around the same time, Douglas McGregor (1960) had distinguished the competing virtues of Theory X and Theory Y in management. By the 1980s, Michael Porter (1985) was advising firms to position themselves on cost leadership or differentiation, or to focus and thus avoid the dangerous situation of 'being caught in the middle.' For all three of these authors the issue of choice did not lie in leaning comprehensively towards one pole rather than the other. Thus Burns and Stalker recognized that a high-performing firm might combine elements of the mechanistic and organic, and Porter saw the empirical possibility of combining several strategies simultaneously. These early references to competing organizational, managerial and strategic tendencies in organizations have now been reaffirmed by contemporary research and, in particular, the extensive findings from the INNFORM programme of research (Pettigrew and Fenton, 2000a). Thus our research shows that as organizations are seeking higher performance through greater innovation and flexibility, so they are in turn confronted by a series of dualities. The sample of firms in the INNFORM programme were simultaneously building hierarchies and networks; seeking greater performance accountability upwards and greater horizontal integration sideways; and attempting to centralize strategy and decentralize operations.

Other scholars have also indicated the tensions between competing tendencies in the modern organization. Castells (1996) has placed the origins of tensions between hierarchies and networks and centralizing and decentralizing in the rise of the network society. Meanwhile, Dunning (1993) observes the strains between global and local reach in the internationalizing behaviour of firms. The large growth in strategic alliances and the recent wave of mergers and acquisitions have in turn raised the issue of the competing virtues of large size and the potential flexibility of the smaller firm. Increasingly the leveraging of organizational capabilities through investments in human capital and knowledge (Nonaka and Takeuchi, 1995) has emphasized the urgency of balancing vertical and horizontal flows of communication for knowledge creation and diffusion within and between organizations. Growing commercial competition (D'Aveni, 1994) has exacerbated the requirements of both customizing and mass-producing. In summary, it is increasingly necessary to understand innovating organizational practices as bi-modal in that they seek to 'accommodate opposing tendencies and yet function as coherent and cohesive concerns' (Bahrami, 1992: 43). Or to put it in more dynamic terms, innovating organizations are becoming ambidextrous, and need to simultaneously 'implement both incremental and revolutionary change' (Tushman and O'Reilly, 1996: 8).

In the remainder of the introductory chapter to Part 3 of this volume, we seek to achieve two things. First, we explain why dualities have become such an important feature of contemporary organizations and why their analysis has attracted such interest across so many disciplines. Secondly, we review a variety of different perspectives and conceptual languages which have engaged with the dualities phenomenon and show how and why the increasing importance of dualities have created further management challenges for those seeking executive control over large complex organizations.

## THE NATURE OF DUALITIES

Dualistic phenomena are not new; they are not particular to management either. They are pervasive in all the sciences, natural and social. In physics, for instance, current thought has rightly stopped to argue whether light should be seen in particle versus wave modes (Feynman, 1967). Philosophers readily recognize that classical debates between objectivity and subjectivity, or realism and idealism, miss the point of the complexity of approximating truth. Sociologists acknowledge the inescapable intermixing of structure and action to understand behaviour (Giddens, 1985), a viewpoint that is bringing many promising rewards to the understanding of organizational life

(Pettigrew, 1985; Whittington, 1994; Reed, 1997). Psychologists are well aware of the need to consider the interplay of both contextual and intra-personal variables (Sarason, 1988). Economists too are beginning to seriously consider the need to work on assumptions of decreasing and increasing returns (Arthur, 1994), and multiple versus single equilibria (Blaug, 1997). Scientific development marches under the banner of integrating knowledge that spans beyond 'either/or' logics in favour of holistic, 'both/and' approaches. Across many disciplines there is evidence that conundrums previously stated in terms of simple dichotomous choices are now being seen as more complex issues of balancing between dualities.

Many management authors have referred in one way or another to the need to balance competing or contradictory ideas and activities. Various authors have characterized these apparent tensions as paradoxes (Quinn and Cameron, 1988; Handy, 1994b); dilemmas (Hampden-Turner, 1990; McLaren, 1982); dialectics (Mittroff and Linstone, 1993), competing goals and values (Cyert and March, 1992); and dualities (Evans and Génadry, 1999; Pettigrew and Fenton, 2000a). Although these concepts all refer to bipolar concepts, the way they have been used differs markedly between different authors. Janssens and Steyaert (1999: 122) and Westenholz (1993: 41) offer illuminating discussions of some of these similarities and differences. Thus we are told that paradoxes are apparent contradictions that do not necessar-ily call for a choice between contradictory elements. Dilemmas are often seen as either/or situations in which one alternative must be preferred over the other attractive alternative. Dialectics relate to transitional dynamics between the extremes of a continuum of opposites. Competing goals and values implicitly pose the need for actively sharing spaces of decision for opposing parties. Dualities, on the other hand, can be seen as opposing forces that need to be balanced because, even if they are seen as paradoxical or contra-dictory, in fact they are complementary. Paradoxes, dilemmas, dialectics, and conflicting goals and values can all be seen as dualities, but not the other way around. For this reason, we think it is more appropriate to use 'duality' as the guiding concept of this aspect of our research.

The interest in dualities also stretches from the challenges of studying them to the more pragmatic issues of actually seeking to manage dualities in executive situations. This dual challenge is exacerbated by four complexities. First, dualities are increasingly being portrayed as endemic and inescapable features of organizational life. Second, such dualities are raising the spec-trum of increasing levels of uncertainty and complexity to be managed. Third, the balancing actions often necessary to manage dualities are them-selves taking place in dynamic contexts. So, the act of balancing itself is taking place on a moving platform. And finally, the tensions evident in dualities about the content of management are now being overlaid by dualities about the processes of management. Perhaps we should elaborate on these four component parts of the dualities conundrum.

First, dualities have rightly been portrayed as perpetual, inevitable and endemic; one cannot either escape them, or once-and-for-all solve them (Handy, 1994b: 12). Or, as Peiperl puts it, 'the nature of paradox is not easily changed, but the way it is viewed can be' (2001: 146). Dualities are all-pervasive to the point that Evans and Génadry suggest that much of what is problematic and challenging in organizations reflects underlying dualities. Evans and Génadry are, of course, referring just to HR management dualities, but we think that their statement could be expanded to many features of contemporary organizational practice and life (1999: 392). Dualities therefore should be accepted, made sense of, and eventually managed (Handy, 1994b: 12) in an on-going and cyclical journey: 'as researchers learn to comprehend paradox, they may discover other, potentially more intricate, contradictions' (Lewis, 2000: 761).

Second, dualistic thinking can be extremely uncomfortable, untidy, messy, a little out of control, manifesting itself in unexpected twists and consequences (Handy, 1994b: 18, 111). Much of this complexity stems from the fact that most valued qualities of a social system 'have a complementary quality, which together constitute a duality' (Evans and Doz, 1992: 87). Therefore, when moving between the extremes of the dualistic continuum, the issue is not one of choosing between right and wrong, but potentially between right and right. Thus, for example, excessive individualism may lead to lack of co-operation, while insufficient individualism may lead, in turn, not to co-operation, but to conformism. Dualities do not necessarily unveil exact opposites, but 'related though different, almost incommensurable terms that do not easily mix' (Evans and Doz, 1992: 88). However, the fact that dualities add to organizational complexity does not need to be construed in negative terms. On the contrary, 'dualities should be viewed not as threats to consistency and coherence, but as opportunities for creative organization development, learning, and renewal' (Evans and Doz, 1992: 96).

Third, the balancing of dualities has to be addressed in dynamic and spatial terms. Thus complementary dualities need to be balanced in dynamic and not just static terms (Evans and Doz, 1992: 90), and within the social context in which they are embedded (Janssens and Steyaert, 1999: 131). To do so, minimal thresholds are needed between the extremes of the continuum so that focus on a single polarity does not lead to degeneration and crisis. Thus, as Lewis suggests, the way to handle dualities may be through 'exploring rather than suppressing tensions' (Lewis, 2000: 764).

Finally, current empirical and theoretical work on innovating organizations suggests that we need to be sensitive to both the content and process issues associated with dualities. We have already rehearsed examples of the content dualities in discussing the tensions, for example, between global and local, hierarchies and networks, and centralizing and decentralizing, but there are many process dualities in managing change. These include: linking the micro and macro aspects of the change process; encouraging top-down pressure and bottom-up energy for change; mobilizing energy and sustaining it; balancing processes of continuity and change; and making progress in change processes sometimes by escalating issues and sometimes by confining issues (Pettigrew, 1985; Pettigrew and Fenton, 2000a).

## DEALING WITH DUALITIES

Because dualities cover the whole spectrum of organization phenomena, they come in many forms and may require multiple approaches to their management. Poole and Van den Ven (1989) propose four alternative ways to deal with paradox. First, accept the tensions and use them constructively to illuminate the complexity of organizational life. Second, spatially separate the tensions at different levels of analysis (for example, micro and macro) or location (for example, headquarters and subsidiary). Third, separate the tensions across time. Finally, synthesize the tensions by introducing a term that resolves the paradox. Another approach, based more on content (what to do in the face of specific duality tensions), is put forward by Lewis (2000). Lewis, in differentiating learning paradoxes (tensions between the old and the new), organizing paradoxes (tensions of control and flexibility), and belonging paradoxes (tensions between self and other, global and local, and group boundaries), proposes a series of balancing remedies. These include using open discussion and experimentation to absorb complexities, searching for common and expansive goals as a way of adding behavioural complexity, and keeping in place a task focus that values differences and reduces power distance. The authors suggest that a system will increase its capacity to manage dualities in all these ways.

Other writing has followed a processual approach to balancing dualities (Hampden-Turner, 1990; Cyert and March, 1992: 164–6; Evans and Doz, 1992; Evans and Génadry, 1999; Janssens and Steyaert, 1999). This stream of writing, albeit with some differences and emphases among its authors, proposes the following strategies.

1  sequential attention to the duality poles
2  building one duality pole upon the other by layering complementary capabilities on top of existing ones
3  interpenetration and reframing, which means bringing in, respectively, a new specific concept or a more general vision that recognizes the simultaneous operation of opposites and dissolves the tension.

Janssens and Steyaert (1999) suggest that the process of interpenetration or reframing sometimes produces organizational strain that can be alleviated by fostering the intervention of third parties.

Thus far the level of theoretical interest in the subject of dualities and how they might be managed has outstripped the quality and quantity of empirical work on dualities. We have many more conceptual distinctions about dualities and theories about how they might be managed than we have solid empirical studies of the phenomena of dualities in contemporary organizations. However, one important feature of the INNFORM programme has been our interest in the empirical expression of dualities, and it is to this work we now turn.

## EVIDENCE ON DUALITY MANAGEMENT FROM THE INNFORM PROGRAMME

The results of the INNFORM programme strongly support the need to maintain a dualistic approach to contemporary organizational analysis (Whittington et al., 1999; Pettigrew and Fenton, 2000a). The quantitative findings from our survey show that in simultaneously innovating along structural, processual, and boundary dimensions, higher performers mostly embrace the full range of organizing dualities. Furthermore, the case studies already published treat us to an even richer picture of these dualities. Thus in Ove Arup and Coopers & Lybrand (Fenton and Pettigrew, 2000a), there were successive attempts to encourage dependence on the centre and independence from the centre; to promote centralization of strategy and the decentralization of operations; and to empower while holding on to power. Both PSOs were attempting to build strong global brands with all that involved in terms of coherence of identity and standardization of quality, while at the same time permitting customized client offerings in national and regional markets. The development of innovative forms of organizing in the Spanish utility Agbar is a further example (Sánchez-Runde and Quintanilla, 2000). Organization development in Agbar involved finding new balances between centralization and decentralization, continuity and change, and building the hierarchy while encouraging horizontal co-ordination. Fremap, the leading Spanish firm in the mutual insurance sector, illustrated the personnel management complementarities needed to support new organizing arrangements (Quintanilla and Sánchez-Runde, 2000). This case also demonstrated that the implementation of these complementarities had to acknowledge and reflect the new balance of centralizing and decentralizing in people-related matters.

In the following chapters of Part 3 of this volume, new elaborations on the management of dualities are presented. Chapter 11 (by Sánchez-Runde, Massini, and Quintanilla) presents quantitative and qualitative evidence on how firms in the INNFORM programme managed 16 people-related dualities in the areas of organizational culture, work organization, leadership and employees' roles, and HR practices. This set of innovating organizations stress a duality-balancing approach to carefully manage their people. The chapter emphasizes how the people management dualities were themselves managed in an across-the-board, systematic fashion.

Chapter 12 presents quantitative evidence about the extent to which new organizational practices are converging or diverging in firms in Germany, the USA and Japan. In their analysis, Lewin, Massini, Ruigrok, and Numagami move back and forth between the organizational (firm) and ecological (nation state) levels of analysis in exposing the interrelations and dualities between a large number of organizational variables in our sample of innovating firms.

Finally, Achtenhagen and Melin show in Chapter 13 how leading firms ABB, Östgöta Enskilda Bank, and Siemens AG balance the dualities of homogeneity and heterogeneity of organizing arrangements. The authors propose a triple way of balancing, which they typify along three alternative generic strategies which aim to increase homogeneity, decrease heterogeneity, and enhance the capacities of managing the dualities. While the dualities discussed are not new, the ways of simultaneously combining those three strategies reveal the practicalities of benefiting from the balancing between homogeneity and heterogeneity.

## IMPLICATIONS FOR THEORY AND RESEARCH

Understanding and managing dualities represent real challenges to current management theory and practice. The content and process dualities addressed in this introductory chapter have all pointed to the need to find new management knowledge which allows us to understand how dualities are managed in theory and practice. Our own evidence from the INNFORM programme has established that new forms of organizing are supplementing and not supplanting older, more traditional organizational practices. The obvious requirement now is for management thought and action which can come to terms with the new power of the 'ands' of dualities instead of the old simplicities of 'either/or' in the traditionally stated dichotomies of, for example, centralization or decentralization. It is also clear from our research findings that the new complexities of current organizing are placing added demands on the information processing capabilities of individuals and groups in complex organizations. How firms cope with these newer levels of complexity and dynamism we have yet to see. Early results from the INNFORM programme suggest that escalating levels of complexity are creating corresponding hunts for simplifying routines to reduce the complexity, or at least keep it under control (Pettigrew and Fenton, 2000a). It is certainly a possibility that movement from the 'either/or dichotomy' to the 'and duality' will increase levels of uncertainty for decision makers and the potential for internal politics around the constantly moving chess board of organizing.

From a research method point of view the understanding of dualities and their management may require the challenging of customary methods of inquiry. For example, traditional quantitative methods have become accustomed to regress mono-independent variables often upon a single dependent variable. It is highly unlikely that this approach will reveal the actual relationships between variables conceptualized in dualistic terms. Equally well, the qualitative analysis of dualities will only be possible with time series data, which can assess not just the origins and development of dualities, but also their consequential management over time. We need to know much more about what the dualities are, from whence they came, how they evolved, and in what way and why they are capable of being managed. We know from other research on organizational dynamics that such processes are highly contextually sensitive (Pettigrew, 1997a). It thus follows that future research should be formulated in research designs which deliberately build in variations in context in order to properly explore how dualities may differentially appear and be differentially managed in those varying organizational and industry contexts.

Dualities seem to appear in bundles rather than in discrete or easily isolatable units. For example, central and distributed leadership is rarely independent of the balance between centralized and decentralized structuring. We have also seen in the INNFORM programme that dualities such as centralizing and decentralizing, managing hierarchies and networks, and balancing continuity and change can all appear together. The research challenge here is to understand how and why these dualities may emerge together, and how in turn they are capable of being managed together. De facto it is clear that managing bundles of practices is much more complex than managing them separately on a one-to-one basis. Following our research results on the relationship between complementary change and organizational performance it would be interesting to know if the same complementarities logic can be applied to the management of dualities, and with the same performance consequences.

Chapter 11

# People Management Dualities

*Carlos J. Sánchez-Runde,*
*Silvia Massini and*
*Javier Quintanilla*

## INTRODUCTION

New forms of competition require new ways of organizing firm activities.
Many authors have pointed out that traditional forms of organization are
not suited to our rapidly changing environments. Innovating organizations
(Pettigrew and Fenton, 2000a) reduce the limitations of hierarchical and
bureaucratic forms by transforming the liabilities of firm size and
redesigning processes. At the same time, new ways of organizing are
being used in conjunction with trends towards downsizing, delayering,
organizing around smaller business units, increasing the number of profit
centres, and entrusting lower levels with more autonomy (Miles and Snow,
1994: 100–1). In this way, they resemble 'enabling bureaucracies' which
alleviate some negative characteristics of more traditional ways of
organizing (Adler and Borys, 1996).

   A major finding of recent research in innovative enterprises is the
need for balance between traditional and newer arrangements (Whittington
et al., 1999; Pettigrew and Fenton, 2000a). This balance is accomplished
by supplementing, rather than supplanting, the old with the new. Thus,
innovative companies 'accommodate opposing tendencies and
yet function as coherent and cohesive concerns' (Bahrami, 1992: 43).
They simultaneously master apparently contradictory dualities such
as continuity and change, hierarchies and networks, vertical and
horizontal integration, and centralization and decentralization that
empowers employees while holding the ring. Further, they identify

and share knowledge across units that both collaborate and compete (Pettigrew, 1999a).

Duality management has been a recurrent but superficially treated theme in organization theory literature. It has only recently begun to be systematically explored as an important and substantive topic in its own right (Evans and Génadry, 1999; Janssens and Steyaert, 1999). Moreover, there is an acknowledged dearth of thought on the people management implications of the newer organizational forms (Kanter and Eccles, 1992; Quintanilla and Sánchez-Runde, 2000). In this chapter, we aim for a clearer understanding of dualities that affect people management in innovating organizations.

This chapter is organized in four parts. First, drawing from the European INNFORM survey and database, a point will be made about the relevance of people management considerations for the performance of innovating organizations. These considerations directly impact on people management dualities in the areas of organizational culture, leadership, work organization and human resource management (HRM) practices. Our quantitative, survey-based data are extremely valuable in suggesting and pointing to the *what* of people management dualities, but they are not sufficient to explain their *why* and *how*.

To bridge this gap, we use qualitative data from innovating firms actually striving to manage these dualities in the second part of this chapter. We begin by reviewing, at a conceptual level, the state-of-the-art on people management dualities regarding organizational culture, work organization, leadership and personnel practices. Then, we confront these theoretical developments in turn with the rich information obtained from recently published in-depth European case studies from the INNFORM programme (Pettigrew and Fenton, 2000a). In the third part of the chapter we discuss our findings. Finally, we present the implications and challenges ahead for theory development and practice.

## FIRM PERFORMANCE AND PEOPLE MANAGEMENT DUALITIES

Personnel interventions in organizations often follow separate, piecemeal, practice-by-practice modes. In other words, introduction of well-integrated, internally consistent bundles of HRM practices remains a rare event (Osterman, 1994; Lawler et al., 1995). Against this state of things, scholars claim that there is growing evidence of the performance benefits enjoyed by companies that introduce systemic HRM approaches (Macy and Izumi, 1993; Arthur, 1994). Unlike practice-by-practice modes, systemic approaches leverage on mutually reinforcing complementarities between people management initiatives (Ashmos and Huber, 1987; Kerr and Jackofsky, 1989). Complementary, high-performance HRM systems also need to match compatible firm strategies and structures (Caligiuri and Stroh, 1995; MacDuffie,

1995; Cappelli and Crocker-Hefter, 1996; Dunlop and Weil, 1996). Therefore, we need to analyse the performance of HRM systems in the context of innovative organizing and strategizing.

Evidence from the INNFORM programme shows two things in this regard (Whittington et al., 1999). First, two-thirds of the companies surveyed claim increased adoption of innovative HRM practices, such as new internal labour markets (ILMs), teamwork, and mission- and vision-building activities. In fact, over one-third of these companies put a fairly strong emphasis on those innovations.

Second, adopting system-wide innovations leads to two types of performance effects. First, companies adopting simultaneous and consistent change at the triple level of structures, processes and boundaries outperform those adopting piecemeal, separate innovations. Second, change has significant and negative performance effects when it is only partial and changes in structures and boundaries are not accompanied by changes in processes. This finding on the counter-productiveness of partial, subsystemic change is worth noting for two reasons. First, it points to the pivotal role of organizational processes, among which people management considerations become crucial. Second, it signals the need for internal consistency within firm subsystems so that they form a cohesive 'system of subsystems'. In other words, internal consistency within subsystems needs to be coupled with horizontal consistency among subsystems for companies to benefit from a systemic approach to change. This poses special challenges for people management in innovative companies. We will see later that some of the newer arrangements display the seemingly opposing, almost contradictory characteristics of dualities. Now, we present evidence from the INNFORM survey showing the performance impact of new people management initiatives in innovating organizations (details of the design and econometrics of the INNFORM survey can be found in Chapter 7 of this volume).

Our quantitative analysis followed an exploratory, rather than confirmatory approach to hypothesis testing. This is normally regarded as appropriate when dealing with phenomena which have not been addressed to any great extent by extant research. The dependent variable is firm performance relative to competitors. We regressed performance on several sets of independent variables covering different people management activities. These activities included extent of use of ILMs; teamworking arrangements; investment in training and development; mission building activities; proportion of employees with graduate degrees; corporate-wide conferences and seminars; outsourcing of HR practices; and outsourcing of training and development. These variables have been shown in the literature to distinctively characterize innovative firms (Pettigrew and Fenton, 2000a; Whittington et al., 1999). Other variables held in common with traditional organizations, such as staffing and reward practices, and organizational culture and leadership, were analysed in detail through in-depth case studies, and we refer to them in the next section.

To account for alternative explanations we introduced control variables that can also affect firm performance. Control variables included: use of IT; project-based, product/service and functional structures; market share; research and development investments; extent of regional and international presence; reengineering initiatives; and vertical, horizontal and networking linkages.

Table 11.1 presents descriptive statistics and correlations of all the variables included in the alternative models that we analysed at one time or another. Table 11.2 presents our preferred model, with eight variables (four independent variables and four controls), after deleting variables that lacked statistical significance and introduced noise in the model. Alternative models and details of our modelling strategy are available upon request from the second author of this chapter.

A preliminary pattern of HRM activities jointly interacting is found in the correlational analysis of Table 11.1. These activities include: new ILMs, managerial development events, mission-building activities, team forms of work organization, cross-company conferences, internal communication networks, and investments in training development. The resulting 21 pairs are all positive. The only four correlations that are not significant at the 0.5 level involve the presence of investments in training and development; we will come back to this variable later. In general terms, and despite their univariate nature, these findings point to the need for systemic approaches that encompass both main and interactive effects (Fisher, 1989; Ichniowski et al., 1997).

Table 11.2 reports multivariate regression analysis. Our ordered probit estimates indicate that all the independent variables and controls in our preferred model are significant. While overall project structures display a negative coefficient, our three other control variables (market share, intensive use of IT, and structuring company operations along geographical lines) show the expected positive impact on firm performance.

The behaviour of the HRM-independent variables merits closer scrutiny. Two of them show positive performance effects. This is not surprising, since the literature has consistently reported the beneficial consequences of co-operatively working in teams with a shared view of the organization's mission and vision (Levine, 1995; Banker et al., 1996). Interestingly, however, the effects of introducing new ILM concepts, with substantial investments in training and development activities, show counter-intuitive negative signs.

A clear explanation for this phenomenon immediately comes to mind. In particular, one should account for the necessary time-lag between the implementation of these innovations and the attainment of their expected rewards, especially when recently introduced (Huselid and Becker, 1996). Some time-lag performance effects are naturally to be expected from all initiatives that introduce substantial change in the organization. These effects, however, are likely to be stronger in the case of the variables in our model

TABLE 11.1  *Descriptive statistics and correlation matrix*

| Variable | Mean 1 | s.d. | Mean 2 | s.d. | 1 | 2 | 3 | 4 | 5 | 6 | 7 | 8 | 9 | 10 | 11 | 12 | 13 | 14 | 15 | 16 | 17 | 18 | 19 | 20 | 21 |
|---|---|---|---|---|---|---|---|---|---|---|---|---|---|---|---|---|---|---|---|---|---|---|---|---|---|
| 1 Relative performance | 3.64 | 0.99 | 0.61 | 0.49 | | | | | | | | | | | | | | | | | | | | | |
| 2 Internal labour markets | 3.82 | 0.85 | 0.16 | 0.37 | -.03 | | | | | | | | | | | | | | | | | | | | |
| 3 Management development | 3.99 | 0.92 | 0.26 | 0.44 | .06 | -.21* | | | | | | | | | | | | | | | | | | | |
| 4 Mission building | 4.05 | 0.99 | 0.27 | 0.44 | .09 | .22* | .29* | | | | | | | | | | | | | | | | | | |
| 5 Teams | 4.15 | 0.80 | 0.28 | 0.45 | .15* | .17* | .28* | .31* | | | | | | | | | | | | | | | | | |
| 6 Conferences | 3.98 | 0.86 | 0.24 | 0.43 | -.02 | .17* | .30* | .31* | .30* | | | | | | | | | | | | | | | | |
| 7 Internal networks | 4.12 | 0.77 | 0.24 | 0.43 | .15* | .14* | .21* | .33* | .31* | .33* | | | | | | | | | | | | | | | |
| 8 Outsourcing HR | 2.07 | 0.86 | 0.30 | 0.46 | .04 | -.07 | -.03 | -.13* | -.10* | -.03 | -.09 | | | | | | | | | | | | | | |
| 9 Outsourcing training | 3.05 | 0.92 | 0.46 | 0.50 | .09 | -.07 | .03 | -.07 | .00 | -.00 | .05 | .36* | | | | | | | | | | | | | |
| 10 Training and development | 1.88 | 0.98 | 0.27 | 0.45 | -.17* | .11* | .05 | .07 | .07 | .10* | .03 | -.03 | -.02 | | | | | | | | | | | | |
| 11 Research and development | 2.79 | 1.15 | 0.29 | 0.45 | -.07 | -.07 | -.01 | .07 | .03 | -.02 | .07 | -.03 | -.04 | .21* | | | | | | | | | | | |
| 12 Graduate employees | 1.90 | 1.11 | 0.26 | 0.44 | -.01 | .03 | .01 | .02 | .01 | .00 | .07 | .10* | .05 | .26* | .20* | | | | | | | | | | |
| 13 Vertical linkages | 3.40 | 0.75 | 0.31 | 0.46 | .08 | .04 | .09 | .09 | .14* | -.03 | .06 | -.05 | -.00 | .11* | .07 | .04 | | | | | | | | | |
| 14 Horizontal linkages | 3.20 | 0.86 | 0.25 | 0.43 | -.00 | .08 | .00 | .13* | .17* | .01 | .13* | -.03 | -.05 | .10* | .10* | .10* | .54* | | | | | | | | |
| 15 IT | 3.47 | 0.83 | 0.38 | 0.49 | .13* | .20* | .11* | .13* | .11* | .09 | .21* | -.06 | .06 | .15* | .10* | .10* | .27* | .27* | | | | | | | |
| 16 Re-engineering | 3.55 | 0.98 | 0.57 | 0.49 | -.05 | .17* | .18* | .19* | .10* | .08 | .12* | -.07 | -.03 | .05 | .13* | .07 | .06 | .04 | .15* | | | | | | |
| 17 Prod/serv. structure | 4.05 | 1.03 | 0.78 | 0.41 | -.00 | .09 | .10* | .09 | .03 | .06 | .10* | .01 | .01 | .01 | .01 | .04 | .04 | .03 | .10* | .12* | | | | | |
| 18 Geograph. structure | 3.30 | 1.25 | 0.52 | 0.50 | .20* | .05 | .06 | .06 | .02 | .07 | .12* | .07 | .02 | .05 | .02 | .03 | .10* | .07 | .14* | .06 | .00 | | | | |
| 19 Functional structure | 3.56 | 1.09 | 0.58 | 0.49 | .08 | .04 | .07 | .08 | .05 | .02 | .01 | -.04 | .02 | .02 | .04 | -.01 | .20* | .16* | .17* | .12* | -.04 | .21* | | | |
| 20 Project structure | 2.90 | 1.35 | 0.42 | 0.49 | -.01 | .12* | .15* | .17* | .13* | .14* | .14* | -.04 | .02 | .06 | .15* | .10* | .17* | .15* | .18* | .27* | .16* | .16* | .21* | | |
| 21 Market share | 2.69 | 1.68 | 0.37 | 0.48 | .13* | .18* | -.03 | .06 | .02 | .00 | .02 | -.04 | -.05 | .05 | .09 | .01 | -.04 | -.08 | -.01 | .03 | .04 | .06 | -.04 | .04 | |
| 22 Internationalization | 2.99 | 1.57 | 0.24 | 0.43 | .02 | .05 | .03 | .08 | .01 | .06 | .13* | -.04 | -.00 | .17* | .22* | .08 | .04 | .02 | .11* | .05 | .09 | .08 | .00 | .05 | .06 |

N = 394 for cells corresponding to Market Share; N = 251 for cells corresponding to Relative performance; N = 439 for all other cells * p < .05

Mean 1 is the mean in a 1–5 Likert scale; Mean 2 is mean of a binary variable with 1 for companies adopting high levels of organizational innovation (that is, ≥ 4 in a 1–5 Likert scale), it corresponds to the proportion of companies adopting high levels of organizational innovation in the sample

TABLE 11.2   *Results of ordered probit regression analyses*

| Relative performance | Coefficient | Standard Error | Z | P > Z |
|---|---|---|---|---|
| Internal labour markets | −.68123 | .347435 | −1.961 | 0.050* |
| Mission building | .53972 | .290881 | 1.855 | 0.064* |
| Teams | .54966 | .294122 | 1.869 | 0.062* |
| Training and development | −.84606 | .295301 | −2.865 | 0.004** |
| IT | .54984 | .260585 | 2.110 | 0.035** |
| Geographical structure | .74239 | .252266 | 2.943 | 0.003** |
| Project structure | −.42391 | .254990 | −1.662 | 0.096* |
| Market share | .18142 | .084558 | 2.145 | 0.032** |

$N = 234$; $X^2(8) = 36.23$ [0.0000]; Pseudo-$R^2 = 0.0581$; Log likelihood $= -293.58369$; *$p < .05$
**$p < .01$

that have a negative sign, than in the case of those with a positive sign. First, it is only natural that the introduction of new ILMs requires medium to longer term scenarios. We will see later, for instance, that ASEA Brown Boveri (ABB) requires its employees to stay for a minimum of 18 months in one company within the group before they can take advantage of ABB's new ILM policies (Ruigrok et al., 2000b). Therefore, ILMs are likely to require around two or three years before they display significant performance effects. Similarly, long time-lag effects have also been repeatedly reported in the literature in relation to the performance benefits of training and development initiatives (McCall et al., 1988). We believe that this should also explain the non-significance of the correlations in Table 11.1 between investments in training and development on the one hand, and managerial development events, mission building activities, and teamwork on the other.

In summary, inferential evidence from the survey provides two main results. First, our quantitative analysis highlights general patterns of systemic HRM dynamics: this concurs with the more recent conclusions of the HRM literature in general, as reviewed above; it is also consistent with the complementarity dynamics explored in Chapter 7 of this book. Second, the analysis shows that some of the variables have a positive effect on performance, whereas others have negative effects. In particular, we need to explore further the behaviour of new ILMs and investments in training and development. To do this, we need to go beyond the usual caveats and look for supplementary lines of argument. We think that complex duality issues can also explain some portions of performance variance across the INNFORM sample.

To introduce a point here which we will develop further in the next section, let us hint at the nature of the independent variables in our model. To do so, we will focus now on the teamworking variable. In spite of its complexity, this variable shows a straightforward, significant, positive regression coefficient in Table 11.2. Therefore, it should help us in stating a robust reasoning that is only likely to err, if at all, on the more conservative side.

Introducing innovative teamwork arrangements requires some prior reorganization of the work that is done in the firm; this reorganization calls for the balancing of clear assignments and task flexibility. Without clear assignments, employees may not fully know – or may be confused about – what they are expected to contribute to the team. Without task flexibility, employees may find themselves over-constrained by job definitions which are not likely to accommodate the required flexibility of group behaviour. However, the line between clarity and flexibility, crucial as it is for the performance of the team organization, is not easy to draw. Naturally, constructing a definition of variables intended to reveal the statistical co-variation of, in this case, performance and teamwork is not easy to do either. That is, of course, unless the complexity of balancing clarity and flexibility is also incorporated in the measurements. With this, however, we are only scratching the surface of the measurement issue. We do not simply have to account for the clarity/flexibility duality in this variable. There are at least three other dualities impinging on teamworking arrangements that also need to be considered, and we will review these later.

If we now turn to the three other independent variables in our model, a similar scenario appears. Effective mission and vision building cannot be isolated from more fundamental patterns shaping the culture and the leadership processes. Further, as with new ILM features, the performance benefits to be derived from training and development investments demand a systemic view of HRM practices and, again, the balancing of dualities.

This discussion is obviously not intended to downplay the validity of the quantitative analysis. On the contrary, important as the quantitative analysis is in confirming the performance effects of the new organizing trends, it also demands that we move ahead. We are ready to extend our research with richer, qualitative data that throw light on the actual working of people management dualities.

## FUNDAMENTAL PEOPLE MANAGEMENT DUALITIES

A systemic view of the firm suggests that changes in the firm's strategy and structure should be paralleled by changes in the way it manages its personnel (Miles and Snow, 1984; Wright and McMahan, 1992). Allred, Snow and Miles, for instance, point out that 'the evolution of organizational forms has always driven the ingredients and paths of managerial careers' (1996: 17). More generally, virtually all models of organization design stress the need for fitting congruence between strategy, structure and processes; at the heart of these models, people management issues weigh heavily. Organizational culture sets the frame for sustaining and fostering consistency and continuity through change; leadership shapes the overall management of the organization; work organization patterns specify the distribution and functioning of

> **Cultural dualities:**
>     Central culture – Peripheral cultures
>     International culture – National cultures
>     General culture – Specialist cultures
>     Unifying culture – Decentralizing cultures
>
> **Work organization dualities:**
>     Assignment clarity – Task flexibility
>     Defined accountability – Freedom to execute
>     Specialized professionalism – Multidisciplinarity
>     Inter-team adaptability – Intra-team stability
>
> **Leadership and management dualities:**
>     Shared leadership – Concentrated leadership
>     Leadership – Management
>     Encouraged participation – Forced participation
>     Temporality – Trust building
>
> **HR dualities:**
>     Agency – Community
>     Employee segmentation – Generalized commitment
>     Vertical assessment – Networking behaviour
>     Collective sanctions – Reputation preservation

FIGURE 11.1    *Summary of people management dualities*

firm activities. At the end of the day, since it is people who get things done in the organization, the question of how individuals themselves are managed, through a given set of HRM practices, is of the utmost importance.

In this section, we present 16 people management dualities. Figure 11.1 presents these dualities in summary.

Four dualities are discussed in each of the fundamental areas of organizational culture, leadership, work organization and HRM practices. We start with a conceptual review of the state of the art in each area. Then, we introduce the dualities and illustrate their dynamism with evidence from eight recently published, in-depth case studies from the INNFORM programme. For space reasons, we will only provide very summary background information on the firms studied; detailed, in-depth company profiles can be found in Pettigrew and Fenton (2000a).

## Organizational culture and duality management

A landmark of organizational behaviour research since the 1980s, the concept of culture is still extremely complex. Cultures have been portrayed as hard to identify, fuzzy, multifaceted and amorphous (Hall, 1992; Brislin, 1993; Trice and Beyer, 1993; Baligh, 1994). Despite these difficulties, common ground can be found in seeing culture variously as a philosophy that underlies the functioning of the organization, as the basic rules of the game for getting along, and as a feeling or climate conveyed by the physical and structural elements of the organization (Schein, 1980). All of these concepts coalesce around culture as a system of shared values and beliefs guiding the behaviour of organizational members (Deal and Kennedy, 1982). One way or another, all organizations either 'are' (Weick, 1983) or 'have' (Smircich, 1983) cultures, or both.

Cultures are also extraordinarily efficient means of co-ordination and control (Wilkins and Ouchi, 1983: 478) under, among others, two conditions that are especially salient in innovating organizations:

1  when firm transactions take place under ambiguity, complexity and interdependence
2  when subunits develop their own subcultures without weakening the overall culture of the organization as a whole.

Transactions in the new organizations do indeed take place under uncertainty, complexity and interdependence. Uncertainty in individuals' roles and responsibilities derives from two related circumstances. First, the characteristic 'boundarylessness' of the newer arrangements, with its associated ambiguity in the drawing of organizational 'frontiers' within and between units. Second, the absence of well-defined and distinct job descriptions in accordance with traditional forms of labour division. Complexity accrues to innovating enterprises through the changing nature of tasks; these tasks are increasingly knowledge-intensive and hold a stronger international orientation. Finally, interdependence also increases in the new organizations. Innovating firms thrive on inter-unit co-operation, exponential growth of internal and external linkages, and teamworking in project-based structures. We will turn to the challenges of this added uncertainty/complexity/interdependence when discussing the management of work organization dualities.

Let us now focus on the second condition signalled by Wilkins and Ouchi, the balancing of organizational culture and subcultures. Here, we introduce four dualities which can be formulated in the following pairs of concepts: central and peripheral cultures; international and national cultures; general and specialist cultures; and unifying and decentralizing cultures.

First, managing the balance between organizational and subunit cultures is more complex now than in traditional firms. In relation to corporate- wide culture, stronger subcultures emerge quite easily in innovative firms, due to the higher levels of autonomy from central headquarters enjoyed at the periphery. This was an important factor behind the 1999 evolution in ASEA Brown Boveri (ABB, arguably the world's largest producer of engineering products and services). ABB moved from an already innovative matrix structure to an even more innovative divisional network. One of the important reasons for this change was the need to restore a strong common culture to counteract the dominance of subcultures at the triple levels of country organizations, front-line firms, and single business areas within the group.

Second, looser ties between the centre and the peripheral firms within a corporation, create another related, albeit different, cultural duality. An international culture, usually fostered from headquarters, can ignite centrifugal reactions along national lines against what might be perceived as dominating national values at the centre. This duality of international versus national (or regional) culture can be found in the case of Ove Arup, a leading provider of consulting services across all the engineering disciplines, headquartered in London (Fenton and Pettigrew, 2000a). In fact, some of Ove Arup's overseas firms perceive their overall international culture as too UK-centric, and react by creating separate, strong subcultures at the level of their national organizations.

Third, boundaryless firms leveraging on knowledge intensity need to foster the professional ties of their employees to their respective communities of practice. This, in turn, augments the potential flourishing of different, at times even competing, professional subcultures. Multiple professional subcultures need to harmoniously coexist with one another, especially whenever different groups of professionals are required to display co-operative, networking behaviour across specialisms. A balance needs to be reached between what can be termed general (or inter-professional) and specialist (or intra-professional) cultures. In Ove Arup, overall cultural integration above professional subcultures is made difficult, for instance, by the diverging values of industrial and building engineers. Value differences across these specialisms arise in regard to the priority that should be given to profitability, commercial attractiveness, work interest and innovation goals.

Management of the inter- and intra-professional culture interface is especially noteworthy in Ove Arup. Somewhat ironically, Ove Arup confronted the challenges of this duality as a result of having previously solved another, rather more basic duality. This basic duality has been conceptualized in terms of the contrast between organizational and professional cultures (Raelin, 1985), and refers to the possibility of conflicting allegiances to either the organization in which someone is employed, or the profession to which someone belongs. Ove Arup solved the 'dual allegiance' issue by creating specialized skill networks that internalized – and solved – previous dual allegiances to the organization and to the profession. This was accomplished partly by having senior engineers organize technical seminars for junior staff members, and partly by issuing professional publications of internal and external prestige. The organizational 'internalization' of (typically) external professional allegiances had one unintended consequence: Ove Arup needed to devise mechanisms that would alleviate duality tensions between employees from the different specialisms that coexisted within the organization. This is at the heart of the general versus specialist culture duality just mentioned.

Subcultural dynamics can thus be so salient that while organizational culture has traditionally been characterized as each company's idiosyncratic 'way of being', corporate-wide culture in the innovating organization needs rather to operate as a 'way of being one', with an emphasis on the cohesiveness required in these much more multicentred, heterarchical concerns (Hedlund, 1994).

Finally, for cultures to really perform as the glue cementing inter-unit cohesion, clear doses of congruence and acceptance of assumptions and values commonly held by all organizational members are required. This presents innovative firms with a fourth balancing act. Virtually all the companies studied in the INNFORM programme display a decentralizing, participative, entrepreneurial, even democratic spirit informing their cultures. These traits are all charged with high potential for strong subculture proliferation. This proliferation, however, is not necessarily derived from the structuring arrangements discussed in the previous three dualities. There, the need for balance between culture and subcultures originates in, respectively, the granting of autonomy from headquarters to peripheral units, operating at local and international levels, and staffing the firm with people of diverse professional backgrounds. Here, instead, the dynamism of cultures that are participative, entrepreneurial and democratic naturally fosters the flourishing of subcultures besides and beyond contingencies like the ones just mentioned. The need to act both locally and globally, for instance, can be imposed on the whole organization by a top management that acts merely in hierarchical, command and control modes. Obviously, these are not the ways exhibited by the innovating firms in our sample, which explains why innovating firms face further pressures for the simultaneous management of unifying and decentralizing cultures.

Management of the new businesses thus requires the preservation of an equilibrium of centrifugal and centripetal cultural pressures. Cultural duality equilibria should facilitate the simultaneous operation of two things. On the one hand, it needs to foster the proliferation of diverse subcultures that inform the particular modes of empowered subunits (Hedlund, 1994); the introduction of shared leadership and new ILMs at Hilti, which we discuss below, are a case in point. On the other hand, highly entrepreneurial and participative modes also need to foster the prevalence of a cultural umbrella that promotes inter-unit integration (Hastings, 1993), complementary strengths (Powell, 1990) and open communication across levels (Helgesen, 1995). We will also see how Fremap, for instance, achieves this by imposing common task calendars and clear overall managing criteria across highly empowered territorial branches.

## Work organization and duality management

In this section, we analyse the following four dualities in the work organization of innovating organizations: assignment clarity and task flexibility;

defined accountability and freedom to execute; specialized professionalism and multidisciplinarity; and inter-team adaptability and intra-team stability.

Traditional forms of work organization are based on the division of work and thus require jobs to be analysed and designed along strict lines of demarcation, and then grouped into separate functional units (Daft, 1992). With time, jobs are enlarged and enriched, thus alleviating the strain of rigid job demarcations on employees; specialists become responsible for an increased number of still discrete tasks (Miles and Snow, 1994). This form of work organization is reinforced by formal job descriptions and strict boundaries between clearly differentiated units. In this way, stable jobs benefit from a changing pool of incumbents, with 'a clear structure of specialized roles, where individual parts can be changed through recruitment and inter-firm mobility' (Hedlund, 1994: 84).

New structuring patterns demand new forms of work organization. Employees are put in charge of empowered work; they exercise broad judgement and control the resources needed to complete their projects (Miles and Snow, 1994). Organizations become 'de-jobbed' (Bridges, 1994; Brousseau et al., 1996), they adapt more easily to the management of knowledge work, and they facilitate focus on core capabilities (Bridges, 1996). Task content prevails over formal position; specific projects evolve in response to needs as they arise (Helgesen, 1995); multifunctional teams are formed and disbanded through fluid sets of continuously re-negotiated assignments (Ezzamel et al., 1994). Boundary-crossing, along functional and geographical lines, gives teams a virtual character, examples of which can be found in the Agbar Foundation (a unit in charge of co-ordinating the environmental research and development within the *Aguas de Barcelona* group, a major provider in the international market for water services) (Sánchez-Runde and Quintanilla, 2000) and in the top management of Coopers & Lybrand's (now PricewaterhouseCoopers) European Pharmaceutical Network (Fenton and Pettigrew, 2000a).

These general patterns point to the need for balancing clarity in the assignment of work on the one hand, and task flexibility on the other. They mark the structural evolution of Spectrum, a business unit created in 1992 within the Rabobank co-operative group charged with providing cutting edge IT knowledge to the group and its local banks (Van Wijk and Van den Bosch, 2000). Spectrum moved from overall task compartmentalization to organizing through a variable number of clusters and project teams, which are deliberately designed to be small in size. In this way, their members are obliged to network with members of other units to gather the knowledge that they need for their work.

The newer forms of work organizing are not merely suited to the new structural landscape. At Ove Arup, project-team structures are seen less as an option than as the only possible way of organizing work. There, neat linearity from idea through transformation to output in the firm's value chain is not feasible; instead, chaotic and emergent processes are found to characterize efficient work patterns. Projects are large scale and, as in Spectrum, teams need to leverage knowledge that is distributed across units. Of course, this is not exclusive to Ove Arup. We find similar trends in Saab Training Systems, a 300-employee manufacturer of laser-based training simulation products for the defence sector, within the Saab corporation (Müllern, 2000). This company is structured mainly around product contracts and innovation experiences through cross-functional teams. Traditional functions are not departmentalized as such. In fact, 'functional teams' are found only in finance, personnel, testing, and central purchasing.

In these new scenarios, temporary task constellations require permanent pools of people who achieve 'the necessary commonality of communicative codes' (Hedlund, 1994: 84). These codes, in turn, depend on improved forms of organization whereby 'an intensified need for frequent communication and interaction across formal boundaries can be created by vague roles and responsibilities' (Baker, 1992: 404).

The implementation of 'vague roles and responsibilities' confronts companies with a second duality. Re-organizing work requires both defined accountability and freedom to execute. As former ABB CEO Barnevik put it in 1991, managers need 'well-defined sets of responsibilities, and clear accountability' on the one hand, and a 'maximum degree of freedom to execute' on the other (Taylor, 1991: 99, cited in Ruigrok et al., 2000b: 120).

Saab Training Systems' way of dealing with this duality between accountability and freedom to execute involves team-based structures on a major scale. To this effect, the firm fully re-organized its activities through about 40 teams of six to eight employees per team, with each team directly reporting to the management team. Each project is carried out by a constellation of teams led by a business team at the centre and the business team integrates all the other teams taking part in the project. These other teams are in charge of logistic delivery, innovation, design, and so on. Teams that grow to over eight members are automatically split. While teams are endowed with ample operational freedom, they are also firmly constrained through two mechanisms: first, a strict planning process directed by the business team; second, the control of a strong firm manager who is ultimately responsible for overall integration. A way out of the duality is thus found by combining well-defined responsibilities and accountability with operational freedom to execute. Fremap, a medium-large firm leading the Spanish mutual insurance industry, shows a similar pattern (Quintanilla and Sánchez-Runde, 2000). Fremap's employees in the territorial branches are asked to take on increased responsibilities through their own initiative. At the same time, accountability is enforced through the sharing of common, company-wide, task calendars and broad management criteria.

Work in teams dominates the new organizational arrangements. Team members manage their own resources (planning, scheduling, co-ordination with other teams…) resulting in dispersed decision making at the organizational level (Miles and Snow, 1994). At the group level, however, having teams make their own decisions allows them to take a holistic approach to problem solving (Ezzamel et al., 1994).

This phenomenon introduces a third duality in the organization of work: the coupling of specialized professionalism and multidisciplinarity. The holistic, multidisciplinary pole of this duality is illustrated by an expanding tendency in Fremap, where local branch employees became 'integral agents', casting off their previously specialized roles. This trend towards multidisciplinarity was counterbalanced by changes at headquarters. On the one hand, to further empower integral agents, work patterns shifted from formalized command-and-control dynamics to informal influence and coordination. On the other hand, headquarters kept, and even reinforced, a traditional functional structure that thrived on specialization. Multidisciplinarity by integral agents was thus strongly supported by functional structures staffed with specialists at the centre.

Finally, Saab Training Systems shows an extremely interesting way of balancing a fourth duality, namely intra-team stability and inter-team adaptability. In very general terms, employees and organizations always need to strike a balance between continuity and change. The organization of work at Saab Training Systems aims to achieve this precisely through the functioning of its team structure. Continuity is achieved by having employees 'micro-working within teams'; intra-team stability provides individuals with a much needed sense of personal and cultural belonging. Simultaneously, having the organization operate through its 'macro-structuring among teams' allows for inter-team adaptability. In this way, the firm can effectively respond to the changing needs of its customers. Therefore, balancing intra-team stability and inter-team adaptability alleviates some of the pressures of continuity and change at the more aggregate organizational level.

We have seen that new forms of work organization require that companies reconcile four pairs of dualities: assignment clarity and task flexibility; defined accountability and freedom to execute; specialized professionalism and multidisciplinarity; and intra-team stability and inter-team adaptability. For these balancing acts to be feasible, however, two other sets of dualities need to be managed as well. The traditional organization was reinforced by hierarchical controls, chain-of-command discipline, limited feedback, personal supervision, collection of progress reports and formal performance evaluation (Ezzamel et al., 1994; Miles and Snow, 1994). In contrast, co-ordination and control in the new organization unfolds through employee self-discipline shaped by reciprocity, reputation, trust and even friendship (Hastings, 1993; Powell, 1990). The divide is so high, and its implications so broad, that new concepts are needed to understand the changing roles of leaders and employees, and HRM practices. In the next two sections, we introduce the dualities that companies face regarding these new concepts.

## Leadership and employees' roles, and duality management

Leadership has so direct an influence on work dynamics that one can hardly separate innovative work organization from leadership patterns. Therefore, in this section we supplement the analysis of work organization dualities with a discussion of leadership dualities. These dualities are: shared and concentrated leadership; leadership and management; forced and encouraged participation; and temporality and trust building.

Traditional leadership controls and facilitates the utilization of employees' functional expertise through limited participation in routine matters and, in its most progressive forms, joint goal-setting. Innovating leadership broadens the responsibilities of all organizational members by investing in employee development, so that people acquire strategic and change expertise (Miles and Snow, 1994). Leadership moves from 'concentrated' to 'distributed' forms (Handy, 1996; Hastings, 1993).

Hilti is a leading global producer of tools for the construction sector (Ruigrok et al., 2000a) which illustrates how traditional leadership at the centre can be supplemented with leadership that is also shared and distributed. 'Empowerment' at Hilti is seen as still too traditional a concept, for it implies a process of hierarchically 'allowing' employees to take on increased responsibilities. Instead, the term 'shared leadership' is preferred, as an indication that employees are 'empowered' without the authorizing mediation of the top management. Obviously, this does not imply any lack of final responsibility on the part of top management for the destiny of the firm. Rather, it indicates a way of overcoming the contraposition of shared leadership and concentrated leadership.

At Hilti, the exercise of shared leadership is seen as the primary responsibility of employees at all levels; employees are expected to implement their own initiatives and experiments, even at the risk of making mistakes. Tolerance for mistakes is quite ample, with only one constraint: mistakes should provide decision makers with clear learning opportunities, without seriously compromising the financial well-being of the firm. In a word, Hilti takes the stronger approach to shared leadership by demanding, rather than merely allowing, that organizational members exercise higher forms of empowerment. Hilti's balancing of distributed and concentrated leadership goes a step further by urging employees to create and dissolve teams and task-forces at their own initiative. The significance of these initiatives is worth noting; they have a profound impact not only on what employees do at any given time, but also on the organizing structure of the company.

Hand in hand with a renewed approach to leadership, new managerial roles need to be learned by the members of the organization. Metaphorically speaking, managers evolved from 'policemen', to 'father figures', and then to 'mentors' whose job was to keep employees focused on their prescribed assignments (Miles and Snow, 1994). Management was then expected to monitor and allocate resources throughout the organization (Hedlund, 1994). New role-modelling, however, views managers as venture capitalists helping employee entrepreneurs to develop their own initiatives (Miles and Snow, 1994), and evokes the figures of 'catalysts', 'architects' and 'protectors' (Hedlund, 1994).

This indicates the need to manage a second duality: the duality of leadership and management. Some scholars have pointed out the dysfunctional consequences of opposing leadership and management (Kotter, 1988: 21–4), but mainstream organizational behaviour theorists have kept the separation between these two concepts. Innovating organizations are likely to dismiss the divide that confronts the 'doing the right things' of leadership with the 'doing the things right' of management (Bennis and Nanus, 1985: 21). New approaches assume that even the rank-and-file are expected to take full initiative and responsibility for their actions. Reconciling the leadership versus management poles of the duality, all employees, from top to bottom, are asked to combine both roles by 'doing the right things right'.

The overcoming of formally separated leadership and management layers can be seen in Rabobank's Spectrum. At Spectrum, four organizational layers (management team, cluster co-ordinators, project managers and regular employees) coalesce into a single formal managerial layer (the management team, led by Spectrum's top manager). The merging of leadership and management roles is also typical of the team-based structuring of Saab Training Systems, which we discussed in the previous section.

How does this management/leadership process that is both shared and concentrated get started? A third duality, known as 'the paradox of initiation', emerges at this point (Kanter, 1983: 244–5). This duality calls for the balancing of participation that is encouraged and participation that is forced. In traditional organizations, it is extremely unlikely that participation will begin at the sole initiative of those who do not already hold formal authority positions. In innovating enterprises – and Hilti stands out again – the expectation of empowerment is so strong that top management actually imposes participation. The seemingly contradictory, un-participative imposition of participation is not as transitory as it might appear. Shared and concentrated leadership is very demanding in terms of the responsibility it puts on everyone's shoulders; it needs to be continuously maintained in both its 'forcing' and its 'enabling' modes. In Saab Training Systems, the Managing Director is characterized as both demanding and authoritarian in making the team-based, participative organization work.

New forms of organizing also imply new forms of commitment from the employees and the organization. The link between what each party expects from the other, usually referred to as the 'psychological contract', has recently been revised in the light of downsizing experiences and new forms of work organization (Rousseau, 1995; Rousseau and Schalk, 2000). To understand the new tacit and implicit agreements, two circumstances need to be pondered. First, new arrangements present a wider array of intra-organizational agreements. In this sense, firms are more willing to differentiate between types of employees – core and peripheral, for instance – in terms of their criticality for the firm. Of course, managing different types of contracts challenges the consistency of people management practices and processes across the organization. Second, more emphasis is also placed on the variability and temporariness of time commitments. New organizational forms are associated with more precarious relationships between the firm and its employees. Job security and lifetime employment, which were linked to traditional ways of organizing, have been transformed into shorter-term, 'employability' relationships (Bahrami, 1992; Nicholson, 1996; Nohria, 1996).

Participative work requires the full commitment of employees. However, employees sense that the trust and commitment that the firm demands is not always matched to the temporary, even precarious, nature of the new psychological contracts. In summary, new organizations meet a fourth duality in this regard: the need to balance trust building attitudes on the one hand, and temporary work patterns on the other.

Without trust, no company will ever encourage or force employee participation. Nor will employees be assured of the necessary tolerance for any mistakes they might eventually make. Further, collaboration can only be built upon the belief that other members will refrain from opportunistic behaviours. In Fremap, trust in the leadership's motives prevented the blockage of changes which could otherwise have threatened the well-being and employment security of the workforce. Trust, however, is primarily a personal, individual phenomenon which conflicts somewhat with the collective, group-based character and spirit of innovative concerns. Manifestations of these conflicts appear in the non-transferability of trust in the face of the fluidly changing composition of team and project-based structures. These conflicts are exacerbated when accounting for the temporary nature of work arrangements: trust-building takes time and continual relationships. This explains the view that partner replacement within Coopers & Lybrand's Pharmaceutical Network might pose important problems for the operation of the unit, or the fact that individual reputation (that is, the personal driver of trust) strongly determines who is selected in and out of project teams at Ove Arup.

Trust and reputation are endogenously self-reinforcing. Networking among local banks at Rabobank takes place almost exclusively through the general managers. This happens because of the longer tenure of general managers within the group and, correspondingly, their greater acquaintance with other general managers. Since the rest of the employees hardly participate in events that cut across local bank boundaries, their inter-bank networking capabilities barely get a chance of being developed.

Companies need to strike a difficult balance between temporariness and trust building. We have just mentioned that Rabobank deals with this duality by linking trust building with the longer tenure of general managers at local banks; this process operates at the level of the individuals. At group level, we saw in the previous section how intra-team stability in Saab Training Systems forms a viable arena for personal and cultural belonging. This belonging is naturally a fertile ground for the flourishing of trust among team members, even when facing temporary projects. At the level of the overall organization, balancing trust and temporariness requires introducing HRM practices that solve other, related dualities such as agency and community, or employee segmentation and generalized commitment. To these dualities, and two others, we turn in the next section.

### Human resource practices and duality management

The previous sections delineated the dualities facing innovating companies when managing cultural, work organization and leadership processes. To support these innovations, firms make sense of new tendencies in personnel practices by managing four other dualities: agency and community; employee segmentation and generalized commitment; vertical assessment and networking behaviour; and collective sanctions and preservation of reputation. To fully understand these dualities, we first review new tendencies in HRM practice (Sánchez-Runde, 2001).

Personnel selection in traditional firms is based on achieving fit between either the employees and their jobs, or the employees and the culture of the firm (O'Reilly et al., 1991). In turbulent environments, companies are expected to fluidly rearrange their work organization. Therefore, innovating firms look for flexible matches between current organizational demands and the sets of knowledge, skills, and abilities that may be needed in the future. Recruitment is used to build up diverse pools of capabilities from which changing needs may be satisfied. In this sense, the main criterion for selecting applicants relates to the differential value added by prospective employees and their learning potential, even if sacrificing tighter fits to current vacancies (Snow and Snell, 1993).

Acquisition of capabilities that may be needed in the future is also accomplished by training and development programmes that go beyond current job requirements, towards diverse and complementary skills (Miles and Snow, 1994). Individual capital traditionally linked to specialized operations is now supplemented with learning that rests on 'social capital as the medium for coordination within the organization' (Burt, 1997: 360).

During recent years, few processes have changed more conspicuously than those around the management of careers (Arthur and Rousseau, 1996;

Hall, 1996). Employment systems emphasizing paternalistic arrangements (Nicholson, 1996) 'no longer define career paths and employment structures' (Nohria, 1996: 51). The traditional logic 'of vertical coordination no longer exists today' (Arthur and Rousseau, 1996: 4). Vertical movement through the pyramid gives way to lateral mobility in the context of self-managed careers (Nicholson, 1996) that become the individual's, not just the organization's, responsibility (Brousseau et al., 1996). Career flows are also transformed into plural sets of options. The linear patterns of the past are supplemented with 'expert', 'spiral', and 'transitory' configurations which are contingent on the firm's strategizing and structuring. Rigidity evolves into 'cafeteria-style' careers better aligned to the needs of firms and employees (Brousseau et al., 1996). The new careers centre around the following characteristics: cross-functional and international expertise; shared leadership and self-management skills; and personal traits of flexibility, trustworthiness and integrity (Allred et al., 1996). These changes are closely related to those taking place in the organization of work and leadership patterns discussed above.

These innovations affect, in turn, the reward systems. Compensation can no longer be based on job definitions because new patterns of work organization continuously blur job boundaries (Gerhart at al., 1995): pay ceases to be linked to organizational position because companies are less hierarchical and employees' effectiveness 'is based on results and credibility, rather than on formal authority, job descriptions and position in the hier-archy' (Bahrami, 1992: 43). Pay is tied both to performance – at the individual and, most importantly, group level – and the acquisition of new skills (Brousseau et al., 1996; Nicholson, 1996). Paying for both performance and skill acquisition fosters a participative culture and a commitment to employee autonomy and self-management, in line with the new require-ments of work organization and distributed leadership (Lawler, 1992). Further, because of the growing centrality of personal reputation, the man-agement of collective sanctions, the other face of collective rewards, becomes paramount (Jones et al., 1997).

We saw in the previous section that the new psychological contract accounts for four major trends. First, the segmentation of the workforce according to the criticality of different types of employees (which is also reflected in the diversity of cafeteria-style career paths). Second, the consistency-related pressures on the overall approach to people management, which are not precisely alleviated by the need to combine current and future matches between employees and the competencies required by the firm. Third, the variability and diversity of employee and firm commitments; diversity is also related to the proliferation of subcultures along professional lines, as we saw before. Finally, the emphasis on employability over employment security, in line with fluid and temporal teams and projects. All these trends pose a formidable dilemma for companies that demand fully committed, participa-tive and trustworthy collaborators.

HRM practices are the vehicle for the management of a first duality, between 'agency' and 'community'. Agency relates to 'the ability of actors to make decisions and to act out of their interests', whereas community refers to 'the participation of actors in interdependent relations' (Rousseau and Arthur, 1997: 8). This duality is addressed by innovating firms through the introduction of new ILMs. New ILMs actually 'internalize', or bring within organizational boundaries, the otherwise external unfolding of careers across different employers. This internalization operates at the level of the firms within a given corporation, and it alleviates most of the strain caused by the violation of the psychological contracts by companies that have massively retreated from job security commitments (Cappelli, 1999).

The new ILMs respond to agency-community tensions in different and related ways. First, they allow the diffusion of knowledge through employee rotation nationally and internationally, and within and across organizational units. ABB's new ILM, for instance, is open to all employees and grants them the possibility of being hired away from one firm within the group into another, with just two conditions: that they have worked a minimum of 18 months for the previous firm, and that the employee's direct supervisor is properly informed of the move. Second, as in Rabobank and Hilti, ILMs promote the establishment by employees of informal networking connections throughout the corporation, along with a holistic understanding of firm-wide processes. Finally, ILMs fulfil a much needed retaining function, as the ABB case also corroborates, by attacking the paradox of losing valuable employees who might otherwise work within another unit in the group to external organizations.

Innovating organizations respond to the challenges of continual employee training and development with initiatives such as global development programmes in ABB, or the Pharma University in Coopers & Lybrand's Pharmaceutical Network. By so doing, they find a middle way through the traditional 'human capital' paradox first described in the labour economics field. Becker's landmark analysis (1964) pointed out the risks of investing in general versus firm-specific training for employees who might very well leave the company before the organization has had a chance to recover the costs of training and development. This literature advised firms to refrain from providing training that is easily transferable to other firms (Mincer, 1994). This was sensible advice for traditional companies that did not experience the need to balance a second HRM duality between employment segmentation and generalized commitment. However, innovating firms cannot disregard the issue so easily. They have to simultaneously combine long-term, overall, integrative commitment across specialisms, and healthy segmentation of skills and capabilities by type of employee. ILMs are also key in the management of this duality. Firms with internalized labour markets do successfully invest in generic development programmes, such as ABB's teamwork and networking programmes, by channelling labour mobility within their broader organization.

A third duality calls for the conciliation of vertical assessment of performance and networking behaviour. Performance and reward practices directly impact on this issue, and firms are still struggling to find the appropriate treatment, for two reasons. First, performance evaluation and compensation systems need to interact at both individual and group levels of analysis. This is quite satisfactorily managed at Hilti and Saab Training Systems, whose performance appraisal and reward policies are fully integrated with their respective team structures. Second, the interaction between individual and group levels also affects, and is affected by, the locus of work organization. The work organization here, let us repeat once more, extends to each specific unit and to the corporation as a whole. Performance of consultants at Coopers & Lybrand's Pharmaceutical Network, for instance, is evaluated according to behaviour at the level of the country firm to which each consultant is assigned. This poses obvious threats to the dynamism of behaviours that take place within the network, beyond strict single-country firm boundaries. The result is only natural: a clear bias in behaviour towards the country firm level. At the end of the day, the country, not the network management, is the locus where decisions are made in regard to each consultant's compensation and promotion.

Finally, another duality derives from the intermixing of individual and group levels of analysis; it affects the dynamics of collective sanctions on the one hand, and the need to preserve personal and team reputations on the other. We have already seen that trust and reputation are very delicate interpersonal processes, critical for the functioning of teams, and difficult to sustain amid fluid and changing patterns of work. Collective sanctions include several forms of social ostracism and punishment, such as vetoing the participation in a project of individuals who have displayed unco-operative, opportunistic behaviours in the past. Collective sanctions, by their very nature, seriously threaten the preservation of reputation. In the innovating firm, this is tantamount to cutting the individual off from the formal and informal network that gives life to the organization. Because of this, collective sanctions at Coopers & Lybrand, and at Ove Arup, for instance, while formally viable, are very rarely imposed. Further, imposing collective sanctions against consultants who do not fully contribute to their networks could be seen as contradicting the democratic and integrative spirit of the cultures upon which the networks are built. Nevertheless, it is far from clear that inaction in this area is sustainable in the long term. Organizations still need to find a middle path between punishing unwanted behaviours and preserving reputations; if they do not, their effectiveness is likely to suffer.

In summary, we have seen in this section that new HRM practices have the potential to resolve the dualities of agency and community, employment segmentation and generalized commitment, vertical assessment and networking behaviour, and collective sanctions and preservation of reputation. ILMs are extremely helpful with regard to the first two dualities; the last two, however, are not yet as completely worked out and understood. This is an area where we hope that innovating firms will make more progress in the future.

## DISCUSSION

The preceding sections show that duality challenges impose severe constraints upon innovative firms. These firms have to simultaneously balance seemingly opposite, contradictory phenomena, while competing in extremely difficult environments. Balancing the traditional and the newer arrangements requires change management expertise that supplements, rather than supplants, antagonistic patterns. Supplementation change processes are not as simple as those that follow an 'either/or' logic of substitution. The firms in this study show that a more sophisticated change capability is needed to implement the integrating 'and' logic of complementation that dualities demand.

Cultural dualities basically refer to the tensions between overall culture and the subcultures in the organization. Subcultures are born out of internally consistent subsets of values and beliefs along structural, national and professional divides. Structurally, different units develop their own ways of looking at organizational phenomena. Nationally, units in different geographical locations adhere to diverse national and/or regional values variously affecting sensemaking that is both particular to the units in the region, and common throughout the corporation. Professionally, knowledge-intensive companies aim at integrating the specific values and beliefs of plural professionalisms and communities of practice that need to collaborate in multidisciplinary projects.

Obviously, the benefits of strong subunit cultures need to be balanced with the imperatives of an equally strong – if not stronger – unifying corporate-wide culture that helps to integrate the organization in a whole that is greater than the sum of its component parts. Managing these dualities is a sensitive issue for all the INNFORM companies: it involves managing employees' dual allegiances to both of the different units to which they may simultaneously belong (as we have seen in Coopers & Lybrand and ABB), as well as to their units and the organization as a whole (Ove Arup is a special case in point).

Another source of centrifugal cultural pressures comes from the need for a strong common culture ('a way of being one') while content-wise adhering to decentralizing, participative, entrepreneurial and democratic values. These values, held in common by all the organizations analysed, further promote subculture proliferation. This all makes for an even more critical culture–subculture balancing act.

As we have seen mainly in the cases of Saab Training Systems and Fremap, dualities also affect work organization patterns. Boundaryless experiences, such as the ones in Coopers and Lybrand and Agbar, need to combine the flexibility of continuously arranging and rearranging tasks with helping employees to maintain a clear view of what is expected of them. This clarity of assignments lays the foundation for well-defined accountability and responsibility for the work that needs doing, without hurting the freedom to execute that flexible assignments require.

Management of complex, large-scale projects requires collaborative work by diverse groups of specialists in multidisciplinary modes. Reconciling the sometimes diverging approaches and value systems of different specialisms is certainly not easy, but it can be done; Ove Arup provides interesting clues on how to manage this duality. We also saw in Saab Training Systems how team organizing, despite its flexibility, ambiguity and fluidity, can become the locus for a sense of belonging and stability. Most importantly, this is accomplished without hurting the required adaptability to the needs of its customers. The more generic duality of change and stability finds an interesting solution here as well.

Leadership and general management processes also pose new, challenging dualities. Hilti and Rabobank's Spectrum illustrate that innovative organizations cannot afford concentrated leadership patterns that put the responsibility for moving the organization ahead into a few hands. Instead, leadership needs to be shared and distributed at different levels of the firm. This calls for the balancing of the classical leadership–management duality. Truly empowered employees both lead and manage different processes at different organizational levels, especially when performing within innovative working arrangements of the kind reviewed. Empowerment and shared leadership, however, also require strong and authoritative, if not authoritarian, leadership that keeps the firm on a steady course. This form of leadership may even come to impose participative ways of working at all times, and not just in the initial stages (as in Hilti and Saab Training Systems). Working out the tensions of leadership dualities also demands the development of trust among organization members; effective trust building presents the added challenge of time constraints. Generating reasonable levels of trust among employees takes time, and this is difficult to reconcile with the time-limited nature and fluidity of many of the arrangements used by innovative firms to organize work (Fremap).

Finally, this chapter also emphasizes the dualities involved in the management of HRM practices. Paramount here is the agency–community duality, which, as we have seen, relates to many of the tensions brought about by the latest personnel management trends in recruitment, selection, career, and reward and performance management. HRM considerations also lie at the heart of issues such as the need to simultaneously hold company-wide, undivided loyalties, while addressing the segmentation of the workforce. Examples of segmentation abound with regard to core and peripheral employees, dual allegiances to organizational units and the organization as a whole, or differing professional subcultures.

Internalizing previously external labour markets helps companies like ABB, Rabobank and Hilti to navigate through these dualities. However, as Coopers & Lybrand and Ove Arup illustrate, many firms still struggle with performance and reward management dualities. These dualities require the balancing of performance assessment that is made centrally and that affects networking behaviours taking place out of the centre, as well as the corresponding granting of rewards and punishments (Saab Training Systems and Hilti provide interesting counterpoints in this regard). Also worth noting are the effects of collective sanctions. These sanctions have the dual effect of effectively addressing issues of unco-operative and opportunistic behaviour, while tarnishing reputations and inducing internal tensions.

We have reviewed the general operation of 16 people management dualities, and the ways in which some organizations in the INNFORM programme address them, but we need to understand that these dualities cannot be understood in isolation. Rather, they appear together in companies that simultaneously effect change at the triple level of boundaries, processes and structures (Pettigrew and Fenton, 2000a). This means that duality management cannot be expected to succeed unless addressed systemically. Instead, we are inclined to predict that simultaneous management of the full set of dualities that we have presented in this chapter will show complementarity effects similar to those discussed in Chapter 7. This certainly adds more complexity to the management of innovating firms, but it may also bring the rewards of higher performance.

## IMPLICATIONS FOR PRACTICE AND RESEARCH

The duality approach implies a departure from traditional thinking. The older approach is anchored in an 'either/or' logic emphasizing the substitution of the old by the new. As such, traditional thinking is, at best, extremely partial: it only stresses one end of the duality continuum. This over-simplification of organizational dynamics is further compounded by the resulting impossibility of ever addressing duality tensions – which are basically ignored – in a systemic way. Sadly enough, this is, in general terms, hardly new in the field.

Management and organization theory has so far not been sensitive enough to the requirements of a truly systemic view of organizations. Systemic approaches, where they have been emphasized, have mostly underlined the need to consider the interactive, multiplicative effects of separate practices upon the organization as a whole. In so doing, however, they have only contemplated the interrelations within sets of separate practices, rather than encompassing the interactions that result from combining the opposing, seemingly contradictory tendencies generated by dualities inside and across separate practices. The older systemic view tried to balance the interactions between 'single-continuum' practices. Our new view of the firm needs to account for 'dual-continuum' interactions within and between practices. It goes without saying that this is no small task. It forces researchers and scholars to substantially rethink our theories.

Dualities affect not only the content of management theories; they also place new demands on how such theories are tested. Virtually all quantitative model testing strategies rely on assessing the effects of 'mono-independent variables' on 'mono-dependent variables'. That is, development of the variables tends to focus on single-continuum characteristics of the constructs at hand. Dualities, in contrast, require more complex variable development and modelling, so that causal relationships can be ascertained. This is an area that certainly merits further thinking and research.

We have seen that dualities are so widespread in organizations, that they may become the cornerstone of analysis for the development of powerful, sophisticated audit tools. These tools should improve pattern recognition in organizations, and help managers and consultants better understand people management phenomena in innovating companies. The duality approach to people management has other implications for practitioners as well. Managing dualities is certainly more complex than managing 'monolities'. Managers may need to strengthen their learning capabilities to deal with the newer organizational realities. Since one person cannot easily master all the requirements of the newer landscape, managers may need to work together in teams even more than they are used to doing. Also, change capabilities are further challenged by the need to keep dualistic modes.

The traditional 'supplanting' approach basically requires one-time change capabilities: once the new is in place, change finishes and only maintenance activities are required until other change initiatives come to the fore. In contrast, the 'supplementing' duality approach requires that the old and the new coexist over the longer term. Managers need to keep holding both sides of the continuum, continuously. This is obviously an important challenge for the innovating organization. But the firms in our study show that, overall, this challenge can be satisfactorily addressed.

## ACKNOWLEDGEMENTS

Qualitative evidence supporting the arguments of this chapter comes from eight recently published case studies from the INNFORM programme (Pettigrew and Fenton, 2000a). For this, and for their insightful comments, we are greatly indebted to their authors. They are: Evelyn Fenton and

Andrew Pettigrew for Ove Arup and Coopers & Lybrand; Winfried Ruigrok, Leona Achtenhagen, Mathias Wagner and Johannes Rüegg-Stürm for ABB and Hilti AG; Raymond van Wijk and Frans van den Bosch for Rabobank; Tomas Müllern for Saab Training Systems; and Javier Quintanilla and Carlos Sánchez-Runde for Fremap and Agbar. We also acknowledge support in time and expenses from the Research Unit of IESE Business School, University of Navarra.

Chapter 12

# Convergence and Divergence of Organizing:

## Moderating Effect of the Nation State

*Arie Y. Lewin, Silvia Massini,*
*Winfried Ruigrok and*
*Tsuyoshi Numagami*

## INTRODUCTION[1]

The strategy and organization literature on organization adaptation and selection assumes that theories have universal application independent of the institutional constraints of nation state configuration. Institutional theory does explicitly incorporate the role of the state (the largest organization in the population) on organization change through coercive and normative isomorphic pressures. The focus, however, is on institutional forces as primary universal forces of change. In this chapter we consider the extent to which strategizing and organizing adaptation practices reflect specific country institutional configurations (Lewin et al., 1999) and whether these practices are converging or continue to diverge across the nation states of Germany, Japan and the USA.

Percy Barnevik, the founding CEO of ABB, exemplifies the ever-present challenge of managing paradoxes: 'ABB has three internal contradictions. We want to be global and local, big and small, decentralized with centralized reporting' (Taylor, 1991). The competing value model (Quinn and Cameron, 1983; Quinn and Rohrbaugh, 1983) provides the basis for describing organizations' structural and procedural preferences as they resolve conflicts involving two-value dimensions: the first relates to finding a balance along the internal–external orientation dimension; the second relates to finding a balance along the centralization–decentralization of decision making dimension. Their model accommodates infinite strategizing and organizing combinations – dualities – and their change over time. For example Quinn and Cameron (1983) show that young entrepreneurial firms have a preference for decentralized structures and decision-making procedures combined with a strong external orientation. As such firms mature and grow in scale, their managerial focus shifts internally to emphasize standardization of decision-making routines and to a preference for more centralized structures and centralized control. The implications of the competing values model are that managing paradoxes – dualities – are ever-present realities. Moreover, at any point in time the specific combinations of strategizing and organizing routines will vary as a reflection of their individual preferences along the two dimensions of internal–external orientation and centralization–decentralization.

In this chapter we first explore the extent to which companies in Germany, Japan and the USA are experimenting with and adopting management practices and forms of organizing which reflect a convergence towards achieving greater capacity of organizational flexibility. Second we explore the differences in structuring flexible organizational forms (reflected in implementation of structure, processes and boundary changes) across the three countries. We analyse the changes in strategies and organizing over the four-year interval represented in the INNFORM survey, and assess the extent to which the trends reflect the moderating effect of the institutional configurations of the three countries and whether the changes portend convergence or continued divergence in management practices. The findings from the INNFORM survey are also compared with another study of companies in the three countries (Droege, 1995) that surveyed expectations of changes in strategy and organizing for the period overlapping the INNFORM survey (1993–96).

The discourse on whether prevalent management practices reflect specific nation state configurations as determined by historical, cultural, political, economic and social factors has been receiving increasing attention in the literature. This research literature involves diverse social science disciplines, theoretical perspectives and levels of analyses (Lammers, 1978; Fligstein, 1985; Chandler, 1990; Lewin, 1999; and Lewin et al., 2003). At the organizational level, Chandler (1990) advanced the thesis that national institutional factors such as history, legal environment, and educational system affected the rise and character of the modern industrial enterprise. For example, Calori et al. (1997) demonstrated on the basis of a comparative historical analysis that the French preference for centralization of decision making compared to the UK preference for delegation is rooted in the differences of the ideology and design of their respective national education systems. In essence Calori et al. (1997) argued that that the nation state configuration (in this instance the design and enactment of the educational system) are reflected in managerial practices. Similarly Kogut and Walker (2001) have shown differences in patterns of diversification strategies between Germany, France and the USA, which they trace to differences in the structure of capital markets and governance regimes. At the individual level, for example, Weber et al. (1998) obtained significant differences in managerial preferences for risk taking between managers from China and the USA. Their analysis of proverbs from the popular culture of the two countries demonstrated the moderating effect of cultural differences on risk preferences.

More generally, a strong argument can be made that nation states evolve unique configurations of political institutions, social compacts, educational systems, institutional structures (for example, capital markets) and corporate governance systems that reflect a collective enactment of a nation culture, values and history. Moreover, the specific nation state configuration legitimizes particular business systems (Chandler, 1990; Hofstede, 1993; Whitley, 1994; Meyer et al., 1997; Lewin et al., 1999; and Lewin et al., 2003), and is reflected in the governance structure, employment relationship and other management practices of enterprises and public institutions (Bendix, 1956; Child and Kieser, 1979; Kogut, 1991; Guillén, 1994; and Whitley, 1996; Baron, 1996; Calori et al., 1997; Djelic, 1998). Therefore, following Lewin et al. (1999) we expect that the pattern of management practices involving strategizing and organizing will differ across the three countries in the survey.

Institutional systems evolve in response to emerging macro forces of change (for example, technological advances, social movements, and so on) and as a consequence of exchange relationships with the enterprise systems embedded within the nation state (Lewin and Volberda, 1999; Lewin et al., 1999; Katz and Kahn, 1978 and Meyer et al., 1997). For example, advances in IT and the emergence of the internet age have the potential to radically affect the institutional structure (for example, emergence of global electronic capital markets) and enable new organizational forms. Chandler, for example, argued that the multidivisional form (M form) emerged in response to technological advances in transportation (railways) and communications (telephone and telegraph) which created the opportunity for structuring organizations suitable for managing across time and space. In the context of the INNFORM project, we assume that the forces propelling the transition to the post-industrial age parallel those that propelled the transition to the industrial age. Now, as then, they involve multiple forces, independent origins and trajectories whose impact crystallizes over long time horizons.

The volatility and dislocations associated with the transition have increasingly stressed the ability of organizations to adapt. Managers worldwide have been increasingly experiencing failure of practices which have worked in the past and have been experimenting with changes to strategy and organizing intended to increase organizational capacity for flexibility and adaptivity. In the sections that follow we summarize the differences in institutional configurations and management practices for the USA, Germany and Japan, present the results of analysing the INNFORM survey in terms of convergence and continued divergence of managerial practices to increase organizational flexibility, and compare our findings with the Droege (1995) survey of managers' expectations of changing managerial practices.

## NATIONAL CONTEXT AS A MODERATING VARIABLE

The moderating effects of institutional configurations may explain why cross-country adaptations do not necessarily converge around *identical* organizational features or management practices. The different institutional configurations may lead to *adaptation trade-offs*, contingencies that enable firms embedded within their national institutional system to pursue the same objective of enhancing their capacity for flexibility and adaptivity by implementing different strategic and organizational changes (Toffler, 1970).

Institutional environments have been conceptualized in various ways. Whitley (1994, 1996) advanced the concept of the business system to refer to the legal, social, political and educational environment of which companies are part and which shape their strategic and organizing actions. Ruigrok and van Tulder (1995) introduced the concept of industrial systems to refer to the strategies of large firms with relation to bargaining partners (suppliers, workers and trade unions, distributors and dealers, financiers and governments). Hofstede (1980) and Hampden-Turner and Trompenaars (1993) introduced several dimensions of national culture shaping the collective thinking and behaviour of individuals. Table 12.1 summarizes these features for the USA, Germany and Japan.

The differences summarized in Table 12.1 are expected to affect management practices in a number of ways. On a relative basis, the US environment indicates that the higher the degree of environmental institutionalizing, the lower the degree of freedom for firms to adapt their structures, processes and boundaries. The implications are that US companies have higher flexibility in restructuring their organizations relative to German and Japanese firms. Moreover, the higher the degree of environmental institutionalization, the more likely that firms will report fewer radical changes in structures, processes and boundaries. As a consequence the variation in firm strategic and organizing responses is expected to be higher for US firms compared to German and Japanese firms.

## ANALYSIS OF RESULTS

Using the results from the INNFORM survey, we evaluate changes in organizational structures, processes and boundary adaptations in the USA,

TABLE 12.1   *Comparison of institutional arrangements in the USA, Germany and Japan, mid-1990s*

| | USA | Japan | Germany |
|---|---|---|---|
| [Institutional factors] | | | |
| Founding conditions | • Diversity<br>• Abundant resource<br>• Huge domestic market<br>• Puritanism<br>• Market competition | • Homogeneity<br>• Shogunate era (1603–1868)<br>• Confucianism<br>• Strong government | • Early industrialization<br>• Financing through banks<br>• Cartelization<br>• Worker participation |
| Role of government | • Encourage market competition<br>• Low industrial policy | • Encourage agreement<br>• High industrial policy<br>• Guidance | • Encourage stability<br>• Direct intervention |
| Legal system | • Transparent<br>• Flexible<br>• Adversarial litigation<br>• Facilitates impersonal transactions | • Flexible<br>• Conciliable litigation<br>• Facilitates relationship-based transactions | • Transparent<br>• Inflexible<br>• Facilitates both types of transactions |
| Capital market | • Market for control of ownership<br>• Highly developed | • Market for stability of ownership<br>• Moderately developed | • Market for stability of ownership<br>• Moderately developed |
| Education system | • Decentralized<br>• Diverse | • Centralized<br>• Homogeneous<br>• Strong meritocracy | • Centralized<br>• Vocational system |
| Culture | • Individualism<br>• Heterogeneous | • Collectivism<br>• Homogeneous | • Moderate collectivism<br>• Homogeneous |
| Managerial practices | | | |
| Governance system | • Separation between ownership and management<br>• Strong institutional holdings<br>• Shareholder-oriented<br>• One-board system | • Cross-holdings among firms<br>• Stakeholder-oriented<br>• One-board system<br>• Formation of group | • Bank holdings<br>• Stakeholder-oriented<br>• Dual-board system |
| Authority and control | • Emphasis on roles and tasks<br>• Top-down | • Emphasis on both authority and roles<br>• Top-down and bottom-up | • Emphasis on power and authority<br>• Top-down |

*(Continued)*

TABLE 12.1    *(Continued)*

|  | USA | Japan | Germany |
|---|---|---|---|
| Employment relationship | • Employment-at-will<br>• External labour market<br>• Non-participative<br>• Performance and market based<br>• Largest gap between top and bottom | • Lifetime employment<br>• Internal labour market<br>• Participative<br>• Seniority based<br>• Smallest gap between top and bottom | • Long-term employment<br>• Participative<br>• Performance and seniority based<br>• Moderate gap between top and bottom |
| Strategic paradigm | • Short-term oriented<br>• External growth<br>• High managerial autonomy | • Long-term oriented<br>• Internal growth<br>• Incremental growth<br>• Low managerial autonomy | • Long-term survival<br>• Internal growth<br>• Moderate managerial autonomy |

*Source*: Lewin, *et al.* (1999: 543); Hofstede (1980).

Germany and Japan between the 1992–93 to 1996–97 period[2] in the sections that follow. We analyse the data to determine the extent to which the nation state configuration of the US, Germany and Japan moderates the organizational change strategies of managers in these countries. The details of the INNFORM survey have been elaborated in Chapter 1 of this volume, as well as in Whittington et al. (1999).

We have argued that managerial practices reflect the nation state institutional configurations within which the companies and industries are embedded. We have also argued that managers' choices in adapting their organizations when faced with changing technological, environmental and competitive conditions (increased global competition) is affected by the institutional constraints within which they are embedded. Following Lewin et al. (2003) we argued that, overall, the US institutional configuration has greater flexibility in accommodating changes that involve industry restructuring, entry and exit from lines of business, and changes to the employment relationship, and is more timely in adapting formal institutional constraints, to technological, social and political forces. The higher institutional flexibility of the USA endows American companies with higher degrees of freedom in adapting their structures, processes and boundaries. Relative to the USA, Japanese and German companies face a wider range, but differing, institutional restraints. Overall, therefore, we expect to observe higher rates and more types of changes for US companies (as indicated by the responses to the INNFORM survey) relative to German and Japanese companies.

The analyses in this chapter are further informed by a comparison (where possible) with the study by Droege (1995). The Droege study involved a mail survey in Europe, the USA and Japan, carried out in 1993. It surveyed managers in the USA, Germany and Japan regarding their *expectations* for a range of organizational adaptations quite similar to the ones dealt with in the INNFORM survey. The Droege survey led to some 1100 useable responses. Response rates were 28.5 per cent in Germany, 10.3 per cent in the rest of Europe, 13.2 per cent in Japan, and 10.5 per cent in the USA. Where possible, we compare the actual changes as found in the INNFORM survey with the *expected* changes summarized and reported in the Droege survey.[3] We treated the Droege data set separately from the INNFORM survey and do not carry out any new analyses with the Droege data set, in order not to exacerbate problems of cross-national research.

### Similarities and differences

Figures 12.1, 12.2 and 12.3 summarize the similarities and differences between managerial practices in the three countries on the three major organizational dimensions of structure, processes and boundaries. It is clear that for the base year of 1992–93 some differences and similarities are quite striking and that these are maintained through 1996–97 but instances of new differences also emerge. For example, in 1992–93 no significant differences are observed between firms in the three countries on the use of projects, extent of strategic decentralization, use of IT systems, deployment of EDI and reliance on a dominant business. The implication being that on these dimensions the moderating effect of nation institutional configurations is not significant. It also suggests that certain managerial practices diffuse globally, largely unimpeded, although the specific deployment of the technology could differ contextually. Examples of significant differences include the use of strategic alliances, extent of operational decentralization, extent of labour force unionization, and reliance on functional organization. The higher reported frequency in the application of strategic alliances in the USA is not surprising. It reflects the greater strategic flexibility that the US institutional configuration makes possible and the greater importance that US managers attribute to exploring and finding new business opportunities (Lewin et al., 2003; Sakano and Lewin, 1999). Similarly the difference in the role of unions is not surprising considering the embeddedness of unions (albeit in different form) in Germany and Japan relative to the USA where the influence of unions had been in decline since the mid 1960s. It is also noteworthy that on certain dimensions significant differences emerge between 1992–93 and 1996–97. For example, by 1996–97, differences in the use of projects become significant and differences in the deployment of strategic alliances become even more pronounced.

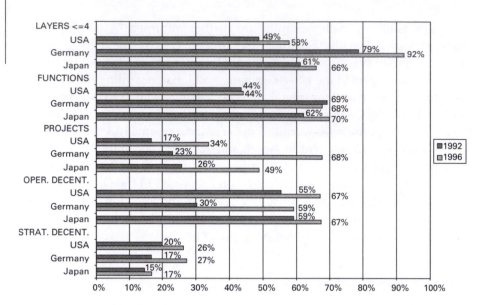

FIGURE 12.1    *Organizational structures in the USA, Germany and Japan 1992–93 and 1996–97*

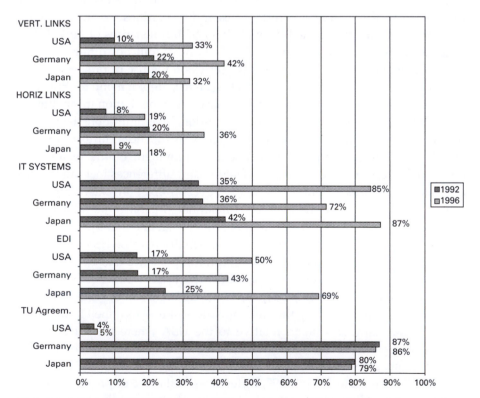

FIGURE 12.2    *Organizational processess in the USA, Germany and Japan 1992–93 and 1996–97*

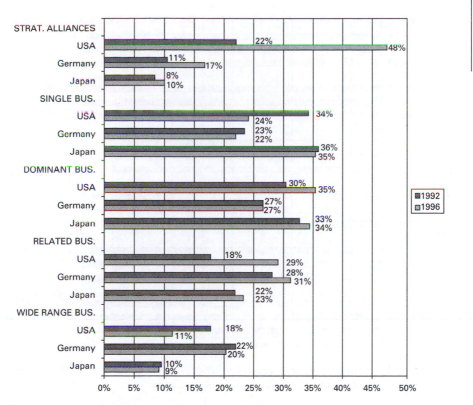

FIGURE 12.3    *Organizational boundaries in the USA, Germany and Japan 1992–93
and 1996–97*

Figures 12.4, 12.5 and 12.6 classify the changes in structures, processes and boundaries on the basis of an imputed binary measure of radical or incremental change (Pettigrew et al., 2000). An examination of these charts clearly supports our expectation that US managers are much more likely to implement radical changes when compared to Germany and Japan. It also supports our arguments that Japan will have the lowest frequency of radical changes. The notable deviations are several instances when German managers implement the highest proportion of radical changes. These include implementation of operational decentralization, strategic decentralization, management training and development, outsourcing and strategic alliances. These findings are discussed in greater detail in the sections that follow.

In the section that follows we consider the changes along the three dimensions of structure, processes and boundaries in greater detail. In addition where feasible we include comparisons with the results for the Droege (1995) survey of managerial expectations in 1993.

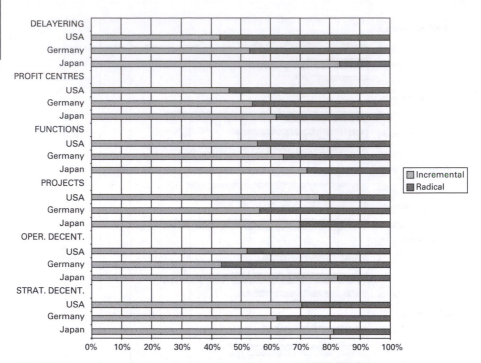

FIGURE 12.4 *Incremental and radical changes in organizational structures, 1992–93 to 1996–97*

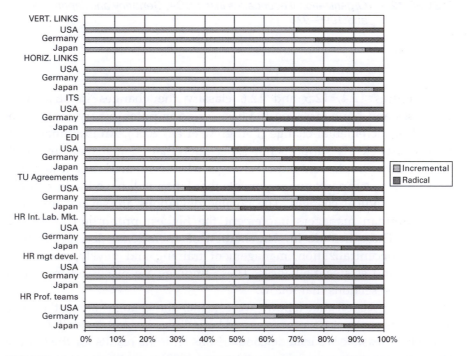

FIGURE 12.5 *Incremental and radical changes in organizational processes 1992–93 to 1996–97*

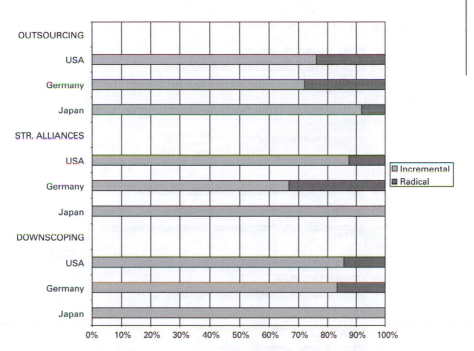

FIGURE 12.6 *Incremental and radical changes in organizational boundaries 1992–93 to 1996–97*

## Structural Innovations

Figure 12.5 shows that over the 1992–93 to 1996–97 period, most companies based in the USA, Germany and Japan reported making no structural changes. Two striking exceptions relate to the dramatic increase in the introduction of profit centres and the very significant increase in the use of projects by German companies. These findings are somewhat at odds with firms' expectations in 1993 (as reported in Droege, 1995), when 31, 81 and 63 per cent of US, German and Japanese companies respectively agreed with the statement that traditional organizational concepts should be replaced by flexible structures, and only 2, 4 and 4 per cent of US, German and Japanese firms respectively claimed that they had already accomplished such flexible structures (Droege, 1995: 159). Based on the INNFORM survey, companies have been much less likely to adjust structures than processes. One reason for this is that structural arrangements are more persistent and often are continued while the charter of the unit could be changed (Galunic and Eisenhardt, 1996). The one significant exception relates to the use of profit centres whose frequency of use increased significantly in the US. Processes, however, may be modified more easily.

However, in some cases the changes reported in Figure 12.7 may not be that significant. For instance, while only 16 per cent of Japanese companies

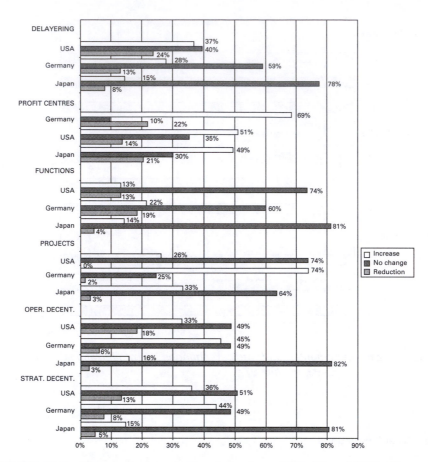

FIGURE 12.7   *Changes in organizational structures 1992–93 and 1996–97*

and 45 per cent of German companies reported having decentralized operational decision making, Japanese companies indicated significantly higher levels of operational decentralization both in 1992 and 1996 than their German counterparts (see Figure 12.1).

By focusing on changes in Figure 12.7, we can identify levels of variation by country along the six structure indicators. This variation is highlighted in subsequent discussion by calculating a 'linear distance' measure of variation (that is, the weighted difference between 'no change' and the changes that did take place) per country (Table 12.2). A comparison of the type of changes in terms of radical or incremental clearly shows that Japanese managers consistently prefer incremental over radical changes (Figures 12.4, 12.5, and 12.6).

### Delayering

In 1993, 80 per cent of US companies, 66 per cent of German companies and 45 per cent of Japanese companies reported their intentions to reduce layers in their hierarchies (Droege, 1995: 153). Figure 12.7 shows that almost 37 per cent

TABLE 12.2    *Variation in organizational changes in the USA, Germany and Japan 1992–93 to 1996–97*

| | Linear distance | | | Quadratic distance | | |
|---|---|---|---|---|---|---|
| | USA | Germany | Japan | USA | Germany | Japan |
| **Structures** | | | | | | |
| Delayering | 1.50 | 0.69 | 0.27 | 23.76 | 1.41 | 0.38 |
| Profit centres | 55.10 | 8.57 | 3.57 | 72163.3 | 584.02 | 116.13 |
| Functions | 0.35 | 0.60 | 0.24 | 0.53 | 1.06 | 0.34 |
| Projects form | 0.32 | 1.14 | 0.49 | 0.45 | 2.03 | 0.79 |
| Operational decentr. | 0.79 | 0.85 | 0.21 | 1.45 | 1.64 | 0.27 |
| Strategic decentr. | 0.67 | 0.74 | 0.23 | 1.04 | 1.23 | 0.31 |
| **Processes** | | | | | | |
| Vertical links | 1.12 | 0.92 | 0.63 | 1.71 | 1.24 | 0.70 |
| Horizontal links | 1.10 | 0.89 | 0.61 | 1.79 | 1.14 | 0.65 |
| IT Systems | 1.29 | 1.19 | 0.97 | 2.78 | 2.42 | 1.58 |
| EDI | 1.13 | 0.94 | 0.90 | 2.07 | 1.52 | 1.46 |
| TU agreements | 3.57 | 3.53 | 3.40 | 54.84 | 73.91 | 11.40 |
| HR internal labour mkt | 0.63 | 0.87 | 0.65 | 0.89 | 1.25 | 0.80 |
| HR mgt development | 0.82 | 1.19 | 0.65 | 1.23 | 1.89 | 0.77 |
| HR professional teams | 0.95 | 1.23 | 0.70 | 1.51 | 1.89 | 0.86 |
| **Boundaries** | | | | | | |
| Outsourcing | 0.78 | 1.02 | 0.73 | 1.09 | 1.45 | 0.84 |
| Strategic alliances | 0.54 | 0.24 | 0.10 | 0.85 | 0.34 | 0.10 |
| Downscoping | 0.49 | 0.24 | 0.06 | 0.62 | 0.27 | 0.06 |

*: The distances in the USA excluding the top and bottom extremes in the profit centres are 21.73 for the linear distance and 3337.79 for the quadratic distance.
*Source:* INNFORM Programme

of US companies did reduce layers, implying that 43 per cent did not implement their intentions. Almost 28 per cent of the German companies indicate that they have reduced layers, again suggesting that nearly 40 per cent did not implement their intentions. Figure 12.4 classifies the change responses as radical or incremental. The US companies report implementing more radical delayering changes as compared to German companies or Japanese companies, which were the most incremental. Judging from these data, US companies were more successful in reducing organizational layers than their German counterparts. One disclaimer to be made, however, is that the average size of US companies in the INNFORM survey was larger than the average German company size. These size differences may overstate the extent to which US companies did reduce layers. At the same time, almost one-fourth of US companies indicated to have *added* layers, as a result of which US firms show by far the highest degree of variation (Table 12.2). This corresponds with our expectations, and is consistent with the analysis of Lewin et al. (2003) that German companies may be constrained by embedded institutional arrangements affecting the employment relationship and labour involvement in the co-determination of strategic changes.

According to the Droege survey, approximately 45 per cent of Japanese companies in 1993 expected to reduce layers. The INNFORM data indicate that only 14.5 per cent of Japanese companies did reduce layers, and when they did, they mostly opted for incremental rather than radical changes. It is more difficult for Japanese firms to reduce layers per se, since Japanese managers have allegiance to managers of higher rank as well as to managers of similar rank, who previously occupied their position, and who have been transferred to another position due to job rotation. Thus, delayering in Japanese companies would also require reducing horizontal, not just vertical, management levels (Fruin, 1992). The concept of 'delayering' may be easier to implement in a US and European context than in Japanese firms, because in Japanese companies management layers are closely interlinked with issues of seniority and horizontal networking. Thus delayering requires making changes in an embedded social network, a significantly slower and more traumatic process.

### Profit centres

In 1993, over 50 per cent of German companies and almost 45 per cent of Japanese companies, surveyed by Droege, indicated that establishing profit centres would become more important. This contrasts with only 17 per cent of US companies expecting that profit centres would become a more important organizational feature (Droege, 1995: 170–2). By establishing profit centres, firms may increase control transparency and enhance individual business units' market orientation, without restructuring divisional or authority structures. The Droege study suggests the low US expectation may reflect US companies' longer experience with establishing profit centres, and their awareness of its limitations, such as the difficulties of introducing and managing transfer pricing between relatively autonomous company units.

However, Figure 12.7 shows that companies in all three countries introduced profit centres into their organizations. Although the Droege survey indicated that US managers had a low expectation of increasing the application of profit centres, our results show a 69 per cent increase. Moreover, US companies were the most active implementing radical changes. German and Japanese companies implemented profit centres at about the same rate, although German companies recorded higher percentages of radical as opposed to incremental change. As compared with US companies, a much higher percentage of German and Japanese firms indicated no change over the period investigated, which corresponds with our expectations that the process of implementing structural changes in Germany and Japan is more cumbersome and requires more time. The 'do it fix it' attitude of US managers is also a factor in their willingness to make radical changes.

## Functions

The Droege study reported that in, 1993, 15 per cent of US, 16 per cent of German companies and 34 per cent of Japanese companies indicated that they saw a need for strengthening their functional orientation. These low percentages are not surprising. A functional orientation is strongest in single-business firms (which have less difficulty in reconciling the three dimensions of products × markets × functions). The INNFORM as well as the Droege survey was sent to large firms, which due to their size include a higher share of multi-business firms. Also, these low percentages reflect the thinking of the 1990s. The management literature of that period suggested that firms should overcome a strict functional orientation and move toward multi-functional teams and employees.

In line with these expectations, Figure 12.7 shows that the majority of US, German and Japanese companies do not report any changes in the significance of a functional orientation. In the case of the USA, the reduction of functional orientation in some companies was offset entirely by an increase in other companies. German and particularly Japanese companies show a moderate increase in the importance of a functional orientation, though largely based on incremental changes (Figure 12.4). Again, a very high proportion (81 per cent) of Japanese companies indicated no change in their functional orientation. This is inconsistent with Japanese firms' expectations in 1993.

## Projects

The Droege (1995) study does not report any quantitative data on US, German or Japanese expectations in 1993 regarding future importance of project-based forms of organizing. However, it did indicate that German companies in particular regarded project-based forms of organizing as a promising avenue that could sharpen customer focus and even facilitate subsequent structural changes (Droege, 1995: 54).

The majority of US and Japanese companies report no significant changes in the role of project-based forms of organizing. Only German companies report a clear, often radical increase in the use of project-based forms of organizing. This development is related in Germany to the dramatic increase in implementing profit centres and to the emergence over the 1990s of the so-called *management holding* structure. The management holding structure can be seen as a hybrid between the holding company structure and the multidivisional form. It consists of a head office (*Konzern*) with legally independent subsidiaries that may or may not be tied together by company-specific markets, technologies or resources (Bühner, 1991). An essential part of this development has been to devolve operational and strategic decision making to these legally autonomous units (see below). The advantages of the German management holding structure are that it facilitated company-internal restructuring by reducing the bargaining power of trade unions (which was no longer concentrated at the corporate level), by creating greater financial transparency (demanded by investors), and by exposing company units directly to their relevant markets (which was often missing in conglomerate structures) (cf. Frese and Teuvsen, 1998). At the same time, however, decentralization called for new ways to manage the interlinkages *(Schnittstellenmanagement)* between the newly autonomous units. Project-based forms were one of the prominent organization solutions that were implemented during the 1990s. Thus, project-based forms were an organizational adaptation response to the specific restructuring trajectory dealing with the German institutional environment (trade union strength, emancipating investors, and more critical customers) (Frese, 2000).

**Decentralization of operational and strategic decision making**
The trends described above were already observed in 1993, when 83 per cent of German firms indicated they intended to greatly increase emphasis on individuals' own responsibility (Droege, 1995: 153). When asked to what extent companies intended to delegate decision making, US companies scored the highest, with around 55 per cent expecting that they would do so over the coming years. Of German companies, almost 45 per cent indicated such intentions, and over 35 per cent of Japanese companies indicated that they expected to delegate decision making (1995: 172).

In the INNFORM survey, organization decentralization is split into operational and strategic decision making. Figure 12.7 shows that changes in the US and Germany are relatively similar. The fact that German companies report higher levels of radical change (Figure 12.4) most probably reflects the rise of the management holding model and also the relative low levels of decentralization in the base year. For operational decentralization the USA and Japan were similar, 55 per cent, and Germany was at 30 per cent.

The higher proportion of radical operational decentralization in Germany very likely reflects the perception of the bold changes entailed in shifting to the holding model, decreasing union power, and focus on customer orientation. These were radical changes for Germany, but were already integral elements of the management logic in the USA and Japan.

**Process Innovations**

Figures 12.7 and 12.8 present a striking contrast between the categories of structures and processes. Over the 1992–93 to 1996–97 period, companies in all three countries report much stronger changes in re-designing processes than structures. The significance of process changes such as strengthened internal linkages, new IT and EDI (electronic data interchange) systems

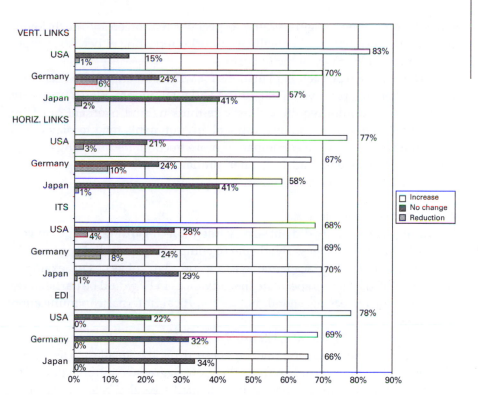

FIGURE 12.8   *Changes in organizational processes 1992–93 to 1996–97*

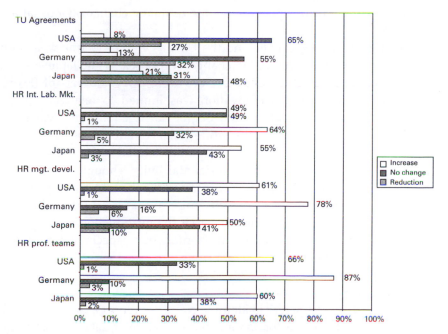

FIGURE 12.9   *Changes in HR practices and trade union agreements 1992–93 to 1996–97*

and HR innovations (Figure 12.9) is especially reinforced by much lower percentages of companies in the three countries reporting either 'no change' or a reduction along any of the indicators.

There are two possible explanations for why companies have been very active in changing processes. First, process adaptations are often more easily adopted. They do not require a drastic re-thinking and overhaul of entire company structures. Second, institutional environments tend to play a less determining role. This leaves companies more freedom for intruding change and *ceteris paribus* will lead to greater similarity in restructuring patterns across the USA, Germany and Japan.

### Vertical and horizontal linkages

The Droege (1995) study did not survey intentions regarding changes in vertical or horizontal linkages. The theme of company internal linkages rose in prominence following academic writing on the subject. For example, Hedlund (1994) began to speculate that advances in IT would be particularly conducive for increasing lateral, not just vertical, internal communication structures.

According to Figure 12.8, US firms report the strongest increases in vertical and horizontal linkages, and Japanese firms the smallest. The strong increase in the USA probably reflects the more aggressive introduction of IT systems in the US over the period investigated (see also below). US firms reported more change, and particularly more radical changes than German and Japanese firms, suggesting that over the 1992–93 to 1996–97 period the 'physiology' of US firms underwent some dramatic changes (Ghoshal and Nohria, 1993).

Japan is clearly lagging behind the USA as well as Germany, as indicated by the very high levels of 'no change' responses. While Japanese auto and electronics manufacturers in the 1980s were early adopters of flexible manufacturing systems, this innovation was limited to relatively simple systems (such as robots with limited degrees of freedom) and was never extended to the administrative and 'white collar' environment.

Figure 12.8 indicates that US companies tended to be slightly more active in establishing vertical than horizontal links. Though this does not hold for Germany, the same pattern was found for the wider European survey (Ruigrok et al., 1999). These results suggest that head offices in many countries were slow in comprehending that the introduction of IT systems not only enabled new modes of horizontal, but especially for vertical communication to emerge.

### IT and EDI systems

Over two-thirds of companies in all three countries report a clear increase in the adoption of IT systems for sharing and exchange of data. The similarity of this trend across the US, Germany and Japan is striking, since US firms could be expected to have implemented IT innovations at an earlier stage than their German or Japanese counterparts. However, the INNFORM data presented here only provides information regarding levels of change, not about absolute levels of IT implementation. The one noticeable difference between the three countries is that in the USA, a much higher percentage of companies report a radical increase in the introduction of IT systems than in Germany and Japan. This could suggest that US companies are in the midst of introducing next generation IT technologies such as client-server and enterprise resource planning (ERP) systems possibly ahead of companies in Germany and Japan.

A somewhat similar picture emerges when looking at the adoption of EDI systems. The Droege study found that in 1993, 10 per cent of German companies agreed with the statement that data processing networks between suppliers and producers are important. However, 41 per cent of German companies agreed that such networks would become more important in the future (1995: 85). In Europe, German companies reported the highest pace of change in introducing EDI systems, based on Germany's traditional manufacturing strengths compared with other European economies (Ruigrok et al., 1999). However, when compared with the USA and Japan, the USA again reports the strongest and most radical increases in implementing EDI systems.

### Human resource practices

Figure 12.9 presents the range of survey questions associated with HR utilization. The legal status of unions and the extent to which workers were covered by agreements with unions is an element of the configuration of countries. There are obvious institutional constraints affecting the ability of companies to reduce trade union influence.

Figure 12.2 indicates that in 1993 the number of US workers covered by trade unions is significantly lower than in Germany and Japan. In the US, the mid point of companies responding had only 4 per cent of their employees covered by trade union agreements. The respective number of employees covered by trade unions in Germany and Japan is 87 per cent and 80 per cent. Of course, in Germany such agreements are negotiated with national unions whereas in Japan the agreements are mostly negotiated with enterprise unions. Not surprisingly the reduction in the USA of workers covered by trade unions was the smallest. More surprisingly is the difference in the workers covered by trade union agreements between Japan and Germany (48 per cent versus 32 per cent). This finding is consistent with the embedded position of German trade unions in the institutional configurations of Germany.

One possible explanation for the higher Japanese decrease in employees covered by trade union agreements relates to outsource workers to affiliate companies, many of which do not have enterprise unions. This practice in theory reduces head count at the parent company but in reality reduces head count for the firm. Overall, the change effect involving the number covered by trade union agreements was not significant.

There was no significant difference between the three countries on the two measures of variation for employees covered under trade union agreements (Table 12.2). The linear measure of variation yielded scores of 3.57, 3.53 and 3.40 respectively for the USA, Germany and Japan. The results were equally not significant for the quadratic measure of variation. The inescapable conclusion has to be that the involvement of unions in all three countries cannot be changed in the short term.

In 1993, the Droege team asked US, German and Japanese respondents about their intentions to institute cross-departmental teams. There are differences for this item, with 60 per cent of Japanese firms, 65 per cent of German firms and 77 per cent of US firms indicating their intention to do so. The interpretation of these figures is not necessarily obvious. For example, the lower percentage for Japanese firms may reflect earlier progress implementing cross-departmental teams (cf. Clark and Fujimoto, 1991).

Figure 12.9 indicates that companies in all three countries were in the process of increasing the effectiveness of their internal labour markets through planned transfer of employees and skills between subunits. Most of the changes, however, were incremental rather than radical. It is quite conceivable that the relatively strong trade union influence in Germany has played a role here, with trade unions supporting initiatives that preserve employment and enhance career prospects for their members. A similar motivation exists in Japan, where employees have been increasing their efforts to honour lifetime employment commitments (tacit not contractual) which required intensifying efforts in planned transfers and training. The surprising finding relates to the USA, where internal labour market practices are not as advanced as in Germany and Japan. Primarily because high worker mobility and voluntary turnover serve to reduce the effectiveness of such practices as planned transfers and training, the 49 per cent increase in such practices suggests that American managers are recognizing the need for leveraging the social capital of their employees.

## Boundaries

Company boundaries may be adjusted through outsourcing activities formerly performed in-house, strategic alliances, and through divestitures, mergers and acquisitions (see Figure 12.10). These activities are clearly subject to institutional constraints and therefore will be more limited in

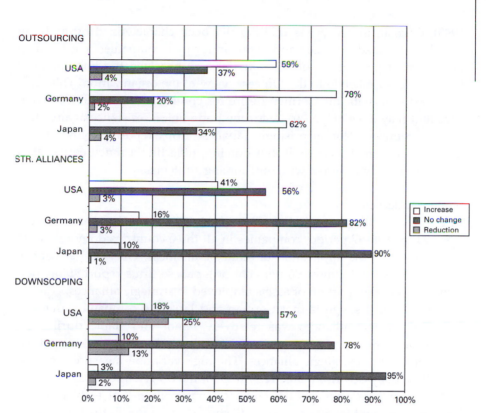

FIGURE 12.10   *Changes in organizational boundaries 1992–93 to 1996–97*

comparisons to adjusting corporate processes. Moreover we expect that the levels of variation for changing firm boundaries will be highest in the USA.

### Outsourcing

In 1993, a significant proportion of German and Japanese managers expected to significantly increase their levels of outsourcing in the future (49 and 47 per cent, respectively), in contrast to US firms whose expectations were significantly lower (21 per cent). Droege argues that outsourcing involves a strong element of learning; once companies have developed outsourcing as a management strategy, they will push its application further (1995: 83).

On average, companies in all three countries report an increase in outsourcing activities over the 1992–93 to 1996–97 period. The increase is most notable in Germany, however, reflecting a radical re-orientation in German management logic relating to manufacturing, very much influenced by the 'Japanese' management model (Womack et al., 1990; Womack and Jones

1995). German industry has traditionally been characterized by a strong *Mittelstand* of medium-sized and highly innovative companies. The German management perspective of the mid 1990s emphasized the imperative of integrating, suppliers into the 'process' view of the organization. This logic was consistent with the German desire for control and uncertainty avoidance and may have helped to overcome trade union resistance against further outsourcing. Not surprisingly Japanese firms report the lowest and mostly incremental increase in outsourcing, reflecting a much earlier start and evolutionary progress with outsourcing strategies.

### Strategic alliances

In the age of alliance capitalism, it is most striking to find that over the 1992–93 to 1996–97 period, companies in all three countries do not seem to have embraced the application of strategic alliances. Over 80 per cent of German firms, and almost 90 per cent of Japanese firms report stable percentages in the proportion of assets employed in strategic alliances.

Figure 12.3 suggests that German and Japanese companies' involvement in strategic alliances was relatively minor and stable during the 1992–93 to 1996–97 period. In contrast, US companies greatly increased their involvement with strategic alliances. The high variation measure for strategic alliances by US firms (Table 12.2), 0.54 for the US versus 0.24 for Germany and 0.14 for Japan, reflects the empirical observation that eight industry groupings account for 80 per cent of all strategic alliances in the USA. These industries include biotechnology, telecommunications, semiconductors, pharmaceuticals and scientific instrumentation. These rapidly developing industries were far more developed in the USA at the time of the survey.

### Downscoping

Consistent with our expectations, US companies exhibit the highest proportion of divestiture and restructuring activities (18 per cent for the USA versus 10 per cent for Germany and 3 per cent for Japan). A possible explanation discussed in Sakano and Lewin (1999) relates to the scale and scope of the capital markets in the three countries. The capital markets in the USA have the capacity to finance a wide range of mergers and acquisitions deals. In addition, ever since the break-up of the conglomerate form a new breed of investment banks has been stimulating such deals as a means to growing investment banking fees. Relative to the USA the German and Japanese capital markets in 1992–96 had almost no capacity for financing merger and acquisition deals across the entire risk/return range. In addition, as Sakano and Lewin (1999) note, Japanese firms used related diversification strategies as a means of maintaining employment for workers who have become redundant in declining business units. Again, the measures of variation (Table 12.2), the USA 0.49, Germany 0.24, and Japan 0.06, are consistent with the role and structure of the capital in the institutional configurations of the three countries.

## CONCLUSIONS

Overall, the results are supportive of the general proposition investigated in this chapter. The individual country analyses support our general expectation, that dualities of organizing and strategizing practices are observable at the country level (in both time periods) and that the mix of those practices does change over the four-year period of the study. We also observe a convergence towards adopting structural and process routines associated with greater flexibility. The results support (as we expected) significant differences between US, German and Japanese firms. US firms showed the highest levels of variation on structural and technology intensive indicators. By contrast, German firms reported stronger adaptations and higher levels of variation along non-structural and non-institutionalized indicators where management has higher levels of discretion. German firms reported a higher pace of change on issues of project and process orientation, and on implications of the development of the management holding organization form – itself an institution-induced restructuring trajectory.

Japanese firms reported markedly less variance: they tended to report 'no change' or only 'incremental change' more often than the German and especially the US firms in the sample. However, this may be partly the result of the selection of variables, which largely reflect a North American and European logic of restructuring. Finally, it appears to be much easier for companies to raise flexibility by adjusting company processes than by adapting structures, or even firm boundaries.

The findings discussed in this chapter suggest several directions for future research. The first relates to developing more fine-grained explanations for the emergence of equifinal best-in-class managerial practices (for strategizing and organizing) across countries. In other words, each nation state institutional configuration may breed management duality models which are, for all intents and purposes, equally effective but reflect different country constraints.

Second, the debate around convergence–divergence is far from a resolution. Although for the sample firms analysed in the INNFORM project and the four-year interval we observe some convergence, the overall results support divergence reflecting country differences and path dependencies. However, it remains to be seen whether the transition to the internet age and to a significantly more globally interdependent world will greatly favour convergence to new managerial practices including convergence of country institutional configurations.

## NOTES

[1]This chapter has benefited from discussions at the AIB meeting in Sydney, Australia 2002.

[2]The number of firms in the US, Germany and Japan are respectively 79, 69 and 257.

[3]The Droege survey was carried out in association with Professors Erich Frese in Germany, Toshiyoshi Shimuzu in Japan, and Arie Lewin in the USA. Droege is a German management consultant company.

Chapter 13

# Managing the Homogeneity–Heterogeneity Duality

*Leona Achtenhagen and Leif Melin*

## INTRODUCTION

For a number of years, the economic landscape has been characterized by high environmental uncertainty and rapid change (cf. Huber, 1990), leading to high levels of complexity for organizations to master (cf. Bleicher, 1999). In this changing economic landscape, innovative organizing practices seem to be an increasing factor for competitive success (cf. Frese and von Werder, 1994; Whittington et al., 1999). The consequences of environmental uncertainty are manifested in reduced predictability of the form and character of organizations (cf. Stacey et al., 2000: 18). A perceived loss of control is evident, as complexity is seen as a loss of organizational control 'when no one can sensibly and comprehensively account for all of it' (Czarniawska-Joerges, 1992: 36).

The level of perceived intra-organizational complexity is nurtured by tensions from the coexistence of opposing forces in the organization (cf. Gustavsson et al., 1994; Bouchikhi, 1998). When new ideas challenge existing practices in organizations tensions erupt. In an attempt to become more responsive to environmental complexity by increasing internal flexibility, many companies add new organizing principles to the 'old' organization. The findings from the INNFORM programme show that many European companies rely on numerous organizational practices simultaneously, for example, on functional *and* project-based orientations (Whittington et al., 1999; Ruigrok et al., 1999). As a result of supplementing rather than supplanting the 'old' with the 'new', companies increase their internal complexity by simultaneously following opposite orientations, for example, stability and flexibility; centralization and decentralization; or standardization and differentiation. In this context, 'new' practices are not necessarily unprecedented practices. They might also be new in that they display new combinations of known practices (cf. Fenton and Pettigrew, 2000a). In an attempt to make its organization more flexible the German media giant Bertelsmann AG has added cross-unit project teams to its traditional divisional structure. The aim was to identify potential synergies and learning opportunities between units as well as to increase the level of internal networking, while keeping the old organizational hierarchies intact. As these cross-unit teams challenged the former boundaries of the units, tensions arose. In 2002, the new CEO announced a return to a more centralized organization with clear internal boundaries. Thus, the source of this tension was abolished.

Some authors have suggested that companies might also proactively experiment with their organization in an attempt to match the perceived demands posed by environmental complexity with corresponding organizational practices, which in turn leads to higher degrees of internal complexity (Müller-Stewens and Fontin, 1997). The Swedish company Saab Training Systems developed simulation software for military training and faced the challenge of dramatic and unpredictable changes in customer demands. The company responded by implementing a complex internal team structure, which allowed it to meet new demands and to respond more quickly to environmental changes (for an extensive discussion of this case, see Müllern, 2000 and Chapter 4 of this volume). Yet, this structure created problems for the company's innovativeness: while internal processes became more efficient, innovativeness decreased, leading to internal tension between efficiency and innovation.

Tensions might arise from the simultaneous presence of polar opposites in a company. Polar opposites have been discussed under a range of different labels. The most prominent of these labels are paradox, dilemma, dichotomy, trade-off and duality. In recent years, the management of these tensions has become an increasingly popular research topic (Eisenhardt, 2000), yet, many contributions to-date share problems. First, the conceptualization beyond the labelling of these tensions – often as paradox or dilemma – is still rather unclear. As few clear-cut conceptualizations exist to-date, the same notion is attributed to different meanings by different authors. We will propose a categorization to clearly distinguish between the different notions, as we argue that it is important to understand the nature of different existing tensions. A number of authors have suggested that these tensions could be managed by taking on a 'both–and' perspective (for example, Johnson, 2002: 4). However, as we will show, there is no easy managerial solution for handling these tensions. Second, the contradictions are often viewed as predominantly negative, and only a small (but increasing) number of authors have argued that successfully managing these tensions might have positive outcomes (cf. Poole and Van de Ven, 1989). Here, we will contribute to the existing literature by discussing different strategies for managing tensions and discuss problems deriving from it. Third, most contributions discuss individual structural tensions, such as centralization versus decentralization, but widely neglect a process dimension (Janssens and Steyaert, 1999). They fail to see that different polar opposites form interrelated dynamic systems (see the discussion in Chapter 10 of this volume). We will show that such an interrelated system of polar opposites unites forces that on the one hand increase and on the other hand decrease the environmental predictability for the organization. To better understand these forces at work, we conceptualize what we label the homogeneity and heterogeneity duality. Fourth, many contributions to-date are largely conceptual, and therefore we lack empirical evidence of how organizations might handle tensions arising from polar opposites (Johnson, 1994: 290). By basing this argument on empirical case studies from the INNFORM programme, which illustrate different approaches to handling polar opposites in practice, we aim to contribute to the body of empirical research on managing organizational and managerial tensions.

Thus, in this chapter we attempt to contribute to resolving the weaknesses in the conceptualization of polar opposites and their deriving tensions. We first review relevant literature to categorize previous conceptualizations of the most frequently discussed polar tensions (namely paradoxes, trade-offs, dilemmas and dualities) and to clarify the discussion in this area. Based on this clarification, we argue for our choice of the notion of dualities to discuss tensions that can be fruitfully managed in their entirety. We then conceptualize a more generic duality, that of homogeneity and heterogeneity, a meta-duality which encompasses different dualities on the organizational and managerial level. We argue that these different dualities cannot only be viewed independently, but that they can also be seen as systems of dualities, which are related to each other as well as to the complementary organizational changes (cf. Chapter 10 of this volume). Based on three empirical case studies, we then identify three different approaches of managing the duality. The first approach attempts to increase the level of homogeneity in the organization, and the second aims to decrease heterogeneity. These two approaches have the ultimate aim of reducing perceived intra-organizational complexity by striving for more predictability and 'control'. The third approach attempts to enhance the organization's capacity to successfully deal with perceived complexity, seeking to manage the generic duality of homogeneity and heterogeneity more comprehensively. In the concluding section we will discuss problems and challenges deriving from managing such tensions in the organization.

## CONCEPTUALIZATIONS OF ORGANIZATIONAL TENSIONS

In recent years, polar opposites have received considerable attention and have been assigned a number of different labels. For example, tensions stemming from opposite orientations in the organization have been named dualities (Peters and Waterman, 1982), dilemmas (Hampden-Turner, 1990) and Janusian thinking (Sjöstrand, 1997). We will discuss four different prominent conceptualizations of these orientations. These four categories are: paradoxes, trade-offs, dilemmas and dualities. This discussion is summarized in Table 13.1 later in this chapter.

### Paradox

A paradox describes a counterintuitive, contradictory phenomenon: 'Paradox denotes contradictory yet interrelated elements that seem logical in isolation but absurd and irrational when appearing simultaneously' (Lewis, 2000: 760). Thus, paradoxes are not necessarily based on polarities but on contradictory elements, which might not constitute opposing poles of the same spectrum. The problems of paradoxes are, therefore, not expounded by relating between opposite poles but in reference to themselves. The notion of paradoxes is usually based on a two-tier logic in which a third way out is not given (cf. Luhmann, 1987). As the contradictory elements both operate simultaneously, no choice can be made between them that would dissolve the paradox (cf. Quinn and Cameron, 1988). For example, employees in a factory of hazardous goods might be faced with the demand of ensuring safety and zero accidents, while at the same time being asked to increase production output by 10 per cent annually. The employees could choose to focus on one option, either safety or output, but this choice would not eliminate the second demand – if they chose to maintain tight safety measures, it would be difficult, all things being equal, to increase production. Thus, the employees face the paradox of two contradictory demands which they cannot reconcile. We can conclude that it is not possible to balance between the contradictory elements of a paradox; it is only possible to make an informed decision based on understanding the potential impacts of it. Yet, paradox situations will probably remain surrounded by uncertainty and disagreement on how to get the best of both points of tension (De Wit and Meyer, 1999: 18–19). Alternatively, the paradox could be dissolved by reorganizing the relevant processes. For example, a differently organized production process might decrease safety concerns and allow for an increase of output.

In the past years, the notion of paradox has been used abundantly and not always within its original definition stemming from logic. Rather, many contradictions or tensions within the organizational context have been denominated as paradoxical (for example, Westenholz, 1993; Kahn, 2002). Handy (1994b: 22–43) discusses different paradoxes and proposes to manage them by understanding them better. Referring to a 'paradox of organizations',

Handy argues that organizations pose contradictory demands on their members. Employees would thus increasingly be expected to act autonomously by making their own choices, but, at the same time are requested to be more team oriented and thus to act collectively. Similarly, management would be expected to delegate more decision-making responsibilities and accountabilities, but still maintain control. By understanding the contradiction, this paradox of organizations can be solved on a perceptual level, but yet the underlying tension remains.

## Trade-offs

Trade-offs arise from a gradual substitution between two opposite poles, without implying a division between them. Trade-offs cannot be solved, but an exchange between the two poles is possible, while, in economic terms, the same utility level is maintained (Müller-Stewens and Fontin, 1997: 4). Thus, many different solutions are possible, each reflecting a different balance between the two conflicting pressures – necessarily more of one pole will mean less of the other (De Wit and Meyer, 1999: 18). A typical example of a trade-off is the choice between working life and pension fund payments – the earlier employees decide to retire, the less they will receive as a pension. They could take the decision to work more years and get a higher pension, or they might be able to choose early retirement plans allowing them to leave before the legal retirement age accepting reductions in pension payments. But, there is no option to leave the utility curve connecting the two points. Usually there is no alternative in which a high pension would be paid for a short working life. For companies, then, the only way to manage a trade-off is to make the best possible choice in placing the organization between the two poles, which requires an understanding of the interdependence between both poles. A trade-off necessarily entails considering both poles – choosing just one pole is not a viable option.

## Dilemma

Dilemmas occur when it is difficult to choose between two options which both logically have equally weighted advantages and disadvantages (Fontin, 1997: 28). Unlike paradoxical poles, the two options in a dilemma refer to each other. As the opposite poles are incompatible, dilemmas lead to difficult either-or choices, which – when viewed separately – will not be clearly superior to the alternative choices (De Wit and Meyer, 1999: 18). As the two opposite poles are interrelated, one cannot be seen without the other, and their relationship has to be fully understood to take a satisfactory decision. For example, at first sight it might appear to be the best decision to centralize purchasing, as it permits cost advantages. The dilemma reveals itself when considering the other side of the coin – decentralized purchasing might reduce stock and thus capital lock-up, it may also facilitate procurement planning, and decentralized purchasing units could react faster to changes in demand. To understand and manage dilemmas, information on the dilemma and its embeddedness into organizational practices is needed. Then, a customized decision can be taken to resolve the dilemma. Gathering the necessary information can, for example, take place in workshops, where the different views can be confronted and action plans developed to deal with the specific dilemma.

### Dualities

Dilemmas are sometimes interrelated and can then form entire systems of dilemmas, which we can call dualities. For example, different operational dilemmas would constitute the centralization–decentralization duality. This duality would also encompass other dilemmas in the decisions regarding centralization and decentralization. For example, centralized human resource management (HRM) would ensure consistent HR practices and facilitate cross-unit transfer of people, but decentralized HRM would ensure staffing people with qualifications needed by the units. Similarly, centralized information and communication technologies (ICT) would ensure compatibility of all data and systems, but decentralized solutions would be tailored to the business needs of each unit. Thus, dualities can consist of dilemmas on a more operational level.

Dualities simultaneously consider two opposite principles which might form an entity without becoming a unity: 'A duality … retains two essential elements but … the two elements are interdependent and no longer separate or opposed, even though they are conceptually distinct (otherwise the duality would become a unity)' (Jackson, 1999: 549). Thus, the *opposing yet complementary* nature of the elements is stressed (cf. Evans and Doz, 1992) and these elements are explicitly addressed (Fontin, 1997: 80). Analysing just one pole of the duality does not capture its underlying logic. The challenge is not to choose between the two different poles but to manage their simultaneous existence. For example, results from the INNFORM survey show that many companies do not rely on either ideal–typical hierarchies *or* networks, but rather they combine hierarchies *and* networks (Pettigrew, 1999a: 5). Therefore, in the context of innovative forms of organizing, the language of dualities seems to capture most fruitfully this complementary nature (cf. Pettigrew and Fenton, 2000a).

Janssens and Steyaert (1999) have conducted a comprehensive literature review on dualities: they categorize structural, cultural and personal dimensions of dualities. The authors distinguish between more classic dualities, which have been inherent in organizations for decades, and new dualities, emerging, for example, within innovative forms of organizing. In their view, new dualities would *replace* the old ones. The integration–differentiation duality (cf. Lawrence and Lorsch, 1967b) would, for example, yield to a stability–instability duality, which focuses on change rather than design. Similarly, the top-down–bottom-up duality would be replaced by an internal–external duality resulting from shifting organizational boundaries. Yet, in the INNFORM programme we witnessed the *supplementing* of old organizing principles with new ones (Pettigrew and Fenton, 2000a). We found also that these dualities coexist, rather than replacing each other. Thus, dualities are not necessarily new. Yet, innovative or re-combined organizing practices enhance the importance of dualities in organizations.

Dualities can be managed in their entirety and thus do not require a decision between two options. Examples of dualistic organizing principles would be 'entrepreneurial risk taking *and* calculating behaviour' or 'imaginative *as well as* pragmatic behaviour'. Managing the duality requires conscious attempts by the corporate leaders to avoid striving for the one 'right way' of managing. Instead of establishing a fixed set of rules, a *philosophy* of management could be promulgated. Managing dualities would then reflect a mind-set or a way of thinking (Evans and Doz, 1992). Here, the conventional language of business might quickly reach its limits, as it is the language of fixed strategies and rules which strives to fulfil explicit targets. Instead, a language allowing for ambiguity is needed, which reflects the dualities. Such a language would, for example, stress the existence of one strong organizational identity as well as local entrepreneurial identities or one common culture as well as multiple cultures (Hampden-Turner, 1990).[1] In short, when dealing with dualities, we need a mindset open to organizational ambiguities, allowing for *as well as* rather than *either or* choices. We also need a corresponding language. Nevertheless, employees might attempt to minimize the emergent level of ambiguity by searching for clear and structured processes rather than searching for new ways of doing things, thereby enhancing the managerial challenge of dealing with dualities.

We also agree with Janssens and Steyaert (1999) on the importance of a more processual approach towards dealing with dualities by approaching the tensions from a dynamic and relational perspective, linking them to people in social interactions. In addition to adopting a new managerial language, a third party, such as a mediating person, a group (for example, a consulting team) or an organization (for example, a clearing house), could serve to keep the social interaction going or to un-block relational conflicts arising from dilemmas or dualities (Janssens and Steyaert, 1999). These interventions could help the process of redefining the situation to create space for interaction between the conflicting views. Thus, dualities are dynamic rather than static.

It should be stressed that managing dualities does not imply taking a suboptimal decision, but rather the opposite. A number of our INNFORM cases confirm that managing tensions as dualities can improve the organization's situation, thus not leading to a compromised middle position on the same utility curve, but to a higher position overall. A practical example of managing a duality and thus improving the overall position is the organization of new product development processes. Within product development, an important decision is to what extent the development process should be standardized and formalized. A low level of standardization and formalization might foster innovation and creativity, and lead to higher levels of innovativeness. However, typical drawbacks could be that unchannelled processes exceed the research and development budget, or that over-engineered products are being developed that do not match market needs. A high level of standardization and formalization, on the other hand, might curtail creativity, as the freedom of thinking and developing innovatively is limited by a tight financial budget and time constraints as well as precisely set product requirements. A mediocre compromise decision on this process, which would not take into account the possibility of achieving a higher utility level by managing it as a duality, would be to provide slack resources in the research budget allowing for experimentation with certain features. Managing this tension as a duality could imply establishing an entirely new research and development process allowing for combining the best elements of both sides. Hilti AG has implemented its Time-to-Money process with the idea of managing these tensions as a duality (for a more detailed discussion of this case, see Ruigrok et al., 2000a). This process is clearly different from taking mediocre in-between decisions as well as from choosing just one pole.

Table 13.1 compares the different conceptualizations of organizational tensions and the proposed alternatives for managing them.

Thus we believe the concept and language of dualities are useful for understanding innovating companies, as they allow the analysis of the struggle to accommodate opposing tensions in the organization without suppressing ambiguities. The concept and language of dualities are highly consistent with findings from the INNFORM programme (Pettigrew and Fenton, 2000a: 295). In the INNFORM programme, we witnessed a number of companies employing innovative forms of organizing that attempted to enhance their capability for managing dualities. As we have argued in Chapters 6 to 8 of this book, complementary changes towards innovative organizing practices can create a performance advantage. These organizing practices are tightly related to the need to manage dualities, and we therefore could also expect the management of dualities to be related to performance outcomes.

## THE HOMOGENEITY–HETEROGENEITY DUALITY

Different dualities are often interrelated; they form dynamic systems of dualities, in which the individual dualities might overlap without being the same. For example, the centralization–decentralization duality might be linked to the hierarchy–network duality when networking is facilitated by decentralized decision making, and centralized processes often imply a hierarchical organization. Yet, the dualities are different – we can find many examples of decentralized organizations that do not focus on networking. Until recently,

TABLE 13.1    *Comparing different conceptualizations of organizational tensions*

|  | Defining elements | Example | Managing the tension |
|---|---|---|---|
| **Paradox** | Contradiction between two elements | Focusing on both safety standards and output in dangerous production processes | Accept paradox and understand contradiction to choose best way out, or dissolve paradox by changing relationship between elements |
| **Trade-off** | Many solutions possible between two opposing poles | Trade-off between working lifetime and pension payment | Choose the best combination in each situation; requires an understanding of the impact of both poles |
| **Dilemma** | Two incompatible and interrelated options with often equally weighing pros and cons | Decentralizing versus centralizing the sourcing function | Customized decisions, depending on context; requires exchange of information from different parties involved to make informed decision |
| **Duality** | Two distinct interdependent elements, which are opposing and complementary; they might be a system of individual dilemmas | Entrepreneurial risk-taking and calculating behaviour | Managing dualities in their entirety rather than deciding between options, leading to an *as well as* rather than an *either or* attitude; requires the exchange of information and a new language; a third party might facilitate the process |

the German electrical engineering company, Siemens AG, did not foster net-working and communication across units that were managed in a very decentralized way.

The different dualities often share one characteristic: they simultaneously comprise forces striving towards homogeneity and forces striving towards heterogeneity of organizational and managerial practices. These forces are represented by the two poles of the different dualities. We conceptualize this system of dualities which share the forces striving towards homogeneity and heterogeneity as a more generic duality. We call this meta-duality the *homogeneity–heterogeneity* duality.

Many of the earlier writings on organizational theory implicitly assume homogeneity of organizational and managerial practices, which would serve to reduce internal complexity by aiming to achieve predictability of outcomes and control. Homogeneity is supported by traditional co-ordination mechanisms, such as standardization (for example, by rules and regulations or job descriptions), planning processes and control (for example, by reporting procedures). More recently, the heterogeneity of organizing practices has been discussed mainly in the literature on multinational corporations and their attitude towards subsidiaries (for example, Ghoshal and Bartlett, 1990; Gupta and Govindarajan, 1991; Hedlund, 1994). As individual subsidiaries fulfil more strategic roles, their freedom to apply practices that vary from those of headquarters and of the other subsidiaries increases. Different studies have suggested that greater strategic importance of a subsidiary would lead to higher levels of decentralization of strategic and operational decision-making responsibilities (for example, Birkinshaw and Morrison, 1995). A higher level of decentralization implies more heterogeneity in managerial and organizing practices, as the freedom regarding the choice of organizing principles increases with the decentralization. We identify forces striving towards homogeneity and heterogeneity of organizing practices in many different dualities. Therefore, we have introduced the notion of the meta-duality of homogeneity and heterogeneity as an abstract concept to shed light on the dynamics inherent in many of the different dualities. To clarify this argument, we will now provide further examples of how different dualities are inter-linked into a system of dualities that reflects the characteristics of homogeneity and heterogeneity forces. However, it should be noted that these links do not display a linear cause–effect relationship.

Innovative forms of organizing are often characterized by changes in organizational boundaries related to increased levels of outsourcing and strategic alliances (Pettigrew and Fenton, 2000a). This change of the firm's organizational boundaries implies an opening up to external partners and competitors to co-operate with them. Internal organizational practices are directly influenced by these external partners, as organizational boundaries blur. When units co-operate with different external partners and both sides attempt to optimize their joint work processes, heterogeneity between internal units increases. This practice reflects the duality of co-operating and competing, both with external partners as well as internally.

Internal competition is also enhanced by implementing market mechanisms in the organization, leading to intra-company trade based on market prices and consequently to higher levels of competition among business units for in-house orders (Frese, 1995). Increasing levels of internal competition might shift the locus of competitive advantage from the organizational level to the individual unit, pushing towards more heterogeneity as competitive behaviour differs between units.

The implementation of market mechanisms often goes hand-in-hand with higher levels of decentralization of operational and strategic decision-making power to enable units to work in an autonomous and self-sustained way within the company. Higher levels of freedom in operational and strategic decision-making power can lead to higher heterogeneity in organizational practices when only the goals are set, but the path towards achieving the goals can be freely chosen. Decentralization creates space for the unit to strive for more innovativeness and creative thinking. Consequently, it might also lead to heterogeneous patterns of interpretations of the occurring events, as the control by headquarters would be based less on how tasks are fulfilled and more on that agreed-upon targets are reached, nonetheless reflecting the centralization–decentralization duality.

Decentralization might be facilitated by new roles of management and employees providing the freedom to develop individual ways of acting in the organization, again fostering heterogeneous practices. In addition, the focus on innovation enhances the discussion about the potential positive impact on innovativeness of greater levels of workforce diversity, or heterogeneity. To increase flexibility, many organizations have also reduced their number of hierarchical layers, leading to greater spans of control. Greater spans of control might imply less overall control, again enhancing the freedom to employ diverging operational practices.

Innovative forms of organizing have been claimed to rely heavily on networks (for example, Miles and Snow, 1992, 1995; Ghoshal and Nohria, 1993; Quinn et al., 1996). Some authors have even claimed that the horizontal dimension would become more important than the vertical dimension (for example, Hastings, 1993). The INNFORM research clearly shows that the horizontal dimension becomes more important, but the vertical dimension still is important, hinting at the increasing complexity arising from this duality (Pettigrew and Fenton, 2000a). The INNFORM findings thus underline that companies do not supplant hierarchies with networks but that both coexist. The major role of hierarchy in the organization is to provide order and control, attempting to maintain predictability and the feeling of being 'in control' (Stacey, 1995). Ensuring a certain level of homogeneity, for example reporting practices, can increase this feeling of control and thereby reduce the perceived complexity. But, within networked communities, heterogeneous practices could emerge which would be beyond the processes controlled (or controllable) by hierarchy.

In conclusion, the different changes in organizing practices lead to a number of dualities in the organization, which can be subsumed under the meta-duality of homogeneity and heterogeneity.

TABLE 13.2   *The homogeneity–heterogeneity duality*

| | Defining elements | Example | Managing the tension |
|---|---|---|---|
| **Homogeneity– heterogeneity duality** | Dynamic system of dualities, which encompasses forces striving towards the homogeneity and heterogeneity of managerial and organizational practices | Dualities are interrelated, e.g. the centralization– decentralization duality is related to the hierarchy– network duality | Empirically we identified three strategies to manage the meta-duality: (1) increasing the level of homogeneity, (2) decreasing the level of heterogeneity, and (3) attempting to manage the duality in its entirety |

## EMPIRICAL EVIDENCE OF DIFFERENT APPROACHES TO DEALING WITH THE HOMOGENEITY–HETEROGENEITY DUALITY

We will now introduce three empirical case studies to illustrate different approaches to managing the homogeneity–heterogeneity duality. We identify three major strategies of dealing with this duality. The first strategy is to reduce the level of heterogeneity in order to reduce perceived complexity in the organization. The second strategy is to increase the level of homogeneity, which also aims at facilitating manageability by reducing perceived complexity. Both of these strategies attempt to increase the feeling of being 'in control'. The third and most challenging strategy is that of attempting to manage the system of dualities in its entirety. A prerequisite seems to be the organizational capability to deal with perceived complexity. The three cases presented in this chapter are Siemens Medical Engineering (S-Med), ABB Switzerland and Östgöta Enskilda Bank (ÖEB). These three cases were chosen as their three approaches to, and success with, dealing with dualities differ. Thus, these cases help to develop a clearer picture of generic strategies of dealing with the homogeneity–heterogeneity duality.

The first case company, S-Med, faced the challenge of transforming a highly hierarchical, traditional company into an innovative high-tech company. The transformation was successful, as dualistic tensions were reduced while establishing the feeling of being in control. Only later was the capability to handle the homogeneity–heterogeneity duality more comprehensively was built up. The second case, ABB Switzerland, consciously introduced dualistic tensions into its organization after the merger of Asea and Brown Boveri. Yet, the company continuously struggled to build up the capability to manage them. The third case, ÖE Bank, introduced dualistic tensions into its organization and from the beginning clearly focused on developing the corresponding capability to manage dualities.

## Siemens Medical Engineering

Siemens AG is a multinational player in electrical engineering and electronics, with firm roots in its home country Germany. In 2001, Siemens AG's 484 000 employees generated sales of 87 billion euros. This case study focuses on the S-Med business area as of 1998. Early in 2001, the area was renamed Siemens Medical Solutions. In 2001, S-Med achieved sales of 7.2 billion euros and employed 29 900 people (see also Chapter 4 of this volume).

For a long time, Siemens had the image of a rather slow-moving, traditional company with a steep hierarchical structure. However, in 1993 a company-wide programme was started to enhance productivity and to speed up processes. At that time, a number of business units faced severe crises and turnarounds were attempted. S-Med was one of the areas to succeed with a fast turnaround. S-Med is an interesting case to study as it started to experiment with innovative organizing modes in response to the company crisis.

In the late 1980s and early 1990s, the situation of Siemens AG was characterized by a number of challenges. On the one hand, it had to meet the demands of large customers (for example, governments) to provide highly engineered, customized products. On the other hand, Siemens offered a broad range of standardized consumer products, but was lacking market and cost orientation. Instead, it often offered over-engineered products. Long development times and 10 000 headquarters' staff positions led to an unfavourable cost structure. In response to the diverse range of products and customers, the company was highly decentralized. But due to a large number of hierarchical ranks and overstaffed management, decision making was slow. In addition, innovativeness and flexibility were hampered by a large number of committees.

At this stage it was recognized that the company needed to be reorganized. In order to create smaller, more entrepreneurial units, the former six business units were split into 19 areas. Thus, the level of homogeneity of organizing practices within each unit could be increased. Functions were now organized within the units, and only regional sales were still managed separately. Thereby, direct access to resources was assigned to the units; synergies were only attempted where this did not imply an increase in organizational complexity. In processes such as research and development, manufacturing and sales, synergies were neglected in favour of attempting to achieve flexibility and speed (Mirow, 1995: 21).

In 1993, a benchmarking study revealed that Siemens showed higher cost levels than competitors and a lower adaptability to change. Thus,

Siemens faced the challenge of infusing a more performance-oriented spirit into the still slow-moving company. As the new structure had been implemented only a few years earlier, it was decided to optimize the existing structure. This created a number of dualities in the company, as old and new organizing practices would now often coexist. As a result of the analyses, the company-wide 'top' programme was initiated ('top' stands for time-optimized processes). The aim of the 'top' programme was to enhance productivity by reducing cycle times, hierarchical layers and interfaces. After a slow start, the programme was perceived to be quite successful. This 'success' was attributed to the fact that the 'top' provided a powerful tool that enabled the communication of a consistent set of values and created a common interpretative framework.

> The 'top' programme ... gave us a good communication tool to bring across issues such as empowerment. And our organization depends on communicating. (Business unit manager)

At that time, S-Med faced additional pressure as a result of demographic and health policy changes as well as requirements by the US Food and Drug Administration (FDA) to enable S-Med's products to be marketed in the USA. On the technological side, combined diagnosis and treatment systems were developed, which were enabled by ICT. In addition, the trend shifted towards providing healthcare solutions, for example, by building fully equipped and networked hospitals. This trend is reflected in the new name of the business area, 'Siemens Medical Solutions'. This focus on solutions demanded a closer co-operation between the formerly more independently operating units.

In the mid 1990s, S-Med introduced a process-based organization structure. This organization structure was based on a number of core processes, which took over the former role of the business functions, as well as projects cutting across the processes. The core idea was to reduce the importance of hierarchy. In addition, the need for networking was seen, yet, networking was fostered only to a limited degree, as controllability was also aimed for:

> Informal contacts exist, but are not explicitly supported. The idea of the process organization is to work in modules in order to limit the need for contacts. The process is structured well enough so that informal contacts are not needed for the work flow. (Service process co-ordinator)

Within this new process structure, the linking role between processes and projects is clearly assigned to co-ordinators, who shall 'be in control' and mediate between the different viewpoints. Resources are assigned to the processes, as processes would be in place longer than temporary projects. Clearly assigned resource responsibilities aim to limit the room for political games and negotiations. But, different processes can compete for resources:

> There is competition for resources, and process managers compete for fulfilling the targets. This creates a high potential for conflicts. But we established forums to discuss these conflicts. We need to get rid of the old functional orientation. We should try to tackle problems, rather than blaming each other. (Business unit manager)

Thus, forums were created to allow for similar interpretations of the issues under discussion to emerge. Overlapping teams could reach mutual agreements on the projects and processes by sharing interpretation patterns of the on-going activities.

New managerial practices were introduced, which were initiated after getting rid of previous positions. Now, co-operation was fostered and newly introduced feedback rounds included the open discussion of failures and weaknesses. These topics had previously been completely avoided. However, even though the focus on co-operation has increased and the role of employees in the business units was extended, much energy is still spent on getting things moving internally. Today's leadership style and HR strategy have gone through very different stages, experimenting with the polar opposites of empowerment and control. The traditional Siemens leadership style, in which co-operation was not asked for or even allowed, had been superseded by the exact opposite:

> ... the stage of co-operative leadership with maximum empowerment – that did not work at all. The co-operative style led to a grass-roots democracy that was no longer goal-oriented. Everybody interpreted it as they wished, for example, as finally having enough time for extended coffee breaks. In result, the authoritarian pole took over again. But now we have reached an ideal degree of empowerment which fosters productive work. (Head of business unit)

Here, we witness the difficulty of moving towards managing the polar opposites of 'empowerment and holding the ring' as a duality (Pettigrew, 1999a), which acknowledges both poles at the same time. S-Med achieved this only after an iterative process of experimenting, before a position could be reached that allowed for a higher level of productivity by combining elements of both sides. One crucial prerequisite for reaching this state was recognized only after unsuccessfully experiencing the tension – that joint interpretation patterns were needed. Learning to manage the duality of specialist and generalist orientations followed a similar pattern: when moving to the new process-oriented structure, more focus was put on specialist training. This caused problems whenever someone was absent from work. Thus, a new rotating scheme was developed to cover all specialist jobs with at least one other person, balancing between specialist and generalist know-how while broadening everybody's knowledge base.

Overall, heterogeneity was limited when possible, with the aim of staying 'in control' of the process, for example, by clearly designing new processes and roles. In addition, a second strategy of increasing the level of homogeneity can be seen, that is, by employing the 'top' programme as a communication tool across units. Only after the company had experimented for some time with increasing homogeneity and reducing heterogeneity, was focus put on expanding the capability of the organization to deal with the forces driving towards homogeneity and heterogeneity as a duality. In conclusion, within S-Med, managing dualities required a tedious learning process, in which we observed experimentation with different practices until the dualities were understood to a degree which allowed them to be managed more comprehensively.

In this case study, we witnessed the struggle of introducing innovative organizing modes and the opposing tensions arising from them. The co-ordinator role between processes and projects can be interpreted as a 'third entity' (Janssens and Steyaert, 1999) to moderate between the two conflicting views of the formerly hierarchically oriented functional structure that now forms the processes and the cross-functional project teams. But while the co-ordinator could support smooth work processes, this strategy did not enable the unit itself to enhance its capability to deal with the duality. Yet, it enabled the unit to explore and learn about the tensions deriving from the new organizing principles, and to develop confidence in them. The joint forums established to discuss the tensions serve as a platform in which joint interpretation patterns can be created and used, helping the unit to handle dualistic tensions. Thus, creating and recreating interpretation patterns to facilitate dealing with the duality is an on-going process.

In this chapter, we argue that the homogeneity–heterogeneity duality is a meta-duality in the sense that it comprises different dualities which are interrelated and which share forces that strive towards more homogeneous or heterogeneous organizing practices. Table 13.3 exemplifies a system of dualities that can be identified in the S-Med case study.

The different dualities presented in Table 13.3 are clearly interrelated, for example, the freedom of deciding on work processes is linked to the responsibility assigned to project teams. The 'poles' listed on the left side of the table contain forces striving towards more heterogeneity, while those on the right contain forces striving towards more homogeneity. For example, communication forums facilitate the creation of joint (and thus more homogeneous) interpretation patterns. The table emphasizes that dualities are interrelated and that they share the characteristic of containing forces striving towards homogeneity and heterogeneity. This justifies our conceptualization of a meta-duality.

The S-Med case suggested that dualities are not opposing and mutually exclusive poles between which an organization has to choose, but rather that it is possible to combine these poles in a complementary way. This will be further discussed in the case study of ABB. After the merger of Asea and Brown Boveri, ABB introduced a highly complex structure, which incorporated

TABLE 13.3   *Exemplifying the homogeneity–heterogeneity duality in the S-Med case*

| Forces striving towards *heterogeneity* | Forces striving towards *homogeneity* |
| --- | --- |
| Empowerment<br>– more freedom to decide on work processes | Holding the ring<br>– maintaining control |
| Decentralization within unit<br>– responsibility assigned to project teams | Centralization within unit<br>– tight co-ordination of processes<br>– 'top' as central programme |
| Process-based organization<br>– processes and projects form a matrix | Hierarchy<br>– resource allocation |
| Competition<br>– resources assigned to competing projects | Co-operation<br>– communication forums |

organizational tensions. Since the merger, the company has struggled hard in the attempt to handle the arising complexity.

## ABB

The potential and risk of attempting to manage the complementary character of the homogeneity–heterogeneity duality can be illustrated by the case of ABB – the former prime model of innovative organizing (for example, Bartlett and Ghoshal, 1993; Barham and Heimer, 1998) that has recently declined so seriously.[2] In this case study, we focus on the company's struggle with its organizational tensions as of late 1998, based on 24 personal interviews that were conducted in the international holding as well as within ABB Switzerland. For a more detailed discussion of ABB's organization and its changes over time, see Ruigrok et al. (2000b). As of 2001, this Swedish-Swiss professional engineering group employed almost 157 000 people and achieved a turnover of US$23.7 billion.

In 1988, the company was formed by a merger between the two former arch-rivals, Swedish ASEA and Swiss Brown, Boveri & Cie. (BBC). ASEA contributed superior profit performance, sophisticated management controls and aggressive marketing, while BBC brought in a strong order book and high tech expertise. The geographical markets of the two companies largely complemented rather than competed with each other. ABB faced the challenge of building one entity out of two companies which not only had considered each other as rivals, but which were based on very different organizing principles: ASEA was a very decentralized company that was organized in profit centres, while BBC was a more hierarchical and traditionally organized company.

A matrix structure was chosen for the merged company with the aim of preparing ABB to 'think global, and act local' (Bartlett and Ghoshal, 1995: 470). Thus, with the merger a high degree of heterogeneity was explicitly chosen, to gratify both the geographical and the product axes.

> The business segments are now stronger than the regions. Before, the regions were stronger. If segments have a problem, top management focuses on it. The drawback of the matrix is that problems are always a mix of region and segment problems. Yet, if there is a problem in a segment in a certain country, it might be very difficult to solve that problem in that country, if the country is strong. (Manager, ABB Structured Finance)

The statement above already hints at the highly political character of ABB's matrix structure. Here lies a major challenge for ABB. To manage the internal complexity, decentralized units had been created, which in turn gave room for high levels of micro-politics.

> Due to its structure, ABB is highly political. To have a successful career here, you need to be successful in the market and in the internal politics. (Manager, ABB Enertech)

The company is characterized by a large product range in a number of different businesses, operating locally in very different markets in a highly decentralized way.

> For the type of business ABB is in, it is a necessity to have this kind of organization, because of the number of countries we are active in. In many countries we need to be present as a local company. Still, it is our goal not to duplicate knowledge bases between countries. (Vice-president, Corporate Development)

At the same time, the units are tightly aligned to allow for economies of scale and scope and for joint appearance in product markets. Heterogeneity in this case is a direct response to the different market needs. Homogeneity is attempted by aligned reporting structures and control.

> We see a difference between decentralization and independence; we have strict follow-ups and monthly reporting. The units are interdependent, because some companies have some of their work done in other countries, as they could not do everything themselves. The units are not dependent on the international holding for that, but they are under supervision. We call this 'freedom under supervision': as long as you perform well there is entrepreneurial freedom. We want entrepreneurial people who maximize business in certain areas, but how they do it is up to them. (Manager, international holding)

Here, ABB is facing a clear struggle. On the one hand it has a high degree of decentralization, on the other hand it employs strict control, showing the limits of the decentralization. This tension becomes also clear in the following statement by Göran Lindahl, Barnevik's successor as CEO of ABB: 'There is only one irrevocable issue within ABB, our targets. Here we do not compromise. How we reach the targets, however, is open and part of the decentralized approach. Every profit centre has the freedom to decide on the most adequate way to fulfil its customer needs' (Lindahl, 1999: 8) (author translation).

Since its merger, the company has struggled with managing the heterogeneity–homogeneity forces, the tension of which had been consciously introduced. The former CEO, Percy Barnevik, stated that the company needed to combine the opposing orientations of global–local, big–small, and decentralized–central control. This stresses the attempt to manage the heterogeneity and homogeneity duality.

ABB aimed at limiting complexity by limiting the interaction between its units. The well known 'Missions, Values, Policies' booklet[3] states that organizational borderlines would be defined by profit centres and business areas, which should have as little internal trade with other ABB units as possible. The number of profit centres in the manufacturing chain up to the customers should be kept as low as possible, while allowing for as much external competition as possible in business areas and profit centres.

The strict policy of management by numbers further aims at implementing an important element of homogeneity.

> This is a self-regulating process, and otherwise management would become too complex. However, we must stay attentive not to lose economies by having too many small units. And management by numbers also has some disadvantages. (Manager, ABB Business Development)

The management by numbers opens up for the renegotiation of power positions in the organization:

> There are two strong credos in the organization: 'You are as strong as your figures.' And: 'Strong men win.' (Manager, ABB High Voltage Technologies, Switzerland)

The ABACUS accounting system aimed to facilitate controlling the diverse and decentralized areas through maintaining homogeneous standards and performance measures. But while the ABACUS system allows for 'homogenizing' the financial and accounting procedures, it is based on a compromise that does not fit the needs of all businesses equally well. Especially for the service-based companies it is difficult to rely on a tool developed for heavy industries.

> ABACUS was great as it was the only reporting system for ABB. Everybody has the same sources and figures, there are no contradictions in the figures, which reduces the risk of conflict. Unfortunately, it is deteriorating now. Because of the new IT trends, some managers now want specialities. Here, the initial decision to only have ABACUS has not been kept in focus. (Manager, ABB Structured Finance)

Thus, homogenizing attempts can result in the counter-effect of triggering 'heterogenizing' energies. This reflects the tensions potentially inherent in the homogeneity–heterogeneity duality. Here, ABB did not show the same capability as S-Med to react to the experiences made with dualistic tensions. This might be due to the fact that little focus was put on learning to deal with complexity after the merger.

ABB has attempted to increase the level of homogeneity in its diverse and decentralized group by measures such as around 50 normative directives valid for the entire group and the use of the same logo. The 'Missions, Values, Policies' booklet was to form the basis of ABB's group culture and identity (Bartlett and Ghoshal, 1993: 26). However, as the major management focus was on numbers, little emphasis was put on fostering a culture and identity, as the following quotes underline:

> Not much practice has come out of the 'Missions, Values, Policies' booklet. It would be a good basis to enhance our corporate culture. But top management doesn't take action from it. We would need to balance short-term and long-term goals better. (Manager, ABB Structured Finance)
>
> There is a pressure to make positive statements. But, I feel a loss of culture and trust as well as the absence of identification. (Member, ABB Power Generation, Switzerland)

Often, employees identify with their own unit, rather than with ABB as a group. As most units need to co-operate with other units for their business, a weak joint identity poses a challenge to ABB. The following statement underlines the existence of multiple identities in the organization.

> The loyalty of employees to their unit has increased. But the loyalty to the ABB group has decreased, as employees feel that the group's loyalty towards them is lower, for example, regarding job security. The lower loyalty of employees is a challenge for management, as they have to meet the employees' claims. (Manager, ABB Network Partners)

In a time of change, employees expect the managers to show them the path out of the difficulties. Employees often expect managers at least to understand the entire complexity of ABB's business. However, many managers feel overwhelmed by this demand.

> Presently, many managers feel unsettled about their new roles. They are now supposed to take on the roles as facilitators and coaches, to support employees, to get rid of barriers to change, and to moderate. It is their task to provide space and frame for confronting conflicts. (Member, ABB Personnel and Organization Development, Switzerland)

The importance of communication in this aim has been recognized. However, sharing information and communication turns out not to be an easy task.

> Communication is very important, it is the most important element. Often, too much or too little information is passed on, and it is very difficult to find a balance here. The more you inform, the more information is being demanded … However, tactical limits to this openness

> exist. Our communication is improving, but anxieties continue to exist,
> you can't always say everything, either for business reasons or for
> personal reasons. (Member, ABB Managing Board, Switzerland)

ABB also applied the strategy of reducing heterogeneity by increasing the number of business units some years after the original creation of the matrix. Equally, the number of businesses the group was in was reduced, and the regional layer was broken up to reduce regional principalities and to facilitate cross-unit collaboration. However, ABB also showed some signs of attempting to 'stretch' the organizational capabilities to manage dualities. The operationalization of this strategy, however, turned out to be much more difficult. For example, potential benefits from enhancing diversity were stressed repeatedly, but few measures accompanied these. At the same time, ABB was working on developing shared symbols and to enhance communication, which can be viewed as an attempt to support interpretation patterns that might allow balancing between the two forces.

In this case, we witness an approach very different from the one S-Med chose. ABB decided consciously to introduce high levels of complexity into the organization. They did not overlay the old organizational practices with new ones; instead, they got rid of the old organizational structure of Brown Boveri and designed a dualistic organization. However, managing this dualistic organization proved to be very difficult and was handled with different levels of success. The constant battles that ABB has fought with its organization can retrospectively be interpreted as attempts to improve the capacity to handle the resultant tensions.

> The contradictions within ABB first released enormous energies. Over
> the course of the time, more and more tensions built up, and for a long
> time our change efforts focused on harvesting low hanging fruits.
> (Manager, ABB High Voltage Technologies)

Table 13.4 exemplifies the homogeneity–heterogeneity duality in the case of ABB.

Again, the individual dualities are highly related and share the forces striving towards homogeneity and heterogeneity.

So far, we have seen two very different ways of dealing with dualistic tensions in the organization: S-Med attempted to reduce its perceived internal complexity until it had gained experience in working with the new organizational and managerial practices. However, to what extent complexity can actually be reduced as well as how to deal with communication needs remain important challenges. These will be further discussed in the last section of this chapter. ABB willingly introduced dualities, yet, they did not manage to develop the capability to deal with different interrelated dualities in their entirety very well, and thus with the homogeneity–heterogeneity duality. Instead, they opened room for micro-political conflicts, without creating sufficient forums to resolve these. The challenge to manage these

TABLE 13.4 *Exemplifying the homogeneity–heterogeneity duality in the ABB case*

| Forces striving towards *heterogeneity* | Forces striving towards *homogeneity* |
|---|---|
| Local market presence | Global alignment of business |
| Decentralization<br>– profit centres | Centralization<br>– ABACUS reporting system |
| Multiple cultures/identities<br>– unit-based identification | Unified culture/identity<br>– group-wide logo, directives |
| Managing by facilitating<br>and coaching | Managing by behavioural<br>and output control |

micro-political conflicts will also be discussed in the concluding section to this chapter.

The next case study presents the Swedish Östgöta Enskilda Bank, which successfully introduced dualities in a proactive manner while recognizing the need to foster the internal capability of managing the deriving tensions.

## Östgöta Enskilda Bank

In the case of ÖE Bank, an explicit approach to creating homogeneity as well as heterogeneity in organizing and managerial practices can be identified. Founded in 1837, this Swedish bank has a long history. Its founder believed that the regional economy in the area of Östergötland needed a bank with strong local anchorage and a counterpoint to the traditional Swedish banking industry. In the early 1990s, the Swedish banking industry faced a major crisis that severely hit the rather small ÖE Bank. However, it was one of only two Swedish banks that survived the crisis without the aid of the Swedish government. This fact was celebrated as a success within the bank and served as a main source of self-confidence over the following years. In 1994, the same spirit led the bank to geographically expand outside of Östergötland by establishing branch offices in the form of autonomous provincial banks with strong local profiles. Within five years, six provincial banks with their own local names were started in different parts of Sweden. However, from the beginning the strategy was not to become bigger than necessary in order to offer the customer the impression of being a valued and individual customer in a bank with personalized, quick service (cf. Annual Report, 1997: 5). This strategy required space for local adaptation by the branches, and thus for heterogeneity within the bank. At the same time, the cultural spirit previously nourished by the successful survival of the bank managed to infuse a strong element of homogeneity into the organization as it provided a means of identity. Thus, ÖEB aimed to create a balance between homogeneity and heterogeneity by top management providing the 'homogenous frame' combined with a great deal of local freedom for the geographically dispersed bank offices (for a more detailed discussion of the case, see Chapter 3 of this book).

The heterogeneity–homogeneity duality arose as an incremental response to the strategic choice of expanding the business into the 'empty space' left by the bankruptcy of a number of banks during the industry crisis. However, it was recognized that heterogeneity and homogeneity could hardly coexist without further processual support, but that 'some kind of software must be added, namely relations' (Manager, ÖEB). These relations are based on personal networks between the managers within headquarters and the local banks, relying on confidence in each other as well as on shared ideas of what is possible and what is not. This is important as the local provincial banks received the freedom and responsibility to serve their customers without intervention from the headquarters. Formerly centralized activities were decentralized into the local banks, including the strategy formation and vision realization processes. However, the headquarters has regulated loan decisions to maintain control. By and large, the duality is not considered problematic, but even has a positive notion of adding to the bank's 'flavour':

> We are not the red army. We are several guerilla units that appear in different uniforms (Vice President ÖEB).

Even though personal relations are highly important in managing the duality, in addition high priority has been given to ICT solutions that keep top management well-informed about the outcome of strategic activities in each provincial bank.

While it has to be noted that the rather high degree of heterogeneity within the organization is facilitated by being a network of provincial banks with the possibility of fragmenting its markets geographically, heterogeneity was explicitly chosen and did not implicitly occur. The view in the bank was that the local branches themselves would know where the borders were and would not overstep them, facilitated by the extensive personal interaction among managers. This case underlines that dualities can be willingly created and that they do not necessarily provide a 'threat' which has to be reduced. Rather, the management of a duality can add to the company's success, if interpretation patterns exist that take over the role of co-ordinative 'rules of the game'. When analysing this case in regard to innovative organizing modes, the major change in the organization that allowed it to actively balance homogeneity and heterogeneity is the changed perception of seeing the local branches in their singularity and unity, supported by ICT. Thus, while ICT

TABLE 13.5 *Exemplifying the homogeneity–heterogeneity duality in the ÖEB case*

| Forces striving towards *heterogeneity* | Forces striving towards *homogeneity* |
|---|---|
| Local entrepreneurial cultures<br>– adaptation to local customer demands | Unifying identity<br>– joint realization of the vision |
| Decentralization<br>– both strategic and operational responsibility assigned to provincial banks | Centralization<br>– standardized ICT to facilitate control and regulated risk-taking (on loan decisions) |

managed to expand the organizational capabilities, prerequisites for managing dualities were the expanded managerial perceptive capabilities and support for sharing interpretation patterns. These interpretation patterns were facilitated by achieving a rather homogeneous identification both with the organization overall and with the units in particular. However, maintaining this identity remains a major challenge that will be further discussed in the end section.

The following table exemplifies the meta-duality of homogeneity and heterogeneity in the ÖEB case.

The table above reflects the interrelatedness of the individual dualities as well as the common forces towards homogeneity and heterogeneity. The relationship between the headquarters and the local provincial banks is thereby characterized by a mutual acceptance of the shared responsibility, in which headquarters has the last decision on loans.

## CONCLUSIONS AND DISCUSSION

In the three case studies above, we have illustrated our conceptualization of the homogeneity–heterogeneity duality. The conceptualization of this meta-duality is based on two arguments. First, dualities are not independent but are often related to other dualities. This interrelatedness is grasped by the meta-duality. Second, similar forces striving towards either the homogeneity or the heterogeneity of organizing and managerial practices can be noted in different dualities. These forces can be better understood by analysing the system of the homogeneity–heterogeneity duality.

We identified three generic strategies of dealing with the homogeneity–heterogeneity duality. The first strategy identified in the cases above was to limit the level of heterogeneity. This strategy was operationalized by focusing the organization on similar business areas and by reorganizing into smaller units. In addition, clear rules and regulations and co-ordinator roles were introduced.

Second, the companies increased the levels of organizational homogeneity. This was exemplified by standardizing certain procedures such as accounting and reporting measures and ICT. Fostering socialization mechanisms, such as the transfer of managers between units, training programmes and communication tools, helped to increase homogeneity. Rules for communication with employees and between employees and managers supported these.

Both of these strategies attempted to reduce the complexity arising from the different tensions simultaneously at play. Third, organizations attempted to manage the duality in its entirety. They fostered a new language and capabilities of dealing with the differing orientations at the same time. Companies worked on developing joint interpretation patterns. For that, forums for the discussion of conflicting issues were crucial. Managing dualities in their entirety might require experimenting with practices and learning from them, to adapt to the organizational needs.

Above, we have hinted at the fact that challenges remain from the management of dualities. We will now discuss in more detail the key challenges encountered in the three cases: (1) reducing complexity, (2) managing micropolitical conflicts, and (3) fostering identity-building (cf. also Kühl, 1998).

## The challenge of managing complexity

The move of S-Med towards innovative forms of organizing was characterized by the attempt to reduce levels of complexity. Fewer hierarchical levels and more networking have been propagated by different management writers and consultants as a panacea to a leaner and less complex organization. Time-consuming decision-making processes were simplified by ascribing responsibilities to the respective units. However, innovative organizing principles, in turn, also create a high level of complexity. This is especially the case when new organizing principles overlap the old. S-Med was constantly fighting the risk that the complexity created by the tensions would demand too much from its employees.

Modularization and the networking between different units to assemble the end products appears to be reducing complexity at first sight, as complexity seems to be 'outsourced' to the partners. However, the co-ordination of the entire process adds new complexity. Within S-Med, co-ordination between the different actors was ensured by a co-ordinator role whose aim was to mediate between the different units because the innovative practice of networking seemed to imply a degree of complexity too high to be handled. Thus, innovative practices – introduced to reduce complexity – appear to bring with them a degree of complexity that might be just as high if not higher than before. It remains to be seen whether the level of complexity will really be lower once the 'transitory stage' of simultaneously managing the old and the new is passed. It might be doubtful, as the organizing practices in themselves are highly complex, partly due to their interrelatedness.

### The challenge of micro-political conflicts

In its attempt to manage the dualities arising from the organizational structure that should provide for local and global, small and big, ABB opened up much room for micro-political conflicts. The notion of 'strong men win' was frequently mentioned in the organization, expressing its micro-political character. At the same time, hardly any forums were created where conflicts could be openly solved. To turn to the next superior as a mediator was forbidden, as it was feared that back-delegation of responsibilities would thwart the idea of decentralization. Thus, power struggles could flourish under the surface, increasing the complexity of whom to do business with. With its organization, ABB's top management created the tension between giving up power by decentralizing and holding on to the power so that actions could be taken in case of under-performance. This tension created an arena for power struggles, as the control of important resources can improve the position of some units over others. Here, those units with extensive external contacts themselves have a better position than internal suppliers without the right to sell externally, such as some of ABB's IT service units. The power position is then often held by a key individual. The reduction of hierarchy within innovative forms of organizing almost necessarily leads to a renegotiation of power structures. If this renegotiation does not have an official space (for example, when the issue of discussing power is a taboo), conflicts seethe underneath the surface and create a highly political playing field. If conflicts or power struggles cannot be openly talked about, the idea of open communication as a necessity for innovating organizations is hampered and leads towards a silent rather than a communicative organization (Kühl, 1998: 105). In the case of ABB, the lack of forums for discussing conflicts and to communicate openly and the emerging space for power struggles were problems that were never solved.

### The challenge of identity creation

ÖEB's glue for its decentralized organization was its strong identity. This identity was fostered initially by the pride derived from the fact of being an independent survivor after the banking crisis. However, identities are not static, but dynamic, and in this decentralized organization, not one but many identities exist. The more decentralized an organization is, the less 'protected' is the joint identity from the local identities. The bank is now facing the challenge of maintaining a joint identity without impeding the development of identity in each of the individual provincial banks.

We can conclude from our cases that the existence of dualities in the organization might pose problems if they are perceived differently and no forums exist where these perceptions can be voiced. Innovative organizing modes with a focus on HR practices and communication, as well as an enhanced role of individuals in the organization can facilitate managing the homogeneity–heterogeneity duality. However, our case studies showed that managing dualities might prove problematic when the interpretation patterns differ to a great extent. In response, some of the INNFORM case companies greatly increased the number, extent, and importance of training courses with the aim of jointly developing and sharing views on specific topics, such as existing dualities. It appears that this strategy of dealing with the homogeneity–heterogeneity duality on the one hand makes it more manageable due to its being explicit, but on the other hand is a dynamic learning process of expanding organizational capabilities to deal with the existing duality.

Yet, managing the homogeneity–heterogeneity duality is a difficult task, which few companies actively experimenting with their organizing practices appear to achieve. However, the cases indicate that the capability of the organizations to manage the duality on the level of organizational practices requires an understanding of the underlying paradoxes and the prevailing interpretation patterns in the organization. Understanding the patterns of interpretation allows organizational actors to then work with them. The focus on patterns of interpretation underlines our process view and the importance of language and symbols attached to managing the duality.

## NOTES

[1] Hampden-Turner (1990) uses the notion of dilemma, which our conceptualization however classifies as a duality. Nonetheless, we acknowledge the close connectedness of dilemmas and dualities as discussed above.

[2] As of October 2002, the company is in a severe financial crisis, partly due to the asbestos-related liability of its US-subsidiary, Combustion Engineering.

[3] The booklet was to set the 'rules of the game' after the merger. Bartlett and Ghoshal (1993: 26) suggested that the booklet provided a strong shared vision and corporate culture.

# IV

# Conclusion

# Chapter 14

# Innovative Forms of Organizing:

## Progress, Performance and Process

*Andrew M. Pettigrew*

## INTRODUCTION

Modesty and care are important attributes for any scholar, but they are particularly crucial for scholars of change. Most big questions of innovation and change require the perspective of the comparative historian to even begin to find proximate answers. And yet as scholars of contemporary innovation, we are impatient to find answers to questions which, in the haze of the present, are as difficult to pose as they are to answer. These difficulties, which we openly recognize, have not inhibited us from asking some big questions about the form, character, processes and consequences of organizational innovation at the beginning of the twenty-first century. Crucially our empirical inquiries have opened up the possibility for us to provide answers across space and time. But even with a quantitative database which accesses fairly large samples of organizations in Europe, Japan and the USA, our spatial width is still limited. Unusually our survey instrument had a time comparison built into it, but this only allowed us to compare the emergence of innovative forms between the two time points of 1992–93 and 1996–97. Notwithstanding these limitations, our survey findings represent clear signals about the extent of development of innovative forms of organizing in Europe, Japan and the USA in the 1990s and provide a baseline for subsequent theoretical interpretation and empirical inquiry.

Our research strategy has been to use multiple methods to pose and answer complementary questions and deliver complementary findings. Thus, survey methods and econometric analyses were used to answer the progress and performance questions about the emergence of innovative forms, and case studies of 18 European firms were utilized to examine the managerial and organizational processes of moving from more traditional forms of organizing. The case studies have complemented our survey work in a number of crucial ways. They have allowed us to move beyond the *what* questions of the surveys and examine the *what*, *why*, *how* and *when* of the emergence of innovative forms in particular organizational and country settings. Crucially the cases have revealed the role and consequences of managerial action in championing and resisting change processes in the firm, the importance and the limitations of leader effects in organizational innovation, and the balancing of exploration and exploitation, and of continuity and change, in long-term change processes. Some of the cases are used to provide case illustrations or studies to illuminate theoretical points (as in Chapters 3, 4, and 13 of this volume). Elsewhere (as in Chapters 5 and 8 of this volume) cases are used to provide a long-term process analysis of cycles of organizational innovation in firms.

Of the three theoretical themes in this volume only one, complementarities, change and performance, was deductively built into the study. The complementarities theme was one of the positive benefits of the interdisciplinary character of the original Warwick team. We hope that the econometric analysis offered in Chapter 7 is justification of the potential of that kind of interdisciplinary collaboration. But another side of that collaboration allowed us, in turn, to first question and develop the static and aprocessual character of prevailing theorizing about the economics of complementarities. We use the extended case examples of BP and Unilever in Chapter 8 to show how complementarities are built and re-built in organizations over successive generations of leaders. These data allow us to theorize in processual terms about complementarities in action and this represents a novel turn in theoretical and empirical work on complementarities.

Juxtaposing large qualitative data sets alongside survey data has also brought further advantages. The nomothetic approach of the survey required us to be specific about how we defined and measured innovative forms. This we chose to do so by focusing in on changes in structures, processes and boundaries and by measuring three elements of each of the three comparative variables (see Figure 1.1 in Chapter 1). All this was crucial in providing both a simple conceptual framework for the programme of research and a standardized measuring instrument across the three regions for our international study. However, with the formality, explicitness and deductive character of this framework also comes inflexibility. Here again the use of the complementary idiographic case method has permitted us two additional and quite crucial intellectual advantages. In the case analysis in this volume, and in our previous book *The Innovating Organization* (Pettigrew and Fenton, 2000a), we have applied the structures, processes and boundaries framework, but have also used those cases to develop and extend the framework. This is evident in our analysis of network forms of organizing (Fenton and Pettigrew, 2000c; Ruigrok et al, 2000a; Van Wijk and Van den Bosch, 2000); in explorations of leadership in innovative forms in Ruigrok et al., 2000b and Achtenhagen, Melin and Müllern (Chapter 3 in this volume), and the more explicit treatment of a broader range of strategic variables as in Pettigrew and Whittington and Fenton and Pettigrew (Chapters 8 and 9 in this volume).

Most crucially, the case method has also provided the interpretative freedom to establish and build the other two major conceptual themes of this volume: organizing/strategizing, and managing dualities in the innovating organization. As we outlined in Chapter 1, the literature on innovative forms of organizing has been theoretically and linguistically diverse. It has also been empirically incomplete relying on often-repeated case examples of exceptional examples in particular sectoral and country settings. Our international comparative work has clearly attempted to deal directly with that deficiency. Existing theoretical work on innovative forms has also covered, and thereby attempted to absorb, many levels of analysis, and yet remains to be united under an overarching theory or perspective.

The theoretical diversity is, of course, interacting with the empirical incompleteness and both are being nourished by the emergent character of innovative forms of organizing. It remains a clear and notable challenge to study and make sense of a target which is ever moving. But emergent responses to an emergent setting require new languages, new distinctions and the juxtaposition of older distinctions. Our organizing/strategizing theme is not just a play on words, but, as we indicated in Chapter 2, is now necessary both to capture changing firm responses to a changing context, and a series of linked theoretical advances in the social and management sciences. Following Weick (1979) our insistence on the verb forms of organizing and strategizing (and the corresponding downplaying of the nouns of organization and strategy) is necessary to capture the continuous processes involved in moving towards and moving along such strategies and forms. Our equal insistence on the oblique mark between organizing/strategizing gives due emphasis to them as a single duality rather than seeing them as separable building blocks in organizational analysis and managerial action. Verbs keep things moving and dualities recognize the inseperability of much contemporary thought and action in organizational life.

The organizing/strategizing duality has, of course, brought other ideas front stage. When these two constructs had been treated as separate notions, organization was customarily regarded as the poor cousin of strategy. By juxtaposing them as a duality and giving emphasis to their dynamic quality, organizing has been uplifted on to an equal footing. The case study evidence in Chapters 5, 8 and 9 of this volume justifies this treatment of organizing. Indeed our studies of professional service organizations (Chapter 9) and BP and Unilever (Chapter 8) allow us to conclude that in certain organizations the form of organizing may almost be synonymous with the strategic development of the enterprise.

Juxtaposing organizing/strategizing has also allowed us to examine the leadership and learning consequences of innovative forms of organizing. In Chapter 3 we use the cases of Östgöta Enskilden Bank and Hilti AG to examine the changing patterns of firm leadership occasioned by innovative forms. The evidence from both cases underlines how the framing, sensegiving and sensemaking processes change with the introduction of innovative organizing. The movement in both cases (albeit in different ways) was from a pattern of more unidirectional, top-down leadership towards a more inclusive leadership process which involved many more participants in the 'reciprocal sensemaking activities' of the organizing/strategizing process. But this process was not unbounded. The opening up of the leadership process was always within boundaries. We observed a certain level of decentralizing of strategic decision making, but in the context of a centrally created and enacted strategic frame. So our primary duality of organizing/strategizing has opened up the related duality of centralizing/decentralizing. Empowering was occurring, but only in context of strengthening the strategic framework at the centre.

In Chapter 4, Achtenhagen, Melin and Müllern take this argument a stage further and discuss the learning implications of innovative forms. The cases of Siemens, Saab and Trumpf are used with effect to demonstrate how and why more flexible learning cultures are needed as organizations seek to become more innovative in their forms and processes. All three cases illustrate and exemplify how and why a more generalist learning culture is needed to foster a more continuous and flexible approach to change. Again the varying pattern of support and resistance to both the learning culture and innovative forms gives emphasis to the divergent responses of firms to the need for change, an issue which we shall return to in discussing convergence and divergence in patterns of organizational innovation at the nation state and regional levels of analysis.

The third theme in this volume, managing dualities in the innovating organization, emerged with great clarity in our survey findings, and as we shall shortly emphasize, became a great consequential issue in the treatment of our case study findings. The notion of competing and apparently contradictory tendencies is well embedded in the writing on complex organizations. As Sánchez-Runde and Pettigrew indicate in Chapter 10 of this volume, dualistic phenomena are also pervasive in all the sciences, natural and social. It has been Castells (1996) who has brought this thinking together in his monumental treatment of the rise of the network society. Castells has placed the origins of tensions between hierarchies and networks and centralizing and decentralizing in the rise of the network society. The empirical studies encapsulated in this and our previous volume on the INNFORM programme (Pettigrew and Fenton, 2000a) clearly show the increasing need to understand innovating organizational practices as bi-modal. Our empirical findings also reveal that the executive control of large complex organizations is much about accommodating opposing tendencies while also thinking and acting holistically about the continuous processes of organizing/ strategizing in the firm (see Chapters 8, 11 and 13). A further executive challenge is to retain control over the burgeoning cycles of complexity which arise as organizations seek to balance several dualities over time. (Achtenhagen and Melin, Chapter 13 of this volume and Pettigrew and Fenton 2000b).

Following this introduction, we provide a summary and concluding commentary around the main findings and ideas in the INNFORM programme. There is no attempt to provide a Herculean synthesis of six years of international collaborative research. Instead, we limit ourselves to signalling some of the key findings and ideas to take from our programme of research. We organize these observations around the three key questions of our work. What progress has been made in the 1990s in the emergence of innovative forms in Europe, Japan and the USA? What are some of the consequences of these patterns of organizational innovation for both the performance of organizations and their capacities to take on further cycles of organizational change? And what were some of the key managerial process issues in implementing such forms? In answering these progress, performance and process questions we shall naturally draw upon the three theoretical themes emblematic of this volume: organizing/strategizing; complementarities, change and performance; and managing dualities in the innovating organization. In addressing the question of progress in the development of innovative forms, we will give special emphasis to debates about the extent to which organizational forms and practices are converging or diverging in different parts of the world.

## PROGRESS, PERFORMANCE AND PROCESS IN THE EMERGENCE OF INNOVATIVE FORMS

### Progress

Behind and beneath the contemporary rhetoric of change can we discern the outlines of a fundamental change in forms of organizing at the beginning of the twenty-first century? If change was indeed occurring, was it uniformly evident across our three elements of structures, processes and boundaries, or was more profound change occurring in some elements more than others? Was there convergence or divergence in the patterns of change across the three nations/regions? Were we seeing parallel change, convergent change, or divergent change across the three regions? Was there any evidence of differential pace of change across the regions, albeit from different starting points in 1992? And for those commentators and analysts who had prophesied revolutionary change in the emergence of innovative forms, were these forms supplanting or supplementing existing organizational practices? These are some of the central progress questions from which we wish to draw together some concluding observations and ideas. But before the empirical assessment, we should step back to examine some of the interpretive debates about the emergence of innovative forms.

Although it might be sensible to confine our discussion of the content of changes in organizational form to a broad spectrum of organizational and inter-organizational practices, we must go deeper and wider to understand why, when and how those changes are occurring, and why there might be variation in any pattern of emergence. There is now a long tradition of embeddedness thinking in the social sciences which rightly seems to connect the transformation of organizations to broad social, economic, political and institutional changes. This is not the place to review these social science literatures, but the interested reader may wish to refer to Granovetter (1985), Castells (1996), Jervis (1997), Dacin et al. (1999), DiMaggio (2001) and Lewin and Kim (2003). These various theoretical traditions are in different ways preoccupied with multi-level analysis which draw attention to 'the nested and constitutive aspects of context', Dacin et al. (1999: 319). In the more particular work on organizational embeddedness, the units of analysis may vary from populations of firms, through various features of the institutional configurations of nation states, to the social organization of economies and management. The different theoretical traditions also vary in the extent to which context is treated as mere constraint on organizational change, whether organizational action can in turn reshape the context, or whether emergence is a product of context and action (Pettigrew, 1985). Studies in this embedded tradition may also recognize the strength or intensity of embeddedness, the interplay between different features and levels of context, and their co-evolutionary character (Pettigrew, 1985; Lewin et al., 1999). There is also a clear recognition that the exploration of the various levels of context on organizational evolution requires historical, comparative and longitudinal analysis (Pettigrew, 1990; Abbott, 1997; Perlow, 1998; Whitley, 1999). Throughout all this highly contextual writing, there is the further unifying imperative that the progress of organization development cannot be explained just by appeals to managerial action and associated drives for efficiency and effectiveness. Context does matter; space and time do matter in accounting for the emergence of new forms of organizing.

Within this tradition of embedded social science there is one theoretical and empirical debate which is particularly germane to our interest in innovative forms of organizing. That debate concerns the extent to which there is an emerging convergence or divergence of organizational forms. At its most specific, the argument is about the extent to which particular historical legacies and institutional configurations of different nation states and regions may influence the diffusion of organizational practices. Useful elaborations of the debate are to be found in Berger and Dore, 1996, Mayer and Whittington, 1999, DiMaggio, 2001, Bryce and Singh, 2001, and, of course, Lewin et al. in Chapter 12 of this volume. There are also parallel discussions of the extent to which human resource practices are converging and diverging across nation states and regions (Brewster et al., 1996; Brewster, 2003).

Looking across these theoretical discussions (and occasionally comparative empirical findings), it is easy to find the theoretical arguments for convergence, but much harder to identify the empirical evidence to support the thesis of regional, never mind worldwide, convergence in organizational forms and practices. Thus in a review chapter Bryce and Singh (2001) offer a 'cautious stance' on the debate, but in the end conclude firmly that any 'global convergence of network forms is not likely to occur in the near future' (2001: 184). They note that since political, legal and economic structures are at the foundation of institutional selection environments, if global convergence of forms is to occur, it must be preceded by convergence in these underlying structures. They see no prospect of this in the short term. In the same volume Westney (2001) uses an argument about the tight coupling between institutional arrangements in Japan to argue for the retention of nation-specific organization practices, and especially so in Japan because of its highly embedded and interconnected configuration of institutions.

Unbridled by evidence from a particular society, DiMaggio (2001) takes a more even-handed posture. He notes that different nation states vary in their degree of internal institutional cohesion and interdependence and that the less tightly integrated they are and the greater proportion of newer industries they have in their economy, the more receptive they may be to ideas and imitation from the international competitive system and the international marketplace for management ideas. So the global organizational field will fall upon more or less receptive nation state and regional and organizational contexts, and the direction and pace of organizational change will continue to be shaped by convergent and divergent forces leading to different mixtures of convergent and divergent outcomes in different settings, at different times, in different parts of the world.

There are clear dangers of ignoring nation state and regional differences in organization form (as our own findings show), but it is equally important to be sensitive to any tendencies to parallel change, or a common trajectory of change, even though there may not yet be a convergent outcome to proclaim (again as our own findings show). In their careful empirical study of the strategy and structure of European firms, Whittington and Mayer (2000) show some level of convergence has occurred in organization form in parts of Europe. They produce findings demonstrating that the diffusion of the divisional structure has effectively suppressed indigenous forms in some European countries. Thus in the mid 1990s, 75 per cent of the top 100 French firms, 70 per cent of the top 100 German firms and 89 per cent of the top 100 UK firms were divisionally organized. They also found that businesses in all three countries were diversifying their strategy and decentralizing their structure regardless of the different nation state institutional arrangements. 'The engineering-oriented and bank-connected Germans are just as diversified as the financially driven British. The statist, hierarchical French are even more divisionalized than the Federal Germans' Whittington and Mayer, 2000: 219. The Whittington and Mayer study is both an empirical and a theoretical counterpoint to the, at times over-determined, writing of the divergency scholars, but the weight of evidence is so strong in the divergent capitalism camp that their voice must be heard too.

In what follows we shall signal some of the more important progress findings on the emergence of innovative forms. In so doing we will directly address how those findings inform the convergence/divergence debate. The fact that we were careful only to survey indigenously owned firms in our localities means we can engage with that debate. The spatial and temporal width of the INNFORM programme has allowed us to reveal both macro-level convergence forces and combinations of more macro and micro forces at nation state and organization levels, which help to expose both diversity of organization innovations and different rates of change in different regions and nations.

We conclude that there are strong drivers for convergence and some evidence of convergence, at least in terms of a common trajectory of change, but from different starting points and with some variation in pace across the three nations/regions. But this evidence for parallel change has not yet overturned the weight of history and the more enduring impact of nested institutional arrangements which continue to sustain divergent organizational practices in our three nations/regions. So our research findings illustrate or exemplify the convergence/divergence conundrum, but in no sense overturn or resolve it. We would expect the conundrum to continue as rates of change at the institutional level are bound to be slower than equivalent change processes at the organizational level. Variations in receptivity for change at nation state and organization levels of analysis will continue to promote diversity in the content and pace of change. This contextual variability will interact with variations in managerial and organizational capability to inhibit any drift or determinism towards convergence in innovative forms of organizing.

The INNFORM survey instrument allowed comparison of trends in innovative forms in Europe, Japan and the USA over the periods 1992–93 to 1996–97. Here we offer a brief summary of the main findings on changes in structures, processes and boundaries, discuss how these dimensions tend to cohere together and draw some conclusions.

The main generic conclusion across the three dimensions of change and the three regions is of a common direction of change, but from different starting points and with considerable variation in pace of change over the time period 1992 to 1997. European and US organizations show much higher percentages of radical change compared with their Japanese comparators (see Figures 1.3, 1.4 and 1.5 and Tables 1.1 and 1.2 in Chapter 1, and also Table 1.2 in Chapter 1). The figures referenced in Chapter 1 clearly show that most organizations were moving towards an increasing adoption of the innovations measured in our survey. The relatively low percentages in the 'against the trend' category for all three regions in Table 1.2 confirms that there is parallel change occurring between 1992–93 and 1996–97.

Of the four logics of organizing measured in the INNFORM survey (product, geography, function and project), we took the project-based structure to be the closest to the characterization of (internal) innovative forms in the literature. If we found over this period an overwhelming change towards project-based structure this would represent some evidence for the new supplanting the old. If, however, any rise in the project form was occurring alongside the corresponding adoption of the other three logics of organizing then this was some evidence to support a more incremental pathway – organizations would be supplementing the old with the new, and not supplanting the old with the new. The clear picture in Figure 1.7 is of a rise in the emergence of project forms of organizing in all three regions with Japan having the highest adoption rate in 1996 from the highest baseline in 1992. However, the very substantial rise of project forms in Europe, Japan and the USA does not appear to be at the expense of other logics of organization. The message from these findings is of new forms of organizing supplementing rather than supplanting existing forms.

The other notable generic finding across Europe, Japan and the USA in the period 1992 to 1997 is of considerably more process changes than structure changes. (See Table 1.2 and Figures 12.4, 12.5, 12.6 and 12.8 in Chapter 12.) This finding and conclusion picks up the crucial theme of the rise of network and process forms of organizing in the 1990s captured so strongly in the writings of, for example, Denison (1997) and Powell (2001).

The strong evidence of process changes in increases in horizontal and vertical interactions, in new human resource practices which facilitate networking and skill exchange, and IT which supports networking and communication, should not, however, detract from the evident structural changes. Albeit from a different starting point in 1992, there was evidence of further moves towards flatter, more fluid and decentralized structures in Europe, the USA and Japan. Boundary changes were also evident. Increased levels of outsourcing and alliance formation occurred, but much more strongly in Europe and the USA than in Japan. (See Table 1.2 and Figure 12.9.)

However, as we have stressed throughout this volume, these signs of a common trajectory of change need to be addressed alongside the continuing divergence in forms of organizing between Europe, Japan and the USA. Our baseline data for 1992 showed statistically significant differences between our Japanese sample and their European comparators and many of these differences were perpetuated through to 1996–97 (see Table 1.2). Thus, by 1996–97 there were statistically significant differences between Europe and Japan (taller hierarchies, higher use of IT, more operational decentralization, and more project organization in Japan). The statistically significant differences between Europe and the USA in 1996–97 were taller hierarchies, more IT investment, and more strategic alliances in the USA.

Although they are not reported in this volume, we have carried out some within-European comparisons of the emergence of innovative forms. Ruigrok et al. (1999) are able to show some comparative statistical analysis between the UK, the German-speaking countries of Germany, Austria and Switzerland, the North European countries (defined as Scandinavia, the Netherlands and Belgium) and South European countries consisting of France, Italy and Spain. In terms of changing internal structures between 1992 and 1996, Ruigrok et al. (1999) found insignificant across-regional differences in delayering, a big rise in project-based organization across Europe, but especially so in the German-speaking countries, strongest operational decentralization in the UK and a big emphasis on the strategic decentralizing in the German speaking world. In the period under investigation there was a strong growth of innovative HR practices across Europe, but the fastest pace of change in IT investment and in horizontal and vertical networking was in the German-speaking countries. In terms of boundary changes there were strong increases in outsourcing throughout Europe, with the German-speaking firms reporting the highest increases. Interestingly, of the companies engaging in alliances, Southern European firms (France, Italy and Spain) reported the highest asset involvements.

In Chapter 7 of this volume we used the nine indicators of structure, process and boundary change to allow us to compare the adoption of composite and systematic changes in Europe, Japan and the USA. Of course, since the composite variables are built from the individual elements that show differences across the regions we would expect to find difference also in the composite and systemic variables. Consistent with the descriptive results on innovation adoption in Chapter 1, our composite analysis in Chapter 7 found strong regional differences in the adoption of multiple and systemic changes. The proportion of Japanese companies adopting multiple and systemic changes are always significantly lower than Western companies, confirming the lower degree of change not only in individual organizational dimensions, but also in multiple dimensions (see Table 7.3, Chapter 7). The second important finding on systems of changes is that higher than expected percentages of companies introduce systemic changes within organizations in Europe compared to the USA and Japan. (See Table 7.4.) The smaller size of European companies compared to US organizations may be behind this finding (see Table 7.5). We also found stronger evidence of systemic changes in the regional breakdowns of Europe, especially in the UK, where firms are relatively smaller. It seems plausible to relate this finding to the size of the organization: medium-sized organizations may be more likely to change in multiple dimensions compared to very large firms. However, there may be other institutional factors which affect the adoption of bundles or systems of organizational changes and some of these were discussed in Chapter 12 of this volume.

Aside from this limited treatment of size as a contingency, we also explored any links between knowledge intensity and internationalization on patterns of organizational innovation. The one common result across the three localities of Europe, Japan and the USA is that a high degree of internationalization increases the probability of engaging in strategic alliances. Elsewhere, the statistical associations between internationalization and knowledge intensity vary from one organization innovation to another. In Europe, high knowledge intensity increases the probability of organizing by projects, introducing a high degree of strategic decentralization and downscoping; in the USA it increases the probability of intensifying horizontal linkages, and in Japan it does not have any effect on the probability of adopting organizational innovations. Meanwhile, in Europe highly internationalized firms are more likely to introduce high strategic decentralization, invest in IT, outsource and engage in strategic alliances. In Japan, highly internationalized companies, in addition to strategic alliances and IT, are also more likely to develop stronger vertical linkages. In the USA, there is a strong statistical association between alliance formation and degree of internationalization.

These empirical findings are among the first to map the extent of the emergence of innovative forms of organizing across three important parts of the globe. They help to provide a baseline for further empirical inquiry, to engage with theoretical debates about convergence and divergence of organizational practices across the globe, and to set some of the context for the INNFORM's wider interest in performance and process questions in the emergence of innovative forms. The findings should also be considered in the light of the limited response rates and the exploratory design of the INNFORM survey instrument. We now move on to consider the performance and process questions of our work and some of the conclusions we can draw from our other empirical findings and ideas.

## Performance

Every action has it consequences, some intended and realized, others emergent and yet still beneficial, and others unintended and possibly punishing in their effects. The careful analyst of change and innovation needs always to be curious about consequences, although the literature on change is rather stronger in illuminating the content and process of change than it is in examining the relationship between change processes and outcomes

(Pettigrew, 2000; Pettigrew et al., 2001). The comparative and longitudinal study by Pettigrew and Whipp (1991) is still one of the few pieces of published research which investigates the relationship between change strategies and the financial performance of companies. As we embarked on the INNFORM programme in 1996 we also discovered that the mapping deficiencies in the literature on innovative forms were compounded by the absence of any evidence seeking to link changes in organizational structures, processes and boundaries to the performance of the firm. Exploring the innovation–performance link thereby became a central aim of the INNFORM programme.

We should give due credit to Martin Conyon and Simon Peck, the two original industrial economists in the Warwick team, for introducing us to the economics of complementarities. We explore theoretical work on the relationship between complementarities, change and performance in Chapter 6 of this volume. In turn, we then present our econometric results in Chapter 7 and the more qualitative and processual developments of our findings in Chapters 8 and 9. In this section of Chapter 14 we offer two examinations of the consequences of innovation in organization forms. First, we use the econometric results of Chapter 7 to draw out some essential conclusions about the innovation-performance link. Second, we explore some aspects of our dualities theme. As we explain in Chapters 10, 11 and 13, an existing tendency for contemporary organizations to experience dualities has been compounded by widespread experimentation with systems of innovative organizational change, and this has created increased levels of complexity which in turn has to be managed. Of course, innovative forms of organizing also have consequences for change and learning processes in the firm and we will return to explore some of these in the final process section of this chapter.

Milgrom and Roberts (1995: 181), the pioneers of complementarity theory within economics, defined complementarities as existing when 'doing *more* of one thing *increases* the returns to doing *more* of another' (emphases in original). Applied to the strategic, structural and technological variables of the firm, this amounts to a notion of internal synergy. Investing in one variable makes investing in another more profitable, setting off a potential virtuous circle of high performance. The key implication is that choice variables should not be thought of discretely, but as belonging to potentially integrated systems of mutually reinforcing elements. Everything in the business should fit smoothly together. Thus Milgrom and Roberts (1995) analyse in detail how the long-run success of Lincoln Electric relies upon a coherent system bringing together the interdependent elements of low-cost strategy, piece rates, permanent employment, high earnings, internal promotion, firm-specific training and old plant and equipment. None of these elements would necessarily make business sense taken individually and the absence of any one of them would damage substantially the benefits of the remainder (see Chapters 6 and 7 for further elaboration).

There are now many theoretical developments of complementarities thinking (see, for example, Rivkin, 2000; Porter and Siggelkow, 2002; Sigglekow, 2002a). However, the central theoretical proposition is that high-performing firms are likely to be combining a number of practices at the same time and that the performance payoffs to a full system of practices are greater than the sum of its parts, some of which taken on their own might even have negative effects. So there is a positive and negative performance implication built into complementarities thinking. The probability is that full system moves will deliver performance benefits, while there is a corresponding probability that singular or partial moves will not only not deliver performance improvements, but may produce a weakening of performance.

As we explain more fully in Chapter 7, we had to use a combination of objective and perceptual measures of performance. The performance data for the UK used changes in the return of capital employed between 1992 and 1996. However, the measure for performance for the rest of the sample is derived from the questionnaire. It is a 1 to 5 scale of self-reported changes in performance in the four-year period 1992 to 1996. This information was used for Continental European firms because of the difficulty of obtaining reliable and comparable published financial performance data in Continental Europe. These questions were also included in the US survey. Previous research has shown high levels of convergence between objective and perceptual measures of performance (Dess and Robinson, 1984; Hart and Banbury, 1994). The absence of performance data for our Japanese sample meant that we could not conduct the innovation–performance analysis for Japanese companies.

We have conducted two analyses of the innovation–performance relationship from the INNFORM survey. The first analysis was published in 1999 by Whittington et al. This analysis was restricted to the European sample of companies and offered a dual inductive and deductive analysis, but with the ordered Probit modelling providing only a static analysis of the relationship between innovation systems and performance. However, both the inductive and deductive analyses were strong and encouraging and made us optimistic of what we might find in the more sophisticated and dynamic analysis produced in Chapter 7.

The inductive analysis separated out the upper and lower quartile companies and established an innovation profile for each set of organizations. The correlation analysis showed a much denser set of related organizational innovations amongst the high performers group than amongst the low performers. We concluded from this analysis that high performers are doing more things together than low performers, and not leaving anything out (Whittington et al., 1999: 593). The deductive analysis followed the Ichniowski et al. (1997) approach of measuring systems of innovations. The four systems were defined in a very similar fashion to Chapter 7 of this volume. The deductive analysis confirmed the potential of the inductive approach.

Whittington et al. (1999) found a positive association between performance and the most comprehensive of the four systems (System 1: structures plus processes plus boundaries). Also consistent with the notion of complementarities were the dangers of partial change, as evidenced by the negative performance associated with System 4 change: changing structures and boundaries, but omitting processes.

These early results on complementarities and performance have now been corroborated and extended by the analysis in Chapter 7. In Chapter 7 we are able to examine a larger and more international sample than in Whittington et al. (1999), (a pooled sample of 538 Western firms, UK plus Continental Europe, plus the USA) instead of just a European sample. We also offer more discrete international comparisons, the pooled Western sample of firms compared with the UK, firms in German-speaking countries and our small (but non-response biased) sample of US firms. Crucially in Chapter 7 we build on the Whittington et al., 1999 analysis and make full use of the time dimension to analyse the effect of multiple interrelated organizational *changes* on corporate performance *changes* in the period 1992–93 to 1996–97. To the best of our knowledge there are no other published studies of this kind in the literature.

Table 7.10 in Chapter 7 provides the summary of the Massini and Pettigrew regression results. The main conclusions are:

- The pooled analysis indicates that the adoption of a full set of changes in structures, processes and boundaries (System 1) increases the probability of improving corporate performance.
- However, the adoption of partial systems, structures and processes (System 2), or processes and boundaries (System 3), is likely to reduce performance.
- Considering individual organizational innovations, our results show very strong positive association between outsourcing and enhanced performance and a strong association between vertical and horizontal linkages and enhanced performance. But interestingly project forms of organizing has a clear negative impact on performance where it is introduced in isolation from other possible related changes.
- The cross country and regional analyses identify specific patterns of complementarities. In the UK we found strong evidence of the harmful effect of introducing partial systems of structural and process changes (System 2). These results are in marked contrast with the pattern for German speaking countries, where System 2 is strongly and positively linked to performance, and System 4 has a negative effect. US companies (as in the pooled sample) demonstrate a strong positive link between the full system change (System 1) and also display the negative effect of partial systems of change (System 2).

These findings, like all those found in the social and management sciences, have their limitations. These are acknowledged and discussed in Chapter 7. However, in 2002 they represent the most extensive application of complementarities theorizing to the study of organizational change and performance. In the final process section of this chapter we take the theoretical, empirical and practical aspects of our work on change and performance several steps forward by unravelling some of the conclusions from Pettigrew and Whittington in Chapter 8. Here we use our case study data of BP and Unilever over the time period 1985 to 2002 to analyse the *what, why, how* and *when* of complementarities in action, an aspect of the theory and practice of complementarities barely touched upon in previous research.

Our research findings on innovative forms of organizing paint a picture of greater organizational uncertainty and complexity. It is to this feature of the consequence of innovation to which we now wish to turn. Although it is now well acknowledged that the new competitive landscape of firms is a great driver of change, we suspect that the more potent cause of complexity in firms lies in the responses firms make to the accumulating external pressure. Through space and time we have discovered a variable tendency for firms to be changing their structures, processes and boundaries. These often simultaneous and complementary innovations are increasingly triggering the bipolar systems of thinking and acting we have characterized in Chapters 10 to 13 of this volume as dualities. These dualities are now appearing more as bundles than discrete, isolatable phenomena. The dualities are multiple and interdependent and promote highly customized action in local contexts which create further variety through time, which in turn has to be managed. All this is happening on a moving platform where the outcomes of action, in turn, appear on a platform which itself is moving. Innovations which may have been conceived as solutions may end up being perceived as problems as the cases of Siemens and ABB in Chapter 13 so sharply portray. Innovation journeys are always incomplete, always in process, never quite there. Changes by definition provoke unexpected effects which may be accommodated, even managed, but are rarely controllable. There is also the issue of perspective and perception. Initiators of innovations may feel the positive exhilaration of tackling a just cause. For others, the change may mean a bruising encounter with the devil. All these dynamics are likely to be magnified by the almost continuous processes of innovating discerned in our 18 case study organizations. Living with constant change (organizing/strategizing and not organization and strategy) means there are always multiple loose ends. A core driver of this experience of wrestling with order and disorder is the challenge of managing multiple dualities in the modernizing organization.

The quantitative results from the INNFORM survey show that in making complementary sets or systems of innovations in their structures, processes and boundaries, many of our firms are exposing themselves to a cluster of dualities. We can see an even richer picture of these dualities in action in our case studies. These are well brought out in Chapters 11 and 13 of this volume and in the more extended case examples analysed in Pettigrew and Fenton (2000a). Thus in Ove Arup and Coopers & Lybrand there were successful attempts to encourage dependence on the centre and independence from the centre; to promote the centralization of strategy and the decentralization of operations; to empower while holding on to power. Both professional service organizations were attempting to build strong global brands with all that involved in terms of coherence of identity and standardization of quality, while at the same time permitting customized client offerings in national and regional markets (Fenton and Pettigrew, 2000b; 2000c).

In Chapter 11 Sánchez-Runde, Massini and Quintanilla discuss and illustrate a range of 16 interdependent and consequential people management dualities across the four domains of organization culture, work organization, leadership and management and human resources. The Spanish-based utility AGBAR is a clear example of the incorporation of dual principles of organizing. Organization development in AGBAR involved finding new balances between centralization and decentralization, continuity and change, and building the hierarchy while encouraging horizontal co-ordination. Fremap, the other Spanish case, drew out clearly how new human resource policies and practices were simultaneously centralizing and decentralizing people-related matters. This recognition that the complementarities in new forms of organizing are not just about multiple '*whats*' of change, but also involve multiple '*hows*' of changing is a novel feature of our research findings. There are many process dualities in managing change. These include: linking the micro and macro aspects of the change process; encouraging top-down pressure and bottom-up energy for change; mobilizing energy and sustaining it; balancing processes of continuity and change; and making progress in change processes sometimes by escalating issues and sometimes by confining issues (Pettigrew, 1985; 1998b).

This clustering of content and process dualities in innovating organizations does not appear on the evidence from our research to be surfacing formulaic solutions. On the contrary, given the highly contextual nature of change and learning processes, it is rather easier to identify local and customized solutions. Thus in Chapter 13, Achtenhagen and Melin are able to pinpoint three quite different accommodating strategies to what they portray as the meta-level duality of homogeneity and heterogeneity. In Siemens-Med there was an attempt to accommodate by increasing the levels of homogeneity. In ABB the strategy was to attempt to decrease heterogeneity, whilst in the Östgöta Enskilda Bank the preferred and more ambitious approach was to enhance the bank's capacity to deal with perceived complexity and thereby manage the duality in a more holistic fashion. As per the theme of this section of Chapter 14, each of these strategies in turn generated further consequences which had, in turn, to be managed. As we have emphasized so strongly in the organizing/strategizing part of this volume, in the contemporary context organizations are best appreciated now not as end states, but as the continuously recreated and ever precarious product of human activities.

Having portrayed the responses of the innovating organization as a generator of rising levels of complexity and uncertainty, it seems logically consistent to at least consider an accommodating strategy in terms of a hunt to find simplifying routines. We have explored this theme in Pettigrew and Fenton (2000a). The BP case provides some excellent examples of these simplifying routines which range from the qualities of holistic thought and action of the top leaders; executive skill in offering clear, simple and evocative messages; through periodic attempts to reduce burgeoning levels of network complexity; to the attempt to use IT solutions to facilitate intra-organizational communication. Strengthening the quality of the dialogue between the strategic centre and the business units in the organizing/strategizing process is also a crucial area of organization capability building. Although our research findings raised the significance of the management of dualities as an issue, and have documented the rise of sets of dualities in the modernizing firm, there is a big research agenda here for other scholars to build upon. We need more research on the varieties of management strategy in use in different localities to sense, accommodate, and lead organizations through further cycles of innovation.

## Process

The belated interest in history and time in the social and management sciences has brought with it a greater variety and sophistication of process analysis in the study of organizational innovation and change. Some of this variety is evident in the measured and real time analysis of change displayed in the Minnesota Innovation Research Program (MIRP) (Van de Ven et al., 1989; 1999). There is also the micro-process work of Langley (1999) and her colleagues, and the multi-level co-evolutionary theoretical and empirical work of Lewin and his collaborators. (Lewin et al., 1999; Lewin and Volberda, 1999). The Warwick tradition of process research on organizational and strategy change rests on the view that theoretically sound and practically useful research on change should explore the contexts, content and process of change together with their interconnections over time. This focus on changing rather than change presented scholars with a dual challenge: (1) to attempt to catch reality in flight, and (2) to study long-term processes in their contexts in order to elevate embeddedness to a principle of method (Pettigrew, 1985; 1990; 1997a). These challenges in turn require a series of linked analytical opportunities. The focus now needs to be on long-term change processes and not just change episodes. Those continuous processes are seen as embedded in multiple levels of context and a product of, and producing those contexts. Processes are themselves multilayered and have their own logic, trajectory and pace and the asymmetries between the different levels of context with their own processes is itself a driver of change. The recognition of this interactive field of cause and effect necessitates a move away from the variables paradigm with its neat demarcation of dependent and independent variables towards a more holistic form of analysis and explanation. And, of course, the only way to expose this interactive field of context and action is to have a sufficiently long time series to reveal the mutuality of context and action. Thus the definition of process guiding our work has been the analysis of sequences of individual and collective events, actions, and activities unfolding over time in their contexts.

The reader by now will have noticed a variety of different approaches and treatment of process in this volume. Our organizing/strategizing theme is an explicit attempt not only to theorize about this duality, but also how the duality works itself through time in the context of the new landscape of competition, and the emergence of the modernizing firm. The case studies in Chapters 3 and 4 extend this generic theorizing about processes of organizing/strategizing into the micro-processes of leading and learning. A similar set of case studies on the management of dualities reveal both the causes and consequences of those dualities and some of the actions taken to accommodate or manage these new sources of organizational complexity. Chapters 11 and 13 use case studies to illuminate these issues of duality management, but they do not offer process analyses. For more extended case analyses offering an embedded treatment of process over time we need to focus in on the concluding messages derivable from Chapters 8, 9 and 5 of this volume.

Linking patterns of change process to organizational performance is a big intellectual challenge and one we have taken up in the INNFORM programme. In Chapter 8 Pettigrew and Whittington built upon the somewhat static theoretical and empirical base of the economics of complementarities. We had noted in Chapter 6 that the path-breaking work of Milgrom and Roberts (1990, 1995) was weak on both how systems of complements were built up, sustained and reconfigured, and also how that building process delivered performance improvement. Although the Milgrom and Roberts case study of Lincoln Electric had an implied view of process (particularly a concept of strong, central leadership) in no sense were they able to analyse how that leadership process was expressed through time to deliver and sustain the performance improvement that theory of complementarities so eloquently sketched. Our contribution has been a twin one. As we demonstrated in Chapter 7, we have been able to statistically corroborate some of the central *what* propositions of the Milgrom and Roberts work. Crucially, we have been able to build upon this econometric analysis to pose and then answer some complementary *how* questions. In Chapter 9 we explored how complementary change was constructed in four professional service organizations and in Chapter 8 we offered the first published examples of the processes of building complementary change to deliver performance enhancement.

We were interested in answers to the following kinds of questions. Was complementary change intended, or did it emerge from a more loosely composed process of learning-by-doing? If the process was intendedly holistic, what were the initial set of complements and how were they subsequently built over time? What role did history, culture and performance crises play in the timing and extent of complementary change? What was the sequence of changes over time and indeed was the change process as much sequential and overlapping as simultaneous? Was there any evidence of the cycling and recycling of change attempts to build complements over the long term? Did we observe performance declines before performance improvements, and if so how did the leadership system cope with such problems of transition? And if as we expected building complements and driving up performance was a long-term process, how was that process enabled or disabled by leadership succession?

The extended case examples of BP and Unilever in Chapter 8 offer some interesting similarities and differences about complementarities in action. Although both cases demonstrate a clear link between complementary change and performance improvement there were important differences in the trajectory of change in the two companies. The BP case was more intendedly holistic than Unilever and, at times, more revolutionary in its character, although not for a long time in its performance effects. The Unilever trajectory can certainly be portrayed as holistic towards the end of the process we analysed, but overall it was more a process of sequential and overlapping change than it was simultaneous change. There were also differences in the change sequence with BP starting with modest boundary changes, then, in Project 1990, featuring large attempts at structure and culture change. These were then followed in the Simon and Browne eras by major strategic, system and process change. Unilever meanwhile started with a long and fairly incremental process of strategy and boundary changes, then followed this with modest process changes, culminating in the large-scale structure, governance and systems changes of the FitzGerald era.

What is strikingly similar about complementarities in action in both companies is the time, the persistence and patience it took before the assembling of the complements as a mutually reinforcing whole began to kick-in and deliver the performance improvements. BP and Unilever clearly demonstrate that complementary change means not just doing lots of things together, but doing them consistently and staying the course. Given the negative consequences of incomplete systems, it takes courage and persistence to press on through the J-curve of performance and reap the full benefits of complementary change. Above all, complementary change is not about great vision but about great delivery. Maintaining successes in such processes is itself about delivering success. And in delivering success, leader effects are important.

The BP and Unilever cases very clearly show that leaders can make a positive difference to organizational performance. They also demonstrate that it can take two or three generations of leaders often displaying different personal styles, competences and degrees of risk taking, but pursuing some consistency in philosophy and action, to deliver enhanced performance. The BP and Unilever cases are essentially about intergenerational leader effects. Duration of leader in post and the careful management of leader succession are at the heart of leading continuity and change, and the skilful management of continuity and change is at the core of the relationship between leadership, change and performance.

Although in Chapter 9 we make no attempt to link complementary change with performance, our comparative survey of four professional service organizations (PSOs) corroborates many of the process issues in the BP and Unilever cases. Our analysis of complementarities in Chapter 9 examined through time the what, why, how and when of the movement of four PSOs from federal, informally networked organizations towards more formal global network structures with corresponding systems and management styles, and with aspirations to co-align processes. All four cases displayed similar drivers for change and also a similar sequencing with again a change process which was jointly emergent and international. The cases also demonstrated the organizing/strategizing duality with continuous organizing being seen as almost equivalent to the process of strategy development. All four cases also shared the problem of what we described as process lag, the failure of process changes to keep up with the realigning of strategy, boundary, structure and systems changes. The four cases also illustrated our dualities theme and the hunt to reduce complexity arising from the difficulties of managing multiple dualities. The main variability in organization development between the four cases was in the pace of change towards globally networked organizations. We explained this variability in speed of change from a mixture of historical antecedents, market positioning, leadership, and size.

The chapter offered by the Erasmus team (Dijksterhuis, van den Bosch and Volberda – Chapter 5) provides a holistic and dynamic analysis of the home banking division of the Dutch international financial institution, ING. Although the method is again contextual and temporal the theoretical lens here focuses much more on the perceptions, beliefs and change actions of decision makers. The authors of Chapter 5 are able to confirm the potential of seeing organizing and strategizing as complementary activities even if they do not also treat organizing/strategizing as a single duality. They give due emphasis to the limits to the discretion of managers in change processes arising from environmental constraints and the path-dependent nature of some firm re-orientation activities.

While encouraging further research, we can offer some key concluding messages that we hope both scholars and practitioners will take forward.

Above all, the new models of organization are not simple panaceas, universal and complete solutions. We insist in this volume on much greater complexity. Thus there are similar trajectories internationally, but countries differ in starting points, pace and details of change. Organizational innovations are supplementing rather than utterly supplanting old forms of organizing. Yet above these kinds of complexity there are also some patterns – patterns of complementarity, of duality and of constancy. Innovative forms of organizing are complex because complementarities demand the construction of full systems of reinforcing innovations, a process that we have seen is typically prolonged and sometimes precarious. They are complex too because of dualities. Leaders must empower within their organizations while holding together coherent systems of complementarities. Strategizing and organizing are no longer separable within neat sequences but bound together almost indistinguishably. Finally, organization is never complete. The pattern of constancy is emphasized in our longitudinal case studies, revealing repeated waves of organizing and reorganizing. This constant process of change and renewal means that, while scholars and managers can take forward certain key messages, there will always be a need for more research on innovative forms of organizing. We hope other scholars will build on this work and, in the belief that understanding how we produced our knowledge is as important as appreciating its content, we now turn to offer some perspective on the social production of knowledge in the INNFORM programme of research.

# Chapter 15

# Co-producing Knowledge and the Challenges of International Collaborative Research

*Andrew M. Pettigrew*

## INTRODUCTION

Contemporary writing on the natural, social and management sciences indicates some fundamental changes in the social production of knowledge (Gibbons et al., 1994; Ziman, 1994; Pettigrew, 1997b; Nowotny et al., 2001). The changes include who is involved in the production of knowledge, the process of knowledge production and types of available knowledge, new levels of international collaboration in research, and new settings and opportunities for knowledge production, dissemination and use. This thesis of a change in the character of knowledge production rests on a broad-ranging theoretical and empirical argument. Nowotny et al. (2001) characterize this as a co-evolutionary process between science and society. The elements of the change are many, but the most often detailed include:

- a more porous boundary between science and society
- a resultant loss of researcher autonomy
- a breakdown of assumptions about unitary views of science and linear notions of the scientific process
- a greater range of participants in the knowledge-development process and greater pluralism of research practice
- a greater recognition of the localized (in time and space) character of research practice and outcomes

- a wider recognition of the emergent rather than planned views of the research process
- a recognition of the complex interactions between multiple stakeholders in the research process and a more contested landscape for evaluating the quality and relevance of research processes, outputs and outcomes.

These elements and the forces driving them are themselves contested. Even the advocates of a change thesis, such as Gibbons et al. (1994) and Ziman (1994), recognize that the process is still emergent, that the rate of change varies in different national and disciplinary communities and that responses are predictably customized to local institution, profession and resource conditions (see also Whitley, 2000). So the debate about convergence and divergence of organizational forms and practices across nation state boundaries is mirrored in the debate about convergence and divergence of knowledge production between scientific communities in different parts of the world. The normative attraction of the divergent science position is linked to the pragmatic virtues of pluralism in social science (Morgan, 1983; Pettigrew, 2001). One of the lessons learned from the natural history of the development of the social sciences is that there can be no one best way of framing, producing, disseminating and using knowledge.

The force of these debates about a new social production of knowledge is also penetrating the various fields of management. A recent special issue of the *British Journal of Management* (Hodgkinson (ed.), 2001) is a useful place to find the variety of perspectives which exist in the UK and USA. The even more recent edited collection on *Collaborative Research in Organizations* offers a more Continental Western European set of experiences (Adler et al., 2003). A distinctive and novel, but certainly not unique feature of the INNFORM programme, was that it featured two crucial areas of collaboration and partnership. The first and most notable of these was collaboration between university teams across nine universities located in three continents. The second was the involvement of PricewaterhouseCoopers in the co-funding, co-production and co-dissemination of our research. This kind of partnering between those in university and non-university settings is now an increasing feature of knowledge production in the management fields, and is frequently tied to the aspiration that management knowledge should meet the double hurdle of scholarly quality and relevance (Pettigrew, 1997b; MacLean et al., 2002). The debates on collaboration are also multifaceted, but within them are a number of partially contested assumptions. First of all there is the view that collaborative knowledge production is intrinsically superior to unrestrained competition; second, collaboration offers greater efficiency and value-for-money in the use of public and private sector research funds; and third, collaboration can add real, tangible value in scholarly research. Through collaboration we can deliver research outcomes not possible from solo or single-team scholarship. The INNFORM experience is certainly corroborative of the third of these views. The knowledge generated by the INNFORM programme could not have been achieved by a single team located in a UK-based university.

As co-ordinator and co-leader of the INNFORM programme I felt strongly that we should try to capture some of the learning from the experience of the programme while it was still fresh in our minds. Our two collaborative themes – scholarly collaboration between geographically dispersed teams, and the co-production and dissemination of knowledge between those in university and non-university based settings – raise major challenges for those who participate in such inquiries. With greater international collaboration and user engagement come new opportunities, but with them also come greater complexities and transaction costs in the research process. Do the benefits outweigh the cost? What additional intellectual, social and political skills are demanded of everyone in these kinds of knowledge production? What are the special challenges imposed on those who seek to co-ordinate or lead this kind of research, and how do we prepare future generations of scholars to be motivated and skilful in collaborative research? These are some of the questions raised in this chapter.

There are four sections to this chapter. First I review aspects of the literature on the special challenges of international collaborative research. This section also picks up the related literature on the structure and dynamics of geographically dispersed and co-located teams. In section two I use these literatures to interrogate aspects of the INNFORM experiences. Some lessons are derivable from the INNFORM programme and these are identified from the perspective of various members of the team. Section three provides a short analysis of the PricewaterhouseCoopers–INNFORM engagement and some of the lessons for the co-production of knowledge. The fourth and final section offers a brief conclusion.

## SOME CHALLENGES OF INTERNATIONAL COLLABORATIVE RESEARCH

Knowing now some of the complexities and transaction costs of international inquiry in the social and management sciences, it seems a reasonably pragmatic to ask – why bother? Five arguments can be assembled in support of international collaborative research. They range from epistemological arguments about the social production of knowledge 'after modernism', through empirical arguments about the importance of space and time shaping the world, to the view that research collaboration can be a more efficient and effective form of knowledge production. The fourth argument starts from the premise that international collaborative research is more intellectually, socially and politically demanding and thereby requires big commitments and higher risk. But then the argument turns the corner and contends that collaborative scientific inquiry is now so common in the natural and engineering sciences that we as management scholars can ill-afford to be left behind in terms of skill and capacity building in how to carry out international collaborative and comparative research.

The 1995 report from the Science Policy Research Unit (SPRU) by Hicks and Katz (1996; 1997), on the changing shape of British science, notes some very interesting trends in UK scientific publication. The SPRU statistics confirm the now well-recognized fact that university-based scientists have long since lost their monopoly supplier position as knowledge workers. The statistics also reveal the tremendous increase in national and international scientific collaboration during the 1980s. The SPRU findings were able to conclude that in 1991, 40 per cent of published papers involved collaboration between researchers in different institutions compared with 28 per cent in 1981. Meanwhile, international scientific partnerships involving UK researchers increased by 75 per cent in the 1980s. The SPRU authors predicted that, by the year 2000, more than 50 per cent of the UK's scientific papers will each be produced by three or more researchers working in more than two institutions.

This pattern of scientific research is, of course, partly energized by the extremely high capital costs of big science. Researchers have to agree to share and barter equipment in order to remain in certain scientific fields. Another driver is the development of meta-level institutions such as the European Union, the European Space Agency and the Airbus Consortium. The management of dispersed research and development collaboration is now crucial in university, industry and government-based science (Boutellier et al., 1999). There are no equivalent statistics on the social and management sciences, but the normal assumption is that large-scale international inquiries are fewer in the social sciences than the natural sciences. Notable management research examples on both sides of the Atlantic include the GLOBE leadership research (House et al., 2002), the NOFIA work on new forms of organizing (Lewin et al., 1999), the CRANET research on international human resource management (Brewster et al., 1996; Tregaskis et al., 2003) and, of course, this INNFORM programme.

But what are the special demands created by international collaborative research in the social and management sciences? To answer this question we need to examine two related bodies of literature. The first group of writing focuses on the generic problems of cross cultural or comparative management and organization analysis. Notable contributions here include Roberts (1970), Sekaran (1983), Redding (1994), Inkeles and Sasaki (1996), Kohn (1996), and Cavusgil and Das (1997). The other stream of research and writing moves on from the general methodological problems of international comparative inquiry to examine the special problems of conducting comparative work by means of teams of participants from different international localities. Examples of this writing include Teagarden et al. (1995), Easterby-Smith and Malina (1999), Brewster et al. (1996) and Tregaskis et al. (2003).

The main generic methodological problem in cross-cultural comparative research is equivalence; comparing like with like. The equivalence issue permeates the whole cycle of the research process and can affect comparability of concept definition, variable identification, operational definitions, instrument design, sample selection, sample treatment and analysis. (McDonald, 2000; Collinson and Pettigrew, 2003). As we shall see, the equivalence issue affected the INNFORM programme most obviously in the definition and operationalization of the survey variables and led to some customization of the survey instrument especially for the Japanese context. Sampling was also important and we were careful to only sample locally owned organizations in the geographical localities of our work so we were identifying indigenous representatives of each setting. There are also major interpretive issues in all cross-cultural research. These issues range from over-generalization beyond data set or time period, to the very difficult issues of distinguishing between the effects of cultural, institutional, and political/economic conditions on the comparative dimension to be explained. Although having an international team conducting the comparative research creates its own dynamics and challenges, the presence of team members who in the sample are 'insiders' for each nation state is a major advantage in dealing with some of the difficult issues of concept definition, operationalization and interpretation.

The recent rise in the number of international collaborative research projects has encouraged team members from those projects to write instructively about their experiences. Thus Teagarden et al. (1995), Brewster et al. (1996) and Tregaskis et al. (2003) have all drawn some useful lessons from collaborative research using survey methods, and Easterby-Smith and Malina (1999) draw upon case study research involving Chinese and UK academics from five different universities. The survey research teams pinpoint the normal difficulties of survey design, survey administration and equivalence of survey variables and translations across countries. They also note the centralizing opportunities enabled by the analysis of survey findings, but also the need to customize the survey instrument to local conditions. Tregaskis et al. (2003) draw on the work of Turati et al. (1998) to argue how important the 'cognitive referential systems' are of team members in giving rise to divergent ways of thinking in the international team. This divergence is both a strength and a potential weakness of such teams. If there is some level of shared vision and trust, the divergent thinking can be a source of creativity and interpretive variety. If trust is low, the divergent thinking potential can create an ambiguous information management and exchange environment which can escalate conflicts and misunderstandings.

The Easterby-Smith and Malina (1999) account of their case study based research confirms the key role that trust and good communication between team members play in the fate of international research collaborations. However, they note that the more open-ended character of idiographic case research leaves much more scope for different ontological and epistemological positions to endanger the development of shared understandings and trust between team members, and between those team members and other key stakeholders in the research process. Prescriptively they argue that creating space for reflexive dialogue between the international team members would have improved the research process in their case example. Thus they contend that creating space for more dialogue would have allowed greater opportunities 'to exchange expectations, assumptions and feelings as the project progressed. It would have required a willingness to share surprises, to allow assumptions to be challenged, to be sensitive to the nature and effect of cultural stereotypes, and above all, to build further on mutual trust and respect' (Easterby-Smith and Malina, 1999: 85).

Although the literature on international collaborative research in management is limited and scattered, this is not the case with the now expansive work on geographically dispersed teams, transnational teams, virtual teams and co-located teams. Notable recent writing in these traditions include Galegher et al., 1990; Snow et al., 1996; Sessa et al., 1999; Jarvenpaa and Leidner, 1999; Maznevski and Chudoba, 2000; Majchrzak et al., 2000 and Cramton, 2001. This work is illuminating for our interest in the structure, dynamics and outcomes of international collaborative research and had I known about it and read it prior to or during the INNFORM programme, I would have been that much better prepared for some of our own experiences. But some definitions are needed. A transnational team is generally taken to mean a work group composed of multinational members whose activities span multiple countries (Snow et al., 1996). A geographically dispersed team (GDT) is one 'whose members are dispersed across distance and time, are linked together by some form of electronic technology, and physically interact with each other rarely, or not at all' (Sessa et al., 1999: 10). Meanwhile co-located teams (CLTs) are teams typically operating in the same location with close-physical proximity, whose members can have face-to-face contact on a regular basis (Sessa et al., 1999: 20). The INNFORM programme team had the virtue of dispersed and co-located team characteristics with the strengths and weaknesses of each team mode to some extent complementary and compensating for one another.

GDTs are an evolved form of teamworking, not an entirely new entity. The development of information and communication technologies in the last ten years have, however, been decisive in spreading the possibilities of GDTs. Much of the analytical vocabulary traditionally applied to CLTs can be readily applied to GDTs. Thus issues of structure, size, composition, task characteristics, interpersonal processes, communication and commitment, team cohesion and trust, and team outcomes and success are important in both types of teams. The big challenge for GDTs is that their team members are separated by time and distance. The distance effects are also multi-dimensional with the research literature giving special emphasis to geographical, cultural, psychological and temporal aspects of distance.

These distance factors create special challenges for GDTs in terms of communication, co-ordination and leadership, which in turn impact on the development and sustainability of trust, which may then affect problem solving and conflict resolution, and ultimately task accomplishment.

Drawing upon evidence of transnational teams in business settings, Snow et al. (1996) conclude that 'successful teams are characterized by leaders and members who trust each other, are committed to the team's mission, can be counted on to perform their respective tasks, and enjoy working with each other', (Snow et al., 1996: 61). Crucially the Snow et al. (1996) study also highlighted the importance of team selection. Given the difficulties of building shared assumptions and trust into GDTs, one way to handle that problem is to pre-select for those characteristics. As we shall see, hand picking the INNFORM team was a critical factor in its success.

But if careful selection is a necessary condition to increase the possibilities of success, what are some of the important sufficient conditions? Several studies refer to the varieties of leadership necessary to make GDTs work. Armstrong and Cole (1995) note the unexpected reactions of team members to decisions in GDTs, and how conflicts can easily rise up from nowhere and escalate quickly. The complex negotiations which occur in international collaborative work can easily lead to misunderstandings which can just as easily lead to offence. These dynamics make leading and co-ordinating GDTs much like walking on egg shells. And yet Armstrong and Cole (1995) conclude that leading a distributed team requires focus and discipline. 'Decisions need to be made clearly, not reversed, and reliably followed up over time' (Armstrong and Cole, 1995: 208). Several authors comment on the distributed nature of leadership in GDTs with different team members potentially offering different forms of leading at different times (Snow et al., 1996; Sessa et al., 1999.) Maznevski and Chudoba (2000) take a dynamic view of the leadership process in global virtual teams and chronicle the importance of team leaders building a rhythm of communication and co-ordination which serves as a 'heartbeat' for the team and provides some elements of continuity and identity.

In two very insightful papers, Cramton (2001) and Sole and Edmondson (2002), bring together many of the issues about GDT team dynamics and structure around the themes of mutual and situated knowledge. Cramton (2001) argues that a combination of the physical dispersion of collaborators and frequent use of communication technology tend to negatively affect the means by which people establish mutual knowledge. This mutual knowledge is defined as knowledge that collaborators share in common and know they share. In turn mutual knowledge 'is a precondition for effective communication and the performance of co-operative work' (Cramton, 2001: 349). The challenge in a GDT is to create some of the conditions that lead to the shared reality, which builds the mutual knowledge, which in turn can nourish the common ground that will positively impact on task performance. Cramton's work revealed the ubiquitous nature of failures of mutual knowledge in GDTs and the negative consequences for 'blaming' and stereotyping in the teams. Cramton also noted the important role that occasional face-to-face meetings and telephone contacts can have in moderating such negative dynamics, but only if they were associated with related processes of building team identity through aligning goals and incentives.

The Sole and Edmondson (2002) paper catalogues the inherently problematic nature of GDTs and leads to the implicit conclusion that the more attractive and effective mode of team-working may be one which combines the advantages and disadvantages of geographically dispersed and co-located teams. Sole and Edmondson argue that co-location is a source of common identity and activity, and that proximity facilitates the development of transactive memory – the knowledge of what others know. This situated knowledge is critical to problem solving ability and yet is not normally readily available unless GDTs encourage co-location and re-location between geographically dispersed team members. As we shall see, the INNFORM team offered a combination of geographical dispersion and distant communication, with the face-to-face advantages of co-location. The advantages thus created to build mutual and situational knowledge were expanded by the movement of team members between the geographical locations. All this helped to build a sufficient level of commitment, trust and identity that kept the INNFORM team together long enough to deliver its desired outputs, and create some level of aspirations for future work together.

## EXPERIENCING THE INNFORM PROGRAMME OF RESEARCH

The purpose of this section of the chapter is to provide a limited multi-perspective account of the natural history of development of the INNFORM programme from its inception in 1995, through its funding in 1996, to the completion of this summative book in January 2003. I will also offer an assessment of the success of the programme as seen by some of the key participants, and through the UK Economic and Social Research Council (ESRC), the wider social science and management research communities. The aim throughout is to identify some of the main intellectual and social/managerial challenges of this kind of complex, collaborative research; to discuss how some of those challenges were managed; and to identify major points of learning by doing. All social science research activities are different and they are certainly all more or less successful on a variety of dimensions. The INNFORM programme is certainly neither uniquely successful, or entirely representative of research practice in management research, but it is I believe worthy of discussion for the lessons that can be learned by other scholars attempting this kind of collaborative research with both international scholarly partners, and an industrial partner.

As a co-founder, co-ordinator and co-leader of the programme I have had a central place in the process. This positioning has given me a unique participant observation perspective, but also a partial, and therefore limited view. In order to offer a wider perspective on the INNFORM programme I have made use of a broader set of resources. These include:

- The e-mail and other correspondence between myself and team members and funders.
- Notes of programme meetings.
- The evaluation of the ESRC co-ordinator during the programme, and the ESRC evaluation process at the end of the funding in late 2000.
- In December 2002, I wrote to five of the INNFORM co-leaders asking them for their summative views of the six aspects of the INNFORM experience. Had the programme been a success or failure, and, if so, why and how? What had they learned about the conduct of this kind of inquiry? What kinds of outcomes and impact had materialized? What issues about team selection, team process, and team commitment can they now see to be critical? Did their motivation and commitment change over time and, if so, why, and with what implications? And finally, what are the critical leadership/co-ordination issues they can now see to be important for this kind of international collaborative research?
- Finally, I have drawn upon the literatures in the previous sections of this chapter to offer some interpretation of the narrative account.

The PricewaterhouseCoopers perspective on the INNFORM work is outlined in the penultimate section of this chapter. Throughout, in so far as it is possible, I maintain the anonymity of teams and team members.

The INNFORM programme began as a research project proposal submitted to the ESRC's Innovation Research Programme in March 1995. This proposal by Pettigrew, Whittington and Conyon was titled 'The new internal network organization: process and performance' and involved the three main progress, performance and process aims carried through into the larger research activity that we re-labelled the INNFORM programme in 1998. The original Warwick team were notified of the success of the proposal in 1995 and we commenced the work in March 1996 with the appointment of the two initial Warwick-based research staff, Drs Evelyn Fenton and Simon Peck. The European office of Coopers & Lybrand agreed to co-fund the research up to £75 000 over three years. The original ESRC contribution was £200 000 over three years. In addition, £30 000 was committed from the consortium of industrial sponsors who supported the Centre for Corporate Strategy and Change (CCSC) of Warwick Business School. At that time Pettigrew was the founding director of the Centre. As the project widened, so all of the international teams put financial and people resources into the programme.

The original project was more limited in scope and participation than the eventual programme. The surveys were to be targeted to the UK, Continental Western Europe and Japan and complemented by a set of European case studies. At the time of the project proposal submission there were four original participants: the Warwick team, two European teams and the Japanese team. We were fortunate that the original representatives of the Dutch and Japanese teams were Visiting Fellows at the CCSC during 1995 and contributed to the project design from the very outset. The original Dutch representative then moved to St Gallen in Switzerland and led the German-speaking part of the work from that base. During 1996 the replacement Dutch representatives joined the project and around the same time the Swedish team joined. With the agreement of all team members, the Spanish team joined in March 1997, and the US representative joined later in 1997 (again with team agreement) to carry out the US survey. This survey was made possible by an additional grant from Coopers & Lybrand in 1997. Later the ESRC provided a supplementary grant to merge and analyse the US survey data. Coopers & Lybrand (by then incorporated into the new entity of PricewaterhouseCoopers) also awarded a further grant in December 1998 to support the dissemination of the research. These additional awards meant that the Warwick team had continuous funding for two full-time research staff from March 1996 until January 2001. Simon Peck left Warwick in September 1998 and was replaced by Dr Silvia Massini in January 1999. Silvia has done a fine job in analysing the survey data since January 1999 and has played a prominent role in the data analysis and writing for this volume.

Team selection is critical, even fateful, for the progress and performance of an international group of researchers who are for much of the time geographically dispersed. Our strategy here was to encourage intellectual and cultural diversity, but to seek personal compatibility and ease of communication by working with people with whom we already had had a working relationship. For the most part this strategy worked well, although we did have tensions with one of the two teams who were new to the overall group. The leader of one new team commented:

> Selection is critical and this is evidenced by the loss of X team. There is a danger of getting involved with people you don't know … But we had a 50 per cent success rate for the two teams who were not previously engaged with the group. If there had only been a 50 per cent success rate across all the teams this would have been a disaster. This tells us something.

More broadly, another team leader said:

> Most country team leaders had had a previous working relation with the Warwick team, often because they had worked at Warwick for some period of time. This made it easier to understand other

> members' intentions, to make oneself understood to other team members, and to define a dominant logic within the project.

All the co-leaders acknowledge the necessary condition of appropriate team selection, but there are other necessary and sufficient conditions to create team success. Building a dominant logic in a dispersed team with intellectual, cultural, resourcing, capacity and organizational differences is a multi-faceted issue which warrants its own complementarities type of analysis and action (Harvey et al., 2002). Aside from the central issue of finding, retaining and motivating talent, any dispersed and co-located international team also needs a clear but adaptable research mission and aims; a sense of focal leadership, but also some element of shared leadership; mechanisms to build a strong and continuing rhythm in the team over time; an incentive and reward system with flexibility to incorporate the different needs of different generations in the team; and the energizing effect of some level of individual and collective success.

Much of the INNFORM's mission and aims were built into the 1995 ESRC proposal which benefited from the shaping process of the Japanese co-leader, one of the European leaders, and PricewaterhouseCoopers. The more structured methodology and positivistic orientation of the survey process and analysis provided a shared task and a common intellectual spine for project development. Although the first draft of the survey instrument was prepared in Warwick, subsequent drafts which led up to the standard instrument, benefited from feedback from all the teams. The Japanese and US teams had some scope to customize the survey instrument, and all the teams were fully engaged in the process of adapting the administration of the survey to the different geographical localities. This meant not just translating and back-translating as appropriate, but also customizing the letter accompanying the survey for the requirements of each location; addressing this letter to fit local etiquette; and handling any subsequent phone calls to build up response rates in an appropriate local fashion. This was demanding work, but it was a common task handled in a way which met the requirement for standardization and customization.

So a level of intellectual coherence was provided by the structural spine of the survey. This survey and its associated conceptual framework, (see Figure 1.1. in Chapter 1) provided a common task and a common language which built a platform for the case study work. The more idiographic approach of case studies demanded more open-ended discussion and debate and these debates were a critical source of creativity in building up and extending the original theoretical base of the programme. In Chapter 14 I mention a number of examples of these theoretical and empirical developments. But creativity itself demands structure and structuring (Amabile, 1996), and the structural spine of the survey and its associated conceptual framework were an important backdrop for the intellectual developments on the idiographic side of the INNFORM programme.

Maznevski and Chudoba (2000) insightfully discuss the importance of building a temporal rhythm in virtual teams. 'Effective global virtual team outcomes are a function of appropriate interaction incidents and the structuring of those incidents into a temporal rhythm' (2000: 489). Anticipating the Maznevski and Chudoba findings, we used a series of two- or three-day meetings to provide the 'heartbeat' of the INNFORM programme. These meetings were important in a task sense for agreeing objectives, monitoring progress, building up the theoretical and empirical base of the work, and then looking forward into the future. The meetings thereby created momentum and tied together the past, present and the future. In this way they also helped to create continuity, change and identity for the programme as a whole. The meetings were also a crucial source of interpersonal bonding, confirming relationships and renewing others, perhaps endangered by inattentiveness. These were also occasions when some of the most difficult political decisions were made to identify and resolve periodic tensions, of which more below.

In the period from the first three-day INNFORM workshop in October 1996, until the last one (which was for one day) in February 2001, nine meetings were held. The meetings were spread throughout the European locations with smaller group meetings also being held, one in Japan, and two in the USA. In addition to these meetings, a further nine meetings were held at important dissemination events attended by most team members. However, these meetings were often of only a three or four hour duration and nearly always focused on the requirements of the conference, with only limited discussion time for wider issues. The main meetings, in retrospect were much more important and fulfilling, with the conference meetings keeping the programme ticking over but hardly contributing in any deep way to the rhythm of the programme. As financial resources for the programme began to wane in 2000–02, and people's commitment was affected by competing demands, so the number of meetings declined. All this is predictable and may be inevitable in projects and programmes, but the loss of rhythm was decisive in reducing commitment. All the co-leaders commented on the loss of rhythm in the programme after 2000, for example:

> Regarding co-ordination, I am convinced that the superior means of co-ordination in international programmes like this is in meetings, where all the team members meet personally with open discussions and decision making on all critical issues. In the first stage we met rather often with many debated discussions of the survey questions fostering better quality. Then I think we met too seldom during the last three years.

Another co-leader linked the issues of motivation, commitment and co-ordination, but recognized the problems of reconciling them:

> Research of this kind is a mixed motive endeavour. People enter for
> different reasons and seek different outcomes. But somehow the
> sense of collective endeavour has to override these different motives
> and the different levels of commitment that go with the different
> motives ... By the end people were beginning to start new other
> things and this led to conflicting loyalties ... We began to move on to
> other things in our mind.

Our meeting schedule contributed to team coherence, but resource
constraints and competing demands meant we probably did not have
enough high-quality meetings throughout the lifecycle of the programme.
Nevertheless, the team events we had were without doubt crucial for
relationship building and intellectual debate, solving political problems, and
maintaining commitment, agreeing plans and objectives and celebrating
success.

Building and maintaining motivation, commitment and coherence is
itself a continuous and thereby precarious process. It is much like the process
of organizing/strategizing we witnessed in our research – always becoming,
never complete, and constantly requiring thought and attention. In this
sense the transaction costs of international collaborative inquiry can be
stretched as far as you wish to let them go. This is one of the great Achilles'
heels of international research – the danger of all process and no outcome.
Mindful of this, the success criteria for the INNFORM programme were at
the forefront of discussions from the very outset. These discussions of outputs and targets, which were encapsulated in a critical path for the project
and then programme, also necessitated the explicit discussion of how publications were to be shared and intellectual property rights agreed over the
data. Discussions were held on these crucial issues, first of all in the Warwick
team in April 1996, then among all the international teams at the first workshop in October 1996. These agreements were then put in writing and
amended, as appropriate or not, as the Spanish and US teams entered the
programme. The guidelines created on those occasions held the ring until
early 2000, when new guidelines were discussed and agreed. This process
was crucial and I would recommend anyone contemplating international
collaborative work of this kind to contract early and explicitly about publishing and intellectual property rights.

Collective and individual success in creative activities is the great
enabler and energizer. Perceived success is a great builder of commitment and
identity. Shared success is not easy to cultivate and maintain in a GDT with
many interests and motives to satisfy. Our strategy from the outset was to look
for win–win situations for as many of the wider team as was possible. We had
three mechanisms to achieve this. One was co-publishing in journal articles, of
which we could have achieved more; a second was bidding for symposia at
major academic gatherings such as the Academy of Management, Strategic
Management Society and European Group for Organization Studies. Here we

were very successful in competitive circumstances. This achieved visibility and impact for our work in refereed conditions. As important, these symposia allowed four or five papers to be presented from the INNFORM programme with sometimes visibility for upwards of eight to twelve members of the overall team. This collective effort and collective display, in turn, led to collective success and collective reinforcement. These symposia were of enormous value in building the internal and external identity of the INNFORM programme. They were also important stepping stones to journal articles and to the two books we have now published from the research.

Holding a diverse team together for six years with the resources running out and with competing loyalties is a great challenge. Our double book contract with Sage Publications was a critical part of our strategy for holding the team together and for delivering outputs which we hoped would have an impact. Both books were focal points for constructive and continuing effort and have and will become emblematic of the INNFORM research aspirations. The effort to produce both books was very considerable. This effort illustrates well the combination of individual and shared leadership so necessary in international collaborative research.

Our earlier brief discussion of leadership processes in GDTs identified the apparently dual nature of leadership requirements. On the one hand, there was a leading-from-the-front dimension which involved shaping strategy and building and maintaining the team rhythm (Maznevski and Chudoba, 2000), together with focus, discipline and clear discussion making and follow through (Armstrong and Cole, 1995). On the other hand, there was also evidence of the importance of building shared reality and common ground which would facilitate deeper dialogue and enhanced trust (Cramton, 2001). Snow et al., 1996 also pinpointed the importance of different forms of leadership in the team at different points in time. It seems there is a prima-facie case for both directive and democratic leadership and for singular and dispersed leadership in international collaborative activities. Fashioning such a leadership process in a team with culturally laced views of appropriate leader behaviour is another major challenge. Thus on the more structuring end of the continuum one was faced with views such as:

> [We needed] through preparation of the joint meetings, including agendas and a clear sense of what has to be accomplished. I remember various meetings that were as such cosy, but in terms of output not productive.

While on the more democratic end:

> Leadership is crucial. However, I believe a programme like this could have been still more successful with a more collective, collegial type of leadership ... A more collective leadership fosters both more dialogue and more motivation from involved teams.

Another co-leader commented on the changing pattern of leadership over time from what he described as a singular leadership to a confused, shared leadership, which was productive. He elaborated by pointing again to the dual requirements:

> In the end you need one person to be ultimately responsible and to be constantly energizing and driving the work forward. But it is also useful to have elements of shared leadership and the divergent contributions that come from this.

Another co-leader painted a picture I can recall all too clearly: 'Personal authority is very important; continued relentless co-ordination and chasing; some smoothing of ruffled feathers was required too'.

But the real leadership tests come when the unexpected comes to the surface, or when one group, for whatever reason, challenges the espoused values of the overall group:

> Occasional opportunism and rivalry are bound to appear. In such cases, it is important for the research co-ordinator to strive for as complete information as possible, to balance his own and the wider group interests, and to be seen to propose some kind of procedural justice.

There were, in fact, three dramas in the development of the INNFORM programme which mobilized the attentions of all the national teams. One was a case of perceived 'free riding' which, when challenged, led to the early exit of one of the teams. The second arose from problems of accessing the survey data from one of the national teams. The third was again perceptually driven and again contestable, but involved perceptions of opportunism by one of the teams. Our review of research on GRTs signalled how cultural mis-understandings and mis-attributions can both surface and escalate problems and lead to an unproductive atmosphere of blaming (Jarvenpaa and Leidner, 1999; Sessa et al., 1999; Cramton, 2001). All these processes surfaced around our three dramas and effectively delayed the problem solving which helped to resolve or accommodate the problems.

It should be clear that the transaction costs of international collaborative research are extremely high, and with or without the duality of directed and shared leadership, many of these costs are borne by the overall team leader/co-ordinator. In my view these costs are worth bearing because of the satisfactions and collegiality of this sort of inquiry, and also with the realization that the knowledge generated could not have been achieved in any other way.

Having examined some of the processes and dynamics of the INNFORM programme, is it possible to make any reliable assessments of its success? Evaluating research is also precarious and is dependent not just on the criteria of evaluation, but also on who is doing the evaluation, and when. At this early stage we have only one independent summative review of the research. That was carried out by anonymous reviewers appointed by the main funders of the research, the ESRC. In November 2000 the ESRC evaluation process deemed our final report 'outstanding' on the four point scale 'outstanding', 'good', 'problematic' and 'unacceptable'. The ESRC define outstanding as 'high quality research making an important contribution to the development of the subject. An outstanding grade indicates a project has fully met its objectives and has provided an exceptional research contribution well above average or very high in relation to the level of the award'. To give some perspective to this grading, on average 20 per cent of all the ESRC final reports from all research disciplines are awarded the outstanding grade, and 12 per cent of the ESRC awards for management research receive the outstanding rating (Evaluation Division of the ESRC).

I asked the INNFORM team members, senior and more junior, about their views of success and failure and received some very interesting commentary using quite different criteria of evaluation:

> I think it was clearly a success. I would do it again. This is the ultimate view of success, despite the difficulties. We also have relationships to carry forward into the future. ... But it was a reasonable success in terms of publications. (Co-leader A)

> It was partly a success experience. A number of excellent teams were brought together and good data from both the survey and case studies were produced. Some very interesting results have been developed ... It was partly a failure experience, not being able to keep the whole set of teams together. (Co-leader B)

> On the whole it was a success, in absolute terms for sure. In input/output terms significantly less so, as the co-ordination and travel effort was considerable and the academic output in terms of journal articles perhaps less than we would have originally wished. This might be too narrow an output measure. I learnt a lot more personally from being in a network, and we have all built/consolidated international links. A lot of the sheer fun came from these links ... my learning is that interdisciplinarity is painful, takes a lot of time to absorb the benefits of, requires big effort in terms of mutual respect, but is ultimately worthwhile. (Co-leader C)

> In my view the research collaboration was definitely not a failure, but also not the success I expected because of the moderate direct research output and the unproductive frictions within the research group. (Co-leader D)

> It has been a success because of the multiple perspectives and different backgrounds of the people. We've also produced some clear outputs, the two books, many articles and the multiple presentations to international scholarly gatherings. On a personal level for me, it has also been a success. I learnt a great deal about the content and process of doing this kind of international work. (Co-leader E)

This account of the INNFORM programme is perhaps tilted too much to the perspectives and experience of the senior members of the overall team. We should not forget that the middle ranks of all the national teams played an irreplaceable part in the task and social dimensions of the work. I have already mentioned the crucial role that Simon Peck and Silvia Massini played on the survey side of the project. For a time the other Warwick based Research Fellow, Evelyn Fenton played an equally important role in day-to-day contact between the international teams and in laying down and codifying some of the methodological and analytical frameworks for our case study work. Other important team members included the four doctoral students who worked with us and who achieved their doctorates through the INNFORM experience. In retrospect I can see how crucial to team success were the on-going cross country, informal relationships between the middle and more junior members of the wider INNFORM team. It was at this level that much of the local and situated knowledge (Sole and Edmondson, 2002) of the team was shared, understood and utilized. In that sense most of the shared learning on the INNFORM programme was occurring in a rather natural and informal way between and among the middle and more junior members of the team. These opportunites were enhanced by some of the doctoral students and team members circulating between the teams and thereby transferring knowledge and skill across the INNFORM network. It is now clear that this transfer of people and ideas was essential to uncover what Cramton (2001) has described as the hidden profiles of GDTs. Of course, the INNFORM experience was also a great learning experience for these doctoral students. As one commented:

> It was a great learning opportunity to be involved in a big project and see how the different academics and schools approached and handled the same problem. ... It opened me up. I have been in a particular school with a particular Professor with very particular views. I could see from several other very senior Professors that there were different research orientations and styles. For me this was very helpful – almost liberating. It allowed me more freedom and was a crucial step in my development. ... It also opened up the academic world for me with a network of scholars that I can return to for help and to work with.

So the INNFORM programme substantially achieved its explicit goals of knowledge development, but also offered personal learning and development for all the different experience levels in the team. But what of the other important dimension of engagement for the INNFORM programme, the co-production of knowledge with PricewaterhouseCoopers? It is to this partnership engagement we now turn.

## ENGAGING RESEARCH WITH PRACTICE

Appropriately enough at a time of change, the relationship between science and society is also undergoing change. Earlier in this chapter I noted some of the dimensions of this change and drew attention to the liberating thoughts of Gibbons et al., 1994 and Nowotny et al., 2001. These debates are now firmly centre stage in the various fields of management (Hodgkinson, 2001). Elsewhere I have articulated my own position in these emerging views of the strengths and weaknesses of management research (Pettigrew, 1997b, 2001). It is the duty of the intellectual in society to make a difference, but the management research communities throughout the world have a long way to go to realize the potential they may have to make a difference. Realizing that potential is much tied up with aspirations to conduct research which meets the double hurdle of scholarly quality and relevance. New opportunities to do precisely that are now appearing with the wholesale questioning of modernist science. Central to this critique of modernism are the arguments and evidence used to undermine scientific claims for rationality, universalism and autonomy. After modernism, and reflecting the more complex, dynamic and internationally conscious world we live in, there is a recognition that any search for general patterns should give much greater significance to temporal and spatial context. Generalizations are hard to sustain over time; they are even tougher to uphold across international, institutional and cultural borders. After modernism, the new excitement to explore time and dynamics will perhaps help to overturn many management researchers' preoccupations with *what is* knowledge and foster a climate where *how to* knowledge is given a higher priority (Pettigrew, 2001). Management research which delivers both *what is* and *how to* knowledge is much more likely to meet the challenge of scholarly quality and relevance. In this volume the most obvious juxtaposition of *what is* and *how to* knowledge is provided in the relationship between the econometric analysis of complementarities in Chapter 7 and complementarities in action in Chapter 8. Both types of knowledge can be valuable, but their value is considerably enhanced when they are located side by side.

A further contention is that the new opportunities for a contextualist and dynamic social science will offer management researchers an additional and attractive bridge to the users of that research. (Pettigrew, 2001). But again this is more of an aspiration than an accomplishment for many of us. And there are many practical difficulties engaging with the range of stakeholders who are potentially interested in management research. These can be variously labelled as users, consumers, funders, co-producers, subjects, gatekeepers and translation of research. Even the user category is diverse, ambiguous and contestable. Drawing on actual accounts of experienced researchers, Robson and Shove (1999) note that user interest in research is fickle and highly time- and context-dependent. Woolgar (2000) has written about the related issue of identifying user needs in research. He notes that user needs are rarely so self-evident that they can be observed and acted upon: 'instead we should accept that user needs rarely pre-exist the efforts and activities of producers to engage with them' (Woolgar, 2000: 169).

Woolgar's (2000) astute observation rests, of course, on the assumption that producers and users of research are two separate categories of person and that production and use are two distinct activities. But this need not be the case. There is the possibility of engaging researchers and users in a collaborative process of co-funding, co-producing and co-dissemination of research and this is precisely what the INNFORM programme had in mind in its relationship with PricewaterhouseCoopers (PWC).

### PricewaterhouseCoopers and the INNFORM Programme

User engagement with research often rests upon quality informal interaction established between researchers and practitioners over long periods of time. It is also often dependent on the institutional position of user and researcher. This was clearly the case with the link with Coopers & Lybrand. I had worked before with Coopers & Lybrand on two previous research projects. One of these had been an ESRC-financed study of the competitiveness of British industry, eventually published in Pettigrew and Whipp (1991). The other project involved Warwick subcontracting a piece of research work to Coopers & Lybrand. We had learned a number of important lessons from these earlier collaborations which were taken into the 1995 ESRC proposal. One of these lessons was about the commitment stake of co-funding. Another was to try and ensure the practitioner presence was built into the original project design and questions, and that a senior practitioner was given access to the on-going project meetings and dissemination activities of the research. This required clear contracting on both sides. The senior practitioner was welcomed in and expected to contribute not just as a co-funder, but also a co-producer and disseminator of knowledge. And the practitioner's presence in the university research environment, and therefore away from the 'day job' at the consultancy firm, was decreed a legitimate activity and part of the reward and recognition system of the senior Coopers consultant who worked with us. There was also an issue of the seniority level of the Coopers research sponsor, and the personal characteristics and motivations of the senior Coopers person who was the week-to-week 'bridge' with the research team. We were fortunate on both accounts. Paul Batchelor, at that time the European Executive Partner of Coopers & Lybrand Europe, was our overall sponsor who committed the financial and political resources; and first Chris David and later David Shaw were the two senior Coopers consultants who worked with us on a week-by-week basis. All three of these individuals had strong conceptual abilities, were interested in ideas, and took a positive view of the potential of management research to have an impact on scholarships and on practice. Issues of team selection are as important on the practitioner side as on the academic side in collaborations of this kind.

Our contacts in Coopers were involved in the project proposal which went to the ESRC in March 1995. In that proposal Paul Batchelor committed his and Chris David's time and £75 000 over three years. Crucially he also noted that their contribution would include:

- expert advice and comment on the overall course of the project and the findings as they materialized
- guidance and support in identifying candidate companies for in-depth case analysis
- guidance and support in the communication and dissemination of findings, particularly throughout the international business community.

Coopers & Lybrand (later PricewaterhouseCoopers (PWC)) delivered on all of these commitments. In terms of access they provided part of their European network as a case (Fenton and Pettigrew, 2000b and Chapter 9 of this volume). In April 1998 they organized a pan-European conference in Brussels on our research findings, which was attended by senior executives and consultants from throughout Europe. David Shaw and I also prepared a PWC White Paper on our research findings, which was circulated throughout PWC worldwide, and we had an article in Volume 1, (1) of the European Business Forum (Pettigrew and Shaw, 2000). I was also provided with the opportunity to present our work to senior executives at one of the regular PWC executive breakfasts in London. In the week-by-week project meetings we also benefited enormously from the wide network of company experiences and consultancy thinking held by our two PWC colleagues. They were also prepared to challenge what they considered to be loose thinking about theory, method and interpretation of findings and tolerated some of the less business-like aspects of our project meetings.

In no sense do we hold up this PWC partnership as typical or exemplary practice. However, it was good experience from which we both learned a great deal. Conscious of this learning potential, I met with one of the PWC consultants at the end of the programme to discuss what they were looking for from co-production and co-dissemination with us, and the extent to which he felt we provided what they were looking for. In retrospect it is clear that although we had contracted very clearly with PWC from the outset about what they would provide by way of support and guidance, we did not contract very clearly at all with them about what their desires and needs were from the partnership. This was probably a mistake, although if we follow Woolgar's (2000) observation that user needs may be very difficult to pre-form and can only be really seen in the context of the research, it might have been difficult to reliably contract about needs. Nevertheless, after the research PWC were able to specify quite clearly their three desires: they were solutions, evidence and promotion.

By solutions they meant a combination of conceptual frameworks, benchmarks, diagnostics and methods. Frameworks and ideas are self-evident, but what of the other three desires? By benchmarking they meant comparable data across firms and industries; by diagnostics they meant survey instruments or frameworks they could use in consultancy practices to diagnose the position of firms; by methods they meant an intervention process they could use to intervene in their client settings in the area of organizational change. It seems we had offering on the first three of these solution desires but not the fourth, intervention methods.

But what about evidence? Here they were looking for broad-based data, which they certainly got. Case studies of best practice from visible organizations was the second evidence desire. Here they had a mixed reaction, some of our cases were very visible across Europe and some were much less so. They also desired industry-specific data and comparisons and here the limited sectoral analysis of our quantitative data set was a frustration to them. They also wanted relevant and topical information. Our data was often relevant, but the relatively slow speed with which the international research progressed meant that we lost some topicality in that process. The key desire that we met, however, was the unusual ability we had to offer in analysis of performance outcomes (as in Chapter 7 of this volume), and the analysis of the processes which delivered those outcomes, (as in Chapter 8). These are a powerful combination of findings which have great practical value and PWC were able to quickly absorb them into their consultancy practice. When I pointed out that all social science research with a dependent variable of performance is contestable, our PWC colleague commented:

> We prefer contestable results than the researcher who said, 'we can't get perfect or near perfect data, let's not bother posing that question and seeking a more limited answer'.

But the big message here is that partnership research with industry which combines quantitative and qualitative data, has a clear dependent variable, and also examines how the outcomes are produced through a process analysis are likely to be perceived to be of scholarly quality and relevance. The juxtaposition of *what* knowledge with *how to* knowledge was a major strength of our research strategy which substantially affected the quality of the industry partnership.

The third set of PWC desires were encapsulated under the label of promotion. Here there were three interrelated issues. First, they valued the independence and reputation of the research team and team leaders. Second, they valued the promotion possibilities of capturing the findings early because of their involvement in the production of the knowledge. The co-production process allowed PWC to understand the ideas behind the data, to have a deeper appreciation of the strengths and the limitations of the data, and to build the ideas into their practice that much earlier than if they had waited for the normal timescale of academic publishing. Of course, on the promotion front they were also interested in attention-grabbing themes.

Here our work on complementarities, process and performance provided the best opportunity, and we collaborated with PWC on a number of occasions to do precisely that.

## CONCLUSION

After modernism we are entering a period of experimentation and learning in the social production of knowledge. As an interdisciplinary set of fields with the requirement to meet the double hurdle of scholarly quality and relevance, management research is particularly well placed to engage with this experimentation and learning. But as we widen and deepen our concept and practice of scholarship, we need also to be more open and reflective about that practice. The INNFORM programme has pushed the boundaries of scholarship out on a number of interrelated fronts. We have approached our theme of innovative forms of organizing from an interdisciplinary and an international perspective. We have used multiple methods to produce complementary findings. We have delivered *what* knowledge and *how to* knowledge, and we have taken seriously spatial and temporal context in our analyses. We have engaged in a form of collaborative inquiry which has mobilized the attentions of nine universities on three continents. We have entered a partnership with PWC for the co-funding, co-production and co-dissemination of knowledge. Finally, we have sought to be open and reflective about our practice, recognizing that we do not claim our work is exemplary, merely that it has been novel and challenging.

In many respects our practice has mirrored our findings. We have claimed that our findings have not discovered dualities, but merely shown that in developing innovative forms of organizing our sample of organizations has further accelerated the creation and impact of these dualities. In turn, the emergence of bundles of dualities in the same organization have created a new level of complexity which has had to be managed, often by periodic hunts for simplifying routines and solutions. What is striking to me about this account of our practice of knowledge production is how many of the dualities we observed in our companies have also been present in our collaborative inquiry. So we have had to have elements of a hierarchy and a network. We have faced simultaneous pressures to centralize and decentralize, and we have been standardizing and customizing, and balancing needs for continuity and change in our activities and relationships.

I see these bundles of dualities being expressed in a number of challenges. A central one of these is to be aware of the complexities created by the bundles of dualities, and to keep some level of control over the transaction costs of the processes of the programme, including the demands of delivering the programme outcomes. These challenges raise the issue of the leadership process in this kind of international inquiry. Here we have identified some further dualities. Notable among these is the simultaneous pressure for forms of directed and democratic leadership, and singular and shared leadership. This volume would have never appeared without someone taking charge of the process and driving that process. Equally well, the book is very much a shared endeavour, and the volume is that much more creative for the shared way in which it was designed and delivered.

The success of the INNFORM programme rests on a multiple set of factors – a complementary system of mutually reinforcing elements. As we saw in Chapter 8, complementary change means not just doing lots of things together, but doing them consistently and staying the course. Above all, complementary change which enhances performance is not just about great vision, but is about delivery. A plea for more openness and more pluralism in research conduct is a noble thought which is captured well in the old Platonic adage that the unexamined life is not worth living. But awareness is nought without action, and collective action in creative processes is among the most challenging action of all.

# References

Abbott, A.D. (1988) *The System of Professions: An Essay on the Division of Expert Labour*. Chicago: University of Chicago Press.

Abbott, A.D. (1997) 'Of time and space: the contemporary advances of the Chicago school', *Social Forces*, 75 (4): 1149–82.

Achtenhagen, L. (2001) *Coordination in New Forms of Organising: An Empirical Study*. Diss. Universität St.Gallen.

Adler, N., Shani, R. and Styhrg, A. (eds) (2003) *Collaborative Research in Organizations: Enabling Learning, Change and Theory Development*. London: Sage Publications.

Adler, P. and Borys, B. (1996) 'Two types of bureaucracy: enabling and coercive', *Administrative Science Quarterly*, 41: 61–89.

Allred, B.B., Snow, C.C. and Miles, R.E. (1996) 'Characteristics of managerial careers in the 21st century', *Academy of Management Executive*, 10 (4): 17–26.

Amabile, T.M. (1996) *Creativity in Context*. Boulder, Colorado: Westview Press.

Aoki, M. (1990) 'Toward an economic model of the Japanese firm', *Journal of Economic Literature*, 28 (8).

Argyris, C. (1976) 'Single-loop and double-loop models in research on decision making', *Administrative Science Quarterly*, 21: 363–75.

Argyris, C. and Schön, D. (1978) *Organizational Learning: A Theory of Action Perspective*. Reading, MA: Addison-Wesley.

Armstrong, D.J. and Cole, P. (1995) 'Managing distances and differences in geographically distributed work groups', in S.E. Jackson and M.N. Ruderman (eds), *Diversity in Work Teams*. Washington DC: American Psychological Association.

Armstrong, P. (1985) 'Changing management control strategies: the role of competition between accountancy and other organisational professions', *Accounting, Organization and Society*, 10/2: 129–48.

Arthur, J.B. (1994) 'Effects of human resource systems on manufacturing performance and turnover', *Academy of Management Journal*, 37: 670–87.

Arthur, M.B. and Rousseau, D.M. (eds) (1996) *The Boundaryless Career*. New York: Oxford University Press.

Arthur, W.B. (1994) *Increasing Returns and Path Dependence in the Economy*. Ann Arbor, MI: Michigan University Press.

Ashmos, D.P. and Huber, G.P. (1987) 'The systems paradigm in organization theory: Correcting the record and suggesting the future', *Academy of Management Review*, 12: 607–21.

Axelsson, B. and Easton, G. (eds) (1992) *Industrial Networks: A New View of Reality*. London: Routledge.

Baden-Fuller, C. (1993) 'The globalization of professional service firms: Evidence from four case studies', in T. Aharoni (ed.), *Coalitions and Competition*. London: Routledge: pp. 102–20.

Bahrami, H. (1992) 'The emerging flexible organization: perspectives from Silicon Valley', *California Management Review*, Summer: 35–52.

Baker, W.E. (1992) 'The network organization in theory and practice', in N. Nohria and R.G. Eccles (eds), *Networks and Organizations. Structure, Form, and Action*. Boston: Harvard Business School Press. pp. 397–429.

Bakker, T. (1994) 'Against the tide', *The Banker*, May: 23–4.

Baldwin, T.T., Danielson, C. and Wiggenhorn, W. (1997) 'The Evolution of Learning Strategies in Organizations: From Employee Development to Business Redefinition', *The Academy of Management Executive*, 11: 47–58.

Baligh, H.H. (1994) 'Components of culture: nature, interconnections, and relevance to the decisions on the organization structure', *Management Science*, 40: 14–27.

Banker, R.D., Field, J.M., Schroeder, R.G. and Sinha, K.K. (1996) 'Impact of work teams on manufacturing performance: a longitudinal field study', *Academy of Management Journal*, 39: 867–90.

Barham, K. and Heimer, C. (1998) *ABB – The Dancing Giant: Creating the Globally Connected Company*. London: Financial Times/Pitman.

Barley, S. and Tolbert, P. (1997) 'Institutionalization and structuration', *Organization Studies*, 18 (1): 93–118.

Baron, D.P. (1996) *Business and its Environment*. (second edition) Upper Saddle River, NJ: Prentice Hall.

Barr, P.S. (1998) 'Adapting to unfamiliar environmental events: A look at the evolution of interpretation and its role in strategic change', *Organization Science*, 9 (6): 644–69.

Barr, P.S., Stimpert, J.L. and Huff, A.S. (1992) 'Cognitive change, strategic action, and organizational renewal', *Strategic Management Journal*, 13: 15–36.

Bartlett, C.A. and Ghoshal, S. (1987) 'Managing across borders: new organizational responses', *Sloan Management Review*, 43, Fall: 43–53.

Bartlett, C.A. and Ghoshal, S. (1989) *Managing Beyond Borders*. Boston: Harvard Business School Press.

Bartlett, C.A. and Ghoshal, S. (1993) 'Beyond the M-form: toward a managerial theory of the firm', *Strategic Management Journal*, 14 (Winter Special Issue): 23–46.

Bartlett, C.A. and Ghoshal, S. (1995) 'Changing the role of top management: beyond systems to people', *Harvard Business Review*, May–June, 132–42.

Bartol, L. (1979) 'Professionalism as a predictor of organizational commitment, role stress, and turnovers: a multidimensional approach', *Academy of Management Journal*, 22: 815–21.

Bartunek, J.M. (1984) 'Changing interpretive schemes and organizational restructuring: the example of a religious order', *Administrative Science Quarterly*, 29: 355–72.

Bass, B.M. (1985) *Leadership and Performance Beyond Expectations*. New York: Free Press.

Bass, B.M. (1990) *Bass & Stogdill's Handbook of Leadership*. New York: The Free Press.

Bate, P., Khan, R. and Pye, A. (2000) 'Towards a culturally sensitive approach to organization structuring: where organizational design meets organizational development', *Organization Science*, 11: 197–211.

Baum, J.A.C. (1996) 'Organizational ecology', in *Handbook of Organization Studies*, Clegg, S., Hardy, C. and Nord, W. (eds), London: Sage. pp. 77–114.

Baum, J.A.C. and Singh, J.V. (1994) 'Organization–environment coevolution', in J.A.C. Baum and J.V. Singh (eds), *Evolutionary Dynamics of Organizations*. New York: Oxford University Press. pp. 379–402.

Becker, G.S. (1964) *Human Capital*. New York: Columbia University Press.

Bell, D. (1973) *The Coming of Post-Industrial Society*. New York: Basic Books.

Bendix, R. (1956) *Work and Authority in Industry: Ideologies of Management in the Course of Industrialization*. New York: Wiley.

Bennis, W.G., and Nanus, B. (1985) *Leaders: The Strategies for Taking Charge*. New York: Harper & Row.

Berger, P.L. and Luckmann, T. (1967) *The Social Construction of Reality*. Garden City, NY: Doubleday & Co.

Berger, S. and Dore, R.P. (eds) (1996) *National Diversity and Global Capitalism*. Ithaca: Cornell University Press.

Bettis, R.A. and Prahalad, C.K. (1995) 'The dominant logic: retrospective and extension', *Strategic Management Journal*, 16: 5–14.

Birkinshaw, J. and Morrison, A. (1995) 'Configurations of strategy and structure in subsidiaries of multinational corporations', *Journal of International Business Studies*, 26 (4): 729–53.

BIS (2000) 'International banking and financial markets developments', *Quarterly Review*.

Blackler, F. (1995) 'Knowledge, knowledge work and organizations: an overview and interpretation', *Organization Studies*, 16 (6): 1021–46.

Blaug, M. (1997) *Economic Theory in Retrospect* (fifth edition, first in 1962). Cambridge, UK: Cambridge University Press.

Bleicher, K. (1999) *Das Konzept Integriertes Management: Visionen – Missionen – Programme* [The concept of integrative management: visions – missions – programmes] (fifth edition) Frankfurt/New York: Campus.

Blomquist, C. (1996) *I Marknadens Namn – Mångtydiga Reformer i Svenska Kommuner*. Stockholm: Nerenius och Santérus.

Bogner, W. and Barr, P. (2000) 'Making sense in hypercompetitive environments: a cognitive explanation for the persistence of high velocity environments', *Organization Science*, 11 (2): 212–26.

Boston Consulting Group (2000) 'Global Payments 2000/1', 66 pp.

Bouchikhi, H. (1998) 'Living with and building on complexity: a constructivist perspective on organizations', *Organization*, 5 (2): 217–32.

Bourdieu, P. (1990) *The Logic of Practice*. Oxford: Polity.

Boutellier, R., Cassman, O. and Von Zeowitz, M. (1999) *Managing Global Innovation*. Springer Berlin and Heidelberg-Verlag.

Bouwen, R. and Fry, R. (1991) 'Organizational Innovation and Learning', *International Studies of Management and Organization*, 21: 37–51.

Bower, G.H. and Hilgard, E.R. (1981) *Theories of Learning*. Englewood Cliffs, NJ: Prentice-Hall.

Bowman, E.H. and Singh, H. (1993) 'Corporate restructuring: reconfiguring the firm', *Strategic Management Journal*, 14: 5–14.

Breshnaham, T., Brynjolfsson, E. and Hitt, L. (2002) 'Information technology, workplace organization and the demand for skilled labour: firm level evidence', *Quarterly Journal of Economics*, 117 (1): 339–76.

Brewster, C. (2003) 'HRM: the comparative dimension', in J. Storey (ed.), *Human Resource Management: A Critical Text*. London: Thompson Learning Business Press.

Brewster, C., Tregaskis, O., Hegewisch, A. and Mayne, L. (1996) 'Comparative research in human resource management', *International Journal of Human Resource Management*, 7 (3): 585–604.

Bridges, W. (1994) *JobShift. How to Prosper in a Workplace without Jobs*. Reading, MA: Addison-Wesley.

Bridges, W. (1996) 'Leading the "de-jobbed" organization', in F. Hesselbein, M. Goldsmith and R. Beckhard (eds), *The Leader of the Future*. San Francisco: Jossey-Bass. pp. 11–18.

Brislin, R. (1993) *Understanding Culture's Influence on Behavior*. Fort Worth: TX: Harcourt Brace.

Brousseau, K.R., Driver, M.J., Eneroth, K. and Rikard, L. (1996) 'Career pandemonium: realigning organizations and individuals', *Academy of Management Executive*, 10 (4): 52–66.

Brown, S.J. and Duguid, P. (1998) 'Organizing Knowledge', *California Management Review*, 40 (3): 90–111.

Brown, A.D. and Starkey, K. (2000) 'Organizational Identity and Learning: A Psychodynamic Perspective', *Academy of Management Review*, 25: 102–20.

Bryce, D.J. and Singh, J.V. (2001) 'The future of the firm from an evolutionary perspective', in P. Di Maggio (ed.), *The Twenty-First-Century Firm*, Princeton: Princeton University Press. pp. 161–185.

Bühner, R. (1987) 'Addressing international diversification of West German corporations', *Strategic Management Journal*, 8: 25–37.

Bühner, R. (1991) 'Management holding: ein Erfahrungsbericht', *Die Betriebwirthschaft*, 2: 141–51.

Burgelman, R.A. (1983) 'A process model of internal corporate venturing in the diversified major firm', *Administrative Science Quarterly*, 28: 223–44.

Burns, J.M. (1978) *Leadership*. New York: Harper & Row.

Burns, T. and Stalker, G.M. (1961) *The Management of Innovation*. London: Tavistock Publications.

Burt, R.S. (1997) 'The contingent value of social capital', *Administrative Science Quarterly*, 42: 339–65.

Caligiuri, P.M. and Stroh, L.K. (1995) 'Multinational corporation management strategies and international human resource practices: bringing international HR to the bottom line', *International Journal of Human Resource Management*, 6: 494–507.

Calori, R. (2002) 'Organizational development and the ontology of creative dialectial evolution', *Organization*, 9 (1): 127–50.

Calori, R., Johnson, G. and Sarnin, P. (1994) 'CEO's cognitive maps and the scope of the organization', *Strategic Management Journal*, 15: 437–57.

Calori, R., Lubatkin, M., Very, P. and Veiga, J.F. (1997) 'Modelling the origins of nationally-bound administrative heritages: a historical institutional analysis of French and British firms', *Organization Science*, 8 (6): 681–96.

Cameron, K. (1986) 'Effectiveness as paradox: consensus and conflict in conceptions of organizational effectiveness', *Management Science*, 32: 539–53.

Cappelli, P. (1999) *The New Deal at Work*. Boston: Harvard Business School Press.

Cappelli, P. and Crocker-Hefter, A. (1996) 'Distinctive human resources are firm's core competencies', *Organizational Dynamics*, 24: 7–22.

Castells, M. (1996) *The Rise of the Network Society*, Volume 1. Oxford: Blackwell.

Cavusgil, S.T. and Das, A. (1997) 'Methodological issues in empirical cross-cultural research: a survey of the management literature and a framework', *Management International Review*, 37 (1): 71–96.

Chakravarthy, B.S. and Doz, Y. (1992) 'Strategy process research: Focusing on corporate self-renewal', *Strategic Management Journal*, 13: 5–14.

Chakravarthy, B. and White, R. (2002) 'Strategy Process: Forming, Implementing and Changing Strategies', in A.M. Pettigrew, H. Thomas, R. Whittington (eds), *The Handbook of Strategy and Management*. London: Sage. pp. 182–205.

Chandler, A.D. (1962) *Strategy and Structure: Chapters in the History of the American Industrial Enterprise*. Cambridge, MA: The MIT Press.

Chandler, A.D. (1990) *Scale and Scope: the Dynamics of Industrial Capitalism*. Cambridge, MA: Harvard University Press.

Chattopadhyay, P., Glick, W.H., Chet Miller, C. and Huber, G.P. (1999) 'Determinants of executive beliefs: comparing functional conditioning and social influence', *Strategic Management Journal*, 20: 763–89.

Chia, R. (1995) 'From modern to postmodern organizational analysis', *Organization Studies*, 16 (4): 580–602.

Chia, R. (1997) 'Thirty years on: from organization structures to the organization of thought', *Organization Studies*, 18 (4): 685–708.

Child, J. (1984) *Organization: A Guide to Problems and Practice* (second edition). London: Harper & Row.

Child, J. and Kieser, A. (1979) 'Organization and managerial roles in British and West German companies: an examination of the culture-free thesis', in C.J. Lammers and D. Hickson (eds), *Organizations Alike and Unlike: International and Inter-institutional Studies in Sociology of Organizations.* London: Routledge & Kegan Paul. pp. 251–71.

Ciucci, R. (1995) 'Martin Hilti aufs Wort', in: *Martin Hilti zum 80: Geburtstag* [Martin Hilti on his 80th Birthday], Schaan: Hilti, 17–47.

Clark, K. and Fujimoto, T. (1991) *Product Development in the World Automobile Industry.* Boston: Harvard Business School Press.

Clegg, S. (1999) 'Globalizing the intelligent organization: learning organizations, smart workers, (not so) clever countries and the sociological imagination', *Management Learning*, 30 (3): 259–80.

Cohen, W.M. and Levinthal, D.A. (1990) 'Absorptive capacity: a new perspective on learning and innovation', *Administrative Science Quarterly*, 35: 128–52.

Cohen, M.D., March, J.G. and Olsen, J.P. (1972) 'A garbage can model of organizational choice', *Administrative Science Quarterly*, 17: 1–25.

Collins, J.C. and Porras, J.I. (1991) 'Organizational vision and visionary organizations', *California Management Review*, 34 (1): 30–52.

Collins, J.C. and Porras, J.I. (1994) *Built to Last: Successful Habits of Visionary Companies.* New York: Harper Business.

Collinson, S. and Pettigrew, A.M. (2003) 'Methodological and analytical issues in international comparative research', Working Paper, Coventry, UK: Warwick Business School.

Conger, J.A. and Konungo, R.N. (1987) 'Towards a behavioral theory of charismatic leadership in organizational setting', *Academy of Management Review*, 12: 637–47.

Contractor, F.J. and Lorange, P. (1988) *Cooperative Strategies in International Business: Joint Ventures and Technology Partnership between Firms.* New York: Lexington Books.

Contractor, F.J. and Lorange, P. (2002) *Cooperative Strategies and Alliances.* Pergamon, Amsterdam.

Cooper, D.J., Hinings, B., Greenwood, R. and Brown, J. (1996) 'Sedimentation and transformation in organizational change: the case of Canadian law firms', *Organization Studies*, 17 (4): 623–47.

Corner, P.D., Kinicki, A.J. and Keats, B.W. (1994) 'Integrating organizational and individual information processing perspectives on choice', *Organization Science*, 5 (3): 294–308.

Coviello, N.E. and McAuley, A. (1999) 'Internationalisation and the smaller firm: a review of contemporary empirical research', *Management International Review*, 39 (3): 223.

Craig, T. (1995). 'Achieving innovation through bureaucracy: lessons from the Japanese brewing industry', *Organization Science*, 38 (1): 8–36.

Cramton, C.D. (2001) 'The mutual knowledge problem and its consequences for dispersed collaboration', *Organization Science*, 12 (3): 346–71.

Crossan, M.M., Lane, H.W. and White, R.E. (1999) 'An organizational learning framework: from intuition to institution', *Academy of Management Review*, 24: 522–37.

Cyert, R.M. and March, J.G. (1963) *A Behavioral Theory of the Firm*. Englewood Cliffs, NJ: Prentice-Hall.

Cyert, R.M. and March, J.G. (1992) *A Behavioral Theory of the Firm*, (second edition, first edition 1963). Oxford: Blackwell.

Czarniawska, B. (1997) *Narrating the Organization*. Chicago: The University of Chicago Press.

Czarniawska-Joerges, B. (1992) *Exploring Complex Organizations: A Cultural Perspective*. Newbury Park: Sage.

Czarniawska, B. and Sevon, G. (eds) (1996) *Translating Organizational Change*. Berlin: De Gruyter.

Dacin, M.T., Ventresca, M.J. and Beal, B.D. (1999) 'The embeddedness of organizations: dialogue and directions', *Journal of Management*, 25 (3): 317–56.

Daft, R.L. (1992) *Organization Theory and Design*. Saint Paul, MN: West.

Daft, R.L. (1999) *Leadership – Theory and Practice*. Fort Worth: The Dryden Press.

Daft, R.L. and Weick, K.E. (1984) 'Toward a model of organizations as interpretive systems', *Academy of Management Review*, 9: 284–95.

Damanpour, F. and Evan, W. (1984) 'Organizational innovation and performance: the problem of organisational "lag"', *Administrative Science Quarterly*, 29: 392–409.

D'Aveni, R. (1994) *Hypercompetition: Managing the Dynamics of Strategic Manoeuvring*. New York: Free Press.

Davidson, A. (1997) 'The Davidson Interview: Niall FitzGerald', *Management Today*, November: 50–54.

Day, J. (2001) 'Organizing for growth', *McKinsey Quarterly*, 2: 4–6.

Deal, T.E. and Kennedy, A.A. (1982) *Corporate Cultures: The Rites and Rituals of Corporate Life*. Reading, MA: Addison-Wesley.

Dean, J.W. and Susman, G.I. (1989) 'Strategic responses to global competition: advanced technology, organization design, and human resource practices', in C.C. Snow (ed.), *Strategy, Organization, and Human Resource Management*. Greenwich, CT: JAI Press. pp. 297–331.

De Certeau, M. (1984) *The Practice of Everyday Life*. Berkeley: University of California Press.

De Certeau, M., Girard, L. and Mayoi, P. (1998) *The Practice of Everyday Life Vol. 2, Living and Cooking*. Minnesota: University of Minnesota Press.

Deloitte Research (1999) 'Millennium top 10: global banking and securities industry outlook'.

Denis, J-L., Langley, A. and Cazale, L. (1996) 'Leadership and strategic change under ambiguity', *Organization Studies*, 17 (4): 673–97.

Denison, D.R. (1997) 'Towards a process-based theory of organizational design' in *Advances in Strategic Management*, Vol.14. Greenwich, CT: JAI Press. pp. 1–44.

Denzin, N.K. (1978) *The Research Act* (second edition). New York: McGraw-Hill.

Dess, G. and Robinson, R. (1984) 'Measuring organisational performance in the absence of objective measures', *Strategic Management Journal*, 5: 265–73.

Dewar, R.D. and Dutton, J.E. (1986) 'The adoption of radical and incremental innovations: An empirical analysis', *Management Science*, 32: 1422–33.

De Wit, B. and Meyer, R. (1999) *Strategy Synthesis: Resolving Strategy Paradoxes to Create Competitive Advantage*. London: Thompson.

Dijksterhuis, M.S., Van den Bosch, F.A.J. and Volberda, H.W. (1999) 'Where do new organization forms come from? Management logics as a source of co-evolution', *Organization Science*, 10 (5): 569–82.

DiMaggio, P. (ed.) (2001) *The Twenty-First-Century Firm: Changing Economic Organization in International Perspective.* Princeton, New Jersey: Princeton University Press.

DiMaggio, P.J. and Powell, W.W. (1983) 'The iron cage revisited: institutional isomorphism and collective rationality in organizational fields', *American Sociological Review*, 48: 147–60.

Dixon, N. (1994) *The Organizational Learning Cycle.* Maidenhead, UK: McGraw-Hill.

Djelic, M.L. (1998) *Exporting the American Model: The Postwar Transformation of European Business.* New York: Oxford University Press.

Dodgson, M. (1993) 'Organizational learning: a review of some literatures', *Organization Studies*, 14: 375–94.

Donaldson, L. (1987) 'Strategy and structural adjustment', *Journal of Management Studies*, 24 (1): 1–24.

Donaldson, L. (1996) *For Positivist Organization Theory.* Sage: London.

Donaldson, L. (1996) 'The normal science of structural contingency theory', in S.R. Clegg, C. Hardy and W.R. Nord (eds), *Handbook of Organization Studies*. Sage: London. pp. 57–76.

Donaldson, L. (2001) *The Contingency Theory of Organizations.* Thousand Oaks: Sage.

Doorduyn, Y. (2001) 'Bij ABN Amro wacht iedereen z'n lot af', *Financieele Dagblad*, August 2.

Downton, J.V. (1973) *Revel Leadership: Commitment and Charisma in the Revolutionary Process.* New York: Free Press.

Drazin, R. and Van de Ven, A.H. (1985) 'Alternative forms of fit in contingency theory', *Administrative Science Quarterly*, 30 (4): 514–40.

Droege, (1995) *Unternehmensorganisation im international en Vergleich: Struktur, Prozesse und Führungssysteme in Deutschland, Japan und den USA.* Frankfurt (Germany)/ New York, NY: Campus Verlag.

Drucker, P.F. (1993) *Post-capitalist Society.* Oxford: Butterworth Heinemann.

Dunlop, J.T. and Weil, D. (1996) 'Diffusion and performance of modular production in the U.S. apparel industry', *Industrial Relations*, 35: 334–55.

Dunning, J. (1993) *Multinational Enterprises and the Global Economy.* Reading, MA: Addison-Wesley.

Dyas, G.P. and Thanheiser, H.T. (1976) *The Emerging European Enterprise.* London: Macmillan.

Easterby-Smith, M. and Malina, D. (1999) 'Cross cultural collaborative research: toward reflexivity', *Academy of Management Journal*, 42 (1): 76–86.

Easton, G. and Araujo, L. (1994) 'Market exchange, social structures and time', *European Journal of Marketing*, 28 (3): 72–84.

Eccles, R.G. and Nohria, N. (1992) *Beyond the Hype.* Boston, MA: Harvard Business School Press.

Eden, C. and Ackermann, F. (1998) *Making Strategy: The Journey of Strategic Management.* London: Sage.

Edvardsson, B., Edvinsson, L. and Nystrom, H. (1993) 'Internationalisation in service companies', *The Service Industries Journal*, 13 (1): 80–97.

Eisenhardt, K. (2000) 'Paradox, spirals, ambivalence: the new language of change and pluralism', *Academy of Management Review*, 25 (4): 703–5.

Eisenhardt, K. and Brown, S. (1999) 'Patching: restitching business portfolios in dynamic markets', *Harvard Business Review*, May–June: 72–80.

Eisenhardt, K. and Martin, J.A. (2000) 'Dynamic capabilities: what are they?', *Strategic Management Journal*, 21: 1105–21.

Ericson, T. (1998) *Förändringsidéer och Meningsskapande – En Studie av Strategiskt Förändringsarbete* (in Swedish with English summary). Linköping Studies in Management and Economics, Dissertation No. 37, Linköping University.

Ericson, T. (2001) 'Sensemaking in organizations – towards a conceptual framework for understanding strategic change', in *Scandinavian Journal of Management*, 17: 109–31.

Ericson, T., Hellqvist, A., Melander, A. and Melin, L. (2000) 'Shaping new strategies in professional organizations: the strategic arena approach'. Paper presented at the 16th EGOS Colloquium, August 2000, Helsinki.

Evans, P. and Doz, Y. (1992) 'Dualities: a paradigm for human resource and organizational development in complex multinationals', in V. Pucik, N.M. Tichy and K.K. Barnett (eds), *Globalizing Management: Creating and Leading the Competitive Organization*. New York: Wiley: pp. 85–106.

Evans, P. and Génadry, N. (1999) 'A duality-based prospective for strategic human resource management', in P.M. Wright, L.D. Dyer, J.W. Boudreau and G.T. Milkovich (eds), *Research in Personnel and Human Resources Management*, Supplement 4. Greenwich, CT: JAI Press: pp. 367–95.

Ezzamel, M., Lilley, S. and Willmott, H. (1994) 'The new organization and the new managerial work', *European Management Journal*, 12 (4): 454–61.

Ezzamel, M., Lilley, S. and Willmott, H. (1996) 'The view from the top: senior executives' perceptions of changing management practices in UK companies', *British Journal of Management*, 7 (2): 155–68.

Fairhurst, G.T. and Sarr, R.A. (1996) *The Art of Framing: Managing the Language of Leadership*. San Francisco: Jossey-Bass.

Fenton, E.M. and Pettigrew, A.M. (2000a) 'Theoretical perspectives on new forms of organizing', in A.M. Pettigrew and E. Fenton (eds), *The Innovating Organization*. London: Sage. pp. 1–46.

Fenton, E.M. and Pettigrew, A.M. (2000b) 'The role of social mechanisms in an emerging network: the case of the pharmaceutical network in Coopers & Lybrand', in A.M. Pettigrew and E.M. Fenton (eds), *The Innovating Organization*. London: Sage. pp. 82–116.

Fenton, E.M. and Pettigrew, A.M. (2000c) 'Integrating a global professional services organization: the case of Ove Arup Partnership', in A.M. Pettigrew and E.M. Fenton, *The Innovating Organization*. London: Sage. pp. 47–81.

Ferner, A., Edwards, P. and Sisson, K. (1995) 'Coming unstuck: in search of the corporate glue in the international professional service firm', *Human Resource Management*, Fall, 34 (3): 343–61.

Feynman, R. (1967) *The Character of Physical Law*. Cambridge, MA: MIT Press.

Fiol, C.M. (1994) 'Consensus, diversity and learning in organizations', *Organization Science*, 5 (3): 403–20.

Fisher, C.D. (1989) 'Current and recurrent challenges in HRM', *Journal of Management*, 15: 157–80.

Fiske, S.T. and Taylor, S.E. (1984) *Social Cognition*. Reading, MA: Addison-Wesley.

FitzGerald, N. (2002) 'Leadership and change: re-awakening the spirit of enterprise', *Presentation to the Goldman Sachs Chief Investment Officer's Conference*, Venice, 15 March 2002: 1–8.

Flier, B., Van den Bosch, F.A.J., Volberda, H.W., Carnevale, C.A., Tomkin, N., Melin, L., Quélin, B.V. and Kriger, M.P. (2001) 'The changing landscape of the European financial services sector', *Long Range Planning*, 34: 179–207.

Fligstein, N. (1985) 'The spread of the multidivisional form among large firms, 1919–1979', *American Sociological Review*, 50: 377–391.

Fligstein, N. and Freeland, R. (1995) 'Theoretical and comparative perspectives on corporate organization', *Annual Review of Sociology*, 21: 21–43.

Floyd, S. and Lane, P. (2000) 'Strategizing throughout the organization: managing role conflict in strategic renewal', *Academy of Management Review*, 25 (1): 154–77.

Fontin, M. (1997) *Das Management von Dilemmata: Ein Ansatz zur Erschliessung neuer strategischer und organisationaler Potentiale* [The Management of Dilemmas: An Approach to Discovering New Strategic and Organizational Potentials]. Wiesbaden: Deutscher Universitätsverlag.

Ford, J.D. and Hegarty, W.H. (1984) 'Decision makers' beliefs about the causes and effects of structure: An exploratory study', *Academy of Management Journal*, 27 (2): 271–91.

Foster G. (1988) 'Core concerns at Unilever', *Management Today*, May: 62–7.

Fox-Wolfgramm, S.J., Boal, K.B. and Hunt, J.G. (1998) 'Organizational adaptation to institutional change: a comparative study of first-order change in prospector and defender banks', *Administrative Science Quarterly*, 43: 87–126.

Fredrickson, J.W. (1986) 'The strategic decision process and organizational structure', *Academy of Management Review*, 11 (2): 280–97.

Fredrickson, J.W. and Mitchell. T.R. (1984) 'Strategic decision processes: comprehensiveness and performance in an industry with an unstable environment', *Academy of Management Journal*, 27 (2): 399–423.

Freeman, S.J. and Cameron, K.S. (1993) 'Organizational downsizing: a convergence and reorientation framework', *Organization Science*, 4 (1): 10–29.

Frese, E. (1995) *Die Grundlagen der Organisation: Konzepte – Prinzipien – Strukturen* (sixth edition) [The Foundations of Organization: Concepts – Principles – Structures]. Wiesbaden: Gabler.

Frese, E. (2000) *Grundlagen der Organisation. Koncept, Prinzipien, Strukturen* (eighth edition). Wiesbaden, Germany: Gabler.

Frese, E. and Teuvsen, L. (1998) 'Market into hierarchy: the restructuring of large German companies', *Mimeo*: 31. Germany: University of Cologne.

Frese, E. and von Werder, A. (1994) 'Organisation als strategischer Wettbewerbsfaktor – Organisationstheoretische Analyse gegenwärtiger Umstrukturierungen', *Zeitschrift für betriebswirtschaftliche Forschung*, Sonderheft, 33: 1–28.

Fruin, M. (1992) *The Japanese Enterprise System: Competitive Strategies and Cooperative Structures*. New York: Oxford University Press.

Fulk, J. and DeSanctis, G. (1995) 'Electronic communication and changing organizational forms', *Organization Science*, 6 (4): 337–49.

Galanter, M. and Palay, T. (1991) *Tournament of Lawyers: The Transformation of the Big Law Firms*. Chicago: University of Chicago Press.

Galegher, J., Kraut, R.G. and Egido, C. (eds) (1990) *Intellectual Teamwork: Social and Technological Foundations of Co-operative Work*. Hillsdale, NJ: Lawrence Erlbaum Associates.

Galunic, D.C. and Eisenhardt, K. (1996) 'The Evolution of intracorporate domains: divisional charter losses in high-technology multidivisional organizations', *Organization Science*, 7 (3): 255–82.

Gavetti, G. and Levinthal, D. (2000) 'Looking forward and looking backward: Cognitive and experiential search', *Administrative Science Quarterly*, 45: 113–37.

Gerhart, B., Minkoff, H.B. and Olsen, R.N. (1995) 'Employee compensation: theory, practice, and evidence', in G.R. Ferris, S.D. Rosen and D.T. Barnum (eds), *Handbook of Human Resource Management*. Cambridge, MA: Blackwell. pp. 528–47.

Ghoshal, S. and Bartlett, C.A. (1990) 'The multinational corporation as an interorganizational network', *Academy of Management Review*, 15 (4): 603–25.

Ghoshal, S. and Bartlett, C.A. (1995) 'Changing the role of top management: from structure to process', *Harvard Business Review*, January–February: 86–96.

Ghoshal, S. and Bartlett, C.A. (1999) *The Individualized Corporation: A Fundamentally New Approach to Management*. London: William Heinemann.

Ghoshal, S. and Moran, P. (1996) 'Bad for practice: a critique of transaction cost theory', *Academy of Management Review*, 21(1): 13–47.

Ghoshal, S. and Nohria, N. (1993) 'Horses for courses: organizational forms for multinational corporations', *Sloan Management Review*, Winter: 23–35.

Gibbons, M.C., Limoges, C., Nowotny, H., Schwartzman, S., Scott, P. and Trow, M. (1994) *The New Production of Knowledge*. London: Sage.

Giddens, A. (1984) *The Constitution of Society*. Cambridge: Polity Press.

Giddens, A. (1985) *The Constitution of Society*. Berkeley, CA: University of California Press.

Ginsberg, A. (1994) 'Minding the competition: from mapping to mastery', *Strategic Management Journal*, 15: 153–74.

Gioia, D.A. (1986) 'Conclusion: the state of art in organizational social cognition: a personal view', in: H.P. Sims and D.A. Gioia (eds), *The Thinking Organization: Dynamics of Organizational Social Cognition*. San Francisco: Jossey-Bass, pp. 336–56.

Gioia, D.A. and Chittipeddi, K. (1991) 'Sensemaking and sensegiving in strategic change initiation', *Strategic Management Journal*, 12: 433–48.

Gioia, D.A. and Mehra, A. (1996) 'Book review: *Sensemaking in Organizations*, by Karl E. Weick (1995)', *Academy of Management Review*, 21 (4): 1226–40.

Gioia, D.A., Thomas, J.B., Clark, S.M. and Chittipeddi. K. (1994) 'Symbolism and strategic change in academia: the dynamics of sensemaking and influence', *Organization Science*, 5 (3): 363–83.

Glaser, B. and Strauss, A. (1967) *The Discovery of Grounded Theory*. Chicago: Aldine.

Glick, W.H., Chet Miller, C. and Huber, G.P. (1993) 'The impact of upper-echelon diversity on organizational performance', in G.P. Huber and W.H. Glick (eds), *Organizational Change and Redesign: Ideas and Insights for Improving Performance*. New York: Oxford University Press.

Goffee, R. and Jones, G. (1996) 'What holds the modern company together?', *Harvard Business Review*, Nov–Dec: 133–48.

Grandori, A. (1997) 'Governance structures, coordination mechanisms and cognitive models', *The Journal of Management and Governance*, 1: 29–47.

Granovetter, M.S. (1982) 'The strength of weak ties: a network theory re-visited', in P. Marsden and N. Lin (eds), *Social Structure and Network Analysis*. Beverly Hills: Sage. pp. 105–30.

Granovetter, M.S. (1985) 'Economic action and social structure: the problem of embeddedness', *American Journal of Sociology*, 91: 481–510.

Granovetter, M.S. (1992) 'Problems of explanation in economic sociology', in N. Nohria and R.E. Eccles (eds), *Networks and Organizations: Structure, Form and Action*. Boston: Harvard Business School Press. pp. 25–56.

Grant, R.M. (1988) 'On "dominant logic", relatedness and the link between diversity and performance', *Strategic Management Journal*, 9: 639–42.

Grant, R.M. (1991) 'The resource-based theory of competitive advantage: implications for strategy formulation', *California Management Review*, 33 (3): 114–22.

Grant, R.M. (1996), 'Toward a knowledge-based theory of the firm', *Strategic Management Journal*, 17 (Winter Special Issue): 109–22.

Gray, B., Bougon, M.G. and Donnellon, A. (1985) 'Organizations as constructions and destructions of meaning', *Journal of Management*, 11 (2): 83–98.

Greene, W.H. (1993) *Econometric Analysis*. Englewood Cliffs, NJ: Prentice-Hall.

Greenwood, R. and Hinings, C.R. (1988) 'Organizational design types, tracks and the dynamics of strategic change,' *Organization Studies*, 9: 293–316.

Greenwood, R. and Hinings, C.R. (1993) 'Understanding strategic change: the contribution of archetypes', *Academy of Management Journal*, 36: 1052–81.

Greenwood, R. and Hinings, C.R. (1996) 'Understanding radical organizational change: bringing together the old and the new institutionalism', *Academy of Management Review*, 21 (4): 1022–54.

Greenwood, R., Hinings, C.R. and Brown, J. (1990) 'Merging professional service firms', *Organization Science*, 5: 239–57.

Greenwood, R. and Lachman, R. (1996) 'Change as an underlying theme in professional service organizations', *Organization Studies*, 17 (4): 563–72.

Greve, H.R. (1998) 'Managerial cognition and the mimetic adoption of market positions: what you see is what you do', *Strategic Management Journal*, 19: 967–88.

Griffiths, D., Boisot, M. and Mole, V. (1998) 'Strategies for managing knowledge assets: a tale of two companies', *Technovation*, 18 (8/9): 529–39.

Grint, K. (2000) *The Arts of Leadership*. Oxford: Oxford University Press.

Grinyer, P. and McKiernan, P. (1990) 'Generating major change in stagnating companies', *Strategic Management Journal*, 11: 131–46.

Grønhaug, K. and Falkenberg, J.S. (1989) 'Exploring strategy perceptions in changing environments', *Journal of Management Studies*, 26 (4): 349–59.

Group of ten (2001) 'The implications of electronic trading in financial markets', January.

Guillén, M.F. (1994) *Models of Management: Work, Authority and Organization in a Comparative Perspective*. Chicago: University of Chicago Press.

Gupta, A.K. and Govindarajan, V. (1991): 'Knowledge flows and the structure of control within multinational corporations', *Academy of Management Review*, 16 (4): 768–92.

Gustavsson, P., Melin, L. and Macdonald, S. (1994) 'Learning to glocalise', *Advances in Strategic Management*, Volume 10B Greenwich: JAI Press: 255–88.

Habermas, J. (1981) *Theorie des kommunikativen Handelns* [Theory of Communicative Action]. Frankfurt: Suhrkamp.

Hall, D.J. and Saias, M.A. (1980) 'Strategy follows structure', *Strategic Management Journal*, 1: 149–63.

Hall, D.T. (ed.) (1996) *The Career is Dead, Long Live the Career*. San Francisco: Jossey-Bass.

Hall, E.T. (1992) *An Anthropology of Everyday Life: An Autobiography*. New York: Anchor.

Hambrick, D.C. (1983) 'Some tests of the effectiveness and functional attributes of Miles and Snow's strategic types', *Academy of Management Journal*, 26 (1): 5–26.

Hambrick, D.C. (1989) 'Putting top managers back in the strategy picture', *Strategic Management Journal*, 10: 5–15.

Hambrick, D.C. and Mason, P.A. (1984) 'Upper echelons: The organization as a reflection of its top managers', *Academy of Management Review*, 9: 193–206.

Hamel, G. (1998) 'Strategy Innovation and the Quest for Value', *Sloan Management Review*, 39 (2): 7–14.

Hamel, G. and Prahalad, C.K. (1996) 'Competing in the new economy', *Strategic Management Journal*, 17: 237–42.

Hammer, M. and Champy, J. (1993) *Reengineering the Corporation*. New York: Harper Business.

Hampden-Turner, C.M. (1990) *Charting the Corporate Mind: From Dilemma to Strategy*. Oxford: Blackwell.

Hampden-Turner, C.M. and Trompenaars, A. (1993) *The Seven Cultures of Capitalism: Value Systems for Creating Wealth in the United States, Japan, Germany, France, Britain, Sweden and the Netherlands.* (first edition). New York: NY: Currency/Doubleday.

Handy, C. (1990) *The Age of Unreason.* London: Arrow Books.

Handy, C. (1992) 'Balancing corporate power: a new federalist organization', *Harvard Business Review*, Nov–Dec, 59: 72.

Handy, C. (1994a) *The Empty Raincoat*, London: Arrow Books.

Handy, C. (1994b) *The Age of Paradox.* Boston, MA: Harvard Business School Press.

Handy, C. (1996) 'The new language of organizing and its implications for leaders', in F. Hesselbein, M. Goldsmith and R. Beckhard (eds), *The Leader of the Future*. San Francisco: Jossey-Bass. pp. 3–9.

Hansen, M.T. and von Oetinger, B. (2001) 'Introducing T-shaped managers: knowledge management's next generation', *Harvard Business Review*, March: 107–16.

Hart, S. and Banbury, C. (1994) 'How strategy-making processes can make a difference', *Strategic Management Journal*, 15: 251–69.

Harvey, D. (1993) *The Condition of Postmodernity.* Oxford: Blackwell.

Harvey, J., Pettigrew, A.M. and Ferlie, E. (2002) 'The determinants of research group performance: towards mode 2?', *Journal of Management Studies*, 39 (6): 747–74.

Hastings, C. (1993) *The New Organization. Growing the Culture of Organizational Networking.* London: McGraw-Hill.

Hay, D. and Morris, D. (1991) *Industrial Economics and Organizations* (second edition). Oxford: Oxford University Press.

Hedberg, B.L.T. (1981) 'How organizations learn and unlearn', in P.C. Nystrom and W.H. Starbuck (eds), *Handbook of Organizational Design*. Oxford: Oxford University Press.

Hedlund, G. (1994) 'A model of knowledge management and the N–form corporation', *Strategic Management Journal*, 15: 73–90.

Helgesen, S. (1995) 'Beyond teams', *Across the Board*, 32 (8): 43–8.

Hendry, J. (2000) 'Strategic decision-making, discourse and strategy as a social practice', *Journal of Management Studies*, 37 (7): 955–77.

Hensmans, M., Van den Bosch, F.A.J. and Volberda. H.W. (2001) 'Clicks vs. bricks in the emerging online financial services industry', *Long Range Planning*, 34: 231–47.

Heracleous, L. and Barrett, M. (2001) 'Organizational change as discourse: communicative actions and deep structures in the context of information technology implementation', *Academy of Management Journal*, 44 (4): 755–78.

Heydebrand, W.V. (1989) 'New organizational forms', *Work and Occupations*, 16 (3): 323–57.

Hicks, D.M. and Katz, J.S. (1996) 'Science policy for a highly collaborative science system', *Science and Public Policy*, 23 (1): 39–44.

Hicks, D.M. and Katz, J.S. (1997) *The Changing Shape of British Industrial Research*, STEEP Special Report No. 6. Brighton, UK: Science Policy Research Unit.

Higgins, L.F. and Ferguson, J.M. (1991) 'Practical approaches for evaluating the quality dimensions of professional accounting services', *Journal of Professional Services Marketing*, 7 (1): 3–17.

Hinings, C.R., Brown, J.L. and Greenwood, R. (1991) 'Change in an autonomous professional organization', *The Journal of Management Studies*, 28 (4): 375–93.

Hinings, C.R. and Greenwood, R. (1988a) 'The normative prescription of organizations', in L.G. Zucker (ed.), *Institutional Patterns and Organizations*. Cambridge, MA: Ballinger Publishing Company. pp. 53–70.

Hinings, C.R. and Greenwood, R. (1988b) *The Dynamics of Strategic Change.* Oxford: Blackwell.

Hinings, B. and Greenwood, R. (1996) 'Understanding radical organizational change: bringing together the old and the new institutionalism', *Academy of Management Review*, 21 (4): 1022–54.

Hitt, M.A., Keats, B.W. and DeMarie, S.M. (1998) 'Navigating in the new competitive landscape: building strategic flexibility and competitive advantage in the 21st century', *Academy of Management Executive*, 12 (4): 22–42.

Hodgkinson, G.P. (ed.) (2001) 'Facing the future: the nature and purpose of management research re-assessed', *British Journal of Management*, Special Issue 12, December 2001.

Hofstede, G. (1993) 'Cultural constraints in management theories', *Academy of Management Executive*, 7: 81–95.

Hofstede, G.H. (1980) *Culture's Consequences, International Differences in Work-Related Values*. Beverley Hills, CA: Sage Publications.

Hopwood, A. and Miller, P. (1994) *Accounting as Social and Institutional Practice*. Cambridge: Cambridge University Press.

Hosking, D.M. and Bouwen, R. (2000) 'Organizational learning: relational-constructivist approaches: an overview', *European Journal of Work and Organizational Psychology*, 9: 129–32.

Hoskisson, R.E. and Hitt, M. (1994) *Downscoping: How to Tame the Diversified Firm*. Oxford: Oxford University Press.

House, R., Javidan, M., Hawges, P. and Dorfman, P. (2002) 'Understanding cultures and the implicit leadership theories across the globe: an introduction to project GLOBE', *Journal of World Business*, 37: 3–10.

Huber, G.P. (1990) 'A theory of the effects of advanced information technologies on organizational design, intelligence, and decision making', *Academy of Management Review*, 15 (1): 47–71.

Huber, G.P. (1991) 'Organizational learning: the contributing processes and the literatures', *Organization Science*, 2: 88–115.

Huff, A.S. and Huff, J.O. (2000) *When Firms Change Direction*. Oxford: Oxford University Press.

Hughes, E.C. (1956) 'The making of a physician', *Human Organization*, 14: 22–25.

Hughes, R.L., Ginnett, R.C. and Curphy, G.J. (1999) *Leadership – Enhancing the Lessons of Experience*. Boston: Irwin McGraw-Hill.

Huselid, M. and Becker, B. (1996) 'Methodological issues in cross-sectional and panel estimates of the estimates of the human resource-firm performance link', *Industrial Relations*, 35: 400–22.

Ichniowski, C. and Shaw, K. (1999) 'The effects of human resource management systems on economic performance: an international comparison of US and Japanese plants', *Management Science*, 45 (5): 704–21.

Ichniowski, C., Shaw, K. and Prenushi, G. (1997) 'The effects of human resource management practices on productivity: a study of steel finishing lines', *American Economic Review*, 87 (3): 291–314.

Inkeles, A. and Sasaki, M. (eds) (1996) *Comparing Nations and Cultures: Readings in a Cross Disciplinary Perspective*. Englewood Cliffs, NJ: Prentice-Hall.

Isabella, L.A. (1990) 'Evolving interpretations as change unfolds: how managers construe key organizational events', *Academy of Management Journal*, 33: 7–41.

Jackson, W.A. (1999) 'Dualism, duality and the complexity of economic institutions', *International Journal of Social Economics*, 26 (4): 545–58.

Jacques, E. (1990) 'In Praise of Hierarchy', *Harvard Business Review*, Jan–Feb: 127–32.

Janis, I. (1982) *Groupthink*. Boston: Houghton Mifflin.

Janssens, M. and Steyaert, C. (1999) 'The world in two and a third way out? The concept of duality in organization theory and practice', *Scandinavian Journal of Management*, 15: 121–39.

Jarillo, J. (1988) 'On strategic networks', *Strategic Management Journal*, 9: 31–41.

Jarvenpaa, S.L. and Ives, B. (1994) 'The global network organization of the future: information management opportunities and challenges', *Journal of Management Information Systems*, 10: 25–48.

Jarvenpaa, S.L. and Leidner, D.G. (1999) 'Communication and trust in global virtual teams', *Organization Science*, 10 (6): 791–815.

Jervis, R. (1997) *System Effects: Complexity in Political and Social Life*. Princeton: Princeton University Press.

Jick, T.D. (1979) 'Mixing qualitative and quantitative methods: triangulation in action', *Administrative Science Quarterly*, December, 24: 602–11.

Johnson, B. (2002): *Polarity Management: Understanding the Paradoxical Wisdom in the Resistance to Our Brilliant Strategies*, Paper presented at the Strategic Management Society Mini-Conference, Rotterdam, August 2002, 17 pp.

Johnson, G. (1994): 'Commentary: learning to glocalize' (P. Gustavsson, L. Melin and S. Macdonald), *Advances in Strategic Management*, Volume 10B: 289–95, Greenwich: JAI Press.

Johnson, G. and Bowman, C. (1999) 'Strategy and everyday reality: the case for the study of "micro-strategy"', paper presented at Egos Colloquium, Warwick, UK.

Johnson, G., Melin, L. and Whittington, R. (2003) 'Micro-strategy and strategising: towards an activity-based view?, *Journal of Management Studies*, 40 (1): 3–22.

Jones, C., Hesterly, W.S. and Borgatti, S.P. (1997) 'A general theory of network governance: exchange conditions and social mechanisms', *Academy of Management Review*, 22 (4): 911–45.

Jurriëns, J.A. and Jesse, J. (1996) 'Research & development, ook binnen banken', *Holland/Belgium Management Review*, 46: 73–83.

Kahn, W.A. (2002) 'Managing the paradox of self-reliance', *Organizational Dynamics*, 30 (3): 239–55.

Kanter, R.M. (1983) *The Change Masters: Innovation and Entrepreneurship in the American Corporation*. New York: Simon & Schuster.

Kanter, R.M. and Eccles, R.G. (1992) 'Conclusion: making network research relevant to practice', in N. Nohria and R.G. Eccles (eds), *Networks and Organizations. Structure, Form, and Action*. Boston: Harvard Business School Press. pp. 521–7.

Katz, D. and Kahn, R.L. (1978) *The Social Psychology of Organizations* (second edition). New York, NY: Wiley.

Kerr, J.L. and Jackofsky, E.F. (1989) 'Aligning managers with strategies: management development versus selection', *Strategic Management Journal*, 10: 157–70.

Ketchen, D.J., Combs, J.G., Russel, C.J. and Shook, C. (1997) 'Organizational configurations and performance: a meta-analysis', *Academy of Management Journal*, 40 (1): 223–40.

Ketchen, D.J., Thomas, J.B. and Snow, C. (1993) 'Organizational configuration and performance: a comparison of theoretical approaches', *Academy of Management Journal*, 36: 1278–313.

Koberg, C.S., Tegarden, L.F. and Wilsted, W.D. (1993) 'Environmental and structural influences on the strategy-making process of banks', *Journal of Applied Business Research*, 9 (3): 58–71.

Kogut, B. (1991) 'Country capabilities and the permeability of borders', *Strategic Management Journal*, 12: 33–47.

Kogut, B. and Walker, G. (2001) 'The small world of Germany and the durability of national networks', *American Sociological Review*, 66: 317–35.

Kohn, M. (1996) 'Cross national research as an analytical strategy', in A. Inkles and M. Sasaki (eds), *Comparing Nations and Cultures: Readings in a Cross Disciplinary Perspective*. Englewood, Cliffs, NJ: Prentice-Hall. pp. 28–53.

Kotter, J.P. (1988) *The leadership factor*. New York: Free Press.

Krackhardt, D. (1990) 'Assessing the political landscape: structure, cognition and power in organizations', *Administrative Science Quarterly*, 35: 342–69.

Kühl, S. (1998) *Wenn die Affen den Zoo regieren: Die Tücken der flachen Hierarchien*, [When Apes Govern the Zoo: The Challenges of Flat Hierarchies] (fifth edition). Frankfurt/New York: Campus.

Kuper, S. (1997) 'Success at the cutting edge', *Financial Times*, November.

Labianca, G., Gray, B. and Brass, D.J. (2000) 'A grounded model of organizational schema change during empowerment', *Organization Science*, 11 (2): 235–57.

Lammers, C.J. (1978) 'The comparative sociology of organizations', *Annual Review of Sociology*, 4: 485–510.

Langfield-Smith, K. (1992) 'Exploring the need for a shared cognitive map', *Journal of Management Studies*, 29 (3): 349–68.

Langley, A. (1999) 'Strategies for theorizing from process data', *Academy of Management Review*, 24: 691–710.

Langley, A., Mintzberg, H., Pitcher, P., Posada, E. and Saint-Macary, J. (1995) 'Opening up decision making: the view from the black stool', *Organization Science*, 6 (3): 260–78.

Lant, T.K. and Mezias, S.P. (1992) 'An organizational learning model of convergence and reorientation', *Organization Science*, 3: 47–71.

Lant, T.K., Milliken, F.J. and Batra, B. (1992) 'The role of managerial learning and interpretation in strategic persistence and reorientation: an empirical exploration', *Strategic Management Journal*, 13: 585–608.

Lash, S. (1990) *The Sociology of Postmodernism*. London: Routledge.

Laughlin, R.C. (1991) 'Environmental disturbances and organizational transitions and transformations: some alternative models', *Organization Studies*, 12 (2): 209–32.

Law, J. (1994) *Organizing Modernity*. Oxford: Blackwell.

Lawler, E.E., III (1982) 'Increasing worker involvement to enhance organizational effectiveness', in P.S. Goodman (ed.), *Changes in Organizations*. San Francisco: Jossey-Bass.

Lawler, E.E., III (1992) *The Ultimate Advantage: Creating the High-involvement Organization*. San Francisco: Jossey-Bass.

Lawler, E.E., III, Mohrman, S.A. and Ledford, G. (1995) *Creating High Performance Organizations*. San Francisco: Jossey-Bass.

Lawrence, P.R. and Lorsch, J.W. (1967a) *Organization and Environment: Managing Differentiation and Fit*. Boston: Harvard University, Graduate School of Business Administration, Division of Research.

Lawrence, P.R. and Lorsch, J.W. (1967b) 'Differentiation and integration in complex organizations', *Administrative Science Quarterly*, 12: 1–47.

Leibinger, B. (1997) 'Mehr Unordnung in Unteruehmen [More disorder to enterprises], in H. and B. von Oetinger (eds), *Wie Kommt daro Neue in die welt*. München/Wien: Hauser. pp. 147–54.

Levine, D.I. (1995) *Reinventing the Workplace*. Washington, DC: Brookings.

Levinthal, D.A. and March, J.G. (1993) 'The myopia of learning', *Strategic Management Journal*, 14, Winter: 95–112.

Levitt, B. and March, J.G. (1988) 'Organizational learning', *American Review of Sociology*, 14: 319–40.

Lewin, A.Y. (1999) 'Application of complexity theory to organization science', *Organization Science*, 10: 215.

Lewin, A.Y. and Kim, J. (2003) 'The nation state and culture as influences on organizational change and innovation', in S.M. Poole and A.H. Van de Ven (eds), *Handbook of Organization Change and Development*. New York: Oxford University Press.

Lewin, A.Y., Kim, J. and Weigelt, C.B. (2003) 'The moderating effect of nation state', in S.M. Poole and A.H. Van de Ven (eds), *Handbook of Organization Change and Development*. New York: Oxford University Press.

Lewin, A.Y., Long, C.P. and Carroll, T.N. (1999) 'The coevolution of new organizational forms', *Organization Science*, 10 (5): 535–50.

Lewin, A.Y. and Volberda, H.W. (1999) 'Prolegomena on coevolution: a framework for research on strategy and new organizational forms', *Organization Science*, 10 (5): 519–34.

Lewis, M.W. (2000) 'Exploring paradox: toward a more comprehensive guide', *Academy of Management Review*, 25 (4): 760–76.

Liebeskind, J. (1996) 'Knowledge, strategy and the theory of the firm', *Strategic Management Journal*, 17 (special issue): 93–108.

Liedtka, J.M., Haskins, M.E., Rosenblum, J.W. and Weber, J. (1997) 'The generative cycle: linking knowledge and relationships', *Sloan Management Review*, 39 (1): 47–58.

Lincoln, J.R. and Kalleberg, A. (1990) *Culture, Control and Commitment*. Cambridge: Cambridge University Press.

Lincoln, J.R. and Nakata, Y. (1997) 'The transformation of the Japanese employment system. Nature, depth and origins', *Work and Occupation*, 24 (1): 33–55.

Lindahl, G. (1999) 'Bereit für die Herausforderung der Zukunft' [Ready for the challenges of the future], *La Vie économique – Revue de politique économique*, 3: 6–9.

Lindell, P., Ericson, T. and Melin, L. (1998) 'Collective thinking in strategic change processes', in M. Hitt, J. Ricart and R. Nixon (eds), *New Managerial Mindsets: Organizational Transfomation and Strategy Implementation*. London: Wiley.

Lorenz, A. (1996) 'Unilever changes its formula', *Management Today*, July: 44–49.

Lowendahl, B. (1997) *Strategic Management of Professional Service Firms*. Handelshojskolens Forlag: Copenhagen.

Luhmann, N. (1987) 'Die Richtigkeit soziologischer Theorie' [The correctness of sociological theory], in: *Merkur*, 41: 36–49.

Luiten van Zanden, J. and Uittenbogaard, R. (1999) 'Expansie, internationalisering en concentratie, 1950–1990', in J. De Vries, W. Vroom and T. De Graaf (eds), *Wereldwijd bankieren: ABN Amro 1824–1999*. Amsterdam: ABN Amro Bank NV. pp. 335–92.

Lyles, M.A. and Schwenk, C.R. (1992) 'Top management, strategy and organizational knowledge structures', *Journal of Management Studies*, 29 (2): 155–74.

Lyotard, J-F. (1984) *The Postmodern Condition: A Report on Knowledge*. Manchester: Manchester University Press.

Maassen, G.F. and Van den Bosch, F.A.J. (1999) 'On the supposed independence of two-tier boards: formal structure and reality in the Netherlands', *Corporate Governance, An international review*, 7: 31–7.

MacDuffie, J.P. (1995) 'Human resource bundles and manufacturing performance: organizational logic and flexible production systems in the world auto industry', *Industrial and Labor Relations Review*, 48: 197–221.

MacIntosh, R. and MacLean, D. (1999) 'Conditioned emergence: A dissipative structures approach to transformation', *Strategic Management Journal*, 20: 297–316.

MacLean, D., MacIntosh R. and Grant, S. (2002) 'Mode 2 Management Research', *British Journal of Management*, 13 (3): 189–208.

Macy, B.A. and Izumi, H. (1993) 'Organizational change, design, and work innovation: a meta-analysis of 131 North-American field studies, 1961–1991', in W.A. Pasmore and R.W. Woodman (eds), *Research in Organizational Behavior*, 7. Greenwich, CT: JAI Press. pp. 235–313.

Maister, D.H. (1993) *Managing the Professional Service Firm*. New York: Free Press.

Majchrzah, A., Rice, R.E., Malhotra, A., King, N. and Ba, S. (2000) 'Technology adaptation: the case of a computer-supported inter-organizational virtual team', *MIS Quarterly*, 24 (4): 569–600.

Maljers, F., Baden-Fuller, C. and van den Bosch, F. (1996) 'Maintaining strategic momentum: the CEO's agenda', *European Management Journal*, 14 (6): 555–61.

March, J.C. and Simon, H.A. (1958) *Organizations*. New York: Wiley.

March, J.G. (1991) 'Exploration and exploitation in organizational learning', *Organization Science*, 2: 71–87.

March, J.G. (1995) 'The Future Disposable Organizations and the Rigidities of Imagination', *Organization*, 2 (314): 427–40.

Markides, C.C. (1996) *Diversification, Refocusing and Economic Performance*. Cambridge, MA: MIT Press.

Massini S., Lewin, A.Y., Numagami, T. and Pettigrew, A.M. (2002) 'The evolution of organizational routines in large Western and Japanese firms', *Research Policy*, 31 (8) and (9): 1333–48.

Mayer, M.C.J. and Whittington, R. (1999) 'Strategy, structure and "systemness": national institutions and corporate change in France, Germany and UK, 1950–93', *Organization Studies*, 20 (6): 933–59.

Maznevski, M.C. and Chudoba, K.M. (2000) 'Bridging space over time: global virtual team dynamics and effectiveness', *Organization Science*, 11 (5): 473–92.

McCall, M.W. and Kaplan, R.E. (1985) *Whatever it Takes: Decision Makers at Work*. Englewood Cliffs, NJ: Prentice-Hall.

McCall, M.W., Lombardo, M.M. and Morrison, A.M. (1988) *The Lessons of Experience: How Successful Executives Develop on the Job*. Lexington, MA: Lexington Books.

McDonald, G. (2000) 'Cross-cultural methodological issues in ethical research', *Journal of Business Ethics*, 27: 89–104.

McGregor, D. (1960) *The Human Side of Enterprise*. New York: McGraw Hill.

McKendrick, D.G. and Carroll, G.R. (2001) 'On the genesis of organizational forms: evidence from the market for disk arrays', *Organization Science*, 12 (6), Nov–Dec: 661–82.

McKinley, W. and Scherer, A.G. (2000) 'Some unanticipated consequences of organizational restructuring', *Academy of Management Review*, 25 (4): 735–52.

McLaren, R.I. (1982) *Organizational Dilemmas*. Chichester, UK: Wiley.

McNulty, T. and Pettigrew, A.M. (1999) 'Strategists on the board', *Organization Studies*, 20 (1): 47–74.

Meindl, J.R., Stubbart, C. and Porac, J.F. (1994) 'Cognition within and between organizations: five key questions', *Organization Science*, 5 (3): 289–93.

Mendelson, H. and Pillai, R. (1999) 'Information age organisations, dynamics and performance', *Journal of Economic Behaviour and Organisation*, 38: 253–81.

Meyer, A.D. and Rowan, B. (1977) 'Institutionalized organizations: formal structure as myth and ceremony', *American Journal of Sociology*, 83: 340–63.

Meyer, A.D., Tsui, A.S. and Hinings, C.R. (1993) Introduction: 'Configurational approaches to organizational analysis', *Academy of Management Journal*, 36 (6): 1175–92.

Meyer, J.W., Boli, J., Thomas, G.M. and Ramirez, F.O. (1997) 'World society and the nation-state', *The American Journal of Sociology*, 103: 144–181.

Mezias, J.M., Grinyer, P. and Guth, W.D. (2001) 'Changing collective cognition: A process model for strategic change', *Long Range Planning*, 34: 71–95.

Miles, M.B. and Huberman, A.M. (1984) *Qualitative Data Analysis*. Beverly Hills, CA: Sage.

Miles, R.E., Coleman, H.J. and Douglas Creed, W.E. (1995) 'Keys to success in corporate redesign', *California Management Review*, Spring: 128–45.

Miles, R.E. and Snow, C.C. (1978) *Organizational Strategy, Structure and Process*. New York: McGraw Hill.

Miles, R.E. and Snow, C.C. (1984) 'Designing strategic human resource management systems', *Organization Dynamics*, 13: 36–52.

Miles, R.E. and Snow, C.C. (1992) 'Causes of failure in network organisations', *California Management Review*, 34 (4) (Summer): 53–72.

Miles, R.E. and Snow, C.C. (1994) *Fit, Failure, and the Hall of Fame*. Free Press: NY.

Miles, R.E. and Snow, C.C. (1995) 'The new network firm: a spherical structure built on a human investment philosophy', *Organizational Dynamics*, 23 (4): 5–18.

Miles, R.E., Snow, C.C., Mathews, J.A., Miles, G. and Coleman, Jr, H.J. (1997) 'Organizing in the knowledge age: anticipating the cellular form', *Academy of Management Executive*, 11 (4): 7–24.

Milgrom P.R., Qian, Y. and Roberts, J. (1991) 'Complementarities, momentum, and the evolution of modern manufacturing', *American Economic Review*, 81: 55–86.

Milgrom, P.R. and Roberts, J. (1990) 'The economics of modern manufacturing: technology, strategy and organization', *American Economic Review*, 80: 511–28.

Milgrom, P.R. and Roberts, J. (1995) 'Complementarities and fit: strategy, structure and organizational change in manufacturing', *Journal of Accounting and Economics*, 19 (2/3): 179–208.

Miller, D. (1986) 'Configurations of strategy and structure: towards a synthesis', *Strategic Management Journal*, 7: 233–49.

Miller, D. (1987) 'The genesis of configuration', *Academy of Management Review*, 12 (4): 686–701.

Miller, D. (1992) 'Environmental fit versus internal fit', *Organization Science*, 3 (2): 505–12.

Miller, D. (1996) 'Configurations revisited', *Strategic Management Journal*, 17: 505–12.

Miller, D., Dröge, C. and Toulouse, J. (1988) 'Strategic process and content as mediators between organizational context and structure', *Academy of Management Journal*, 31 (3): 544–69.

Miller, D. and Friesen, P. (1978) 'Archetypes of strategy formulation', *Management Science*, 24 (9): 921–33.

Mincer, J. (1994) 'Human capital: a review', in C. Kerr and P.D. Staudohar (eds), *Labor Economics and Industrial Relations: Markets and Institutions*. Cambridge, MA: Harvard University Press. pp. 109–41.

Mintzberg, H. (1973) *The Nature of Managerial Work*. New York: Harper & Row.

Mintzberg, H. (1979) *The Structuring of Organizations*. Englewood Cliffs, NJ: Prentice Hall.

Mintzberg, H. (1990) 'The Design School: reconsidering the basic premises of strategic management', *Strategic Management Journal*, 11: 171–95.

Mintzberg, H. and Westley, F. (1992) 'Cycles of organizational change', *Strategic Management Journal*, 13 (special issue, Winter): 39–59.

Mirow, M. (1995) 'Wie können Konzerne wettbewerbsfähig bleiben?' [How can concerns stay competitive?], *Zeitschrift für Betriebswirtschaft*, Ergänzungsheft, 1: 9–25.

Mitroff, I.I. and Linstone, H.A. (1993) *The Unbounded Mind: Breaking the Chains of Traditional Business Thinking*. Oxford: Oxford University Press.

Morgan, G. (ed.) (1983) *Beyond Method: Strategies for Social Research*, Newbury Park, CA: Sage Publications.

Morris, E. (1987) 'Vision and strategy: a focus for the future', *Journal of Business Strategy*, 8 (2): 51–8.

Müller-Stewens, G. and Fontin, M. (1997) *Management unternehmerischer Dilemmata* [The Management of Corporate Dilemmas], Entwicklungstendenzen im Management, IfB-Schriften Universität St. Gallen, Band 15, Schäffer-Poeschel/ Verlag Neue Zürcher Zeitung.

Müllern, T. (2000) 'Integrating the team-based structure in the business process: the case of Saab Training Systems', in A.M. Pettigrew and E.M. Fenton (eds), *The Innovating Organization*. London: Sage. pp. 236–55.

Müllern, T. and Östergren, K. (1997) 'Managing renewal projects in different learning cultures', in R. Lundin and C. Midler (eds), *Projects as Arenas for Renewal and Learning Processes*. Kluwer Academic Publishers.

Müllern, T. and Stein, J. (2000) *Leadership in the New Economy* (in Swedish). Malmö: Liber.

Nahapiet, J. and Ghoshal, S. (1998) 'Social capital, intellectual capital and the organizational advantage', *Academy of Management Review*, 23: 242–67.

Nelson, R.R. and Winter, S.G. (1982) *An Evolutionary Theory of Economic Change*. Cambridge, MA: Belknap.

Newton, J., and Johnson, G. (1998). 'Bridging the gap between intended and unintended change: the role of managerial sensemaking', in M. Hitt, J. Ricart and R. Nixon (eds), *New Managerial Mindsets: Organizational Transformation and Strategy Implementation*. London: Wiley.

Nicholson, N. (1996) 'Career systems in crisis: change and opportunity in the information age', *Academy of Management Executive*, 10 (4): 40–50.

NNI (1997) 'Strategic changes in the financial services industry', *Research Memorandum*, December: 31 pages.

Nohria, N. (1996) *From the M-form to the N-form: Taking Stock of Changes in the Large Industrial Corporation*, Working Paper 96–054, Harvard Business School.

Nohria, N. and Berkley, J.D. (1994) 'An action perspective: the crux of the new management', *California Management Review*, Summer: 70–92.

Nohria, N. and Ghoshal, S. (1997) *The Differentiated Network: Organizing Multinational Organizations for Value Creation*. San Francisco: Jossey Bass.

Nolan Norton Institute. (1998) 'Strategische vernieuwing in de financiële dienstverlening'.

Nonaka, I. (1994) 'A dynamic theory of organizational knowledge creation', *Organization Science*, 5 (1): 14–37.

Nonaka, I. and Takeuchi, H. (1995) *The Knowledge-Creating Company*. New York: Oxford University Press.

Nooteboom B. (1999) *Inter-firm Alliances: Analysis and Design*. London: Routledge.

Normann, R. (1977) *Management for Growth*. New York: Wiley.

Nowotny, H., Scott, A. and Gibbons, M. (2001) *Re-Thinking Science: Knowledge and the Public in an Age of Uncertainty*. Cambridge: Polity Press.

O'Farrell, P.N., Wood, P.A. and Zheng, J. (1998) 'Internationalisation by business service SMEs: An inter-industry analysis', *International Small Business Journal*, 16 (2): 13–33.

O'Reilly, C.A., Chatman, J. and Caldwell, D.F. (1991) 'People and organizational culture: A profile comparison approach to assessing person-organization fit', *Academy of Management Journal*, 34: 487–515.

Orlikowski, W. (2000) 'Using technology and constituting structures: a practice lens for studying technology in organizations', *Organization Science*, 12 (4): 404–28.

Ortner, S.B. (1984) 'Theory in anthropology since the sixties', *Comparative Studies of Society and History*, 26: 126–66.

Osterman, P. (1994) 'How common is workplace transformation and who adopts it?' *Industrial and Labor Relations Review*, 47: 173–87.

Ouchi, W. (1980) 'Markets, bureaucracies and clans', *Administrative Science Quarterly*, 25: 129–41.

Papadakis, V.M., Lioukas, S. and Chambers, D. (1998) 'Strategic decision-making processes: the role of management and context', *Strategic Management Journal*, 19: 115–47.

Parkhe, A. (1991) 'Interfirm diversity, organizational learning, and longevity in global strategic alliances', *Journal of International Business Studies*, 22: 579–601.

Pearlson, K.E. and Saunders, C.S. (2001) 'There is no place like home: managing telecommuting paradoxes', *Academy of Management Executive*, 15 (2): 117–28.

Peiperl, M.A. (2001) 'Getting 360° feedback right', *Harvard Business Review*, 79 (1): 142–7.

Perlow, L.A. (1998) 'Boundary control: the social ordering of work and family time in a high-tech corporation', *Administrative Science Quarterly*, 43 (2): 328–57.

Perrone, V. (1997) 'The coevolution of contexts and structures: the N-form', in T. Clark (ed.), *Advances in Organizational Behaviour: Essays in Honour of Derek S. Pugh*, Aldershot: Ashgate, 145–63.

Peters, T.J. and Waterman, R.H.(1982) *In Search of Excellence*, New York: Harper & Row.

Pettigrew, A.M. (1985) *The Awakening Giant: Continuity and Change in ICI*. Oxford: Basil Blackwell.

Pettigrew, A.M. (1990) 'Longitudinal field research on change: theory and practice', *Organization Science*, 1 (3): 267–92.

Pettigrew, A.M. (1992) 'The character and significance of strategy process research', *Strategic Management Journal*, 13 (Winter special issue): 5–16.

Pettigrew, A.M. (1997a) 'What is a processual analysis?' *Scandinavian Journal of Management*, 13 (4): 337–48.

Pettigrew, A.M. (1997b) 'The double hurdles for management research', in T. Clarke (ed.), *Advancement in Organizational Behaviour: Essays in Honour of D. S. Pugh*, London: Dartmouth Press. pp. 277–96.

Pettigrew, A.M. (1998a) 'Catching reality in flight', in A. Bedeian, *Management Laureates*, Volume 5, Greenwich, CT: JAI Press, 171–206.

Pettigrew, A.M. (1998b) 'Success and failure in corporate transformation initiatives', in R.D. Galliers and W.R.J. Baets (eds), *Information in Technology and Organizational Transformation*, Chichester: Wiley. pp. 271–89.

Pettigrew, A.M. (1999a) 'Organizing to improve company performance', *Hot Topics-Warwick Business School*, 1 (5): 1–4.

Pettigrew, A.M. (1999b) 'Complementarities in action: organizational change and performance in BP Amoco 1988–1999', paper presented to the INNFORM Symposium on Organizing/Strategizing, *US Academy of Management Annual Conference*, Chicago: 9–11 August 1999.

Pettigrew, A.M. (2000) 'Linking change processes to outcomes: a commentary on Ghoshal, Bartlett and Weick', Chapter 12 in M. Beer and N. Nohria (eds), *Breaking the Code of Change*. Boston: Harvard Business School Press. pp. 243–65.

Pettigrew A.M. (2001) 'Management research after modernism', *British Journal of Management*, 12 December special issue: S61–S70.

Pettigrew, A.M., Brignall, S., Harvey, J. and Webb, D. (1999) *The Determinants of Organizational Performance: A Review of Literature*, report prepared for the Department of Health, March 1999 and available from Warwick Business School.

Pettigrew, A.M. and Fenton, E.M. (eds) (2000a) *The Innovating Organization*. London: Sage.

Pettigrew, A.M. and Fenton, E.M. (2000b) 'Complexities and dualities in innovative forms', in A.M. Pettigrew and E.M. Fenton (eds), *The Innovating Organization*. London: Sage. pp. 279–300.

Pettigrew, A.M., Massini, S. and Numagami T. (2000) 'Innovative forms of organizing in Europe and Japan', *European Management Journal*, 18 (3): 259–73.

Pettigrew, A.M. and Shaw, D. (2000) 'How to get the best out of change', *European Business Forum*, Issue 1 (Spring): 37–43.

Pettigrew, A.M. and Whipp, R. (1991) *Managing Change for Competitive Success*. Oxford: Blackwell.

Pettigrew, A.M. and Whittington, R. (2001) 'How to join up change', *People Management*, 11 October, 52–4.

Pettigrew, A.M., Whittington, R., Conyon, M. (1995) 'The new internal network organisation: process and performance', successful proposal to the ESRC. Warwick Business School, University of Warwick.

Pettigrew, A.M., Woodman, R.W. and Cameron, K.S. (2001) 'Studying organizational change and development: challenges for future research', *Academy of Management Journal*, 44 (4): 697–713.

Podolny, J.M. and Page, V.L. (1998) 'Network forms of organization', *Annual Review of Sociology*, 24: 57–76.

Polos, L., Hannan, M.T. and Carroll, G.R. (2002) 'Foundations of a theory of social forms', *Industrial and Corporate Change*, 11 (1): 85–115.

Poole, M.S. and Van den Ve, A.H. (1989) 'Using paradox to build management and organization theories', *Academy of Management Review*, 14 (4): 562–78.

Porac, J.F., Thomas, H. and Baden-Fuller, C. (1989) 'Competitive groups as cognitive communities: the case of Scottish knitwear manufacturers', *Journal of Management Studies*, 26 (4): 397–416.

Porter, M.E. (1985) *Competitive Advantage: Creating and Sustaining Superior Performance*. New York: Free Press.

Porter, M.E. (1996) 'What is strategy?', *Harvard Business Review*, 74 (6): 61–79.

Porter, M.E. and Siggelkow, N. (2002) 'Contextual interactions within activity systems and sustainable competitive advantage', unpublished paper, *Harvard Business School*.

Powell, W.W. (1990) 'Neither market nor hierarchy: network forms of organization', in B. Staw (ed.), *Research in Organizational Behaviour*. Greenwich, CT: JAI Press: 12: pp. 295–336.

Powell, W.W. (2001) 'The capitalist firm in the twenty-first-century: emerging patterns in western enterprise,' in P. DiMaggio, *The Twenty-First Century Firm*. Princeton: Princeton University Press. pp. 33–68.

Prahalad, C.K. and Bettis, R.A. (1986) 'The dominant logic: a new linkage between diversity and performance', *Strategic Management Journal*, 7 (6): 485–501.

Prahalad, C.K. and Hamel, G. (1990) 'The core competence of the corporation', *Harvard Business Review*, May–June: 79–91.

Prokesch, S.E. (1997) 'Unleashing the power of learning: an interview with British Petroleum's John Browne', *Harvard Business Review*, September–October: 147–68.

Quinn, J.B. (1980) *Strategies for Change*. Homewood, IL: Irwin.

Quinn, J.B., Anderson, P. and Finkelstein, S. (1996) 'New forms of organizing', in H. Mintzberg and J.B. Quinn (eds), *The Strategy Process*, New York: Process Hall, 350–62.

Quinn, R.E. and Cameron, K.S. (1983) 'Organizational life cycles and shifting criteria of effectiveness: some preliminary evidence', *Management Science*, 29: 33–51.

Quinn, R.E. and Cameron, K.S. (eds) (1988) *Paradox and Transformation: Toward a Theory of Change in Organization and Management*. Cambridge, MA: Ballinger.

Quinn, R.E. and Kimberly, J.R. (1984): *Paradox, Planning, and Perseverance: Guidelines for Managerial Practice*, in J.R. Kimberly and R.E. Quinn (eds) (1984): *Managing Organizational Transitions*, Homewood, 295–313.

Quinn, R.E. and Rohrbaugh, J. (1983) 'A spatial model of effectiveness: towards a competing values approach to organizational analysis', *Management Science*, 29: 363–77.

Quintanilla, J. and Sánchez-Runde, C.J. (2000) 'New forms of organizing through human resource management: the case of Fremap', in A.M. Pettigrew and E.M. Fenton (eds), *The Innovating Organization*. London: Sage. pp. 208–35.

Raelin, J.A. (1985) *The Clash of Cultures: Managers Managing Professionals*. Boston: Harvard Business School Press.

Ranson, N.S., Hinings, B. and Greenwood, R. (1980) 'The structuring of organisational structures', *Administrative Science Quarterly*, 25: 1–17.

Redding, S.G. (1994) 'Comparative management theory: jungle, zoo or fossil bed?' *Organization Studies*, 15 (3): 323–59.

Reed, M.I. (1997) 'In praise of duality and dualism: rethinking agency and structure in organizational analysis', *Organization Studies*, 18 (1): 21–42.

Reich, R.B. (1991) *The Work of Nations*. London: Simon & Schuster.

Remer, A. (2001) 'Management in Dilemma – von der konsistenten zur kompensatorischen Managementkonfiguration' [Management in a dilemma – from a consistent to a compensatory management configuration], in: *Die Unternehmung*, 55 (6): 353–75.

Rickards, T. (1999) *Creativity and the Management of Change*. Malden, MA: Blackwell.

Rivkin, J.W. (2000) 'Imitation of complex strategies', *Management Science*, 46 (6): 824–44.

Roberts, J. (1999) 'The internationalisation of business service firms: a stages approach', *The Service Industries Journal*, 19 (4): 68–88.

Roberts, K.H. (1970) 'On looking at an elephant: An evaluation of cross-cultural research related to organizations', *Psychological Bulletin*, 74 (5): 327–50.

Roberts, P.W. and Greenwood, R. (1997) 'Integrating transaction cost and institutional theories: toward a constrained-efficiency framework for understanding organizational design adoption', *Academy of Management Review*, 22 (2): 346–73.

Robson, B. and Shove, C. (eds) (1999) *Interactions and Influence: Individuals and Institutions*. Swindon: ESRC.

Romanelli, E. and Tushman, M.L. (1994) 'Organizational transformation as punctuated equilibrium: an empirical test', *Academy of Management Journal*, 37 (5): 1141–66.

Roos, J. and Victor, B. (1999) 'Towards a new model of strategy-making as serious play', *European Management Journal*, 17 (4): 348–55.

Roth, K. and Nigh, D. (1992) 'The effectiveness of HQ-subsidiary relationships: the role of co-ordination, control and conflict', *Journal of Business Research*, 25: 277–301.

Rousseau, D.M. (1995) *Psychological Contracts in Organizations. Understanding Written and Unwritten Agreements*. Thousand Oaks, CA: Sage.

Rousseau, D.M. and Arthur, M.B. (1997) 'The boundaryless human resource function: building agency and community in the new economic era', *Organizational Dynamics*, 25 (3): 7–18.

Rousseau, D.M. and Schalk, R. (eds) (2000) *Psychological Contracts in Employment. Cross-National Perspectives*. Thousand Oaks, CA: Sage.

Ruef, M. (2000) 'The emergence of organizational forms: a community ecology approach', *American Journal of Sociology*, 106 (3): 658–714.

Ruigrok, W., Achtenhagen, L., Wagner, M. and Rüegg-Stürm, J. (2000a) 'Hilti AG: shared leadership and the rise of the communicating organization', in A.M. Pettigrew and E. Fenton (eds), *The Innovating Organization*. London/Thousand Oaks: Sage. pp. 178–207.

Ruigrok, W., Achtenhagen, L., Wagner, M. and Rüegg-Stürm, J. (2000b) 'ABB: beyond the global matrix towards the network multidivisional organization', in A.M. Pettigrew and E.M. Fenton (eds), *The Innovating Organization*. London: Sage. pp. 117–43.

Ruigrok, W., Pettigrew, A.M., Peck, S. and Whittington, R. (1999) 'Corporate restructuring and new forms of organising: evidence from Europe,' *Management International Review*, 39, (July special issue): 41–64.

Ruigrok, W. and van Tulder, R. (1995) *The Logic of International Restructuring*, London (England); New York, NY: Routledge.

Rumelt, R. and Stopford, J.M. (1996) 'Changing managerial logics', unpublished manuscript, Jan: 31pp.

Sakano, T. and Lewin A.Y. (1999) 'Impact of CEO succession in Japanese Companies: a coevolutionary perspective', *Organization Science*, 10: 654–71.

Sánchez-Runde, C.J. (2001) 'Strategic human resource management and the new employment relationships', in J. Gual and J.E. Ricart (eds), *Strategy, Structure, and the Changing Nature of Work*. London: Edward Elgar. pp. 47–78.

Sánchez-Runde, C.J. and Quintanilla, J. (2000) 'Initial steps in the path towards new forms of organizing: two experiences within the group Aguas de Barcelona', in A.M. Pettigrew and E.M. Fenton (eds), *The Innovating Organization*, London: Sage: pp. 256–78.

Sarason, S.B. (1988) *The Making of an American Psychologist: An Autobiography*. San Francisco: Jossey-Bass.

Schatzki, T., Knorr Cetina, K. and von Savigny, E. (2000) *The Practice Turn in Contemporary Theory*. London: Routledge.

Schein, E.H. (1980) *Organizational Psychology*. Englewood Cliffs, NJ: Prentice-Hall.

Schein, E.H. (1992) *Organizational Culture and Leadership*. San Francisco: Jossey-Bass.

Schneider, S.C. and Angelmar, R. (1993) 'Cognition in organizational analysis: who's minding the store?', *Organization Studies*, 14 (3): 347–74.

Schoemaker, P.J.H. (1992) 'How to link strategic vision to core capabilities', *Sloan Management Review*, 34 (1): 67–81.

Sekaran, U. (1983) 'Methodological and theoretical issues and advancements in cross-cultural research', *Journal of International Business Studies*, 14 (2): 61–74.

Senge, P. (1990) 'The leader's new work: building learning organizations', *Sloan Management Review*, Autumn: 7–23.

Sessa, V.I., Hansen, M.C., Prestridge, S. and Kossler, M.E. (1999) *Geographically Dispersed Teams: An Annotated Bibliography*, Greensboro, NC: Center for Creative Leadership.

Sharma, A. (1997) 'Professional as agent: knowledge asymmetry in agency exchange', *The Academy of Management Review*, 22 (3): 758–98.

Sharma, D.D. and Johanson, J. (1987) 'Technical consultancy in internationalisation', *International Marketing Review*, Winter: 20–9.

Siggelkow, N. (2001) 'Change in the presence of fit: the rise and fall, and the renaissance of Liz Claiborne', *Academy of Management Journal*, 44 (4): 838–57.

Siggelkow, N. (2002a) 'Misperceiving interactions among complements and substitutes: organizational consequences', *Management Science*, 48 (7): 900–16.

Siggelkow, N. (2002b) 'Evolution toward fit', *Administrative Science Quarterly*, 47 (1): 125–59.

Silverman, D. (1985) *Qualitative Methodology & Sociology*. Hants: Gower.

Simon, H.A. (1960) *The New Science of Management Decision*. New York: Harper.

Simon, H. (1991) 'Bounded rationality and organizational learning', *Organization Science*, 2: 125–34.

Sims, D., Fineman, S. and Gabriel, Y. (1993) *Organizations and Organizing*. London: Sage.

Sjöstrand, S-E. (1997) *The Two Faces of Management – The Janus Factor*, International Thomson Business Press: London.

Smircich, L. (1983) 'Concepts of culture and organizational analysis', *Administrative Science Quarterly*, 28: 339–58.

Smircich, L. and Morgan, G. (1982) 'Leadership: the management of meaning', *Journal of Applied Behavioral Science*, 18 (3): 257–73.

Smircich, L. and Stubbart, C. (1985) 'Strategic management in an enacted world', *Academy of Management Review*, 10 (4): 724–36.

Snow, C.C. and Snell, S.A. (1993) 'Staffing as strategy', in N. Schmitt and W.C. Borman (eds), *Personnel selection in organizations*. San Francisco: Jossey-Bass. pp. 448–78.

Snow, C., Snell, S.A., Davison, S.C. and Hambrick, D.C. (1996) 'Use transnational teams to globalize your company', *Organizational Dynamics*, Spring: 50–67.

Sole, D. and Edmondson, A. (2002) 'Situated knowledge and learning in dispersed teams', *British Journal of Management*, Volume 13, September, special issue: 517–34.

Stacey, R.D. (1995) 'The science of complexity: an alternative perspective for strategic change processes', *Strategic Management Journal*, 16 (6): 477–95.

Stacey, R.D. (2001) *Complex Responsive Processes in Organizations: Learning and Knowledge Creation*. London/New York: Routledge.

Stacey, R.D., Griffin, D. and Shaw, P. (2000) *Complexity and Management: Fad or Radical Challenge to Systems Thinking?*, London/New York: Routledge.

Starbuck, W.H. (1993) 'Keeping a butterfly and an elephant in a house of cards: the elements of exceptional success', *Journal of Management Studies*, 30 (6) (November): 885–921.

Starbuck, W.H. and Milliken, F.J. (1988) 'Executives' perceptual filters: what they notice and how they make sense', in D.C. Hambrick (ed.), *The Executive Effect: Concepts and Methods for Studying Top Managers*. Greenwich, CT: JAI Press: pp. 35–65.

Suryanarayanan, S. (1989) 'Trends and outlook for U.S. Consulting', *Journal of Management Consulting*, 11: 3–9.

Taylor, W. (1991) 'The logic of global business: an interview with ABB's Percy Barnevik', *Harvard Business Review*, 69 (2): 91–105.

Teagarden, M.B. et al. (1995) 'Towards a theory of comparative management research: an idiographic case study of the best international human resource management project', *Academy of Management Journal*, 38: 1261–87.

Teece, D.J., Pisano, G. and Shuen, A. (1997) 'Dynamic capabilities and strategic management', *Strategic Management Journal*, 18 (7): 509–33.

Thomas, J.B., Clark, S.M. and Gioia, D.A. (1993) 'Strategic sensemaking and organizational performance: linkages among scanning, interpretation, action, and outcomes', *Academy of Management Journal*, 36 (2): 239–70.

Tidd, J., Bessant, J. and Pavitt, K. (1997) *Managing Innovation. Integrating Technological, Market and Organizational Change*. Chichester, UK: Wiley.

Toffler, A. (1970) *Future Shock*. New York: Random House.

Tregaskis, O., Mahoney, C. and Atterbury, S. (2003) 'International survey methodology: experiences from the Cranfield Network', in W. Mayrhofrs, C. Brewster and M. Morley (eds), *Trend in Human Resource Management in Europe*. London: Butterworth Heinemann.

Trice, H.M. and Beyer, J.M. (1993) *The Cultures of Work Organization*. Englewood Cliffs, NJ: Prentice-Hall.

Tripsas, M. and Gavetti, G. (2000) 'Capabilities, cognition, and inertia: evidence from digital imaging', *Strategic Management Journal*, 21: 1147–61.

Tsoukas, H. (1996) 'The firm as a distributed knowledge-system: a constructionist approach', *Strategic Management Journal*, 17 (special issue): 11–26.

Turati, C., Usai, A. and Ravagnani, R. (1998) 'Antecedents of co-ordination in academic international project research', *Journal of Management Psychology*, 13 (3): 188–98.

Tushman, M.L. and Nadler, D. (1986) 'Organizing for innovation'. *California Management Review*, 23: 74–92.

Tushman, M.L. and O'Reilly, C.A. (1996) 'Ambidextrous organizations: managing evolutionary and revolutionary change', *California Management Review*, 38 (4): 8–30.

Uzzi, B. (1997) 'Social structure and competition in interfirm networks: the paradox of embeddedness', *Administrative Science Quarterly*, 42: 35–67.

Vandermerwe, S. and Chadwick, M. (1989) 'The internationalization of services', *The Service Industries Journal*, 9: 79–93.

Van de Ven, A.H., Angle, H.L. and Poole, M.S. (1989) *Research on the Management of Innovation: The Minnesota Studies*. New York: Ballinger/Harper & Row.

Van de Ven, A.H., Polley, D.G., Garud, R. and Venhatanaman, S. (1999) *The Innovation Journey*, New York: Oxford University Press.

Van Looy, B.V., Leliaert, A., De Weerdt, S., Corthouts, F. and Broeckmans, J. (2000) 'Establishing a relational field that fosters learning processes: some tentative propositions derived from trainee experiences', *European Journal of Work and Organizational Psychology*, 9: 189–210.

Van Wijk, R.A. and Van den Bosch, A.J. (2000) 'The emergence and development of internal networks and their impact on knowledge flows: the case of the Rabobank Group', in A.M. Pettigrew and E.M. Fenton (eds), *The Innovating Organization*. London: Sage: pp. 144–77.

Volberda, H.W. (1996) 'Toward the flexible form: how to remain vital in hyper competitive environments', *Organization Science*, 7 (4): 359–75.

Volberda, H.W. (1998) *Building the Flexible Firm: How to Remain Competitive*. Oxford: Oxford University Press.

Volberda, H.W., Van den Bosch, F.A.J., Flier, B. and Gedajlovic, E.R. (2001) 'Following the herd or not? Patterns of strategic renewal in the Netherlands and the U.K.', *Long Range Planning*, 34: 209–29.

Walsh, J.P. (1988) 'Selectivity and selective perception: an investigation of managers' belief structures and information processing', *Academy of Management Journal*, 31 (4): 873–96.

Walsh, J.P. (1995) 'Managerial and organizational cognition: notes from a trip down memory lane', *Organization Science*, 6 (3): 280–321.

Walsh, J.P. and Ungson, G.R. (1991) 'Organizational memory', *Academy of Management Review*, 16: 57–91.

Waterman, R.H., Peters, T.J. and Phillips, J.R. (1980) 'Structure is not organization', *Business Horizons*, June, 14–27.

Weber, E.U., Hsee, C.K. and Sokolowska, J. (1998) 'What folklore tells us about risk and risk taking: cross-cultural comparisons of American, German and Chinese proverbs', *Organization Behaviour and Human Decision Processes*, 75: 170–186.

Weber, M. (1927) *General Economic History*, (trans. F.H. Knight). Glencoe, IL: Free Press.

Weick, K.E. (1969) *The Social Psychology of Organising*, (first edition). MA: Addison-Wesley.

Weick, K.E. (1979) *The Social Psychology of Organising*, (second edition). MA: Addison-Wesley.

Weick, K.E. (1983) Letter to the editor. *Fortune*, 17 October: 27.

Weick, K.E. (1995) *Sense-Making in Organizations*. Thousand Oaks, California: Sage.

Wenger, E. (1998) *Communities of Practice: Learning, Meaning and Identity*. Cambridge: Cambridge University Press.

Werner, H. and Hügli, T. (1995) 'Michael Hilti über Kerngeschäfte, Marktbesitz und Mitarbeiter' [Michael Hilti on core businesses, market ownership and employees], *Index*, 5/6: 20–1.

Westenholz, A. (1993) 'Paradoxical thinking and change in the frames of reference', *Organization Studies*, 14 (1): 37–58.

Westley, F. and Mintzberg, H. (1989) 'Visionary leadership and strategic management', *Strategic Management Journal*, 10 (Summer): 17–32.

Westney, D.E. (2001) 'Japanese enterprise faces the twenty-first century', in P. DiMaggio (ed.), *The Twenty-First Century Firm*, Princeton: Princeton University Press. pp. 105–44.

White, W.R. (1998) 'The coming transformation of continental European banking?' BIS working paper No. 54, June. Basle: Bank for International settlements, Monetary and economic department.

Whitley, R. (1994) 'Dominant forms of economic organization in market economies', *Organization Studies*, 15.

Whitley, R. (1996) 'The social construction of economic actors: institutions and types of firm in Europe and other market economies', in R. Whitley, P.H. Kristensen and E.S. Foundation (eds), *The Changing European Firm Limits to Convergence.* London (England); New York, NY: Routledge.

Whitley, R. (1999) *Divergent, Capitalisms: The Social Structuring and Change of Business Systems.* Oxford: Oxford University Press.

Whitley, R. (2000) *The Intellectual and Social Organization of the Sciences,* (second edition). Oxford: Oxford University Press.

Whittington, R. (1992) 'Putting Giddens into action: social systems and managerial agency', *Journal of Management Studies*, 29 (6): 693–712.

Whittington, R. (1993) 'Social structures and strategic leadership', in J. Hendry, G. Johnson and J. Newton (eds), *Strategic Thinking: Leadership and the Management of Change.* London: Wiley: pp. 181–98.

Whittington, R. (1994) 'Sociological pluralism, institutions, and managerial agency', in J. Hassard and M. Parker (eds), *Towards a New Theory of Organization.* London: Routledge: pp. 53–74.

Whittington, R. (1996) 'Strategy as practice', *Long Range Planning*, 29 (5): 731–5.

Whittington, R. (2002) 'Corporate structure: from policy to practice', in A.M. Pettigrew, H. Thomas and R. Whittington (eds), *The Handbook of Strategy and Management.* London: Sage: pp. 113–38.

Whittington, R. and Mayer, M. (1997) 'Beyond or behind the M-Form?: the structures of European business', in D. O' Neal, H. Thomas and M. Ghertman (eds), *Strategy Structure and Style.* Chichester: Wiley, pp. 241–58.

Whittington, R. and Mayer, M. (2000) *The European Corporation: Strategy Structure and Social Science.* Oxford: Oxford University Press.

Whittington, R., Pettigrew, A.M., Peck, S.I., Fenton, E.M. and Conyon, M. (1999) 'Change and complementarities in the new competitive landscape: a European panel study 1992–1996', *Organization Science*, 10 (5): Sep–Oct, 583–600.

Whittington, R., Pettigrew, A.M. and Ruigrok, W. (1999) 'New notions of organizational "fit"', *Financial Times, Mastering Strategy*, November 29: 8–10.

Whittington, R., Pettigrew, A.M. and Ruigrok, W. (2000) 'New Notions of organizational "fit"', in T. Dixon (ed.), *Mastering Strategy.* London: Financial Times/Prentice Hall: pp. 151–57.

Whittington, R., Pettigrew, A.M. and Thomas, H. (2002) 'Conclusions: doing more in strategy research', Chapter 21 in A.M. Pettigrew, H. Thomas and R. Whittington (eds), *The Handbook of Strategy and Management.* London: Sage: pp. 475–88.

Wilkins, A.L. and Ouchi, W.G. (1983) 'Efficient cultures: exploring the relationship between culture and organizational performance', *Administrative Science Quarterly*, 28: 468–81.

Williamson, O.E. (1991) 'Strategizing, economizing and economic organization', *Strategic Management Journal*, 12: 75–94.

Winter, S.G. and Szulanski, G. (2001) 'Replication and strategy', *Organization Science*, 12 (6): 730–43.

Womack, J.P. and Jones, D.T. (1995) *Lean Thinking: Banish Waste and Create Wealth in your Corporation,* New York, NY: Simon and Schuster.

Womack, J.P., Jones, D.T. and Roos, D. (1990) *The Machine that Changed the World,* New York, NY: Rawson Associates.

Woodward, J. (1965) *Industrial Organization: Theory and Practice*. Oxford: Oxford University Press.

Woolgar, S. (2000) 'Social basis of interactive social science', *Science and Public Policy*, 27 (3): 165–73.

Wright, M., Ennew, C. and Wong, P. (1991) 'Deregulation, strategic change and divestment in the financial services sector', *National Westminster Bank Quarterly Review*, November: 51–64.

Wright, P.M. and McMahan, G.C. (1992) 'Theoretical perspectives for strategic human resource management', *Journal of Management*, 18: 295–320.

Yasai-Ardekani, M. (1986) 'Structural adaptations to environments', *Academy of Management Review*, 11 (1): 9–21.

Yin, R.K. (1984) *Case Study Research: Design and Methods*. Thousand Oaks, CA: Sage.

Yukl, G. (1998) *Leadership in Organizations*. Upper Saddle River, NJ: Prentice-Hall.

Zahra, S.A. and O'Neill, H.M. (1998) 'Changing the landscape of global competition. Reflections on emerging organizational challenges and their implications for senior executives', *Academy of Management Executive*, 12 (4): 13–21.

Zeffane, R. (1992) 'Organization structures: design in the nineties', *Leadership & Organization Development Journal*, 13 (6): 18–23.

Zenger, T.R. and Hesterly, W.S. (1997) 'The disaggregation of corporations: selective intervention, high-powered incentives and molecular units', *Organization Science*, 8 (3): 209–22.

Ziman, J. (1994) *Prometheus Bound: Science in a Dynamic Steady State*, Cambridge: Cambridge University Press.

# Index